Practical
Divinity
Volume 2

Practical Divinity

Volume 2

Readings in Wesleyan Theology

Edited by

Thomas A. Langford

ABINGDON PRESS

Nashville

PRACTICAL DIVINITY
VOLUME 2
READINGS IN WESLEYAN THEOLOGY

This book is printed on elemental-chlorine—free paper.

Library of Congress Cataloging-in-Publication Data

Langford, Thomas A.
  Practical divinity / Thomas A. Langford.
    p. cm.
  Includes bibliographical references and index.
  Contents: v. 1. Theology in the Wesleyan tradition—v. 2. Readings in
Wesleyan theology.
  ISBN 0-687-07382-0 (v. 1. : pbk. : alk. paper)
       0-687-01247-3 (v. 2. : pbk. : alk. paper)
  1. Methodist Church—Doctrines—History.   I. Title.
BX8331.2.L36   1998
230'.7—dc21   98-27227
                                                              CIP

99 00 01 02 03 04 05 06 07 08—10 9 8 7 6 5 4 3 2 1

MANUFACTURED IN THE UNITED STATES OF AMERICA

CONTENTS

Contents

PREFACE

The Methodist theological tradition is being freshly discovered, and this discovery now needs to be explored in depth. Primary source materials provide opportunity for a firsthand encounter with this tradition, yet much important material is not readily available. The selections included in this collection make accessible characteristic writings of important thinkers and discussion of critical issues that have been significant in the formation of Methodist theology.

The Wesleyan tradition is broader than United Methodism, but in order to keep clear focus and to provide enough material for adequate interpretation of historical developments, the concentration is on United Methodism, the dominant stream of the tradition. Only a limited number of particularly important readings have been chosen. This has been done to allow the authors to speak for themselves with some fullness. Short introductions are provided, but the conviction underlying this book of readings is that primary sources are of basic historical importance and must be presented at length if the reader is to discover their worth.

The principles of selection for this volume need to be set forth. Important authors and themes that have played a critical role in the development of Wesleyan theology have been chosen. Where the author is of chief importance, the selection attempts to present both individual distinctiveness and an issue that is important for the continuing tradition. Where the theme has primary importance, a representative writer on that theme has been chosen. To balance these interests in limited space has forced difficult decisions of inclusion and exclusion, but an effort has been made to represent the tradition in accurate ways. Much weight has been placed on the earlier part of the tradition because of the difficulty of obtaining primary documents and the general lack of familiarity with these materials, but theologians selected include some at work today. Overabundance, not paucity of activity, makes decisions about which current materials to include especially difficult. My hope is that all of the selections will lead to further reading.

To survey the Wesleyan theological tradition, to assume responsibility for selecting its leading spokespersons and ideas, and to indicate its historical development constitute a heavy responsibility. It must be emphasized that the Wesleyan tradition is open for interpretation of both its achieved character and its future prospects. This book of readings represents an attempt to open a door through which others may enter and look and learn.

The selections are arranged in chronological order and framed with a brief historical sketch. For a study of these theologians and issues that sets them into an interpretative context, the reader may look to volume 1 of this two-volume work, *Practical Divinity: Theology in the Wesleyan Tradition* (rev. ed., Abingdon Press, 1998). Notes accompanying these articles when first published have been retained where they may be helpful to readers of this volume.

My hope in providing these resources is that they will excite interest in Wesleyan theology and lead to a more thorough understanding and appreciation of the Wesleyan tradition.

TAL

Part I

Early Developments

The immediate successors to John Wesley were characterized by their efforts to reassert principal themes of Wesley's thought. Although the desire was to be faithful, there was little effort simply to repeat what Wesley had said. Rather, the dominant objective was to continue the spirit of Wesley's thought, especially his full-orbed Christian affirmation, his biblical foundations, his sense of the primacy and sufficiency of grace, and his special emphasis on the work of the Holy Spirit. Over time, however, particular challenges evoked some shift of emphasis.

Yet, the primary theological themes found continual expression in the theologians who are represented in these initial selections. John Fletcher, Adam Clarke, Nathan Bangs, and Richard Watson were the leaders and typified the character of early Methodist theology. In all of these writers salvation was central: it was rooted in prevenient grace, was dependent upon God's justifying forgiveness, and reached toward Christian perfection or sanctification. The affirmation of Methodist positions was cast against the backdrop of challenge from other theological positions. Consequently, both the themes addressed and the running dialogue, especially with Calvinism, are prominent. These early Methodists were establishing theological principles, foundations upon which later theology would be constructed.

John Fletcher

After Wesley, John Fletcher (1729–1785) was the first significant theologian in the Methodist tradition. Born in Nyon, Switzerland, he was christened Jean Guillaume de la Flêchère. After joining a Methodist Society he sought ordination in the Church of England and served as vicar of Madeley, Shropshire. Fletcher was distinguished by his piety as well as his theological ability. In the tempestuous decade of the 1770s, his was a clear, balanced, compelling voice. Fletcher became a theological writer when tensions increased between Methodists and Calvinists. In the Conference of 1770, John Wesley had been unclear about the relation of faith and works. Fletcher's carefully wrought theological statement of the contested issues helped clarify Wesley's thought. The selection included in this text comes from his *Checks to Antinomianism:* in this important work Fletcher intended to defend Wesley's commanding interest in morally responsible and mature Christian life. Fletcher was an important progenitor of distinctive Methodist theological emphases because he set the directions for future Methodist theological developments. The "First Check to Antinomianism" is selected from *The Works of the Reverend John Fletcher* (New York: B. Waugh and T. Mason, 1935), I, pp. 11-39.

First Check to Antinomianism

Honoured and Reverend Sir, Before a judge passes sentence upon a person accused of theft, he hears what his neighbours have to say for his character. Mr. Wesley, I grant, is accused of what is worse than theft, *dreadful heresy;* and I know that whosoever maintains a dreadful heresy is a *dreadful heretic;* and that the Church of Rome shows no mercy to such. But may not "real Protestants" indulge, with the privilege of a felon, one whom they so lately respected as a brother? And may not I, an old friend and acquaintance of his, be permitted to speak a word in his favour, before he is branded in the forehead, as he has already been on the back?

This step, I fear, will cost me my reputation, (if I have any,) and involve me in the same condemnation with him whose cause, together with that of truth, I design to plead. But when humanity prompts, when gratitude calls, when friendship excites, when reason invites, when justice demands, when truth requires, and conscience summons, he does not deserve the name of a *Christian friend,* who, for any consideration, hesitates to vindicate what he esteems truth, and to stand by an aggrieved friend, brother, and father. Were I not, sir, on such an occasion as this to step out of my beloved obscurity, you might deservedly reproach me as a *dastardly wretch:* nay, you have already done it in general terms, in your excellent sermon on the fear of man. "How often," say you, "do men sneakingly forsake their friends, instead of gloriously supporting them against a powerful adversary, even when their cause is just, for reasons hastily prudential, for fear of giving umbrage to a superior party or interest?"

These generous words of yours, Rev. sir, together with the leave you give both Churchmen and Dissenters to direct to *you* their answers to your circular letter, are my excuse for intruding upon you by this epistle, and my apology for begging your candid attention, while I attempt to convince you that my friend's principles and Minutes are not heretical. In order to this, I shall lay before you, and the principal persons, both clergy and laity, whom you have, from all parts of England and Wales, convened at Bristol, by printed letters,—

I. A general view of the Rev. Mr. Wesley's doctrine.

II. An account of the commendable design of his Minutes.

III. A vindication of the propositions which they contain, by arguments taken from Scripture, reason, and experience; and by quotations from eminent Calvinist divines, who have said the same things in different words.

And suppose you yourself, sir, in particular, should appear to be a strong assertor of the doctrines which you call a *dreadful heresy* in Mr. Wesley, I hope you will not refuse me leave to conclude, by expostulating with you upon your conduct in this affair, and recommending to you, and our other Christian friends, the forbearance which you recommend to others, in one of your sermons: "Why doth the narrow heart of man pursue with malice or rashness those who presume to differ from him?" Yea, and what is more extraordinary, those who agree with him in all essential points?

I. When, in an intricate case, a prudent judge is afraid to pass an unjust sentence, he inquires, as I observed, into the general conduct of the person accused, and by that means frequently finds out the truth which he investigates. As that method may be of service in the present case, permit me, sir, to lay before you a general view of Mr. Wesley's doctrine.

1. For above these sixteen years I have heard him frequently in his chapels, and sometimes in my church: I have familiarly conversed and corresponded with him, and have often perused his numerous works in verse and prose: and I can truly say that, during all that time, I have heard him, upon every proper occasion, steadily maintain *the total fall of man in Adam,* and his utter inability to recover himself, or take any one step toward his recovery, "without the grace of God preventing him, that he may have a good will, and working with him when he has that good will."

The deepest expressions that ever struck my ears on the melancholy subject of our natural depravity and helplessness, are those which dropped from his lips: and I have ever observed that he constantly ascribes to Divine grace, not only the good works and holy tempers of believers, but all the good thoughts of upright heathens, and the good desires of those professors whom he sees "begin in the Spirit and end in the flesh:" when, to my great surprise, some of those who accuse him of "robbing God of the glory of his grace, and ascribing too much to man's power," directly or indirectly maintain that Demas and his fellow apostates never had any grace; and that if once they went on far in the ways of God, it was merely by the force of fallen nature; a sentiment which Mr. Wesley looks upon as diametrically opposite to the humbling assertion of our Lord, "Without me ye can do nothing;" and which he can no more admit than the rankest Pelagianism.

2. I must likewise testify, that he faithfully points out *Christ as the only way of salvation;* and strongly recommends faith as the only mean of receiving him, and all the benefits of his righteous life and meritorious death: and truth obliges me to declare, that he frequently expresses his detestation of the errors of modern Pharisees, who laugh at original sin, set up the powers of fallen man, cry down the operation of God's Spirit, deny the absolute necessity of the blood and righteousness of Christ,

and refuse him the glory of all the good that may be found in Jew or Gentile. And you will not without difficulty, sir, find in England, and perhaps in all the world, a minister who hath borne more frequent testimonies, either from the pulpit or the press, against those dangerous errors. All his works confirm my assertion, especially his sermons on Original Sin, and Salvation by Faith, and his masterly Refutation of Dr. Taylor, the wisest Pelagian and Socinian of our age. Nor am I afraid to have this testimony confronted with his Minutes, being fully persuaded that, when they are candidly explained, they rather confirm than overthrow it.

His manner of preaching the fall and the recovery of man is attended with a peculiar advantage: it is close and experimental. He not only points out the truth of those doctrines, but presses his hearers to cry to God that they may feel their weight upon their hearts. Some open those great truths very clearly, but let their congregations rest, like the stony ground hearers, in the first emotions of sorrow and joy which the word frequently excites. Not so Mr. Wesley: he will have true penitents "feel the plague of their own hearts, travail, be heavy laden," and receive "the sentence of death in themselves," according to the glorious "ministration of condemnation:" and according to "the ministration of righteousness and of the Spirit which exceeds in glory," he insists upon true believers knowing for themselves, that Jesus "hath power on earth to forgive sins;" and asserts, that they "taste the good word of God, and the powers of the world to come," and that they "are made partakers of the Holy Ghost and the Divine nature; the Spirit itself bearing witness with their spirits that they are the children of God."

3. The next fundamental doctrine in Christianity is that of *holiness of heart and life;* and no one can here accuse Mr. Wesley of leaning to the Antinomian delusion, which "makes void the law through" a speculative and barren "faith:" on the contrary, he appears to be peculiarly set for the defence of practical religion: for, instead of representing Christ "as the minister of sin," with Ranters, to the great grief and offence of many, he sets him forth as a complete Saviour from sin. Not satisfied to preach holiness begun, he preaches finished holiness, and calls believers to such a degree of heart-purifying faith, as may enable them to triumph in Christ, as "being made to them of God, sanctification as well as righteousness."

It is, I grant, his misfortune (if indeed it be one) to preach a fuller salvation than most professors expect to enjoy here; for he asserts that Jesus can "make clean" *the inside* as well as the *outside* of his vessels unto honour; that he hath power on earth "to save his people from their sins;" and that his blood "cleanses from all sin," from the guilt and defilement both of original and actual corruption. He is bold enough to declare, with St. John, that "if we say we have no sin, *either by nature or practice*, we deceive ourselves, and the truth is not in us: but if we confess our sins, God is faithful and just to forgive us our sins, and to cleanse us from all unrighteousness." He is legal enough not to be ashamed of these words of Moses: "The Lord thy God will circumcise thine heart, and the heart of thy seed, to love the Lord thy God with all thine heart, and with all thy soul, that thou mayest live." And he dares to believe that the Lord can perform the words which he spoke by Ezekiel: "I will sprinkle clean water upon you, and you shall be clean: from ALL your filthiness and from ALL your idols will I cleanse you. A new heart also will I give you: I will take away the stony heart out of your flesh, and I will give you a heart of flesh; and I will put my Spirit within you, and cause you to walk in my statutes; and ye shall keep my judgments, and do them. I will also save you from *all* your uncleannesses." Hence it is that he constantly exhorts his hearers "to grow in grace, and in the knowledge of our Saviour;" till by a strong and lively faith they can continually "reckon themselves to be dead indeed unto sin, but alive unto God through Jesus Christ our Lord." He tells them, that "he who committeth sin, is the servant of sin;"—that "our old man is crucified with Christ, that the body of sin might be destroyed, that henceforth we should not serve sin;"—that "if the Son shall make us free, we shall be free indeed;"—and that although "the *law* of the Spirit of life in Christ Jesus" will not deliver us from the innocent infirmities incident to flesh and blood, it will nevertheless make us "free from the law of sin and death," and enable us to say with holy triumph, "How shall we, that are dead to sin, live any longer therein?" In a word, he thinks that God can so "shed abroad his love in our hearts, by the Holy Ghost given unto us," as to "sanctify us wholly, soul, body, and spirit;" and enable us to "rejoice evermore, pray without ceasing, and in every thing give thanks." And he is persuaded, that He who "can do far exceeding abundantly above all that we can ask or think," is able to fill us with the "perfect love which casts out fear; that we, being delivered out of the hands of our enemies," may have "the mind which was in Christ;" be righteous as the *man* Jesus was righteous; "walk as he also walked," and be in our measure, "as he was in the world:" he as the stock of the tree of righteousness, and we as the branches, "having our fruit" from him "unto holiness," and "serving God without fear in true holiness and righteousness all the days of our life."

14

This he sometimes calls *full sanctification*, the state of "fathers in Christ," or the "glorious liberty of the children of God;" sometimes "a being strengthened, stablished, and settled;" or "being rooted and grounded in love;" but most commonly he calls it *Christian perfection:* a word which, though used by the apostles in the same sense, cannot be used by him without raising the pity or indignation of one half of the religious world; some making it the subject of their pious sneers and godly lampoons; while others tell you roundly "they abhor it above every thing in the creation." . . .

On account of this doctrine it is that he is traduced as a Pharisee, a papist, an antichrist; some of his opposers taking it for granted that he makes void the priestly office of Christ, by affirming that his blood can so completely wash us here from our sins, that at death we shall "be found of him in peace, without spot, wrinkle, or any such thing;" while others, to colour their opposition to the many scriptures which he brings to support this unfashionable doctrine, give it out, that he only wants the old man to be so refined in all his tempers, and regulated in all his outward behaviour, as to appear perfect in the flesh; or, in other terms, that he sets up Pharisaic SELF, instead of "Christ *completely* formed in us *as the full* hope of glory." But I must (for one) do him the justice to say he is misapprehended, and that what he calls perfection is nothing but the rich cluster of all the spiritual blessings promised to believers in the Gospel; and, among the rest, a continual sense of the virtue of Christ's atoning and purifying blood, preventing both old guilt from returning and new guilt from fastening upon the conscience; together with the deepest consciousness of our helplessness and nothingness in our best estate, the most endearing discoveries of the Redeemer's love, and the most humbling and yet ravishing views of his glorious fulness. Witness one of his favourite hymns on that subject:—

> Confound, o'erpower me with thy grace;
>   I would be by myself abhorr'd:
> (All might, all majesty, all praise,
>   All glory be to Christ my Lord!)
>
> Now let me gain perfection's height,
>   Now let me into nothing fall;
> Be less than nothing in my sight,
>   And feel that *Christ is all in all.*

15

4. But this is not all: he holds also *general redemption*, and its necessary consequences, which some account *dreadful heresies*. He asserts with St. Paul, that "Christ, by the grace of God, tasted death for every man;" and this grace he calls *free*, as extending itself *freely* to all. Nor can he help expressing his surprise at those pious ministers who maintain that the Saviour keeps his grace, as they suppose he kept his blood, from the greatest part of mankind, and yet engross to themselves the title of *preachers of FREE grace!*

He frequently observes, with the same apostle, that "Christ is the Saviour of *all* men, but especially of them that believe;" and that "God will have *all* men to be saved," consistently with their moral agency, and the tenor of his Gospel.

With St. John he maintains that "God is love," and that "Christ is the propitiation not only for our sins, but also for the sins of the *whole world*." With David he affirms that "God's mercy is over *all* his works:" and with St. Peter, that "the Lord is not willing that any should perish, but that all should come to repentance;" yea, that God, without hypocrisy, "commandeth *all* men, *every where*, to repent." Accordingly he says with the Son of God, "Whosoever will, let him come and take of the water of life freely;" and after his blessed example, as well as by his gracious command, he "preaches the Gospel TO *every creature;*" which he apprehends would be inconsistent with common honesty, if there were not a Gospel FOR *every creature.* Nor can he doubt of it in the least, when he considers that Christ is a king as well as a priest; that we are under a law to him; that those men who "will not have him to reign over them, shall be brought and slain before him;" yea, that he will "judge the secrets of men," according to St. Paul's Gospel, and take vengeance on all them that obey not his *own* Gospel, *and* be the author of eternal salvation to *none but* them that obey him. With this principle, as with a key given us by God himself, he opens those things which are "hard to be understood," in the Epistles of St. Paul, and "which they that are unlearned and unstable wrest, as they do some other scriptures, *if not* to their own destruction, *at least* to the overthrowing of the faith of some" weak Christians, and the hardening of many, very many infidels.

As a true son of the Church of England, he believes that "Christ redeemed him and all mankind;" that "for us men," and not merely for the *elect*, "he came down from heaven, and made upon the cross a full, perfect, and sufficient sacrifice, oblation, and satisfaction, for the sins of the *whole* world." Like an honest man, and yet a man of sense, he so subscribed the seventeenth article as not to reject the thirty-first, which he thinks of equal force, and much more explicit; and, therefore, as the seventeenth article authorizes him, he "receives God's promises in suchwise as they are generally set forth in holy Scripture;" rejecting, after the example of our governors in Church and state, the Lambeth articles, in which the doctrine of *absolute unconditional* election and reprobation was maintained, and which some Calvinistic divines, in the days of Queen Elizabeth, vainly attempted to impose upon these kingdoms, by adding them to the thirty-nine articles. Far, therefore, from thinking he does not act a fair part in rejecting the doctrine of particular redemption, he cannot conceive by what salvo the consciences of those ministers, who embrace it, can permit them to say to each of their communicants, "The blood of Christ was shed for *thee;*" and to baptize promiscuously *all* children within their respective parishes, "in the name of the Father, and of the Son, and of the Holy Ghost," when all that are unredeemed have no more right to the *blood, name,* and *Spirit* of Christ, than Lucifer himself.

Thus far Mr. Wesley agrees with Arminius, because he thinks that illustrious divine agreed thus far with the Scriptures, and all the early fathers of the Church. But if Arminius, (as the author of *Pietas Oxoniensis* affirms, in his letter to Dr. Adams,) "denied, that man's nature is totally corrupt; and asserted, that he hath still a freedom of will to turn to God, but not without the assistance of grace," Mr. Wesley is no Arminian; for he strongly asserts the *total* fall of man, and constantly maintains that by nature man's will is only free to evil, and that Divine grace must first prevent, and then continually farther him, to make him willing and able to turn to God.

I must, however, confess, that he does not, as some *real Protestants*, continually harp upon the words FREE grace, and FREE will; but he gives reasons of considerable weight for this. (1.) Christ and his apostles never did so. (2.) He knows the word *grace* necessarily implies the *freeness* of a favour; and the word *will*, the *freedom* of our choice: and he has too much sense to delight in perpetual tautology. (3.) He finds, by blessed experience, that when the will is touched by Divine grace, and yields to the touch, it is as free to good, as it was before to evil. He dares not, therefore, make the maintaining *free will*, any more than *free breath*, the criterion of an unconverted man. On the contrary, he believes none are converted but those who have a *free will* to follow Jesus; and, far from being ashamed to be called a "free-willer," he affirms it as essential to all men to be "free-willing creatures," as to be "rational animals;" and he supposes he can as soon find a diamond or a flint without gravity, as a good or bad man without free will.

Nor will I conceal that I never heard him use that favourite expression of some good men, *Why me? Why me?* though he is not at all against their using it, if they can do it to edification. But as he does not see that any of the saints, either of the Old or New Testament ever used it, he is afraid to be humble and "wise above what is written," lest "voluntary humility" should introduce refined pride before he is aware. Doubting, therefore, whether he could say, *Why me? Why me?* without the self-pleasing idea of his being preferred to thousands, or without a touch of the secret self applause that tickles the Pharisee's heart, when he "thanks God he is not as other men," he leaves the fashionable exclamation to others, with all the refinements of modern divinity; and chooses to keep to St. Paul's expression, "He loved me," which implies no exclusion of his poor fellow sinners; or to that of the royal psalmist, "Lord, what is *man*, that thou art mindful of him; and the *son of man*, that thou visitest him."

5. As a consequence of the doctrine of general redemption, Mr. Wesley lays down two axioms, of which he never loses sight in his preaching. *The first is*, that ALL OUR SALVATION IS OF GOD IN CHRIST, and therefore OF GRACE;—all opportunities, invitations, inclination, and power to believe being bestowed upon us of mere grace;—grace most absolutely free: and so far, I hope, that all who are called Gospel ministers agree with him. But he proceeds farther; for, *secondly*, he asserts with equal confidence, that according to the Gospel dispensation, ALL OUR DAMNATION IS OF OURSELVES, by our obstinate unbelief and avoidable unfaithfulness; as we may "neglect so great salvation," desire to "be excused" from coming to the feast of the Lamb, "make light of" God's gracious offers, refuse to "occupy," bury our talent, and act the part of the "slothful servant;" or, in other words, "resist, grieve, do despite to," and "quench the Spirit of grace," *by our moral agency.*

The first of these evangelical axioms he builds upon such scriptures as these:—"In me is thy help. Look unto me and be saved. No man cometh unto me except the Father draw him. What hast thou that thou hast not received? We are not sufficient to think aright of ourselves, all our sufficiency is of God. Christ is exalted to give repentance. Faith is the gift of God. Without me ye can do nothing," &c, &c.

And *the second* he founds upon such passages as these: "This is the condemnation, that light is come into the world, and men loved darkness rather than light. Ye always resist the Holy Ghost. They rejected the counsel of God toward themselves. Grieve not the Spirit. Quench not the Spirit. My Spirit shall not always strive with man. Turn, why will ye die? Kiss the Son, lest ye perish. I gave Jezebel time to repent, and she repented not. The goodness of God leads [not *drags*,] thee to repentance, who after thy hardness and impenitent heart treasurest up wrath unto thyself. Their eyes have they closed, lest they should see, and be converted, and I should heal them. See that ye refuse not him that speaketh from heaven. I set before you life and death, choose life! Ye will not come unto me that ye might have life. I *would* have gathered you, and ye *would not*," &c, &c.

As to the *moral agency* of man, Mr. Wesley thinks it cannot be denied upon the principles of common sense and civil government; much less upon those of natural and revealed religion; as nothing would be more absurd than to bind us by laws of a civil or spiritual nature; nothing more foolish than to propose to us punishments and rewards; and nothing more capricious than to inflict the one or bestow the other upon us; if we were not *moral agents.*

He is therefore persuaded, the most complete system of divinity is that in which neither of those two axioms is superseded: He thinks it is bold and unscriptural to set up the one at the expense of the other, convinced that the prophets, the apostles, and Jesus Christ left us no such precedent; and that, to avoid what is termed *legality,* we must not run into refinements which they knew nothing of, and make them perpetually contradict themselves: nor can we, he believes, without an open violation of the laws of candour and criticism, lay a greater stress upon a few obscure and controverted passages, than upon a hundred plain and irrefragable Scripture proofs. He therefore supposes that those persons are under a capital mistake who maintain only the first Gospel axiom, and under pretence of securing to God *all* the glory of the salvation of *one* elect, give to perhaps *twenty* reprobates full room to lay *all* the blame of their damnation either upon their first parents, or their Creator. This way of making twenty *real* holes, in order to stop a *supposed* one, he cannot see consistent either with wisdom or Scripture.

Thinking it therefore safest not to "put asunder" the truths which "God has joined together," he makes all extremes meet in one blessed Scriptural medium. With the Antinomian he preaches, "God worketh in you both to will and to do of his good pleasure;" and with the Legalist he cries, "Work out, therefore, your own salvation with fear and trembling;" and thus he has all St. Paul's doctrine. With the Ranter he says, "God has chosen you, you are elect;" but, as it is "through sanctification of the Spirit and belief of the truth," with the disciples of Moses he infers, "make your calling and election sure, for if ye do these things ye shall never fall." Thus he presents his hearers with all St. Peter's system of truth, which the others had rent to pieces.

Again, according to the *first* axiom, he says with the perfect Preacher, "All things are now ready;" but with him he adds also, according to the *second*, "Come, lest you never taste the Gospel feast." Thinking it extremely dangerous not to divide the word of God aright, he endeavours to give to every one the portion of it that suits him, cutting, according to times, persons, and circumstances, either with the smooth or the rough edge of his two-edged sword. Therefore, when he addresses those that are steady, and "partakers of the Gospel grace from the first day until now," as the Philippians, he makes use of the *first* principle, and testifies his confidence, "that he who hath begun a good work in them, will perform it until the day of Christ." But when he expostulates with persons, "that ran well, and do not now obey the truth," according to his *second* axiom, he says to them, as St. Paul did to the Galatians, "I stand in doubt of you; ye are fallen from grace."

In short, he would think that he mangled the Gospel, and forgot part of his awful commission, if, when he has declared that "he who believeth shall be saved," he did not also add, that he "who believeth not shall be damned;" or, which is the same, that none perish merely for Adam's sin, but for their own unbelief, and wilful rejection of the Saviour's grace. Thus he advances God's glory every way, entirely ascribing to his mercy and grace all the salvation of the elect, and completely freeing him from the blame of directly or indirectly hanging the millstone of damnation about the neck of the reprobate. And this he effectually does, by showing that the former owe all they are, and all they have, to creating, preserving, and redeeming love, whose innumerable bounties they freely and continually receive; and that the rejection of the latter has absolutely no cause but their obstinate rejecting of that astonishing mercy which wept over Jerusalem; and prayed, and bled even for those that shed the atoning blood—the blood that expiated all sin but that of final unbelief.

I have now finished my sketch of Mr. Wesley's doctrine, so far as it has fallen under my observation during above sixteen years' particular acquaintance with him and his works. It is not my design, sir, to inquire into the truth of his sentiments, much less shall I attempt to prove them orthodox, according to the ideas that some *real Protestants* entertain of orthodoxy. This only I beg leave to observe: Suppose he is mistaken in all the scriptures on which he founds his doctrine of Christian perfection and general redemption, yet his mistakes seem rather to arise from a regard for Christ's glory, than from enmity to his offices; and all together do not amount to any heresy at all; the fundamental doctrines of Christianity, namely, *the fall of man, justification by the merits of Christ, sanctification by the agency of the Holy Spirit,* and *the worship of the one true God in the mysterious distinction of Father, Son, and Holy Spirit,* as it is maintained in the three creeds, not being at all affected by any of his peculiar sentiments.

But you possibly imagine, sir, that he has lately changed his doctrine, and adopted a new system. If you do, you are under a very great mistake; and to convince you of it, permit me to conclude this letter by a paragraph of one which I received from him last spring:—

"I always did (for between these thirty and forty years) clearly assert the total fall of man, and his utter inability to do any good of himself: the absolute necessity of the grace and Spirit of God to raise even a good thought or desire in our hearts: the Lord's rewarding no works, and accepting of none, but so far as they proceed from his preventing, convincing, and converting grace, through the Beloved; the blood and righteousness of Christ being the sole meritorious cause of our salvation. And who is there in England that has asserted these things more strongly and steadily than I have done?"

Leaving you to answer this question, I remain, with due respect, Hon. and Rev. sir, your obedient servant, in the bond of a peaceful Gospel,

Madeley, *July* 29, 1771. J. Fletcher

Adam Clarke

Adam Clarke (1760?–1832), a native of Ireland who became a Methodist preacher in his early twenties, was a scholar of the first order and one of the most important theologians of early Methodism. In a remarkable way he combined a life of energetic preaching with serious scholarship, and careful textual work with a broad vision of Christian mission. Known especially for his classical commentaries and linguistic accomplishments (he deciphered language on the Rosetta Stone), he was also a significant theological voice. His *magnum opus* was his *Commentary on the Bible* on which he worked for forty years. He also published sermons and essays on theology such as *The Doctrine of Salvation by Faith* (1816) and *Christian Theology* (1835). The selections included in this collection illustrate, in title and content, characteristic emphases of both Clarke and Methodism in the early nineteenth century. "Justification" and "The Holy Spirit" are taken from *Christian Theology* (London: Thomas Tegg and Son, 1835), pp. 154-60, 167-72, 176-77.

Justification

The following are a few of the leading acceptations of the verb, which we translate "to justify:"—

1. It signifies to declare or pronounce one just or righteous; or, in other words, to declare him to be what he really is: "He was justified in the Spirit," 1 Tim. iii.16. 2. To esteem a thing properly, Matt. xi.19. 3. It sig-

nifies to approve, praise, and commend, Luke vii.29; xvi.15. 4. To clear from all sin, 1 Cor. iv.4. 5. A judge is said to justify, not only when he condemns and punishes, but also when he defends the cause of the innocent. Hence it is taken in a forensic sense, and signifies to be found or declared righteous, innocent, &c., Matt. xii.37. 6. It signifies to set free, or escape from, Acts xiii.39. 7. It signifies, also, to receive one into favour, to pardon sin, Rom. viii.30; Luke xviii.14; Rom. iii.20; iv.2; 1 Cor. vi.11, &c. In all these texts the word "justify" is taken in the sense of remission of sins through faith in Christ Jesus; and does not mean making the person just or righteous, but treating him as if he were so, having already forgiven him his sins.

Justification, or the pardon of sin, must precede sanctification; the conscience must be purged or purified from guilt, from all guilt, and from all guilt at once; for in no part of the Scripture are we directed to seek remission of sins *seriatim;* one now, another then, and so on.

The doctrine of justification by faith is one of the grandest displays of the mercy of God to mankind. It is so very plain that all may comprehend it; and so free that all may attain it. What more simple than this—Thou art a sinner, in consequence condemned to perdition, and utterly unable to save thy own soul. All are in the same state with thyself, and no man can give a ransom for the soul of his neighbour. God, in his mercy has provided a Saviour for thee. As thy life was forfeited to death because of thy transgressions, Jesus Christ has redeemed thy life by giving up his own; he died in thy stead, and has made atonement to God for thy transgression; and offers thee the pardon he has thus purchased, on the simple condition that thou believe that his death is a sufficient sacrifice, ransom, and oblation for thy sin; and that thou bring it, as such, by confident faith to the throne of God, and plead it in thy own behalf there. When thou dost so, thy faith in that sacrifice shall be imputed to thee for righteousness; that is, it shall be the means of receiving that salvation which Christ has bought by his blood.

The doctrine of the imputed righteousness of Christ, as held by many, will not be readily found in Rom. iv., where it has been supposed to exist in all its proofs. It is repeatedly said that faith is imputed for righteousness; but in no place here, that Christ's obedience to the moral law is imputed to any man. The truth is, the moral law was broken, and did not now require obedience; it required this before it was broken; but, after it was broken, it required death. Either the sinner must die, or some one in his stead; but there was none whose death could have been an equivalent for the transgressions of the world but Jesus Christ. Jesus, therefore, died for man; and it is through his blood, the merit of his passion and death, that we have redemption; and not by his obedience to the moral law in our stead: Our salvation was obtained at a much higher price. Jesus could not but be righteous and obedient; this is consequent on the immaculate purity of his nature; but his death was not a necessary consequent. As the law of God can claim only the death of a transgressor—for such only forfeit their right to life—it is the greatest miracle of all that Christ could die, whose life was never forfeited. Here we see the indescribable demerit of sin, that it required such a death; and here we see the stupendous mercy of God, in providing the sacrifice required. It is therefore by Jesus Christ's death, or obedience unto death, that we are saved, and not by his fulfilling any moral law. That he fulfilled the moral law, we know; without which he could not have been qualified to be our Mediator; but we must take heed lest we attribute that to obedience (which was the necessary consequence of his immaculate nature) which belongs to his passion and death. These were free-will offerings of eternal goodness, and not even a necessary consequence of his incarnation.

This doctrine of the imputed righteousness of Christ is capable of great abuse. To say that Christ's personal righteousness is imputed to every true believer, is not Scriptural: to say that he has fulfilled all righteousness for us, in our stead, if by this is meant his fulfilment of all moral duties, is neither Scriptural nor true; that he has died in our stead, is a great, glorious, and Scriptural truth; that there is no redemption but through his blood is asserted beyond all contradiction in the oracles of God. But there are a multitude of duties which the moral law requires, which Christ never fulfilled in our stead, and never could. We have various duties of a domestic kind which belong solely to ourselves, in the relation of parents, husbands, wives, servants, &c., in which relations Christ never stood. He has fulfilled none of these duties for us, but he furnishes grace to every true believer to fulfil them to God's glory, the edification of his neighbour, and his own eternal profit. The salvation which we receive from God's free mercy, through Christ, binds us to live in a strict conformity to the moral law; that law which prescribes our manners, and the spirit by which they should be regulated, and in which they should be performed. He who lives not in the due performance of every Christian duty, whatever faith he may profess, is either a vile hypocrite or a scandalous Antinomian.

God is said to be "no respecter of persons" for this reason, among many others, that, being infinitely righteous, he must be infinitely impartial. He cannot prefer one to another, because he has nothing to hope or fear from any of his creatures. All partialities among men spring from one or other of these two principles, hope or fear; God can feel neither of them, and therefore God can be no respecter of persons. He approves or disapproves of men according to their moral character. He pities all, and provides salvation for all, but he loves those who resemble him in his holiness; and he loves them in proportion to that resemblance, that is, the more of his image he sees in any the more he loves him, and *e contra*. And every man's work will be the evidence of his conformity or nonconformity to God; and according to this evidence will God judge him. Here, then, is no respect of persons. God's judgment will be according to a man's work, and a man's work or conduct will be according to the moral state of his mind. No favouritism can prevail in the day of judgment; nothing will pass there but holiness of heart and life. A righteousness imputed, and not possessed and practised, will not avail where God judgeth according to every man's work. It would be well if those sinners and spurious believers, who fancy themselves safe and complete in the righteousness of Christ, while impure and unholy in themselves, would think of this testimony of the apostle.

As eternal life is given IN the Son of God, it follows it cannot be enjoyed WITHOUT him. No man can have it without having Christ; therefore "he that hath the Son hath life," and "he that hath not the Son hath not life." It is in vain to expect eternal glory if we have not Christ in our heart. The indwelling Christ gives both a title to it and a meetness for it. This is God's record. Let no man deceive himself here. An indwelling Christ, and glory; no indwelling Christ, no glory. God's record must stand.

Who are Christ's flock? All real penitents; all true believers; all who obediently follow his example, abstaining from every appearance of evil, and in a holy life and conversation show forth the virtue of Him who called them from darkness into his marvellous light. "My sheep hear my voice and follow me." But who are not his flock? Neither the backslider in heart, nor the vile Antinomian, who thinks the more he sins the more the grace of God shall be magnified in saving him; nor those who fondly suppose they are covered with the righteousness of Christ while living in sin; nor the crowd of the indifferent and the careless; nor the immense herd of Laodicean loiterers; nor the fiery bigots, who would exclude all from heaven but themselves, and the party who believe as they do. These the Scripture resembles to swine, dogs, goats, wandering stars, foxes, lions, wells without water, &c., &c. Let not any of these come forward to eat of this pasture, or take of the children's bread. Jesus Christ is the good Shepherd; the Shepherd who, to save his flock, laid down his own life.

To forsake all, without following Christ, is the virtue of a philosopher. To follow Christ in profession, without forsaking all, is the state of the generality of Christians. But to follow Christ, and forsake all, is the perfection of a Christian.

Talking about Christ, his righteousness, merits, and atonement, while the person is not conformed to his word and Spirit, is no other than solemn deception.

The white robes of the saints cannot mean the righteousness of Christ, for this cannot be washed and made white in his own blood. This white linen is said to be the righteousness of the saints, Rev. xix.8; and this is the righteousness in which they stand before the throne; therefore it is not Christ's righteousness, but it is a righteousness wrought in them by the merits of his blood and the power of his Spirit.

We must beware of Antinomianism, that is, of supposing that, because Christ has been obedient unto death, there is no necessity for our obedience to his righteous commandments. If this were so, the grace of Christ would tend to the destruction of the law, and not to its establishment. He only is saved from his sins who has the law of God written in his heart, who lives an innocent, holy, and useful life. Wherever Christ lives he works; and his work of righteousness will appear to his servants, and its effect will be quietness and assurance for ever. The life of God in the soul of man is the principle which saves and preserves eternally.

The Holy Spirit

The Witness of the Spirit.—As every pious soul that believed in the coming Messiah, through the medium of the sacrifices offered up under the law, was made a partaker of the merit of his death, so every pious soul that believes in Christ crucified is made a partaker of the Holy Spirit. It is by this Spirit that sin is made known, and by it the blood of the covenant is applied; and, indeed, without this the want of salvation cannot be discovered, nor the value of the blood of the covenant duly estimated.

From the foundation of the church of God it was ever believed by his followers that there were certain infallible tokens by which he discovered to genuine believers his acceptance of them and of their services. This was sometimes done by a fire from heaven consuming the sacrifice; sometimes by an oracular communication to the priest or prophet; and at other times, according to the Jewish account, by changing the fillet or cloth on the head of the scape goat from scarlet to white: but most commonly, and especially under the gospel dispensation, he gives this assurance to true believers by the testimony of his Spirit in their consciences, that he has forgiven their iniquities, transgressions, and sins, for His sake who has carried their griefs and borne their sorrows.

"The Spirit itself"—That same Spirit, the Spirit of adoption; that is, the Spirit who witnesses this adoption; which can be no other than the Holy Ghost himself, and certainly cannot mean any disposition or affection of mind which the adopted person may feel; for such a disposition must arise from a knowledge of this adoption, and the knowledge of this adoption cannot be known by any human or earthly means; it must come from God himself. "With our spirit"—in our understanding, the place or recipient of light and information; and the place or faculty to which such information can properly be brought. This is done that we may have the highest possible evidence of the work which God has wrought. As the window is the proper medium to let the light of the sun into our apartments, so the understanding is the proper medium of conveying the Spirit's influence to the soul. We therefore have the utmost evidence of the fact of our adoption which we can possibly have; we have the word and Spirit of God, and the word sealed on our spirit by the Spirit of God. And this is not a momentary influx: if we take care to walk with God, and not grieve the Holy Spirit, we shall have an abiding testimony; and while we continue faithful to our adopting Father, the Spirit that witnesses that adoption will continue to witness it; and hereby we shall know that we are of God by the Spirit which he giveth us.

"The same Spirit," viz., the Spirit that witnesses of our adoption and sonship, makes intercession for us. Surely, if the apostle had designed to teach us that he meant our own sense and understanding by the Spirit, he never could have spoken in a manner in which plain common sense was never likely to comprehend his meaning. Besides, how can it be said that our own spirit, our filial disposition, bears witness with our own spirit; that our own spirit helps the infirmities of our own spirit; that our own spirit teaches our own spirit that of which it is ignorant; and that our own spirit maketh intercession for our spirit, with groanings unutterable? This would have been both incongruous and absurd. We must, therefore, understand these places of that help and influence which the followers of God receive from the Holy Ghost; and consequently, of the fulfilment of the various promises relative to this point which our Lord made to his disciples.

This Holy Spirit is sent forth to witness with their spirit. He is to bear his testimony where it is absolutely necessary,—where it can be properly discovered,—where it can be fully understood, and where it cannot be mistaken:—viz., in their hearts; or, as St. Paul says, "the Spirit itself beareth witness with our spirit:" The Spirit of God with the spirit of man—spirit with spirit—intelligence with intelligence; the testimony given and received by the same kind of agency: a spiritual agent in a spiritual substance.

This witness is not borne in their passions, nor in impressions made upon their imagination; for this must be from its very nature doubtful and evanescent; but it is borne in their understanding, not by a transitory manifestation, but continually—unless a man by sins of omission or commission grieve that divine Spirit, and cause him to withdraw his testimony—which is the same thing as the divine approbation. And God cannot continue to the soul a sense of his approbation, when it has departed from the holy commandment that was given to it: but, even in this case, the man may return by repentance and faith to God, through Christ, when pardon will be granted and the witness restored.

Wherever this Spirit comes, it bears a testimony to itself. It shows that it is the divine Spirit, by its own light; and he who receives it is perfectly satisfied of this. It brings a light, a power, and conviction, more full, more clear, and more convincing to the understanding and judgment, than they ever had, or ever can have, of any circumstance or fact brought before the intellect. The man knows that it is the divine Spirit, and he knows and feels that it bears testimony to the state of grace in which he stands.

So convincing and satisfactory is this testimony, that a man receiving it is enabled to call God his Father, with the utmost filial confidence. Surprised and convinced, he cries out at once, "Abba, Father! my Father! my Father!" having as full a consciousness that he is a child of God, as the most tenderly beloved child has of his filiation to his natural parent. He has the full assurance of faith; the meridian evidence that puts all doubts to flight.

And this, as was observed above, continues; for it is the very voice of the indwelling Spirit: for "crying" is not only the participle of the present tense, denoting the continuation of the action; but, being neuter, it agrees with the Spirit of his Son; so it is the divine Spirit which continues to cry, "Abba, Father!" in the heart of the true believer. And it is ever worthy to be remarked, that when a man has been unfaithful to the grace given, or has fallen into any kind of sin, he has no power to utter this cry. The Spirit is grieved and has departed, and the cry is lost! No power of the man's reason, fancy, or imagination, can restore this cry. Were he to utter the words with his lips, his heart would disown them. But, on the other hand, while he continues faithful, the witness is continued; the light and conviction, and the cry, are maintained. It is the glory of this grace that no man can command this cry; and none can assume it. Where it is, it is the faithful and true witness: where it is not, all is uncertainty and doubt.

The persons mentioned, Rom. viii.15, 16, had the strongest evidence of the excellence of the state in which they stood; they knew that they were thus adopted; and they knew this by the Spirit of God, which was given them on their adoption; and, let me say, they could know it by no other means. The Father who had adopted them could be seen by no mortal eye; and the transaction, being of a purely spiritual nature, and transacted in heaven, can be known only by God's supernatural testimony of it upon earth. It is a matter of such solemn importance to every Christian soul, that God in his mercy has been pleased not to leave it to conjecture, assumption, or inductive reasoning; but attests it by his own Spirit in the soul of the person whom he adopts through Christ Jesus. It is the grand and most observable case in which the intercourse is kept up between heaven and earth; and the genuine believer in Christ Jesus is not left to the quibbles or casuistry of polemic divines or critics, but receives the thing and the testimony of it, immediately from God himself. And were not the testimony of the state thus given, no man could possibly have any assurance of his salvation which could beget confidence and love. If to any man his acceptance with God be hypothetical, then his confidence must be so too. His love to God must be hypothetical, his gratitude hypothetical, and his obedience also. If God had forgiven me my sins, then I should love him, and I should be grateful, and I should testify this gratitude by obedience. But who does not see that these must necessarily depend on the "if" in the first case? All this uncertainty, and the perplexities necessarily resulting from it, God has precluded by sending the Spirit of his Son into our hearts, by which we cry, "Abba, Father;" and thus our adoption into the heavenly family is testified and ascertained to us in the only way in which it can possibly be done, by the direct influence of the Spirit of God. Remove this from Christianity and it is a dead letter.

The fact to be witnessed is beyond the knowledge of man: no human power or cunning can acquire it: if obtained at all, it must come from above. In this, human wit and ingenuity can do nothing. It is to tell us that we are reconciled to God; that our sins are blotted out; that we are adopted into the family of heaven. The apostle tells us that this is witnessed by the Spirit of God. God alone can tell whom he has accepted; whose sins he has blotted out; whom he has put among his children: this he makes known by his Spirit in our spirit; so that we have (not by induction or inference) a thorough conviction and mental feeling, that we are his children.

There is as great a difference between this and knowledge gained by logical argument, as there is between hypothesis and experiment. Hypothesis states that a thing may be so: experience alone proves the hypothesis to be true or false. By the first, we think the thing to be possible or likely; by the latter we know, experience, or prove, by practical trial, that the matter is true, or is false, as the case may be.

I should never have looked for the "witness of the Spirit," had I not found numerous scriptures which most positively assert it, or hold it out by necessary induction; and had I not found that all the truly godly, of every sect and party, possessed the blessing—a blessing which is the common birthright of all the sons and daughters of God. Wherever I went among deeply religious people, I found this blessing. All who had turned from unrighteousness to the living God, and sought redemption by faith in the blood of the cross, exulted in this grace. It was never looked on by them as a privilege with which some peculiarly favoured souls were blessed: it was known from Scripture and experience to be the common lot of the people of God. It was not persons of a peculiar temperament who possessed it; all the truly religious had it, whether in their natural dispositions sanguine, melancholy, or mixed. I met with it everywhere, and met with it among the most simple and illiterate, as well as among those who had every advantage, which high cultivation and deep learning could bestow. Perhaps I might, with the strictest truth, say that during the forty years I have been in the ministry, I have met with at least forty thousand who have had a clear and full evidence that God, for Christ's sake, had forgiven their sins, the Spirit himself bearing witness with their spirit that they were the sons and daughters of God. . . .

The Holy Spirit in the soul of a believer is God's seal, set on his heart to testify that he is God's property, and that he should be wholly employed in God's service.

As Christ is represented as the ambassador of the Father, so the Holy Spirit is represented as the ambassador of the Son, coming vested with his authority, as the interpreter and executor of his will.

We know by the Spirit which he hath given us, that we dwell in God, and God in us. It was not by conjecture or inference that Christians of old knew they were in the favour of God; it was by the testimony of God's own Spirit in their hearts; and this Spirit was not given in a transient manner, but was constant and abiding, while they continued under the influence of that faith which worketh by love. Every good man is a temple of the Holy Ghost; and wherever He is, He is both light and power. By his power he works; by his light he makes both himself and his work known. Peace of conscience and joy in the Holy Ghost must proceed from the indwelling of that Holy Spirit; and those who have these blessings must know that they have them, for we cannot have heavenly peace and heavenly joy without knowing that we have them. But this Spirit in the soul of a believer is not only manifest by its effects, but it bears its own witness to its own indwelling. So that a man not only knows that he has the Spirit from the fruits of the Spirit, but he knows that he has it from its own direct witness. It may be said, "How can these things be?" And it may be answered, "By the power, light, and mercy of God." But that such things are, the Scriptures uniformly attest; and the experience of the whole genuine church of Christ, and of every truly converted soul, sufficiently proves. "As the wind bloweth where it listeth," and we "cannot tell whence it cometh and whither it goeth, so is every one that is born of the Spirit:" the thing is certain, and fully known by its effects; but how this testimony is given and confirmed, is inexplicable. Every good man feels it, and knows he is of God by the Spirit God has given him.

Nathan Bangs

Nathan Bangs (1778–1862) was the first important theological voice of North American Methodism. Born in Stratford, Connecticut, and self-educated, he participated in the intellectual discussions of his time and wrote extensively on theological issues. He was licensed to preach in 1801 and spent six years in Canada as a Methodist itinerant missionary. In 1820 he was appointed head of the Methodist Publishing Concern in New York and editor of *The Methodist Magazine* (later *The Methodist Quarterly Review*), which post he held from 1820 to 1836. He was also one of the founders of the Methodist Missionary Society. Among his more important publications are *Predestination Examined* (1817), *Methodist Episcopacy* (1820), *Essay on Emancipation* (1840), and *Letters on Sanctification* (1851). As a writer, editor, and denominational spokesman, Bangs provided leadership for the emerging North American church and set trends of theological interest and development. The selections from Bangs' writings indicate two of his central interests: the work of the Holy Spirit and the grace of God in human volitional activity. The selections "On Election" and "On Christian Perfection" are taken from *The Errors of Hopkinsianism* (New York: John C. Totten, 1815), pp. 97-115, 153-58, 183-87, 195-97.

On Election

Rev. Sir,

1. On entering upon the doctrine of election, it is proper to notice the tendency of some of your remarks upon this important point. Your

32

labouring to prove that election is not founded upon works foreseen, is calculated to impress the reader with an idea that we believe it is. This sentiment *you* know was not advocated in the debate; and you also know that the "disputant on the" Hopkinsian "side," laboured to force me to assert and defend the doctrine, that election to eternal life depends on our works. His efforts, however, were unavailing. So far from believing this sentiment, we continually maintain that the election of souls to eternal life, is predicated of the goodness of God; and that, if it depended wholly upon works, no one would see life. It was pure love that moved God to give his Son, and that moved the Son to suffer and die for man. It is pure love that moves the Holy Trinity to begin, carry on, and perfect the work of salvation in the hearts of sinners. But such is the order of God, and the economy of grace, that this work of salvation is not effected without the co-operation of the free volitions of man. *Work out your own salvation with fear and trembling, for it is God that worketh in you, both to will and to do of his good pleasure.* Neither are we justified here as penitent sinners by works, but by faith. *With the heart man believeth unto righteousness. He that believeth and is baptized, shall be saved.* Nor does it follow by consequence from our doctrine, that election to eternal life depends upon our works as its *cause.* It is true, we believe, from the undeviating testimony of scripture, that by the *evidence* of our *good works*, which are the fruits of justifying faith, we are justified in the sight of men here, and in the sight of God at the great day. . . .

6. You only beat the air in your first section, where you say, "It is to be shown that election is not founded on works," p. 58. Here you suppose that our doctrine, either by principle or consequence, makes election to eternal life, depend solely on our works. But this supposition arises from a mistaken apprehension of our doctrine. If a beggar were to receive from the hand of a wealthy benevolent man, something to supply his wants, does it follow that the act of the beggar in receiving the gratuitous donation from his benefactor, is the *foundation,* or *meritorious cause* of his subsistence? By no means. The *benevolence* of the donor, and not the *act* of the beggar, is the source of the poor man's subsistence. Mankind may be fitly compared to beggars, as they stand related to God. He offers them grace: if any comply with the condition of the gospel, and receive the gift of pardon by faith, does it follow that their act of receiving is the foundation of their pardon? It does not. The source of all the *favours* bestowed on fallen men, is in the plenitude of divine goodness. It was infinite condescension in God that caused him to provide a Saviour for sinners, and to accommodate the terms of acceptance

33

and salvation to the weakness of man. The question is not therefore, as your readers might infer, whether our election to eternal life be predicated of *works* or *grace;* but whether grace, the grace of eternal life, be unconditionally bestowed on some, and whether all the rest be unconditionally reprobated to eternal death, without any respect to their wicked works. All the scriptures therefore which you have quoted to prove that *grace* is the *first* and *moving* cause of our salvation, makes nothing against us; and all you say against works being the *foundation* of our election, is wide of the point, as we never held they were. Nevertheless, that *believing* in the Lord Jesus, is the condition of our justification here, as penitent sinners, and that those *good works* which spring from a living, justifying faith, are the evidences both of our justification here and hereafter, is abundantly manifest from scripture. *By grace are ye* (not shall be) *saved, through faith, and that not of yourselves; it is the gift of God, Eph. ii.8. And by him, all that believe are justified from all things, Acts xiii.39. He that believeth on him is not condemned; but he that believeth not is condemned already,* BECAUSE *he hath not believed on the name of the only begotten Son of God,* John iii.18. Who that reads these scriptures can doubt but that faith in Christ is a condition on the performance of which our justification is suspended? Any man who can doubt it, with such plain and positive testimony before his eyes, may turn sceptic and doubt of every thing. If this be so, that our justification is suspended on our believing, that believing is the expressed *condition* of justification, then your doctrine of *unconditional* election to eternal life, is erroneous. And if this part of your system be erroneous, so also must the dreadful counterpart of it be, namely, *unconditional reprobation to eternal death.* In regard to this part of your system, I believe you have quoted no scripture to support it—and you are quite excusable; for indeed there are none to be found.

The word which the translators of our bible have rendered *reprobate,* is *adokimos,* and this comes from *dokimos,* which signifies to *try, prove,* as metals are tried and proved in the fire. It is applied figuratively to man—Previous to justification all men are *adokimos,* reprobates; that is, such as will not bear the test, when their characters are examined by the standard of Christianity. They must first be cast into the refining fire of God's Spirit, until the dross of sin be separated from them, and then they are *dokimos,* elect, or *approved.* This word occurs but eight times in all the New Testament. In 1 Cor. ix.27, Paul saith, *Lest that by any means, when I have preached to others, I myself should be adokimos, a cast-away,* or *reprobate;* one that will not bear the test of examination at the great day;

34

or one that will not be *approved* by his judge. In 2 Cor. xiii.5, 6, 7.—Rom. i.28.—2 Tim. iii.8. and Tit. i.16, it is rendered *reprobate;* in Heb. vi.8, *reject-ed*. Any person who will consult the places where this word occurs, will be convinced that it is used to designate a person whose conduct is dis-approved in the sight of God—Those who have so much of the *dross of sin* about them, that, when weighed in the scale of truth, they *are found wanting*. But the *dokimoi*, the *elect*, it appears, are those of whom God approves. They having been refined in the fire of God's Spirit, and still enduring all the severe trials which come upon them, are found *pure* and *good*, and shall be found unto praise and glory, if they become not, by departing from God, *reprobates*, or cast aways, 1 Cor. ix.27. It appears therefore, that the *reprobates* may become *elect*, and the *elect* may become *reprobates*. Here is no foundation for the doctrine of *eternal* and *uncondi-tional* election and reprobation. . . .

Allowing the accuracy of the above remarks, that the reprobates are such as are *disapproved*, after being *tried*, how can they be reprobated from all eternity, seeing they could not be *tried* before they had an opportunity of *acting*? Can gold be tried before it exists? To say that God *knew* who would stand the test of examination, is no argument in favour of Hopkinsianism. This declares that God's determination respecting the final estates of men, was antecedent to his *knowledge* of them; so that prescience itself is dependent for its existence upon preordination. . . .

God saith concerning the Israelites, *I have chosen you in the furnace of affliction*. Were they in the furnace of affliction before they were born? If not, this *choice* could not have been from all eternity.

8. In Eph. v.6, the Apostle Paul assigns a reason why impenitent sin-ners are finally damned.—"Let no man deceive you with vain words, for *because of these things* cometh the wrath of God upon the children of disobedience." The things to which the Apostle alludes, are mentioned in the preceding verse—*For this ye know, that no whoremonger, nor unclean person, nor covetous man, who is an idolater, hath any inheritance in the king-dom of Christ and of God*. How different the opinion of this Apostle from yours! "It is not," say you, "assigning a sufficient reason for their repro-bation, to say they were wicked, and would not accept of mercy," p. 63. Now sir, either you, or Jesus Christ and the Apostle Paul, are mistaken. Paul saith in the above passage, "The wrath of God cometh on the chil-dren of disobedience, *because* of their wickedness." You say, "This is not a sufficient reason." Paul saith, 2 Thess. ii.10, 11, 12, that sinners are damned *because* they received not the love of the truth *that they might be saved*—and for this *cause* God shall send them strong delusions, that

35

they should believe a lie, that they all might be damned who believe not the truth, but had pleasure in unrighteousness. But you say, this is not a sufficient reason. If the Apostle had believed your doctrine, would he not have said, *they are damned on account* of an *eternal decree of reprobation*, which immutably secured their wickedness, that they might be vessels of wrath and "suitable objects" of eternal indignation? Jesus Christ said, Luke xiii.34, How oft would I have gathered you together, and ye would not? Behold your house is left unto you desolate. *Ye would not* accept of mercy, and therefore ye shall be rejected, i.e. reprobated. You reply, "This is not assigning a sufficient reason for their reprobation." Are then Dr. Hopkins and yourself wiser than Jesus Christ, and his servant Paul! Surely this is being wise above what is written. Were I to quote all the scriptures which assign the wickedness of sinners, and their refusal to accept of mercy as the *cause* of their final condemnation, I should transcribe a great part of the bible. They are fitted, it is true, for destruction; but they fit themselves by abusing the goodness of God, by an obstinate refusal of mercy; in a word, by *not receiving the truth that they might be saved*.

9. Although you strongly assert your belief in unconditional predestination, you seem ashamed of it in the discussion of your subject. For in p. 59 you very modestly say, "But why did the Lord of Angels *suffer* them to rebel?"—and p. 60, "Why were such a part of the Angels suffered to apostatize?" This language, sir, ill becomes the lips of such a rigid predestinarian as you have avowed yourself to be. To hold that God *absolutely decreed*, before the foundation of the world, that precisely so many intelligent beings should apostatize, and that every particular sin of their lives were not only unalterably fixed in the mind of God, but also "brought to pass" by him: and then talk about *suffering* their apostacy, is truly ridiculous. Why not speak out, and ask, Why did God *decree* and *foreordain* that Angels should rebel, and that precisely so many of the human family should apostatize, and remain in their apostacy, and finally be damned. And why not give a categorical answer to these questions, in conformity to your unscriptural doctrine? *Because he would.* Does the absurdity of your doctrine appear so glaringly horrid at some times, that you wish to draw a veil over it?

10. Page 64, "Paul mentions the greatness of his sin, as one reason why he obtained mercy." Is this correct? He is so far from assigning the "greatness of his sin" as a reason why he obtained mercy, that he says, 1 Tim. i.13. But I obtained mercy *because* I did it *ignorantly* and in *unbelief*. These words seem to suppose, that if he had *believed* Christ was the

promised *Messiah*, and if he had *known* him to be the person against whom he acted so violently, he should not have obtained mercy. He says indeed, in v. 14, *And the grace of our Lord Jesus was exceeding abundant with faith and love.* And in v. 16, "Howbeit, for this *cause* I obtained mercy, (not because he had been a great sinner, but *because of the abundance of the grace of Jesus Christ) that in me first Jesus Christ might shew forth all long-suffering, for a pattern to them who should hereafter believe in him to life everlasting.*" The *cause* of which he here speaks, is not that he had been a great sinner, (although he had been even a blasphemer, and a persecutor, and injurious, v. 13.) but that Christ's long-suffering might be manifest,—and that the Apostle might be a pattern to others, not of "indwelling sin," but of faith and purity.—In the whole passage, I cannot discover that the Apostle had the remotest allusion to sin, as a *reason* why he obtained mercy. O sir, what a dangerous sentiment you have advanced! Paul obtained mercy because of the greatness of his sin: Let us *sin* then, may all blasphemers say, that grace may abound. Do not say that this objection was brought against the Apostle's doctrine, as well as against yours; and therefore you teach the same thing. It is a legitimate consequence from your sentiment; but was an unjust reflection upon the Apostle. Paul obtained mercy *because* he was a great sinner. "Well then," says a correct reasoner, "the same *cause* under the same circumstances, will produce the same *effect;* I will therefore be a great sinner, that I also may obtain mercy." Will you undertake to prove that his reasoning is not conclusive?

On Christian Perfection

Rev. Sir,

Having shewn in my former letter, the inconsistency of your doctrine of personal election, I come now to examine what you say respecting "sinful imperfection." It is matter of some surprise, that, after all which has been said and written to the contrary, you should strive to impose upon the public a belief, that we hold, "that saints in this life are as perfect as they will be in heaven," p. 103, note. O sir, is it fair, is it consistent with that *charity which hopeth all things,* thus to misrepresent a body of people! And how do you attempt to prove your assertion? Why, "By the argument which they use in their book of Discipline against the power of death to sanctify," *ibid.* And pray sir, do you really believe in the *power of death* to sanctify? It would seem so by this observation of

37

yours, as also from what you say about Paul's desiring to *die*, because death would put an end to that body of sin under which he groaned.— But from what part of the scriptures do you prove this strange doctrine? Does not John say, 1 John i.7, *The blood of Jesus Christ his Son, cleanseth us from all sin?* Does not the apostle Paul ask, Heb. ix.14, *How much more shall the blood of Christ, who through the eternal Spirit, offered himself without spot to God, purge your conscience from dead works to serve the living God?* In this passage they are said to be purged from dead works, *by the blood of Christ,* that they might serve the living God.—But if they do not serve the living God until purified, and if *death* acts as a purifier, then we do not serve the living God until after death. It is seriously doubted whether a solitary passage of scripture can be found in all the Bible to support the idea, that *death* is the *destroyer* of sin. On the contrary, death is all along represented as a *consequence of sin,* and the last enemy. Shall the effect destroy its cause? And shall the enemy of mankind do the most friendly and beneficial act towards them?—The "arguments," therefore "which we use against the power of death to sanctify," do not necessarily suppose, that we are as sinless in this life, as are the *spirits of just men made perfect.* It is true, we wish to ascribe the glory of our salvation, from the foundation to the top-stone, to Jesus Christ, and not to death; and in this respect we accord with the holy scriptures, which teach us to ascribe honour and glory *unto him that loved us, and washed us in his own blood.*

As the *consequence* which you endeavour to infer from our doctrine, has no connexion with it, so neither do we hold it in *principle.* And you might have convinced yourself of this, if you had taken the trouble of looking in our discipline, instead of quoting merely from recollection, and perhaps from hearsay. To convince you of your mistake, I will transcribe some passages from the discipline, published in 1808. P. 120, After having shewn the difference between the Mosaic economy, comprehending the political, moral, and ceremonial laws, and the Adamic law of innocence; and also shewing the reason why men cannot fulfil the requirements of the latter, the author concludes thus,—"Consequently, no man is able to perform the service, which the Adamic law requires." Compare this with p. 106. "To explain myself a little farther on this head; 1. Not only *sin, properly* so called, that is, a voluntary transgression of a known law, but sin, improperly so called, that is, an involuntary transgression of a divine law, known or unknown, needs the atoning blood. 2. I believe there is no such perfection *in this life,* as excludes these involuntary transgressions, which I apprehend to be naturally consequent on the ignorance and mistakes inseparable from mortality. 3. Therefore *sinless perfection* is a phrase I never use, lest I should seem to contradict myself. 4. I believe a person filled with the love of God, is still liable to these involuntary transgressions. 5. Such transgressions you may call sins, if you please; I do not for the reasons above mentioned." Take another instance from page 123, "But the best of men may say, Thou art my light, my holiness, my heaven.—Through my union with thee, I am full of light, of holiness, and happiness. And if I were left to myself, I should be nothing but sin, darkness, and hell." "The best of men need Christ as their priest, their atonement, their advocate with the Father; not only, as the continuance of their every blessing depends on his death and intercession, but on account of their coming short of the law of love."

From these quotations, all of which are taken from our *discipline,* it is undeniably plain, 1. That we believe that a *perfect christian,* when considered in relation to the Adamic law, falls far short of its requirements; and therefore, on this account, may be denominated a transgressor. 2. But that no man since the fall is under that law, because it is, properly speaking, a law of works; whereas we are under the dispensation of grace. And will you undertake to prove, that the glorified saints in heaven do not perfectly fulfil this law? Are they not perfectly freed not only from sin, but also from all its consequences? At least at the resurrection, when their glorified bodies shall become like unto *Christ's most glorious body.* If you cannot prove this, neither can you prove that we hold to as great perfection *in this life,* as the saints in heaven possess. 3. That such is our situation, surrounded with temptations, the spirit shrouded in a corruptible body, our reasoning powers impaired, that we frequently *involuntarily* transgress the law of love, under which we are; but that these are not *sins,* "properly so called." 4. That therefore we continually need the atoning merits of Christ to wash us, and the Holy Spirit to help our infirmities.—After reading these remarks, it is possible you may think, that, among other sins, which you suppose you momentarily commit, you have been guilty, I hope unintentionally, of the sin of misrepresentation. Having made these observations to remove the misapprehension which may have arisen in the minds of your readers, respecting our ideas of christian perfection, I proceed to examine, in the first place, those texts of scripture with which you attempt to support your doctrine of "sinful imperfection." . . .

II. 1. Having thus cleared the way, by rescuing the sacred scriptures from the "unholy service (to borrow the words of an eminent author) into which they were pressed against their will," I shall attempt to prove our doctrine of evangelical perfection, by an appeal to "unequivocal" texts of holy writ. And let it be remembered, that the point in debate is not whether we are as perfect in this life, as are the glorified spirits; nor whether we may be so perfect as to keep the Adamic law; but whether a *Christian* may arrive to such a state of perfection as to keep the gracious law under which the gospel of Christ places him, so as, in this sense to be delivered from sin. It ought furthermore to be observed, that no man since the introduction of moral evil into our world, is under the Adamic law, (which was a law of works) for justification and salvation. Neither is it a rule of life or of judgment: This point is so clear that it is needless to spend time to prove it. Taking it for granted, therefore, that we are under the *law of liberty*, established by Jesus Christ, I undertake to prove that a Christian, whose heart is thoroughly changed by the Spirit of God, does and must, in order to enter into life, keep it.

2. *But Noah found grace in the eyes of the Lord. Noah was a* JUST *man, and* PERFECT *in his generation, and Noah walked with God*, Gen. vi.8, 9. It may be asked, Why was Noah *just* and *perfect?* Because he found *grace* in the sight of God. It was not therefore from obedience to the Adamic, nor ceremonial law, that he was made perfect, but because he believed God, and faithfully improved the light of the dispensation of grace, under which he lived. He walked with God, like Enoch before him, who walked with God three hundred years, and did not *see death,* for God *translated him;* and before his translation, he had this testimony that he pleased God, Heb. xi.5. If death be necessary to cleanse the heart from sin, and if none can enter heaven without being previously cleansed, what becomes of *Enoch,* who did not *see death.* Here is at least one exception to your doctrine—Is not the prophet Elijah another?

3. You have frequently alluded to Isaiah vi.5. Woe is me, &c. If you had read on to the 7th verse, you would have discovered the doctrine for which we contend. *Then flew one of the seraphims unto me, having a live coal in his hand, which he had taken with the tongs from the altar. And he laid it upon my mouth and said, Lo this hath touched thy lips; and thine* INIQUITY IS TAKEN AWAY, *and thy* SIN IS PURGED. Does not this text undeniably prove the doctrine of a deliverance from sin?—Equally in point are the words of the Psalmist, Psa. ciii.12, *As far as the east is from the west, so far hath he removed our transgressions from us.* Observe that this is not spoken in anticipation of what shall be done at *death;* but it asserts what had already been accomplished.

4. Turn we our attention to the New-Testament writers. *What shall we*

say then, shall we CONTINUE *in* SIN *that grace may abound? God forbid: how shall we that are dead to sin,* LIVE *any longer therein?* Rom. vi.1, 2. How shall we that are *dead* to *sin,* consistently with that character we are called to support, as the servants of God, live any longer in sin!

V. 6. *Knowing this that our old man* IS CRUCIFIED (not shall be crucified at death) *with him, that the body of sin might be destroyed, that henceforth we should not serve sin.* V. 7, *For he that is dead is freed from sin.* V. 11. *Likewise reckon ye yourselves to be dead indeed unto* SIN, *but alive unto God through Jesus Christ our Lord.* V. 12. Let not sin therefore reign in your mortal bodies, that ye should obey it in the lusts thereof. V. 14. For SIN SHALL NOT HAVE DOMINION OVER YOU. No language can be more express, to denote the total destruction of sin from the human heart. "Observe the confidence with which he speaks"—Knowing this—what? Why, *that the old man is crucified, that the body of sin might be destroyed—that they were freed from sin—that they should reckon themselves dead to sin—that sin should not have dominion over them.* How diametrically opposite were the sentiments of this holy Apostle, in regard to deliverance from sin, and your's, sir, who so strenuously plead for its continuance through life! The man who can read the above passages of sacred scripture, and then deny the necessity and possibility of the destruction of sin from the heart in this life, may, with equal propriety, deny every doctrine of the Bible. See also from ver. 18-22, in the last of which it is said, *But now being made* FREE *from* SIN, *and become servants to God, ye have your fruit unto holiness, and the end everlasting life.*

5. The Apostle John bears testimony to the same truth, 1 John i, 6. *If we say that we have fellowship with him, and walk in darkness* (to walk in *sin* is the same as to walk in *darkness*) *we* LIE, *and do not the truth.* Do you not, sir, profess to have fellowship with Jesus Christ? and do you not also profess to live in sin every moment? In which particular are you mistaken? You think you ought not to have the "least mite of charity" for a Christian who professes to be delivered from sin! How different the judgment of St. John. It would seem that he had so little charity for those professors of his day, who said they had fellowship with God, and yet walked in darkness, that with his apostolic plainness, he called them liars. V. 7. *But if we walk in the light as he is in the light, we have fellowship one with another, and the blood of Jesus Christ his Son cleanseth us from* ALL SIN. How much sin is there left when *all* is taken away? And it ought to be observed that the Apostle does not speak of a *future* cleansing, but the blood of Christ *now cleanseth.* Ch. iii.8. *He that committeth sin is of the Devil; for the Devil sinneth from the beginning.* If your doctrine be true, that

41

all must "always sin in thought, word, and deed," then, according to John, all are children of the Devil. Who represents Christ as "vanquished" now? *For this purpose the Son of God was manifested, that he might destroy the works of the devil.* Will you say, that the *very purpose* for which the Son of God was manifested, shall not be accomplished? He came, according to the language of the Apostle Paul, *to redeem us from* ALL INIQUITY, *and to purify to himself a peculiar people, zealous of good works.* If therefore none are *purified*, if none are redeemed from *all iniquity* in this life, the benevolent design for which the Lord Jesus came into the world is not answered. And is it not highly dishonourable to God, to suppose that the express *design* for which he gave his Son; and equally dishonourable to the Son who came to accomplish the same *end*, to say that this desirable *end* is not, in any instance, obtained? . . .

10. You will, without doubt, acknowledge that conviction, justification and sanctification, are all the work of God. And Moses saith, *His work is perfect,* Deut. xxxiii.4. When therefore a sinner is convicted, justified and sanctified, he is *perfectly* convicted, justified and sanctified; for all the *works of God are perfect.* Any thing is perfect, which answers its END. Thus when God finished his work of creation, he pronounced it all *very good,* that is, *perfect;* because each and every part was fitted for the place it was designed to occupy, and to discharge the duties resulting from its relative situation. When souls are born into the kingdom of God, they are said to be *created anew unto good works, which God ordained that ye should walk in them.* To say therefore that adult christians do not walk in good works, but in sin, is to pronounce them *imperfect;* and to pronounce them in this sense imperfect, is to say that God's work is *defective*—that he has not so wrought believers, as to answer the *end* of their new creation. Again, the end for which Christ died for us is, *That he might redeem us from all iniquity, and purify to himself a peculiar people, zealous of good works.* This then is the *end,* the manifest *design* of God in the work of redemption and salvation. To accomplish this *end,* and fit man for this *design,* God works in the hearts of those who believe in Jesus Christ. To say, therefore, that obedient believers are not redeemed from all iniquity, and purified from all sin, "properly so called," is to say that the gracious design of God is frustrated, even towards those who are given to Christ. And that the Apostle in the above passage spoke of being *redeemed from all iniquity in this life,* is undeniably certain, from his adding, *a peculiar people zealous of good works;* unless you absurdly suppose that he meant they should not be *zealous of good works* until after death.—Now, as it is impious to insinuate that the *perfect work of God* is

defective, that his benevolent designs to the world never take effect, so it is absurd to say that believers are not saved from sin. If indeed we were left to ourselves in the work of salvation, we might well despair of an exemption from the curse of the law, and an emancipation from the thraldom of sin. But when we take into consideration, that he who is omnipotent in *power* and unbounded in wisdom and goodness, has undertaken to accomplish this glorious and desirable work, all our fears of its *complete* accomplishment are dissipated. He who worketh in us to *will* and to *do* of his own *good pleasure*, is fully able and abundantly willing to work in us *perfect* faith and love, *perfect* humility and patience, *perfect* meekness and temperance, goodness and forbearance, which are some of the perfect graces which adorn the soul of a christian. *Faithful is he that calleth you, who also will do it,* says Paul, 1 Thess. v. 24.

Richard Watson

Richard Watson (1781–1833), a British Methodist, was the first systematic theologian in Methodism and its most influential spokesman for the first half of the nineteenth century. His *Theological Institutes* (1833) was not only important in British Methodism but was the primary theological text of the North American Methodist ministerial course of study. Watson solidified Methodist theology and set it forth in well-organized detail. The selections included in these readings present an increasingly pervasive theme in Methodist thought: human moral agency. It is necessary to see this theme in relation to the discussion of grace in Fletcher and of the Holy Spirit in Clarke and Bangs and as it is worked out by later writers such as Whedon. The interaction of prevenient grace and human agency is one of the distinctive issues of the Wesleyan theological tradition. Among Watson's more important writings are *An Apology for the Bible* (1796), *A Biblical and Theological Dictionary* (1831), and *Life of John Wesley* (1831). Watson served as secretary to the Wesleyan Missionary Society (1821–25) and as President of the Conference (1826). The selections, "Man a Moral Agent" and "The Justice and Grace of God," are from *Theological Institutes* (London: John Mason, 1858), I, pp. 1-9, 15-16, and IV, pp. 132, 134-38.

Man a Moral Agent

The theological system of the holy Scriptures being the subject of our inquiries, it is essential to our undertaking to establish their divine authority. But before the direct evidence which the case admits is adduced, our attention may be profitably engaged by several considerations, which afford presumptive evidence in favour of the revelations of the Old and New Testaments. These are of so much weight that they ought not, in fairness, to be overlooked; nor can their force be easily resisted by the impartial inquirer.

The moral agency of man is a principle on which much depends in such an investigation; and, from its bearing upon the question at issue, requires our first notice.

He is a moral agent who is capable of performing moral actions; and an action is rendered moral by two circumstances,—that it is voluntary, and that it has respect to some rule which determines it to be good or evil. "Moral good and evil," says Locke, "is the conformity or disagreement of our voluntary actions to some law, whereby good or evil is drawn upon us from the will or power of the law-maker."

The terms found in all languages, and the laws which have been enacted in all states, with accompanying penalties, as well as the praise or dispraise which men, in all ages, have expressed respecting the conduct of each other, sufficiently show that man has always been considered as an agent actually performing, or capable of performing, moral actions; for as such he has been treated. No one ever thought of making laws to regulate the conduct of the inferior animals, or of holding them up to public censure or approbation.

The rules by which the moral quality of actions has been determined are, however, not those only which have been embodied in the legislation of civil communities. Many actions would be judged good or evil were all civil codes abolished; and others are daily condemned or approved in the judgment of mankind which are not of a kind to be recognised by public laws. Of the moral nature of human actions there must have been a perception in the minds of men previous to the enactment of laws. Upon this common perception all law is founded, and claims the consent and support of society; for in all human legislative codes there is an express or tacit appeal to principles previously acknowledged, as reasons for their enactment.

This distinction in the moral quality of actions previous to the establishment of civil regulations, and independent of them, may, in part, be traced to its having been observed, that certain actions are injurious to society, and that to abstain from them is essential to its well-being. Murder and theft may be given as instances. It has also been perceived, that such actions result from certain [afflictions] of the mind; and the indulgence or restraint of such affections has, therefore, been also regarded as a moral act. Anger, revenge, and cupidity, have been deemed evils, as the sources of injuries of various kinds; and humanity, self-government, and integrity, have been ranked among the virtues; and thus, both certain actions, and the principles from which they spring, have, from their effect upon society, been determined to be good or evil.

But it has likewise been observed, by every man, that individual happiness, as truly as social order and interests, is materially affected by particular acts, and by those feelings of the heart which give rise to them; as, for instance, by anger, malice, envy, impatience, cupidity, &c.; and that whatever civilized men, in all places, and in all ages, have agreed to call vice, is inimical to health of body, or to peace of mind, or to both. This, it is true, has had little influence upon human conduct; but it has been acknowledged by the poets, sages, and satirists of all countries, and is adverted to as matter of universal experience. Whilst, therefore, there is, in the moral condition and habits of man, something which propels him to vice, uncorrected by the miseries which it never fails to inflict, there is also something in the constitution of the human soul which renders vice subversive of its happiness, and something in the established law and nature of things which renders vice incompatible with the collective interests of men in the social state.

Let that, then, be granted by the Theist which he cannot consistently deny,—the existence of a supreme Creator, of infinite power, wisdom, goodness, and justice, who has both made men and continues to govern them; and the strongest presumption is afforded,—by the very constitution of the nature of man, and the relations established among human affairs, which, with so much constancy, dissociate happiness from vicious passions, health from intemperance, the peace, security, and improvement of society from violence and injustice,—that the course of action which best secures human happiness has the sanction of his will; or, in other words, that He, by these circumstances, has given his authority in favour of the practice of virtue, and opposed it to the practice of vice.

But though that perception of the difference of moral actions which is antecedent to human laws, must have been strongly confirmed by these facts of experience, and by such observations, we have no reason to conclude that those rules by which the moral quality of actions has, in all ages, been determined, were formed solely from a course of observation on their tendency to promote or obstruct human happiness; because we cannot collect, either from history or tradition, that the world was ever without such rules, though they were often warped and corrupted. The evidence of both, on the contrary, shows, that so far from these rules having originated from observing what was injurious and what beneficial to mankind, there has been, almost among all nations, a constant reference to a declared will of the supreme God, or of supposed deities, as the rule which determines the good or the evil of the conduct of men; which will was considered by them as a law, prescribing the one and restraining the other under the sanction, not only of our being left to the natural injurious consequences of vicious habit and practice in the present life, or of continuing to enjoy the benefits of obedience in personal and social happiness here; but also of positive reward and positive punishment in a future life.

Whoever speculated on the subject of morals and moral obligation, in any age, was previously furnished with these general notions and distinctions; they were in the world before him; and if all tradition be not a fable, if the testimony of all antiquity, whether found in poets or historians, be not delusive, they were in the world in those early periods when the great body of the human race remained near the original seat of the parent families of all the modern and now widely-extended nations of the earth; and, in those early periods, they were not regarded as distinctions of mere human opinion and consent, but were invested with a divine authority.

We have, then, before us two presumptions, each of great weight. First, that those actions which, among men, have almost universally been judged good, have the implied sanction of the will of our wise and good Creator, being found in experience, and by the constitution of our nature and of human society, most conducive to human happiness. And, second, that they were originally, in some mode or other, prescribed and enjoined as his law, and their contraries prohibited.

If, therefore, there is presumptive evidence, of only ordinary strength, that the rule by which our actions are determined to be good or evil is primarily a law of the Creator, we are all deeply interested in ascertaining where that law exists in its clearest manifestation. For ignorance of the law, in whole or in part, will be no excuse for disobedience, if we have the opportunity of acquainting ourselves with it; and an accurate acquaintance with the rule may assist our practice in cases of which human laws take no cognizance, and which the willfully corrupted general judgment of mankind may have darkened. And should it appear either that in many things we have offended more deeply than we suspect, whether willfully or from an evitable ignorance; or that, from some common accident which has befallen our nature, we have lost the power of entire obedience without the use of new and extraordinary means, the knowledge of the rule is of the utmost consequence to us, because by it we may be enabled to ascertain the precise relation in which we stand to God our Maker; the dangers we have incurred; and the means of escape, if any have been placed within our reach.

It is well observed by a judicious writer, that "all the distinctions of good and evil refer to some principle above ourselves; for, were there no supreme Governor and Judge to reward and punish, the very notions of good and evil would vanish away; they could not exist in the minds of men, if there were not a supreme Director to give laws for the measure thereof."

If we deny the existence of a divine law obligatory upon man, we must deny that the world is under divine government; for government without rule or law is a solecism; and to deny the divine government, would leave it impossible for us to account for that peculiar nature which has been given to man, and those relations among human concerns and interests to which we have adverted, and which are so powerfully affected by our conduct;—certain actions and habits which almost all mankind have agreed to call good, being connected with the happiness of the individual, and the well-being of society; and so on the contrary. This, too, has been matter of uniform and constant experience from the earliest ages; and warrants, therefore, the conclusion, that the effect arises from original principles and a constitution of things which the Creator has established. Nor can any reason be offered why such a nature should be given to man, and such a law impressed on the circumstances and beings with which he is surrounded, except that both had an intended relation to certain courses of action as the sources of order and happiness, as truly as there was an intended relation between the light, and the eye which is formed to receive its rays.

But as man is not carried to this course of action by physical impulse or necessity; as moral conduct supposes choice, and therefore instruction, and the persuasion of motives arising out of it; the benevolent intention of the Creator as to our happiness could not be accomplished without instruction, warning, reward, and punishment; all of which necessarily imply superintendence and control, or, in other words, a moral government. The creation, therefore, of a being of such a nature as man, implies divine government, and that government a divine law.

Such a law must be the subject of revelation. Law is the will of a superior power; but the will of a superior visible power cannot be known without some indication by words or signs, in other terms, without a revelation; and much less the will of an invisible power, of an order superior to our own, and confessedly mysterious in his mode of existence, and the attributes of his nature.

Again: The will of a superior is not in justice binding until, in some mode, it is sufficiently declared; and the presumption, therefore, that God wills the practice of any particular course of action, on the part of his creatures, establishes the farther presumption, that of that will there has been a manifestation; and the more so if there is reason to suppose, that any penalty of a serious nature has been attached to disobedience.

The revelation of this will or law of God may be made either by action, from which it is to be inferred; or by direct communication in language. Any indication of the moral perfections of God, or of his design in forming moral beings, which the visible creation presents to the mind; or any instance of his favour or displeasure towards his creatures clearly and frequently connected in his administration with any particular course of conduct; may be considered as a revelation of his will by action; and is not at all inconsistent with a further revelation by the direct means of language.

The Theist admits that a revelation of the will of God has been made by significant actions, from which the duty of creatures is to be inferred; and he contends that this is sufficient. "They who never heard of any external revelation, yet if they knew, from the nature of things, what is fit for them to do, they know all that God will or can require of them."

They who believe that the holy Scriptures contain a revelation of God's will do not deny that indications of his will have been made by action; but they contend that they are in themselves imperfect and insufficient, and that they were not designed to supersede a direct revelation. They hold, also, that a direct communication of the divine will was made to the progenitors of the human race, which received additions at subsequent periods, and that the whole was at length embodied in the book called, by way of eminence, "The Bible." . . .

Now it is not necessary to prove at length, what is so obvious, that if we had no method of knowing the will and purposes of God, but by inferring them from his works and his government, we could have no information as to any purpose in the divine Mind to forgive his sinning creatures. The Theist, in order to support this hope, dwells upon the proofs of the goodness of God with which this world abounds, but shuts his eyes upon the demonstrations of his severity: yet these surround him as well as the other; and the argument from the severity of God is as forcible against pardon, as the argument from his goodness is in its favour. At the best, it is left entirely uncertain; a ground is laid for heart-rending doubts, and fearful anticipations; and, for any thing he can show to the contrary, the goodness which God has displayed in nature and providence may only render the offence of man more aggravated, and serve to strengthen the presumption against the forgiveness of a wilful offender, rather than afford him any reason for hope.

The whole of this argument is designed to prove, that had we been left, for the regulation of our conduct, to infer the will and purposes of the supreme Being from his natural works, and his administration of the affairs of the world, our knowledge of both would have been essentially deficient; and it establishes a strong presumption in favour of a direct revelation from God to his creatures, that neither his will concerning us, nor the hope of forgiveness, might be left to dark and uncertain inference, but be the subjects of an express declaration.

The Justice and Grace of God

If all knowledge of right and wrong, and all gracious influence of the Holy Spirit, and all objects of faith have passed away from the Heathen, through the fault of their ancestors not liking to "retain God in their knowledge," and without the present race having been parties to this wilful abandonment of truth, then they would appear no longer to be accountable creatures, being neither under law nor under grace; but as we find it a doctrine of Scripture that all men are responsible to God, and that the whole world will be judged at the last day, we are bound to admit the accountability of all, and, with that, the remains of law and the existence of a merciful government towards the Heathen on the part of God. . . .

It is allowed, and all scriptural advocates of the universal redemption of mankind will join with the Calvinists in maintaining the doctrine, that every disposition and inclination to good which originally existed in the nature of man is lost by the fall; that all men, in their simply natural state, are "dead in trespasses and sins," and have neither the will nor the power to turn to God; and that no one is sufficient of himself to think or do anything of a saving tendency. But as all men are required to do those things which have a saving tendency, we contend that the grace to do them has been bestowed upon all. Equally sacred is the doctrine to be held, that no person can repent or truly believe except under the influence of the Spirit of God; and that we have no ground of boasting in ourselves, but that all the glory of our salvation, commenced and consummated, is to be given to God alone, as the result of the freeness and riches of his grace.

It will also be freely allowed, that the visitations of the gracious influences of the Holy Spirit are vouchsafed in the first instance, and in numberless other subsequent cases, quite independent of our seeking them or desire for them; and that when our thoughts are thus turned to serious considerations, and various exciting and quickening feelings are produced within us, we are often wholly passive; and also, that men are sometimes suddenly and irresistibly awakened to a sense of their guilt and danger by the Spirit of God, either through the preaching of the word instrumentally or through other means, and sometimes, even, independent of any external means at all; and are thus constrained to cry out, "What must I do to be saved?" All this is confirmed by plain verity of holy writ; and is also as certain a matter of experience as that the motions of the Holy Spirit do often silently intermingle themselves with our thoughts, reasonings, and consciences, and breathe their milder persuasions upon our affections.

From these premises the conclusions which legitimately flow are in direct opposition to the Calvinistic hypothesis. They establish,

1. The justice of God in the condemnation of men, which their doctrine leaves under a dark and impenetrable cloud. More or less of these influences from on high visit the finally impenitent, so as to render their destruction their own act by resisting them. This is proved, from the Spirit having striven with those who were finally destroyed by the flood of Noah; from the case of the finally impenitent Jews and their ancestors, who are charged with always resisting the Holy Ghost; from the case of the apostates mentioned in the Epistle to the Hebrews, who are said to have done despite the Spirit of grace; and from the solemn warnings given to men in the New Testament, not to grieve and quench the Holy Spirit. If, therefore, it appears that the destruction of men is attributed to their resistance of those influences of the Holy Spirit, which, but for that resistance, would have been saving, according to the design of God in imparting them, then is the justice of God manifested in their punishment; and it follows, also, that his grace so works in men, as to be both sufficient to lead them into a state of salvation, and even often actually to place them in this state, and yet so as to be capable of being finally and fatally frustrated.

2. These premises, also, secure the glory of our salvation to the grace of God; but not by implying the Calvinistic notion of the continued and

51

uninterrupted irresistibility of the influence of grace and the passiveness of man, so as to deprive him of his agency; but by showing that his agency, even when rightly directed, is upheld and influenced by the superior power of God, and yet so as to be still his own. For, in the instance of the mightiest visitation we can produce from Scripture, that of St. Paul, we see where the irresistible influence terminated, and where his own agency recommenced. Under the impulse of the conviction struck into his mind, as well as under the dazzling brightness which fell upon his eyes, he was passive, and the effect produced for the time necessarily followed; but all the actions consequent upon this were the results of deliberation and personal choice. He submits to be taught in the doctrine of Christ; he confers not with flesh and blood; he is not disobedient to the heavenly vision; he faints not under the burdensome ministry he had received; and he keeps his body under subjection, lest after having preached to others he should himself become a castaway. All these expressions, so descriptive of consideration, choice, and effort, show that the irresistible impulse was not permanent, and that he was subsequently left to improve it or not, though under a powerful but still a resistible motive operating upon him to remain faithful.

For the gentler emotions produced by the Spirit, these are, as the experience of all Christians testifies, the ordinary and general manner in which the Holy Spirit carries on his work in man; and if all good desires, resolves, and aspirations are from him, and not from our own nature, (and, if we are utterly fallen, from our own nature they cannot be,) then, if any man is conscious of having ever checked good desires, and of having opposed his own convictions and better feelings, he has in himself abundant proof of the resistibility of grace, and of the superability of those good inclinations which the Spirit is pleased to impart. He is equally conscious of the power of complying with them, though still in the strength of grace; which yet, whilst it works in him to will and to do, neither wills nor acts for him, nor even by him, as a passive instrument. For if men were wholly and at all times passive under divine influence; not merely in the reception of it, (for all are, in that respect, passive,) but in the actings of it to practical ends; then would there be nothing to mark the difference between the righteous and the wicked but an act of God,—which is utterly irreconcilable to the Scriptures. They call the former "obedient," the latter "disobedient;" one "willing," the other "unwilling;" and promise or threaten accordingly. They attribute the destruction of the one to their refusal of the grace of God, and the salvation of the other, as the instrumental cause, to their acceptance of it;

and to urge that that personal act by which we embrace the grace of Christ, detracts from his glory as our Saviour by attributing our salvation to ourselves, is to speak as absurdly as if we should say that the act of obedience and faith required of the man who was commanded to stretch out his withered arm, detracted from the glory of Christ's healing virtue, by which, indeed, the power of complying with the command and condition of his being healed was imparted.

Part II

Developing Distinctiveness

Methodism's efforts to express a distinctive theology became increasingly self-conscious as the nineteenth century progressed. What were the Wesleyan movement's dominant themes? A number of theologians attempted to express their understanding of the tradition's characteristic emphases. Phoebe Palmer renewed stress upon sanctification, although with new nuances. Daniel D. Whedon set forth a full range of Methodist doctrines emphasizing their distinctive character. William Burt Pope discussed Methodist doctrine stressing its kinship with catholic Christianity. John Miley structured his understanding of Methodist theology by establishing Theism as his basis, and Milton Terry presented a Methodist understanding of biblical study. Hugh Price Hughes brought a prophetic voice to Methodist social concern. In their efforts to clarify the Methodist positions, these writers not only reaffirmed their received theology but also set new directions.

Phoebe Palmer

Phoebe Palmer (1807–1874) was a lay evangelist who played an important role in the renewal of Methodist interest in Christian perfection. With her sister, Sara Lankford, she held Tuesday meetings for the promotion of holiness in New York City beginning in 1835. The response to these meetings was immediate and their influence extended quickly. The message that Phoebe Palmer taught was that Christian holiness is a promise of the Scriptures and that acceptance of the biblical promises is the event which brings sanctification to an individual's life. She intended to be more explicit about the method which leads to sanctification, to reduce the role of emotionalism, and reinforce assurance of holiness. She found her answer in a "short way," an explicit method which conveyed certainty. Holiness, Phoebe Palmer believed, carries ethical implications, so she became involved in an inner-city rescue mission and in societal moral concerns and she encouraged responsible action. After the Civil War she was a leader in the National Camp Meeting Association for the Promotion of Holiness and continued to be a prominent spokeswoman for entire sanctification. She wrote a number of books, among them *Pioneer Experiences* (1868) and *Four Years in the Old World* (1866). *The Way of Holiness* (1850) is her most important publication; the section that follows introduces her "short way" to the experience of Christian perfection. The selection is taken from *The Way of Holiness* (New York: Lang and Scott, 1851), pp. 17-24.

The Way of Holiness: Is There Not a Shorter Way?

Section I

"Be always ready to give an answer to every man that asketh you a reason of the hope that is within you, with meekness and fear."—Peter.

"I have thought," said one of the children of Zion to the other, as in love they journeyed onward in the way cast up for the ransomed of the Lord to walk in; "I have thought," said he, "whether there is not a *shorter way* of getting into this way of holiness than some of our . . . brethren apprehend?"

"Yes," said the sister addressed, who was a member of the denomination alluded to; "Yes, brother, THERE IS A SHORTER WAY! O! I am sure this long waiting and struggling with the powers of darkness is not necessary. There is a shorter way." And then, with a solemn feeling of responsibility, and with a realizing conviction of the truth uttered, she added, "But, brother, there is but one way."

Days and even weeks elapsed, and yet the question, with solemn bearing, rested upon the mind of that sister. She thought of the affirmative given in answer to the inquiry of the brother—examined yet more closely the Scriptural foundation upon which the truth of the affirmation rested—and the result of the investigation tended to add still greater confirmation to the belief, that many sincere disciples of Jesus, by various needless perplexities, consume much time in endeavoring to get into this way, which might, more advantageously to themselves and others, be employed in making progress in it, and testifying, from experimental knowledge, of its blessedness.

How many, whom Infinite Love would long since have brought into this state, instead of seeking to be brought into the possession of the blessing at once, are seeking a preparation for the reception of it! They feel that their *convictions* are not deep enough to warrant an approach to the throne of grace, with the confident expectation of receiving the blessing *now.* Just at this point some may have been lingering months and years. Thus did the sister, who so confidently affirmed "there is a shorter way." And here, dear child of Jesus, permit the writer to tell you just how that sister found the "shorter way."

On looking at the requirements of the word of God, she beheld the command, "Be ye holy." She then began to say in her heart, "Whatever my former deficiencies may have been, God requires that I should *now* be holy. Whether *convicted,* or otherwise, *duty is plain.* God requires *present* holiness." On coming to this point, she at once apprehended a simple truth before unthought of, i.e., *Knowledge is conviction.* She well knew that, for a long time, she had been assured that God required holiness. But she had never deemed this knowledge a sufficient plea to take to God—and because of present need, to ask a present bestowment of the gift.

Convinced that in this respect she had mistaken the path, she now, with renewed energy, began to make use of the knowledge already received, and to discern a "shorter way."

Another difficulty by which her course had been delayed she found to be here. She had been accustomed to look at the blessing of holiness as such a high attainment, that her general habit of soul inclined her to think it almost beyond her reach. This erroneous impression rather influenced her to rest the matter thus:—"I will let every high state of grace, in name, alone, and seek only to be *fully conformed to the will of God, as recorded in his written word.* My chief endeavors shall be centred in the aim to be an humble *Bible Christian.* By the grace of God, all my energies shall be directed to this one point. With this single aim, I will journey onward, even though my faith may be tried to the uttermost by those manifestations being withheld, which have previously been regarded as essential for the establishment of faith."

On arriving at this point, she was enabled to gain yet clearer insight into the simplicity of the way. And it was by this process. After having taken the Bible as the rule of life, instead of the opinions and experience of professors, she found, on taking the blessed word more closely to the companionship of her heart, that no one declaration spoke more appealingly to her understanding than this: "Ye are not your own, ye are bought with a price, therefore glorify God in your body and spirit which are his."

By this she perceived the duty of *entire consecration* in a stronger light, and as more sacredly binding, than ever before. Here she saw God as her Redeemer, claiming, by virtue of the great price paid for the redemption of body, soul, and spirit, the *present and entire service* of all these redeemed powers.

By this she saw that if she lived constantly in the entire surrender of all that had been thus dearly purchased unto God, she was but an unprofitable servant; and that, if less than all was rendered, she was worse than unprofitable, inasmuch as she would be guilty of keeping back part of that price which had been purchased unto God: "Not with corruptible things, such as silver and gold, but by the precious blood of

Jesus." And after so clearly discerning the will of God concerning her, she felt that the sin of Ananias and Sapphira would be less culpable in the sight of Heaven than her own, should she not at once resolve on living in the *entire* consecration of all her redeemed powers to God.

Deeply conscious of past unfaithfulness, she now determined that the time past should suffice; and with a humility of spirit, induced by a consciousness of not having lived in the performance of such a "reasonable service," she was enabled, through grace, to resolve, with firmness of purpose, that entire devotion of heart and life to God should be the absorbing subject of the succeeding pilgrimage of life.

Section II

"We by his Spirit prove,
And know the things of God,
The things which freely of his love
He hath on us bestow'd."

After having thus resolved on devoting the entire service of her heart and life to God, the following questions occasioned much serious solicitude:—How shall I know when I have consecrated all to God? And how ascertain whether God *accepts* the sacrifice—and how know the manner of its acceptance? Here again the blessed Bible, which she had now taken as her counselor, said to her heart, "We have received not the spirit of the world, but the Spirit which is of God, that we might know the things freely given to us of God."

It was thus she became assured that it was her privilege to *know when she* had consecrated all to God, and also to know that the sacrifice was *accepted*, and the resolve was solemnly made that the subject should not cease to be absorbing, until this knowledge was obtained.

Feeling it a matter of no small importance to stand thus solemnly pledged to God, conscious that sacred responsibilities were included in these engagements, a *realization* of the fact, that neither body, soul, nor spirit, time, talent, nor influence, were, even for one moment, at her own disposal, began to assume the tangibility of living truth to her mind, in a manner not before apprehended.

From a sense of responsibility thus imposed, she began to be more abundant in labors, "instant in season and out of season."

While thus engaged in active service, another difficulty presented itself. How much of self in these performances? said the accuser. For a moment, almost bewildered at being thus withstood, her heart began to

59

sink. She felt most keenly that she had no certain standard to raise up against this accusation.

It was here again that the blessed word sweetly communed with her heart, presenting the marks of the way, by a reference to the admonition of Paul: "Therefore, my beloved brethren, be ye steadfast and unmovable, always abounding in the work of the Lord, forasmuch as ye know that your labor is not in vain in the Lord."

These blessed communings continued thus: If the primitive Christians had the assurance that their labors were in the Lord; and thus enjoyed the heart-inspiring *confidence* that their labors were *not in vain*, because performed in the might of the Spirit, then it is also your privilege to *know* that your labor is in the Lord. It was at this point in her experience that she first perceived the *necessity*, and also the *attainableness* of the witness of *purity of intention*—which, in her petition to God, as most expressive of her peculiar need, she denominated, "The witness that the spring of every motive is pure."

It was by the word of the Lord she became fully convinced that she needed this heart-encouraging confidence in order to insure success in her labors of love. The next step taken was to resolve, as in the presence of the Lord, not to cease importuning the throne of grace until the witness was given "that the spring of every motive was pure."

On coming to this decision, the blessed Word, most encouragingly, yea, and also assuringly, said to her heart, "Stand still, and see the salvation of God!"

Daniel D. Whedon

Daniel D. Whedon (1808–1885) was an American preacher, theologian, author, and editor. Born in Onondaga, New York, he graduated from Hamilton College and served on the faculty of Wesleyan University, Connecticut, and the University of Michigan. Intellectually able and morally sensitive, Whedon originally trained for law and then became a Methodist minister. He was a theological spokesman for the Methodist Episcopal Church as editor of the *Methodist Quarterly Review* (1856–84) and wrote an important study, *The Freedom of Will* (1864), in which he challenged Jonathan Edwards' interpretation of human free agency. He also edited commentaries on the Old and New Testaments (12 vols.). Whedon was instrumental in reshaping Wesleyan theology in North America by placing more emphasis upon human capability and giving less weight to the grounding of this ability in prevenient grace. Utilizing philosophical tools to discuss distinctive qualities of human life, Whedon attempted to reinforce the integrity of human personhood with responsibility for choice and action. In his synoptic treatment, Whedon indicates the distinctiveness of Methodist theological positions. Whedon's "Doctrines of Methodism" needs to be read in connection with the next selection, "Methodist Doctrine," from William Burt Pope, which emphasizes Methodism's relation to catholic Christianity. These articles together represent nineteenth-century Methodism's effort to gain clear self-understanding. "Doctrines of Methodism" is chosen from *Essays, Reviews, and Discourses* (New York: Phillips and Hunt, 1887), pp. 109-46.

Doctrines of Methodism

It is our purpose in the present article to furnish a brief statement of the doctrines of the Methodist Episcopal Church, especially those points in which there exists an issue with Calvinism. As a receiver of those doctrines, it will, of course, be expected, and probably desired, that the writer should present them favorably, and as they are viewed by their advocates. Occasional argumentative issues may be stated, in order that the points of collision may be more easily understood; but it forms no part of our province to *prove* the doctrines presented. It is believed that such a statement, at the present time, may tend to remove misunderstanding, and serve the cause of Christian unity.

In regard to the issue, it may be generally remarked that in those points which more immediately concern the divine government Calvinism affirms more than Arminianism, and that more the latter declines to accept. Both sides, for instance, affirm foreknowledge, freewill, and the necessity of divine grace to salvation; Calvinism superadds to these respectively, foreordination, necessity, and irresistibleness, to which Arminianism declines assent. On points less central, as final apostasy, entire sanctification, and witness of the Spirit, our Arminianism affirms, and Calvinism rejects.

Fundamental Maxim of Divine Government

The fundamental maxim upon which the issue above named is primarily grounded, and from which, if we mistake not, most of the other issues logically result, is the Edwardean maxim, that it is no matter how we come by our evil volitions, dispositions, or nature, in order to responsibility, provided we really possess them. Or we may state the maxim thus: God judges us as he finds us to be, good or evil, and holds us responsible without regard to the means by which we became so. We do not say that all who are considered Calvinists hold this maxim. But upon the acceptance or rejection of this proposition it logically depends, as it appears to us, whether the man *should be* a Calvinist or Arminian. From our rejection of this maxim it is that we differ from some or all the classes of Calvinists on the subject of *free-will, divine sovereignty, predesti-*

62

nation, election, primary responsibility for inborn depravity, partial atonement, and *final perseverance.* To this maxim, that *it is no matter how we come by volitional state in order to its being responsible,* we oppose the counter maxim that *in order to responsibility for a given act or state, power in the agent for a contrary act or state is requisite.* In other words: *"no man is to blame for what he cannot help." Power underlies responsibility.* Non-existence of power is non-existence of responsibility. The only limitation of this principle is the maxim that *self-superinduced inability does not exclude responsibility.* The agent who abdicates his powers we hold to be responsible for his impotence, and for all the non-performances which legitimately result. Our entire axiom, then, is: *all inability to an act or state, not self-superinduced, excludes responsibility.* The man who maintains, counter to this our position, the above-specified Edwardean maxim must, we think, if a logical reasoner, support all the Calvinistic views above enumerated. The man who adopts our maxim is as logically bound to reject them.

Free-Will

When a man transgresses a divine requirement by a wrong volition, the question arises: *Could he have willed otherwise?* He is held by the law penally responsible for the act. If, now, the maxim be true that God regards not the way in which he became possessed of the volition, then no power to the contrary is required. God may create him without power for other volition; may create him in fixed and necessitated possession of the volition, yet may still hold him responsible, and consign him to endless penalty. If, on the other hand, adequate power for a contrary volition must underlie obligation for a contrary volition, and so for responsibility for the actual volition, then there must have existed in the given agent power for a volition contrary to the volition actually put forth.

Methodism has, in accordance with this view, from the beginning maintained this doctrine of free-will. We have ever maintained that it imputes injustice to God to suppose that he holds us responsible for a necessitated act or condition; or that he ever requires an act or condition for which he does not furnish the adequate power. It is the apparent making of this imputation in the various doctrines of Calvinism with which Methodism has taken issue.

Our view of free-will is tolerably well expressed by the formula: "the power of contrary choice." It would, perhaps, be more accurately expressed by the formula furnished and condemned by Edwards (p. 419, Andover Edition, 1840): *"The power of choosing differently in given cases."* The question proposed by Fletcher to Toplady was: *"Is the will at liberty to choose otherwise than it does, or is it not?"* The man who affirms the first member of this question is bound to be an Arminian; the affirmant of the latter member must, as we suppose, logically be a Calvinist. . . .

Our views of responsibility require us, therefore, to affirm fully and unequivocally the doctrine of *the freedom of the will.* With the limitation which we have already indicated in our axiom, every obligatory and every responsible volitional act is a free act; that is, put forth with the adequate power of putting forth a different act instead. . . .

Divine Sovereignty

We hold it to be a doctrine both of natural and revealed religion that God is an omnipotent being, possessed of power for all operations which involve not a contradiction. But any act the expression of which involves a contradiction we consider to be no act at all; so that this exception is not a limitation of divine power, but only a definition of the true idea of omnipotence. God is sovereign over the realm of nature and of free agents; yet in both cases he limits his uniform action by self-circumscribing laws. The laws of nature are the uniform rules of God's action, imposed by himself upon himself. And these self-imposed laws are necessary to the very existence of the kingdom of nature; and they do, in fact, give God his position as sovereign of nature, and therein are necessary to his divine sovereignty. In the realm of free agency, also, God finds, as we think, his highest exaltation as sovereign, by so circumscribing his own modes of action as to leave unviolated the full exercise of the freedom of the agent, so far forth as he is a free and responsible agent. For God to secure absolutely and limitatively the one possible volition of the agent, and yet leave him a free agent, is, in our view, a contradiction; as genuine a contradiction as for God to cause a heavier body to ascend, and yet preserve the law of gravitation. The requirement that God's sovereignty must jealously *cause* and *secure,* as well as limit, every act of the agent in our estimation reduces God from his position as a sovereign to the predicament of a mechanist. He is no longer king of free beings, but a mover of automatons. The highest glory of God as a divine sovereign consists, as we conceive, in his giving the fullest permission for the freest range of responsible agency, though it sweep the scope of half the universe; and yet so taking the wise in their

64

own craftiness, and over-mastering the mighty in their own might, as to accomplish all his own grand designs and produce the best and most glorious possible of ultimate results. . . .

Foreknowledge

It might at first appear fair to say that the reconciliation of fore-knowledge with free agency is *the* difficulty of our theology. Yet there seems to be a great difference, of which a theology ought to avail itself, between the admission of simple foreknowledge and the additional admission of predestination. If the term *predestination* has any proper significance, it implies a strict causative relation between the long past predestinating act and the predestined event. If it becomes any thing less than this, it becomes simply *prerecognition*, with non-prevention in view of some collateral good; which is, properly speaking, foreknowl-edge. The true distinction, in fact, between foreknowledge and predes-tination is, that the former simply cognizes the act which another cause will put forth, while the latter causatively determines its putting forth, purposely excluding, by necessitative limitation, any other act instead. God may be supposed to *foresee* the act because the agent will put it forth; but God cannot properly be said to *predestinate* the action because the agent will put it forth; on the other hand, the agent must perform the act because it is predestinated. The act of the agent cannot properly be free, because it is antecedently limited and determined. . . .

Doctrine of Sin and Guilt

Sin is, according to John, *anomia,* or disconformity to the law; and the term, therefore, though primarily applicable to actual transgression, is nevertheless used, both in theology and Scripture, to designate a moral *state* or *condition* of being. Should, however, a being be placed in such a state otherwise than by his own free act, with full power of acting oth-erwise, for such a state we hold that he could not be strictly responsible, or, with absolute justice, punishable. In such a being there would be *evil, moral evil, sin,* but not responsibility, or desert of penalty. Should such a state of being be brought about by the agent's own free act, the respon-sibility would, we think, exist in full force; or, should the free being in such a state, possessed of full power to act otherwise, nevertheless sanc-tion and appropriate to himself his depraved condition, making it the controlling power of his life, he thereby contracts the responsibility.

65

Such a depraved state, in our view, has never been produced in any being by God, but always by free secondary agents. All responsible sin, therefore, whether of action or condition, arises from the action of free finite beings, in disconformity to the law, and in abuse of their free agency. . . .

The act of the will, put forth with full power otherwise, in intentional disconformity to the law, is actual or *actional sin*. The resultant ethical quality of *condemnability*, which our moral sense sees as inhering in the personality of the agent in consequence of the commission of such sin, we call *guilt*. And as the moral sense can see this guilt solely in the personality of the committing agent, it is impossible for this guilt to be transferred to another personality. Correlative to this *guilt*, the moral sense sees inhering in the person of the guilty *a desert of just punishment*. These correlations are fundamental and axiomatic. *Punishment*, therefore, is no more transferable, literally, than *guilt*. Neither is any more transferable than is a *past act* personally performed by one agent transferable to another agent. When, therefore, an innocent man is said to suffer in the stead of a guilty man, it is only in figurative conception that the guilt and punishment of the guilty are attributed or imputed to the innocent man; the literal fact is, that the innocent man is still innocent, and the endurance by the innocent is simply *suffering*, but not literally, to him, *punishment*.

The Fall and Depravation of Man

In the primordial man, Adam, as in every primordial progenitor, a whole posterity is conceptually enfolded. As in the acorn is inclosed, not only the oak, but a whole descending lineage of oaks, so in our first parent was inclosed a whole system of diverging lineages embracing a race. As his primordial nature shall stand higher or lower, so shall the deduced nature of that race be higher or lower. Under this fundamental law, extended through the whole generative system of creation, and based upon reasons of the highest wisdom, man, with his fellow races, animal and vegetable, is placed on earth. That law, that self-limiting law, God cannot wisely change. Upon the first man he bestows a nature of transcendental excellence, yet with a free and plastic power of self-degradation by sin. As man stands or falls, he stands or falls in his typical character; and his whole race, under the universal lineal law, must bear the same physical, intellectual, and moral type. And with this natural law corresponds the theodicic arrangement. Under the same moral and judicial conditions in which man places himself, must, as we believe, his posterity, if born, be born. . . .

Under these conditions, shall he bring a posterity into existence? He can bring them into existence, by the laws of nature, only with his own character, and, apparently, to his own destiny. For conceptionally, as above stated, his whole race is seminally existent in him. The sentence of condemnation is addressed to him individually, indeed, yet to him, containing his whole race within himself. Shall the individuals of that race, by the prosecution of the natural generative law, be brought by him into personal existence? Man, then, by a second procedure, would consummate the terrible evil of his first procedure. He, under the fundamental laws, in the prosecution of second causes, would plunge a race in endless misery, *naturally* resulting from his unholy procedures. There are but two methods, that we can conceive, of arresting man in his full course of evil-doing. By the first method the full force of the sentence may be executed and exhausted upon himself by the infliction of temporal, spiritual, and eternal death immediately interposed, previous to the production of offspring. God's veracity is thus sustained, and the evil of sin is manifested by the abortion of the race. By the second method, a redemptive system may be interposed, by which, on the continued basis of free agency and probation, man, the whole race, or that part of the race which attains the end of its probation, may be restored to even, perhaps, a higher glory than the Adamic race could have attained. . . .

The Redemption

The introduction of the Redeemer, sequently upon the fall of man, was not a divine afterthought. By a divine predetermination, *conditioned* upon that foreseen apostasy, Christ was the Lamb slain from before the foundation of the world. In view of the compensations by it afforded, expressions of deeper severity toward sin are made than otherwise would have taken place. A Redeemer is introduced who, by a death of infinitely more value than that of Adam and all his race, is entitled to take humanity into his guardianship, and measure out mercy and justice according to the laws of a wise probation: 1. In view of the future atonement, the natural continuity of the human race remains uninterrupted, and a basis is thus afforded for a new system. 2. In view of that same atonement, the Holy Spirit is restored, whereby motives in the direction of spiritual realities may become grounds of action, and their proper improvement may lead to justification and regeneration. Man does not thereby receive any new faculty. He is not even organically *made* to be a free agent; for he never ceased to be such; only spiritual things, and the possibility of pleasing God, are again *brought within the reach* of his free agency. Nor is the Holy Spirit, nor any other influence, normally so brought to bear upon his free agency as to be *irresistible,* or *secured to be unresisted;* since that would be to overwhelm his free agency on the other side. To afford him such aids as render him able to accept salvation without overcoming his ability to reject it, probationarily leaving the decision to his own free-will, is the precise law by which the dealings of God with him are now governed. 3. Though, both in the matter of temporal and eternal death, man still remains under liability, so that, by rejection of the Redeemer, he may come under full execution of the primal sentence, yet by the proper exercise of his free-will, aided by the Spirit graciously bestowed, in accepting and obeying the Redeemer, he may finally attain a glory through Christ, greater, perhaps, than he lost through Adam. . . .

So far as we can see, these statements present the antithesis between our loss through Adam and our gain through Christ, in full accordance with its presentation by Paul in the fifth chapter of Romans. By the sin of the former, we incur death and judgment unto condemnation, and are made sinners. By the righteousness of the latter, we receive life and justification, are made righteous, attaining a grace much more abundant than the previous sin. And inasmuch as we are made sinners antecedently to the atonement, without the power of being other than sinners, we can be held in that case as responsible sinners only by a conceptual imputation of sin. Under the atonement, that conceptual imputation is continued only as the logical antithesis to the conceptual imputation of righteousness to the guilty through the atoning righteousness of Christ.

Righteousness and Grace in the Redemption

In regard to parts, if not the whole, of the provisions of the redemption, as thus stated, it will be said that they are but provisions of justice and not of grace. If powers were necessary in order to the fulfillment of requirements, God was bound, in righteousness, to grant them; and, in justice, could not withhold them; and they are therefore not gracious. Nevertheless, we hold that such provisions are none the less by grace because by righteousness. Benevolence is the goodness of God exhibited in nature; grace is the goodness of God exhibited in redemption. And as God could not be justified in the works of nature without appealing to the proofs of benevolence, it might be said that "God is bound to furnish that benevolence; and it is therefore no benevolence, but mere righteousness." Nevertheless, it is none the less benevolence because necessary to justify God's righteousness. The righteousness and the grace are but different views of the same thing.

. . . Every endowment that man receives, by nature or redemption, even though it be the basis of a duty and a requirement, is none the less a gratuity. God gives the grace, and imposes the requirement, because it is a grace; nor does the requirement abolish the grace.

Nature and Extent of the Atonement

. . . Christ died for all men, and for every man, and for no one man more than for another. The personal, voluntary reception of the atonement, in its full conditions, by the sinner himself, constitutes the difference between one man and another in the obtainment of its benefits. A fountain stands for the entire inhabitants of a town, for one man no more than for another; and the personal drawing and drinking of the water may constitute the only difference in the enjoyment of its benefits. The atonement itself is universal and irrespective; the personal appropriation, by which the individual sinner secures his share of its benefits, is in each case particular.

Justification by Faith

The method by which the sinner appropriates a share of the benefits of the atonement personally to himself is comprehensively said to be *by faith.* By the works of the law, that is, by a Christless morality, can no flesh be justified. The law finds us in sin and in depravity, made responsible by volitional action, and reveals our sin unto us. When its perfectness is comprehended, all hopes of meeting its full demands must die within us. We can, therefore, only hope for salvation by the acceptance of the offered atonement for past sins and future short-comings.

The *faith which justifies* implies the belief of the intellect, the accord of the affections, and the submissive acceptance by the will. By this entire act of the whole soul the sinner surrenders himself to Christ for salvation. The sincerity of this faith implies the full renunciation of sin by repentance, and the full self-commitment to obedience to Christ. This act of the sinner is accepted of God, and is imputed to him for righteousness. By the law of the redemptive kingdom, he stands justified before God for all his sins past; the record of condemnation is blotted out, and his name is enrolled in the Lamb's book of life. In accordance with the conditions of the atonement, the Holy Spirit is now imparted unto him, not merely in its convicting, but in its witnessing, enlightening, strengthening, and sanctifying power. . . .

The gracious influences of the Spirit ever precede our action, working within us both to will and to do, and are ever graciously given more abundantly upon our action; so that in attaining justifying grace God and man previously cooperate.

Though the *convicting* influences of the Spirit are often, for a time, to a degree *irresistible*, measurably awakening the conscience and convincing the reason, in spite of our resistance, yet neither is the influence that results in saving faith, nor the saving grace which follows properly irresistible by the will. Justifying faith is voluntary and free. The soul is normally able to withhold it; nor is the operation of the Spirit such as necessitatively to secure it.

We are not saved by the *merit* of faith. Faith may indeed be considered in one sense as a *work*, a good work, a right work, the rightest work which, in the case, the sinner can perform. It has in itself the same sort of *good desert*, or ethical merit, as we ascribe to every act which in its given place is morally right. The contrary act would be morally wrong. And it is because of the meetness and ethical fitness and moral rightness in the case, that faith is selected as the proper medium of reconciliation and acceptance. *Yet the value of this faith is not such as that it merits the salvation* sequently bestowed upon it. Abstractly, God might rightfully drop the being into non-existence at the instant of its accomplished faith. The sinner has presented no equivalent for the salvation he receives, and he is truly saved by the free and abounding grace of God. . . .

Possibility of Apostasy

In full consistency with that doctrine of human freedom and responsibility which pervades our theology, we maintain that, inasmuch as we were free in first performing the conditions of salvation, so we are free in the continuance or cessation of their performance. The volition by which we accepted the terms, we could have withheld; neither our probation nor our freedom on that test-point has ceased at our conversion. Amid the temptations, the unbeliefs, and the backslidings of life, the test-question may again and again recur, whether we shall hold fast our first faith; and there still exists the same freedom for decision for either alternative. . . .

We affirm, indeed, that God grants full enabling grace to persevere. He protects us so that none can snatch us from our Father's hand, nor separate us from the love of God; he keeps, supports, and guards; he confirms us when we are strong, and raises us when we are fallen; but he performs all this for us, not as *things*, but as *agents* from whom the consenting accordance and co-operation are conditionally presumed, both in the promise and performance of all these preserving acts of grace. After all these gracious aids on the part of God, there still remains, by the very nature of free agency, an ultimate element of *selfhood*, which alternately decides whether or not that grace shall be in vain. That free selfhood intrinsically remains, however it may sometimes objectively be circumscribed, through the entire existence of the self. . . .

Regeneration

We have said that, consequent upon our justification, the Holy Spirit is imparted unto us no longer in its mere convicting power, but in its enlightening, quickening energy; giving us not, indeed, a new organic faculty, but the power and disposition, with our existing faculties, freely to love God with all our heart, and our neighbor as ourselves. This is regeneration. Though always concomitant with justification, it is in the order of nature consequent. So truly *new* is this gift by the Holy Spirit, so new and powerful are the views, feeling, purposes of the man, that it is said he is a new creature; that all things with him are made new; that he is born anew, born of God, regenerated. He is now a child of God— a member of the justified family of God.

We thus hold that regeneration *succeeds* justification. It is the unregenerate who is first convinced of sin by the Holy Spirit, who considers upon his wicked ways and seeks repentance, who examines the law of God and the Gospel of Christ in order to learn the method of escaping the wrath to come, who bows in penitent prayer for the continuing guidance of the Holy Spirit in order to the accomplishment of the work, and who does at successive points receive, in consequence of these his preparatory doings, the gracious aid of God. To the question, can these actions of the unregenerate man be holy, and so acceptable to God, we seem to ourselves to have abundant answer. They are not holy in the absolute sense of the word; and yet in their place they are acceptable and accepted by God, as by him prescribed to the man in his case. . . .

Regeneration is the act of God. It presupposes conditions previously performed by the man; but in the work itself God is the doer, and man the submissive recipient. It presupposes anterior justification, and the performance, by the free-will of the sinner, of all the conditions requisite to the work. The Holy Spirit aids in those conditioned acts, but, except, perhaps, at particular points, never necessitates. The sinner acts as a free, responsible agent, and his free agency, so far forth as it exists and extends, excludes necessitation or predestination as its contradictory. Upon the decision and choice of the man as a free agent it ultimately depends whether the condition be performed and salvation attained, or rejected and eternal death incurred. This is the *great alternative point* of man's free probation. From his own essential and central self is the decision most freely made; upon his own central and essential self must the eternal responsibility rest. And, hereby, though man be condemned, God shall be justified.

Witness of the Spirit

Where God performs directly the work of justification and of regeneration, is it not to be expected that he will as directly give notice of so wonderful a mercy? And this thought suggests the reasonableness of the doctrine of the witness of the Spirit, directly testifying to us that we are born of God.

The *witness of our own spirit* is that self-judgment which we are rationally able to pronounce, in the light of consciousness and Scripture, that we are the children of God. This is a logical inference, drawn from the fruits we find, by self-examination, in our minds and external conduct.

But besides this, is there not felt in every deep religious experience, a simple, firm assurance, like an intuition, by which we are made to feel calmly certain that all is blessedly right between God and our own soul? Does not this assurance seem to come into the heart as from some outer source? Does it not come as in answer to prayer, and in direction, as if from him to whom we pray? Scripture surely makes the assuring and witnessing act of the Spirit to be as immediate and direct as the justifying or regenerating acts. Hereby then, we have the *witness of God's Spirit*, concurrent with the *witness of our own spirit*, testifying to the work of our justification and adoption. "The Spirit itself beareth witness with our spirit that we are the children of God." Rom. viii, 16. . . .

Entire Sanctification, or Christian Perfection

. . . Through a maturity of Christian experience and the fullness of the Spirit imparted, the spiritual powers of the faithful Christian may be so strengthened that he may, and often does, maintain, through grace, for a longer or shorter period, a permanent state of the undiminished fullness of his acceptance with God, and under no more actual condemnation than at the moment of his justification.

Every thing which has attained the normal completeness of its own class or kind is rightly called *perfect*. Not after an ideal, but a normal standard, we speak of a *perfect egg*, a *perfect chicken*, a *perfect full-grown fowl*. There may be a perfect child or a perfect man. And every thing which is wanting in none of the normal complement of qualities, in normal degree, is *perfect* in its class. Now the Christian who has attained to the description of our formula, is at the normal standard of a *perfect* man in Christ. We use an abundantly scriptural term in calling this a state of Christian *perfection*. It is a state in which all the normal qualities of the Christian are permanently, or with more or less continuity, possessed in the proper completeness. And as this spiritual strength and power over and against sin, derived from the Holy Spirit, is *sanctification,* so in the completeness which we have described, it is not improperly, perhaps, by us called entire sanctification.

Of this state of sanctification, the actual divine acceptance, in its uncondemning fullness, is, according to our present statement, the actual standard. With how much short-coming from the perfect law this is in any case possible, the Spirit is itself in every case judge. It may, therefore, not be possible to answer this question by antecedent words, especially to a metaphysician, demanding absolute exactness; and in this fact, perhaps, consists the basis of the complaint often made by theologians, that they cannot understand the thing we attempt to describe.

The evangelic law requires love with all our present feeble powers to God, and to our neighbor as ourselves. As we are unable to love God with full Adamic powers, the perfect law even then condemns us. Moral weaknesses contracted by past sinful habits, moral ignorances resulting from our own past fault, prejudices of which we are more or less unconscious, nervous irritabilities and physical idiosyncrasies, may produce condemnation from censorious man, where there is still acceptance from him who "knoweth our frame." So far as the will is concerned, Mr. Wesley excluded from the sanctified state all "voluntary transgressions;" but it is questionable whether under the term "involuntary" he did not really include countless numbers of minuter *volitions*, inevitably escaping from our moral weakness, in spite of our most vigorous tone of spiritual purpose and spiritual activity. With how much of all these "infirmities" the uninterrupted fullness of the divine approbation can consist, it is, as we before remarked, impossible in human words exactly to define, even if we could exactly conceive. Thus much, at any rate, is fully certain, that Leighton correctly describes it as an "imperfect perfection." Ample work, doubtless, is found from these short-comings for a permanent exercise of the most *perfect* repentance, as well as the most perfect faith in the blood of Christ. Ample reasons will be found for praying, "Forgive us our trespasses." Ample verge there is for all those texts of Scripture which affirm that there is none that "sinneth not;" that is, in the wider sense of the word "sin." Nor is there any difficulty in understanding how the most exalted of our Christian saints, in the light of the pure and perfect law, looking at themselves with the eye of a sanctified conscience, can scarce find words sufficient to express their deep humiliation, not only for the depths of the fall of their own nature, but for their own short-comings and for their sins against infinite purity.

But the law is our school-master to drive us to Christ. And yet when in Christ it is not our duty to keep our shuddering eyes perpetually fixed upon the *school-master*. Greater spiritual power, as well as higher spiritual joy, can be derived from dwelling in Christ, and holding up before ourselves the measure of Christian holiness we can attain through him. A goal is thus set up for our holy ambition; a positive standard for which we may labor. Thence a more cheerful piety arises in him who contemplates what he may gain through Christ than in him who is ever trembling under the lash of the law, and who is ever exclaiming, "I am all sin, and nothing but sin." Hence, as the doctrine of apostasy constitutes a real warning against backsliding and sin, so the doctrine of Christian perfection is a living incitement to progressive holiness.

Conclusion

Upon the whole, the writer of this article has doubtless failed in his task if he has not made it conceivable to a candid examiner from the other side that our Arminianism is a well-defined, symmetrical system, which a mind possessed of the broadest logical consistency may reasonably be imagined to accept as the best approximation to a satisfactory solution of the facts of the divine government. It is an attempt to show the reconcilability of the divine sovereignty in the plenitude of its holiness with the freedom and responsibility of man, by a method securing the divine honor, and affording the most powerful motives for human piety. . . .

William Burt Pope

William Burt Pope (1822–1903) was the North American continent's first contribution to British Methodist theology. Born in Nova Scotia, Pope returned to England where he received his education and entered the Methodist ministry. Shy and retiring by nature, he was an excellent scholar, prodigious student, and a writer with a fine literary style; he became theological tutor at Didsbury College, Manchester, in 1867. Catholic in his religious sensibility and theological interest, he expressed Methodist theology in a manner which utilized the resources of the wider Christian tradition while also understanding himself to be hewn from the rock of Wesleyan Methodism. Among his books are *The Person of Christ* (1871) and *Sermons, Addresses, and Charges* (1878). His chief theological writing was the three-volume *Compendium of Christian Theology* (1875–76). This work is the most important statement of British Wesleyan theology from the last half of the nineteenth century. The following article was included in *The Wesley Memorial Volume* (1880), a publication that represented an effort to assess Wesley and the Methodist Movement. "Methodist Doctrine" is taken from *The Wesley Memorial Volume*, ed. J. O. A. Clark (New York: Phillips & Hunt, 1880), pp. 168-90.

Methodist Doctrine

The term Methodism was, some hundred years since, a watchword of contempt for a body of fanatics supposed to hold some new religious doctrines, to profess some strange experiences, and to arrogate to themselves a peculiar commission from Heaven. To many it is a watch-word of reproach still. But it has, nevertheless, rooted itself firmly in the nomenclature of the Christian Church. Evangelical Christendom generally agrees with those who bear it to accept the term as a human designation of a system of thought and action which it has pleased the Head of the Church to take into his plans for the spread of his kingdom in these later days. Its history has produced a very general conviction that the Holy Spirit, the Lord and Giver of life ecclesiastical, has added this to the corporate bodies of our common Christianity. Meanwhile, not solicitous about the judgments of men, it is commending itself to God by doing faithfully the work appointed for it in the world. Its sound—or rather, the sound of the Gospel by its lips—has gone out into all the earth. It is slowly diffusing its leaven through almost every form of corrupt Christianity; it is silently impressing its influence, acknowledged or unacknowledged, upon the uncorrupt Churches of Christendom; while, as an independent and self-contained organization, it is erecting its firm superstructure in many lands.

This last fact implies that the system has its varieties of form. Methodism is a genus of many species. The central term has gathered round it various adjectives or predicates which express more or less important differences. But the term itself remains a bond of union among all these; a bond which will be, as it has been hitherto, permanent and indestructible, if the type of doctrine of which it is the symbol shall be maintained in its integrity. For, though Methodism began as a life, that life was quickened and nourished by its teaching; its teaching has sustained it in vigor; and to its teaching is mainly committed its destiny in the future. The object of the following pages will be to indicate briefly, but sharply, that type of doctrine. It must be premised, however, that there will be no systematic exhibition of its tenets illustrated by definitions, quotations, and historical developments generally. The scope assigned to this paper in the programme of the present volume allows only of a few general remarks.

The subject takes us back to the beginning of the great movement. There are two errors which we have at once to confront: that of assigning a doctrinal origin to the system, and that of making its origin entirely independent of doctrine.

The founders of Methodism—*sit venia verbo*—did not, like the Reformers of the sixteenth century, find themselves face to face with a Christianity penetrated through and through by error. They accepted the doctrinal standards of the English Church; and the subscription both of their hands and of their hearts they never revoked. What is more, they adhered to the emphatic interpretation of these standards as contained in liturgical and other formularies. Nothing was further from their thought than to amend either the one or the other in the dogmatic sense. Though they clearly perceived that certain truths and certain aspects of truth had been kept too much in the background, and therefore gave them special prominence, they never erected these revived doctrines into a new confession. They did not isolate the truths they so vehemently preached; but preached them as necessary to the integrity of the Christian faith. The strength of their incessant contention was this, that men had ceased to see and feel what they nevertheless professed to believe. It was a widespread delusion concerning the Revival in the last century, and it is not quite exploded in this century, that its promoters pretended to be the recipients and organs of a new dispensation: modern Montanists, as it were, deeming themselves the special instruments of the Holy Ghost, charged to revive apostolic doctrines and usages which had been lost through intervening ages. Neither earlier nor later Methodism has ever constructed a creed or confession of faith. It never believed that any cardinal doctrine has been lost; still less, that its own commission was to restore such forgotten tenets. Its modest and simple revivals of early practice are such as Christian communities in all ages have felt it their privilege to attempt; but these have never touched the hem of the garment of Christian primitive truth. To sum up in one word: Methodism, as the aggregate unity of many bodies of Christian people, is not based upon a confession, essentially and at all points peculiar to itself, which all who adhere to its organization must hold.

On the other hand, it is no less an error to disregard the theological character which was stamped from the very beginning on this branch of the great Revival. Never was there a work wrought by the Holy Ghost in the Christian Church which was not the result of the enforcement of Christian truth; and never was such a work permanent which did not lay the foundations of its durability in more or less systematized doctrine. Now it was one of the peculiarities of Methodism that it threw around all its organization, and every department of it, a doctrinal defense. The discourses which produced so wonderful an effect in every corner of England were, as delivered, and are now, as preserved, models of theological precision. There is not one of them which does not pay the utmost homage to dogmatic truth; and it is a fact of profound importance in the history of this community, that the very sermons which, under God, gave the movement its life, still form the standard of its theological profession. No more remarkable tribute to the connection between ecclesiastical life and ecclesiastical doctrine can be found in the history of Christendom. It is customary to ascribe the stability of the new economy to the wonderful organizing genius of its founder; it may be questioned whether his zeal for solid dogma has not a right to be included. Certain it is, that early Methodism had a sound theological training; theology preached in its discourses, sang in its hymns, shaped its terms of communion, and presided in the discussions of its conferences. Hence its stability in comparison of other results of the general awakening. The mystical Pietists of Germany, quickened by the same breath, threw off, to a great extent, the fetters of dogmatic creed; they retired from the external Church, disowned its formularies, gathered themselves within a garden doubly inclosed, cultivated the most spiritual and unworldly personal godliness, but made no provision for permanence and for posterity. Methodism, on the other hand, while steadily aiming at the perfection of the interior life kept a vigilant eye on the construction of its peculiar type of theology. That was always in steady progress. It had not reached its consummation when the old Societies of the eighteenth century were consolidated into the Church of the nineteenth. But all the elements were there: some of them, indeed, indeterminate and confused; some of them involving troublesome inconsistencies; others of them giving latitude for abiding differences of opinion; but on the whole supplying the materials of what may now be called a set type of confessional theology.

For that type no name already current can be found; in default of any other, it must be called the Methodist type. But that term is no sooner written than it demands protection. It may seem at once to suggest the idea of an eclectic system of opinion. But, apart from the discredit into which this word eclectic has fallen, whether in the philosophical or in the theological domain, it is not applicable here. The staple and substance of Methodist theology is essentially that of the entire Scripture as interpreted by the catholic evangelical tradition of the Christian Church. It holds the three Creeds, the only confessions of the Faith which ever professed to utter the unanimous voice of the body of Christ on earth; and, so far as these three Creeds were ever accepted by universal Christendom, it accepts them, with only such reservations as do not affect doctrine. Among the later confessions—the badges of a divided Christendom—it holds the Articles of the Church from which it sprang:

holds them, that is, in their purely doctrinal statements. The eclectic hand has done no more than select for prominence such views of truth as have been neglected; never has it culled from this or that Formulary any spoil to make its own. It has no more borrowed from the Remonstrant Arminians than it has borrowed from the Protestant Lutherans. It agrees with both these so far as they express the faith of the New Testament; but no further. It has had, indeed, in past times a conventional connection with the name Arminian; but its Arminianism is simply the mind of the Catholic Church down to the time of Augustine; and with the historical Arminianism that degenerated in Holland it has no affinity. It might be said, with equal propriety or want of propriety, that it has learned some of its lessons from Calvinism. Certainly it has many secret and blessed relations with that system; not with its hard, logical, deductive semi-fatalism, over which Absolute Sovereignty reigns with such awful despotism, but with its deep appreciation of union with Christ, and of the Christian privileges bound up with that high principle.

But to return. The simple fact is, that any truly catholic confession of faith must seem to be eclectic: for there are no bodies of professed Christians, even to the outskirts of Christendom, which do not hold some portions of the truth; while it may be said that many of them hold some particular truth with a sharper and more consistent definition of it than others. But a really catholic system must embrace all these minor peculiarities; and in proportion as it does so, it will seem to have borrowed them. In this sense, the defenders of Methodist theology admit that it is eclectic. They claim to hold all essential truth; to omit no articles but those which they consider erroneous; and to disparage none but those which they deem unessential. This, of course, is a high pretension, but it is not a vainglorious one; for surely it is the prerogative of every Christian community to glory in holding "the faith once delivered to the saints." And as it is with the doctrines, so it is with the spirit, of Methodist teaching. In this also it is, after a fashion, eclectic, as it sympathizes with those who make it their boast that they know no other theology than the biblical, and is as biblical as they. It also agrees with those who think that divinity is a systematic science, to be grounded and organized as such; while with almost all its heart it joins the company of Mystics, whose supreme theologian is the interior Teacher, and who find all truth in the experimental vision and knowledge of God in Christ.

We have to say a few words upon certain peculiarities in the doctrinal position of Methodism. But it is a pleasant preface to dwell for a moment on the broad expanse of catholic evangelical truth, concerning which it has no peculiarities, or no peculiarities that affect Christian doctrine. To begin where all things have their beginning, with the being, triune essence, and attributes of God; his relation to the universe as its Creator and providential Governor; his revelation of himself in nature: this supreme truth it holds against all atheism, antitheism, pantheism, and materialism. The unity of mankind, created in the image of God; fallen into guilt and depravity in Adam; restored through the intervention of the Son of God, who offered a vicarious atonement for the whole race, and is now carrying on the holy warfare for man, and in man, and with man, against the personal devil and his kingdom of darkness: this it holds against all who deny the incarnation of the divine Son, one Person in two natures forever. The divinity and economical offices of the Eternal Spirit of the Father and the Son, the source of all good in man; the inspirer of all holy Scripture; the administrator of a finished redemption to sinful men convinced by his agency on their minds, justified through faith in the atonement which he reveals to the heart, and sanctified to the uttermost by his energy within the soul, operating through the means of grace established in the Church over which he presides, and revealing its power in all good works done in the imitation of Christ: all this it holds against the Pelagian, Antinomian, and Rationalist dishonor to the Holy Ghost. The solemnities of death, resurrection, and eternal judgment, conducted by the returning Christ, and issuing in the everlasting severance between good and evil, the evil being banished from God's presence forever, and the good blessed eternally with the beatific vision: all this, too, it holds with fear and trembling, but with assured confidence that the Judge will vindicate his righteousness forever. In this general outline we have all the elements of the apostles' doctrine and the truth of God. And with regard to these substantial and eternal verities, the system of doctrine we now consider is one with all communions that may be regarded as holding the Head. . . .

The doctrine of the most Holy Trinity might seem to be one in which there is no room for variety of sentiment among those who hold it: that is, the great bulk of the Christian world. But that doctrine is deeply affected both in itself and in its relation to the universe generally, and the economy of redemption in particular, by the view taken of the eternal Sonship of the second Person. Those who would efface the interior distinctions of generation and procession in the Godhead surrender much for which the earliest champions of orthodoxy fought. They take away from the intercommunion of the divine Persons its most impressive and affecting character; and they go far toward robbing us of the sacred mystery which unites the Son's exinanition [humiliation] in heaven with his humiliation as incarnate on earth. Now, we lay claim to no peculiar fidelity here, nor would this subject be mentioned, were it not that Methodism has had the high honor of vindicating the eternal Sonship in a very marked manner. It has produced some of the ablest defenses of this truth known in modern times; defenses which have shown how thoroughly it is interwoven with the fabric of Scripture, how vital it is to the doctrine of the incarnation, and how it may be protected from any complicity with subordinational Arianism. The transition from this to the person of Christ in the unity of his two natures if obvious. And here two remarks only need be made: first, that our doctrine—we may say henceforward our doctrine—is distinguished by its careful abstinence from speculation as to the nature of the Redeemer's self-emptying, simply holding fast the immutable truth that the Divine Son of God could not surrender the essence of his divinity; and, secondly, that in the unity of his Person he was not only sinless but also incapable of sin. Any one who watches the tendencies of modern theology, tendencies which betray themselves in almost all communities, and watches them with an intelligent appreciation of the importance of the issues involved, will acknowledge that this first note of honest glorying is not unjustified.

Turning to the mediatorial work which the Son became incarnate to accomplish, we have to note that the Methodist doctrine lays a special emphasis on its universal relation to the race of man, and deduces the consequences with a precision in some respects peculiar to itself.

For instance, it sees in this the true explanation of the vicarious or substitutionary idea, which is essential to sound evangelical theology, but is very differently held by different schools. There are two extremes that it seeks to avoid by blending the truths perverted by opposite parties. The vague generality of the old Arminian and Grotian theory, which makes the atonement only a rectoral expedient of the righteous God, who sets forth his suffering Son before the universe as the proof that law has been vindicated before grace begins to receive transgressors, was very current in England when Methodism arose. This was and still is confronted by the vigorous doctrine of substitution, which represents Christ to have taken at all points the very place of his elect, actually for them and only them, satisfying the dreadful penalty and holy requirements of the law. Throughout the whole current of Methodist theology there runs a mediating strain, which, however, it would take many pages to illustrate. It accepts the Arminian view that the holiness of God is protected by the atonement; but it insists on bringing in here the vicarious idea. The sin of Adam was expiated as representing the sin of the race as such, or of human nature, or of mankind: a realistic conception which was not borrowed from philosophic realism, and which no nominalism can ever really dislodge from the New Testament. . . .

The blessings of the Christian covenant, administered and imparted by the Holy Ghost, which constitute the state of grace, are so simply set forth in the New Testament that there is not much room for difference of opinion among those whose views of the atonement are sound. We hold them, in common with all who hold the Head, to be one great privilege flowing from union with Christ, in whom we are complete; and that this great privilege of acceptance is administered both externally and internally. But, as we are dwelling on shades of difference, we may observe that the Methodist theology lays more stress than most others upon the fact that in every department of the common blessing there is both an external and an internal administration. . . .

But this leads to the doctrine of the Witness of the Spirit, which has been sometimes regarded as a Methodist peculiarity. By many it is set down as a specimen of what may be called an inductive theology; that is, as a formula for certain experiences enjoyed by the early converts of the system. Now, there can be no question that there is some truth in this. The experiences of multitudes who felt suddenly and most assuredly delivered from the sense of condemnation, enabled to pray to God as a reconciled father, and conscious of their sanctification to his service, may be said to have anticipated the confirmation of the word of God. They first read in their own hearts what they afterward read in their Bibles. For that the induction of experience coincides in this with biblical induction is most certain. That it is the privilege of those who are new creatures in Christ Jesus, and have passed from death unto life, to know the things that are freely given them of God, cannot be denied by any who, with unprejudiced eyes, read the New Testament. In fact, the general principle is admitted in all communions, the differences among them having reference either to certain restrictions in the evidence itself, or to the medium through which it is imparted. A large portion of Christendom unite this witness with sacramental means and ordinances; making personal assurance of salvation dependent on priestly absolution, either with or without a sacrament devised for the purpose. Another, and almost equally large body of Christian teachers, make this high privilege a special blessing vouchsafed to God's elect as the fruit or reward of long discipline and the divine seal upon earnest perseverance; but, when imparted, this assurance includes the future as well as the past, and is the knowledge of an irreversible decree of acceptance which nothing can avail to undermine however much it may be occasionally clouded. The Methodist doctrine is distinguished from these by a few strong points which it has held with deep tenacity from the beginning. It believes that the witness of the Spirit to the spirit in man is direct and clear; distinct from the word, and from the faith that lays hold on the word, though closely connected with both. It is not separated from the testimony which is believed; for, implicitly or explicitly, the promise in Christ must be apprehended by faith. But faith in this matter is rather trust in a Person than belief of a record; and that trust is distinct from the assurance He gives, though that assurance follows so hard upon it that in the supreme blessedness of appropriating confidence they are scarcely to be distinguished. While the faith itself may be always firm, the assurance may be sometimes clouded and uncertain. Neither can co-exist with lapse into sin; and therefore the witness may be suspended, or may be indeed finally lost. It is the assurance of faith only for the present; only the assurance of hope for the future. It may be calm in its peace, or may be quickened into rapture. But it must be confirmed by the testimony of a good conscience; while, on the other hand, it is often the silencer of a conscience unduly disturbed. It is, to sum up, in all types of Methodist theology—whatever abuses it may suffer in some Methodist conceptions of it—no other than the soul's consciousness of an indwelling Saviour through the secret and inexplicable influence of his Holy Spirit.

Perhaps the most eminent peculiarity of the type of doctrine called Methodist is its unfaltering assertion of the believer's privilege to be delivered from indwelling sin in the present life. Its unfaltering assertion: for although varying very much on some subordinate matters of statement as to the means of attainment and the accompanying assurance, it has always been faithful to the central truth itself. Its unfaltering assertion: for in the maintenance of this it has met with the most determined hostility, not only from such opponents as deny the doctrines of grace generally, but also from those whose evangelical theology in general and whose high sanctity give their opposition a very painful character and make it very embarrassing.

It cannot be too distinctly impressed that the one element in the Methodist doctrine that may be called distinctive, is the article that the

83

work of the Spirit in sanctifying believers from sin—from all that in the divine estimate is sin—is to be complete in this state of probation. This is the hope it sees set before us in the Gospel, and this, therefore, it presses upon the pursuit and attainment of all who are in Christ. This is, in the judgment of many, its specific heresy; this, in its own judgment, is its specific glory. . . .

Another is the doctrine of the sacraments. Methodist teaching has, from the beginning, mediated here between two extremes which need not be more particularly defined: in that mediation keeping company with the Anglican Formularies, and the Presbyterian Westminster Confession, both of which raise them above mere signs, and lay stress on their being seals or pledges or instruments of the impartation of the grace signified to the prepared recipient. All its old standards, including its hymns, bear witness to this; they abundantly and irresistibly confirm our assertion as to the sacramental idea generally. As to the two ordinances in particular, there can be no doubt that the sentiments of the various Methodist communions run through a wide range. Recoil from exaggerated doctrine has led many toward the opposite extreme; and a large proportion of their ministers put a very free construction upon their standards, and practically regard the two sacraments as badges simply of Christian profession, the Eucharist being to them a special means of grace in the common sense of the phrase. There is a wide discretion allowed in this matter, and the wisdom of this discretion is, on the whole, justified. With that question, however, we have nothing to do here; our only object being to state the case as it is.

But this essay must be closed, leaving untouched many subjects which naturally appeal for consideration. Something ought to be said as to the controversial aspect of this theology. But leaving that for other essays, we have only to commend the general principles of the Methodist theology to any strangers to it who may read these pages. They will find it clear and consistent, on the whole, as a human system, worthy of much more attention than it usually receives from the Christian world; and, what is of far more importance, they will find it pervaded by the "unction from the Holy One," which is the secret of all truth and of all edification.

Milton S. Terry

Milton S. Terry (1846–1914) was a professor of biblical studies at Garrett Biblical Institute. His *Biblical Hermeneutics: A Treatise on the Interpretation of the Old and New Testaments* (1883) was an important contribution to American Methodism's acceptance of the historical-critical study of the Bible. Under the guidance of Terry and others, such as Hinckley G. Mitchell (1846–1920), Episcopal Methodism found the new approach to Scripture an acceptable way of investigating the biblical message. There was resistance in some quarters, but by the First World War Methodist theology was characterized by its utilization of these critical resources. The presentation by Terry indicates some central issues in the discussion during the period of transition. The chief points of controversy were the authority of Scripture, the relation of the Word of God to the words of the Bible, the nature of historical change relative to the unchanging will and Word of God, and the authenticity of human transmission of the biblical text. The selection included is a pamphlet, *Methodism and Biblical Criticism* (New York: Eaton and Mains; Cincinnati: Jennings and Graham, 1905).

Methodism and Biblical Criticism

The chief characteristic of Methodism, as an epochal religious movement of modern Christianity, is the emphasis it has put upon self-conscious spiritual life. "Our main doctrines, which include all the rest," said John Wesley, "are Repentance, Faith and Holiness. The first of these we account, as it were, the porch of religion; the next is the door; the third is religion itself." At Wesley's first Conference, in 1744, the first two days were devoted to the question of what should be the chief staple of Methodist preaching, and the unanimous conclusion was that they should keep clear of all theological subtlety, and make prominent the doctrines of repentance, faith, justification, sanctification, and the witness of the Spirit. And this has been the glory of Arminian Methodism for over a hundred and fifty years. Wesley's thirteen discourses on the Sermon on the Mount declare that wonderful sermon of our Lord to be "the sum of true religion." And I may add that first, last, fundamental and positive, the source of the life and power of Methodism, is her firm immediate hold on the Supernatural. Her abiding watchword for living and for dying is, "The best of all is, GOD IS WITH US."

Another notable feature of Methodism is the broad, catholic spirit it has shown. Among John Wesley's sermons we find one entitled "A Caution Against Bigotry." It is immediately followed by another on "The Catholic Spirit." This providential founder of Methodism was accustomed to boast of the liberality of Methodism. We do not impose human opinions, he often argued, as a test of membership in our societies. "One condition, and one only, is required, a real desire to save their souls. Where that is, it is enough." In a letter to the Rev. Mr. Venn he says: "I impose my notions upon none. I will be bold to say there is no man living farther from it. I make no opinion the term of union with any man. I think and let think. What I want is holiness of heart and life. They who have this are my brother, sister and mother." In his *Journal* of May, 1778, he writes: "There is no other religious society under heaven which requires of men, in order to their admission into it, nothing but a desire to save their souls. The Methodists alone do not insist on your holding this or that opinion, but they think and let think. I do not know any other religious society, either ancient or modern, wherein such liberty of conscience is now allowed, since the age of the apostles. Here is our glorying; and a glorying peculiar to us."

But it must not be supposed from these utterances that either Wesley or his followers made light of fundamental truths. In his sermon on the "Catholic Spirit" he declares that the true catholic spirit is "not speculative latitudinarianism. It is not an indifference to all opinions: this is the spawn of hell, not the offspring of heaven." It was agreed at the first conference that the great, practical, fundamental doctrines of

Christianity should be the main substance of the Methodist preaching and teaching. The simplicity and self-evidencing authority of their principal doctrines, and the conviction that such truths needed only a fair hearing to be generally accepted, made those fathers of Methodism perfectly willing to allow all reasonable liberties of thought.

What I wish here and now to note is that this wide liberty of opinion,—the boast and glory of John Wesley in the organization of his societies,—*was at that time a new thing under the sun*. The whole world was publicly challenged to show another religious body like it under the wide heaven. Other churches had their prescriptive and proscriptive creeds, and confessions, and dogmatic tests of membership. But Wesley was gifted with the spiritual discernment to anticipate Neander in contending that "it is the *heart* that makes the theologian." His sole great question was, "Is thy heart herein as my heart? If it be, give me thy hand."

From this rapid glance at the fundamental and characteristic position of Methodism as to spiritual life and catholicity I pass to a notice of the pre-eminence it has always assigned the Holy Scriptures as the supreme rule of faith and practice. Originating within the Church of England, it naturally and most loyally accepted the declaration of the sixth of the historic 39 Articles, which declares that "the Holy Scriptures contain all things necessary to salvation; so that whatsoever is not read therein, nor may be proved thereby, is not to be required of any man that it should be believed as an article of faith." In his sermon on "God's Vineyard," Wesley says that the first four Oxford Methodists were each of them "a man of one book. God taught them all to make his word a lantern to their feet and a light in all their paths. They had one, and only one, rule of judgment with regard to all their tempers, words and actions, namely, the oracles of God. They were one and all determined to be Bible Christians." There is, then, and there can be no question as to the high place the Bible holds in the estimate of Methodism.

But when we ask, Who is the authorized interpreter, or who are the authorized interpreters, of these scriptures for the Methodist world, what shall we say? Is John Wesley our Pope to pronounce *ex cathedra* what critical opinions must be accepted as to the origin and composition of the different books of the Bible? Are his Notes on the New Testament and his other expositions a finality for us in exposition? Must we be open to censure if we decline to accept all he affirms in his sermon on "The Cause and Cure of Earthquakes?" May one not be a good, loyal Methodist, sound in doctrine and discipline, and yet reject the teaching of Wesley in his famous sermon on the brute creation, that by reason of the sin of Adam the whole animal world has been made subject to pain and all manner of evils, and even insects and worms lost the high intelligence they previously possessed, but that they are all hereafter to be delivered from this deplorable condition, and that when man is made equal to angels, the kid and the cow and the wolf may be made equal to what we are now?

Now, in the full light of the actual teachings of the founders of Methodism and of the relevant facts of some four generations of Methodist history, we may safely affirm the proposition that, aside from those fundamental truths which formed the staple of Methodist preaching, there exists no prescriptive creed, confession, law, rule or standard of Methodism which defines or determines our liberty of thought and opinion on matters of biblical criticism and interpretation. Accepting the canonical Scriptures, both of the Old Testament and the New, as given by inspiration of God, and profitable for comfort, for teaching, for reproof, for correction and for instruction in righteousness, all questions of higher and of lower criticism are to be treated as matters of personal opinion. Whether it be a question of criticism or interpretation on which all the Methodist fathers agree, or a question on which they differ, no one among us, whether he be minister or layman, is necessarily shut up to any such opinion of the fathers. To contend for the contrary of this statement would seem to be the extreme of presumption. The question of the authorship of any particular book, or set of books, is not a matter of essential doctrine. Every Methodist commentator on the Epistle to the Hebrews, so far as I know, from John Wesley to D. D. Whedon, maintains the Pauline authorship. But must that uniformity of opinion be therefore regarded as a finality of investigation, so that if one, following the steady drift of scholarly opinion for the last forty years, finds that no distinguished commentary on Hebrews, except Whedon's, that has appeared for half a century past, accepts that older view, he is not at liberty to follow the all but unanimous modern opinion because Wesley, and Clarke, and Benson, and Coke, and Watson, and Whedon thought otherwise? Surely on such a question, and with such facts before him, no one is bound even by the unanimous opinion of revered fathers, when upon careful examination he discovers other views and other arguments of more convincing and more satisfactory character.

But if on critical questions in which the fathers were agreed we claim the right of differing from them in opinion, much more may we claim that liberty on matters wherein they differed among themselves. Let us first notice what Wesley says about himself as an expositor of the New Testament. His "Explanatory Notes upon The New Testament" occupy no secondary place among the Methodist standards. If there is anything of the nature of authoritative interpretation of any part of the Bible among the Methodists, it is these "Notes" of Wesley on the New Testament. And yet, in the Preface of his work, the author observes three things which we do well to consider. 1. First he expresses his own deep sense of inability and want of learning, experience, and wisdom for the important task. 2. Then he advises the reader that his *notes* were not principally designed for men of learning, who are provided with many other helps; but he writes for plain, unlettered men. 3. He furthermore informs us that he has appropriated most of his comments from a work of Bengel, a German professor and critic, who had died some three years before the date of his Preface to the "Notes."

Let us now ponder for a moment the significance of these utterances of Wesley as against the supposition that a faithful and loyal Methodist preacher is not at liberty to differ from the views of the founder of Methodism in matters of biblical criticism and interpretation. No matter what new discoveries have been made since 1754, no matter what contributions have been made to biblical science during a hundred and fifty years, no matter how clear and convincing other views than those of Wesley have become to scores and hundreds of "men of long and deep experience in the ways and word of God," at whose feet Wesley says in that same Preface he would like "to sit and to learn," no matter if half or two thirds of the best known scholars of Christendom outside of Methodism offer other critical opinions which they believe better conserve the views of Christ and of Paul, and "justify the ways of God to man;" no matter if all the world think otherwise, no honest Methodist can think otherwise and continue as a consistent member or minister of the Methodist Church! I am slow to believe that we have any among us who would seriously presume to maintain a position so unreasonable. What! After all that we have quoted from Wesley himself, his boast of the liberty of opinion enjoyed in his societies, his emphatic repetition of the phrase "think and let think," and in spite of his disclaimer in the Preface to his New Testament "Notes" of any superior wisdom and ability as an expounder of the Scriptures, shall we rise up in these later days and forbid the liberty which he extolled?

We turn next to examine a few specimens of Wesley's critical opinions. In his first note on the New Testament, speaking of the genealogy of Jesus Christ and its difficulties as compared with that of Luke, he observes that "if there were any difficulties which could not easily be removed, they would rather affect the Jewish tables than the credit of the evangelists." "Nor was it needful that they should correct the mistakes, if there were any." He further argues that, as their chief aim was to show "that Jesus was of the family from which the promised seed was to come," these New Testament genealogies, even if they contained errors, would have "had more weight with the Jews for the purpose than if alterations had been made by inspiration itself." I cannot but imagine what a turmoil would be made in some quarters if only some radical "higher critic" should publish such a statement as this. For this very first comment of John Wesley on the New Testament involves the following propositions: (1) The Jewish Tables of Old Testament genealogy may contain some mistakes. (2) Such mistakes would not invalidate but might even be a help in accomplishing the purpose of the evangelists with Jewish readers. (3) Even divine inspiration itself employed in correcting the records would have been less effectual in influencing the Jews in this matter. (4) Would it not logically follow that, if any errors exist in the Old Testament records, and if they can be made to serve a good purpose, it may be better even for divine inspiration to let them stand for such supposable good uses rather than correct them?

In the textual criticism of the New Testament Wesley did not hesitate to make changes where occasion seemed to him to require it. He tells us in his Preface that he embodied in his text those various readings which Bengel had shown to have a vast majority of ancient copies and translations on their side. But as one noteworthy example of his following the great German critic into error, observe what he says about the text of the "three heavenly witnesses" in John V, 7: "What Bengelius has advanced concerning the authority of the controverted verse will abundantly satisfy any impartial person." The same opinion is in substance repeated in his sermon "On the Trinity," which he bases on this questionable passage. Coke and Benson adopt the view of Wesley, but Adam Clarke, who stands pre-eminent as critic and commentator among the older Methodists, tells us that this famous text "is wanting in every manuscript of this epistle written before the invention of printing, one excepted. It is wanting in both the Syriac, all the Arabic, Ethiopic, Coptic, Sahadic, Armenian, Slavonian; in a word, in all the ancient versions but the Vulgate; and even of this version many of the most ancient and correct manuscripts have it not." In Dr. Whedon's commentary on the passage, published 24 years ago, we read: "Scholars are agreed, at the present day, that this entire verse is not genuine; being a late interpolation and not the words of St. John." In the Revised Version of our Bible this text is omitted, and there is not an intimation even in the margin that it ever existed. . . .

Wesley's comments on the Psalms are comparatively few and meager, but we should make mention of the fact that in his "Sunday Service of the Methodists in North America" he took great liberty in abridging the Psalter, and he wrote in the Preface: "Many psalms are left out, and many parts of others, as being highly improper for the mouths of a Christian congregation." In his Preface to the Psalms he observes that these ancient songs of Israel are not all from David, but by many different authors of various times, some in the time of the Babylonian exile. It is notorious that Adam Clarke was very bold in questioning the Davidic authorship of the 23d and 51st Psalms, which have been all but universally attributed to the great king of Judah. He declares his opinion that the 23d psalm was written after the captivity, and he cites Bishop Horsley and Dr. Kennicott to show that the title to psalm 51 is misplaced, and that it must have been written during the captivity. He is very positive in the conviction that, whether the title be misplaced or not, the last two verses of the psalm do not fit the subject of the preceding verses nor the times of David. They are rather a prayer of some one of the captives in Babylon for the redemption of Zion and the rebuilding of Jerusalem. It is also a noteworthy fact that Clarke questioned the Solomonic authorship of Ecclesiastes, pointing to the fact that the style is that of writers who lived after the exile, and declaring his opinion that the attempts to deny this are often trifling and generally ineffectual. . . .

The foregoing facts have been presented to show the glaring impropriety, not to say the absurdity, of anyone now pretending that we, earnest and loyal Methodists of the twentieth century, are not at liberty to accept the interpretations of Scripture and the critical views prevalent in our time, if they are seen to differ from those of the founders and fathers of Methodism. Observe, it is no question of any of the great practical truths of Arminian Methodist theology that we are here discussing. There has never been in the entire history of our Arminian Methodism any considerable dispute over matters of fundamental doctrine. Our record in this respect is that of a beautiful and glorious unity of faith. No doctrine of religion enunciated in our 25 Articles, or in our General Rules, or in any other recognized standard, is compromised by the differences of opinion among the fathers, or among the sons, on such matters of biblical criticism as we have been presenting. If any one is persuaded in his mind that Adam Clarke's views on a critical question are preferable to those of Wesley, he ought to feel at full liberty to adopt them. He may with equal liberty prefer to abide by the views of Wesley or some other. That is his right as an honest Methodist, and his plain duty as a conscientious Christian. And if we find that on some critical questions the drift of opinion is away from the views universally accepted in Wesley's time, and contrary to those maintained by all the early Methodists, no faithful student of the Holy Scriptures should feel himself tied up to old opinions when he sees or believes them to be superseded by a better exposition. . . .

It is a noteworthy fact that Wesley put the personal experience of the witness of the Spirit above all other evidences of Christianity. He maintained that the conversion of a soul to God is essentially miraculous. "I suppose," he writes, "that all who allow there is any such thing believe it to be supernatural. And what the difference is between a supernatural and a miraculous work, I am yet to learn." It was the prevailing custom of the orthodox apologetics of Wesley's time to lay stress first of all on the "external evidences" so called, especially the historicity of the miracles recorded in the Bible. In fact, the main argument in the Deistic controversies of the eighteenth century rested upon the question of the traditional genuineness and authenticity of the books which recorded the miracles and the prophecies. But nothing in all the writings of John Wesley is more remarkable than what we read in his famous "Letter to Dr. Conyers Middleton," where he argues and insists that the internal witness of the Spirit is of a higher grade than any external and traditional testimony. He boldly declares that what he "experiences in his own breast" is of greater weight than anything which appeals to him merely from without. And so he contrasts the two in the following manner:

1. First, he argues, traditional evidence is weakened by length of time; it must pass through many hands, in a succession of ages. But no length of time can possibly affect the strength of this internal evidence.

2. Traditional evidence is extremely complicated and taxes the brains of men of strong and clear understanding. But the internal experience is so plain and simple that a child may feel all its force.

3. Tradition stands a great way off, and gives account of what happened long ago. The inward evidence is intimately present, at all times, in all places. "It is nigh thee, in thy mouth and in thy heart."

4. Even if it were possible for the historic foundation of Christianity to be shaken (which of course Wesley nowhere concedes), still he contends that the internal evidence would remain firm and unshaken.

5. "I have been sometimes almost inclined to believe," he writes, "that the wisdom of God has, in most later ages, permitted the external evidence of Christianity to be more or less clogged and incumbered for this very end, that men (of reflection especially) might not altogether rest there, but be constrained to look into themselves also, and attend to the light shining in their hearts."

6. "Without this I cannot but doubt whether they can long maintain their cause." More stress, he urges, must be put on the internal evidence. It will be an advantage to the Christian cause, and "perhaps the speediest and the only effectual way of bringing all reasonable Deists to be Christians." Thus he puts his great emphasis on the intrinsic value of the Christian faith, and asks: "What reasonable assurance can you have of things whereof you have no personal experience?"

In all this we cannot but note how remarkably John Wesley anticipated the trend of modern critical thought in placing the internal above the external evidences of Christianity. He thus adopted in substance the same position and argument as the late Professor Bruce, who says: "It must be confessed that miracles cannot be offered as evidences of Christianity now with the confidence with which they were employed for this purpose by the apologists of the past age. Men do not now believe in Christ because of his miracles; they rather believe in the miracles because they have first believed in Christ. For such believers Christ is his own witness, who accredits everything connected with him: scripture, prophecy, miracle. Those who are in this happy position need no help from apologists." . . .

In like manner Wesley maintained the necessity of personal inspiration of every true believer to understand the deep things of God. In his letter to the Rev. Mr. Potter he argues that one must have "a particular and immediate inspiration before he can either understand, or preach, or live the gospel." "But," says Mr. Potter, "the Scriptures are a complete and sufficient rule. Therefore, to what purpose could any further inspiration serve? The supposed need of it is highly injurious to the written word." To which Mr. Wesley replies: "High sounding words! But, blessed be God, they are only *brutum fulmen* (empty sound); they make much noise, but do not wound. 'To what purpose could any further inspiration serve?' Answer yourself: 'To enlighten the understanding and to rectify the will.' Else be the Scriptures ever so complete, they will not save your soul. . . . When you say yourself, 'The Spirit is to teach us all things, and to guide us into all truth,' judge you, whether this is to 'explain, or to supply, the written word.'"

93

And so, in one way and another, did that good man of God empha-size the truth that the Scriptures are not an end in themselves, but a means to an end. And that end is the cultivation of spiritual life. And this has been the accepted view of our Methodism from the beginning. We must seek the divine illumination of the Spirit in order to a proper and profitable understanding of the Holy Scriptures.

I have not been able to find in Wesley's works any dogma or theory of biblical inspiration. Bengel's note on 2 Tim. III, 16, is: "Scripture was divinely inspired, not merely when it was written, God breathing through the writers, but also while it is being read, God breathing through the Scripture, and the Scripture breathing him." Wesley's note is as follows: "The Spirit of God not only once inspired those who wrote it, but continually inspires, supernaturally assists, those that read it with earnest prayer. Hence it is so profitable for doctrine, for instruction, etc."

There is nothing in our Articles of Religion which so much as names a theory of inspiration, but the fifth article affirms (not the inerrancy, nor the infallibility, but) the SUFFICIENCY of the Holy Scriptures for a knowledge of salvation. . . .

When, now, it is asked what the attitude of modern Methodism should be toward modern biblical criticism, our answer is, That which it has been from the beginning, and that which has been our boast and glory from the time of Wesley until now: "We think and let think." We act according to the apostolic precept: "Prove all things; hold fast that which is good." Among the things now quite generally maintained by biblical scholars are the following opinions touching the various books of the Bible:

1. The Bible is not so much a single book as it is a great library, a col-lection of books of very different dates and authorship.

2. Of a considerable number of the books the authorship is unknown, and opinions vary as to their origin and relative value.

3. Many of these books are of composite origin. The composite char-acter of the Pentateuch, of Joshua, Judges, Samuel, Kings, Chronicles, Ezra, Nehemiah, the books of Isaiah, Zechariah and Proverbs, is quite generally conceded.

4. The compilation of the Book of Psalms, as it now appears in our Bibles, was the work of the post-exile leaders of the Jewish people.

5. The biblical writers have employed nearly all the forms of literary composition which appear in the other great literatures of the world. We find various styles of prose writing, and also poetry, parable, riddle, symbol, fable and proverb. We also find in these scriptures various types and grades of religious thought.

6. No divine authority, either of Jesus, or of the prophets or apostles, has ever fixed the limits of the biblical canon.

7. The contents of these Scriptures, taken as a whole (whether one accept the Palestinean or the Alexandrian canon of the Old Testament), furnish us with a priceless record of the progressive revelation of God in and through the Jewish people. Therefore we call these holy scriptures "oracles of God;" the things which "God spoke of old time unto the fathers in the prophets by divers portions and in divers manners." . . .

I cannot better close this paper than by citing the words of the Rev. Dr. W. T. Davison, a well known leader among the Wesleyans of England, and late president of the British Conference, in an article which appeared in "The Methodist Times" of February 4, 1904. He therein expressed his general approval of Canon Driver's recent work on the book of Genesis, and declares "that we cannot read these early chapters of the Bible precisely as our fathers did. The literalist who believes that by a miracle the serpent spoke in the garden, and that the deluge covered the whole globe, is apt to assume that it is he alone who accepts the Bible as true, whereas his principles of interpretation are really at fault. . . . Methodism will not be behindhand in this work (of criticism and interpretation). Rashness is not characteristic of us as a community, and rashness in such matters is little short of wickedness. But timidity is not goodness, and obscurantism is not helpful or kind. The Spirit of truth who inspired the writers of the Sacred Scriptures, and who guided our fathers to read and expound them, will still guide us as we seek to know and teach the whole truth, and nothing but the truth. And it is written—the Master himself has said it—'The truth shall make you free.'"

John Miley

John Miley (1813–1895) reflects the intersection of evangelical faith and scientific sensibility as these found expression in the final decades of the nineteenth century. He maintained that theology explores the data of religious experience and is, in this sense, scientific. Miley attempted to be both a natural and a dogmatic theologian. The immediate experience of God is basic; the Scriptures clarify and provide normative interpretation of that experience.

Miley designated his position "Ethical Arminianism." Utilizing the inheritance shaped by D. D. Whedon and others, Miley made free personal agency the foundational principle of his work. His chief theological writing was the two-volume *Systematic Theology* (1893). This systematic statement was a well-structured, thorough discussion of cardinal theological issues from Miley's perspective. The selections included in this reader are selected from *Systematic Theology* and represent central themes in Miley's thought, namely his basic theistic principles and doctrine of the atonement. In his discussion of the atonement he develops a distinctive form of the governmental theory and argues for the sufficiency of the atonement for all people. Miley is distinct among Methodist theologians of his time in making theism and Christology coordinate themes. These Miley selections are taken from *Systematic Theology* (New York: Hunt and Eaton, Cincinnati: Cranston & Cuttis, 1894), Library of Biblical and Theological Literature, vols. V & VI: "Theism," V, pp. 57-66; 68-70; "Sufficiency of the Atonement," VI, pp. 195-202, 218-21.

Theism

I. The Sense of Theism

1. *Doctrinal Content of the Term.*—Theism means the existence of a personal God, Creator, Preserver, and Ruler of all things. Deism equally means the personality of God and also his creative work, but denies his providence in the sense of theism. These terms were formerly used in much the same sense, but since early in the last century deism has mostly been used in a sense opposed to the Scriptures as a divine revelation, and to a divine providence. Such is now its distinction from theism. Pantheism differs from theism in the denial of the divine personality. With this denial, pantheism can mean no proper work of creation or providence. The philosophic agnosticism which posits the Infinite as the ground of finite existences, but denies its personality, is in this denial quite at one with pantheism. The distinction of theism from these several opposing terms sets its own meaning in the clearer light. Creation and providence are here presented simply in their relation to the doctrinal content of theism. The methods of the divine agency therein require separate treatment. Nor could this treatment proceed with advantage simply in the light of reason; it requires the fuller light of revelation.

2. *Historic View of the Idea of God.*—Religion is as wide-spread as the human family and pervades the history of the race. But religion carries with it some form of the idea of God or of some order of supernatural existence. There is no place for religion without this idea. This is so thoroughly true that the attempts to found a religion without the notion of some being above us have no claim to recognition in a history of religion. But while religion so widely prevails it presents great varieties of form, especially in the idea of God, or of what takes the supreme place in the religious consciousness. Such differences appear in what are called the ethnic religions, the religions of different races. Of these James Freeman Clarke enumerates ten. Some make the number greater, others less. However, the exact number does not concern our present point. In the instances of Confucianism, Brahmanism, and Buddhism there are wide variations in the conception of God, and equally so in the other ethnic religions. As we look into details these variations are still more manifest. In view of the objects worshiped, the rites and ceremonies of the worship, the sentiments uttered in prayer and praise, we must recognize very wide differences of theistic conception. The case is not really other, because so many of these ideas are void of any adequate truth

of theism. They are still ideas of what is divine to the worshiper and have their place in the religious consciousness. We can hardly think that in the low forms of idolatry there is nothing more present to religious thought and feeling than the idol. "Even the stock or stone, the rudest fetich before which the savage bows, is, at least to him, something more than a stock or stone; and the feeling of fear or awe or abject dependence with which he regards it is the reflex of a dim, confused conception of an invisible and spiritual power, of which the material object has become representative."

3. *Account of Perverted Forms of the Idea.*—These perverted forms arise, in part, from speculations which disregard the imperative laws of rational thinking, and, in part—mostly, indeed—from vicious repugnances to the true idea. When God is conceived under the form of pantheism, or as the Absolute in a sense which precludes all predication and specially denies to him all personal attributes, the idea is the result of such speculation as we have just now characterized, or a creation of the imagination. In either form the idea is just as impotent for any rationale of the cosmos as the baldest materialism. Neither has any warrant in rational thought. When God is conceived under the forms of idolatry the conception is from a reaction of the soul against the original idea. The reaction is from a repugnance of the sensibilities to the true idea, not from any discernment of rational thought. This is the account which Paul gives of the source and prevalence of idolatry. His account applies broadly to the heathen world. "When they knew God, they glorified him not as God, neither were thankful; but became vain in their imaginations, and their foolish heart was darkened." Thus closing their eyes to the light of nature in which God was manifest, they "changed the glory of the uncorruptible God into an image made like to corruptible man, and to birds, and four-footed beasts, and creeping things." It was because "they did not like to retain God in their knowledge."

4. *Definitive Idea of God.*—A definition of God that shall be true to the truth of his being and character is a difficult attainment. This must be apparent whether we study definitions as given, or the subject of definition. God is for human thought an incomprehensible Being, existing in absolute soleness, apart from all the categories of genus and species. Hence the difficulty of definition. The true idea cannot be generalized in any abstract or single principle. As the Absolute or Unconditioned, God is simply differentiated from the dependent or related; as the Infinite, from the finite. The essential truths of a definition are not given in any of these terms. As the Unknowable, the agnostic formula is purely neg-

ative and without definitive content. Absolute will cannot give the content of a true idea of God. In order to the true idea, will must be joined with intellect and sensibility in the constitution of personality. Some of the divine titles have the form of a definition, but are not such in fact. God is often named the Almighty, but this expresses simply his omnipotence, which is only one of his perfections. Another title is Jehovah, which signifies the eternal, immutable being of God; but while the meaning is profound the plenitude of his being is not expressed. "God is love." There is profound truth here also; but the words express only what is viewed as supreme in God.

The citation of a few definitions may be useful. "The first ground of all being; the divine spirit which, unmoved itself, moves all; absolute, efficient principle; absolute notion; absolute end."—*Aristotle.* This definition conforms somewhat to the author's four forms of cause. It contains more truth of a definition than some given by professedly Christian philosophers. "The moral order of the universe, actually operative in life."—*Fichte.* Lotze clearly points out the deficiencies of this definition. It gives us an abstract world-order without the divine Orderer. "The absolute Spirit; the pure, essential Being that makes himself object to himself; absolute holiness; absolute power, wisdom, goodness, justice."—*Hegel.* "A Being who, by his understanding and will, is the Cause (and by consequence the Author of nature; a Being who has all rights and no duties; the supreme perfection in substance; the all-obligating Being; Author of a universe under moral law; the moral Author of the world; an Intelligence infinite in every respect."—*Kant.* "*God* is derived incontestably from *good* and means the Good itself in the perfect sense, the absolute Good, the primal Good, on which all other good depends—as it were, the Fountain of good. Hence God has been styled the Being of beings (*ens entium*), the supreme Being (*ens summum*), the most perfect Being (*ens perfectissumum s. realissimum*)."—*Krug.* "The absolute, universal Substance; the real Cause of all and every existence; the alone, actual, and unconditioned Being, not only Cause of all being, but itself all being, of which every special existence is only a modification."—*Spinoza.* This is a pantheistic definition. "The *ens a se,* Spirit independent, in which is embraced the sufficient reason of the existence of things contingent—that is, the universe."—*Wolf.* These citations are found in the useful work of Krauth-Fleming. Some of them contain much truth, particularly Hegel's and Kant's. The serious deficiency is in the omission of any formal assertion of the divine personality as the central reality of a true definition. On the other hand, too much account is made of the divine agency in creation and providence. This agency is very properly included in a definition of theism, particularly in its distinction from deism and pantheism, but is not necessary to a definition of God himself.

We may add a few other definitions. "God is the infinite and personal Being of the good, by and for whom the finite hath existence and consciousness; and it is precisely this threefold definition—God is spirit, is love, is Lord—this infinite personal Good, which answers to the most simple truths of Christianity." Martensen gives the elements of a definition substantially the same. "God is a Spirit, infinite, eternal, and unchangeable, in his being, wisdom, power, holiness, justice, goodness, and truth." Dr. Hodge thinks this probably the best definition ever penned by man. Personality is the deepest truth in the conception of God and should not be omitted from the definition. With this should be combined the perfection of his personal attributes. All the necessary truths of a definition would thus be secured. Hence we define thus: *God is an eternal personal Being, of absolute knowledge, power, and goodness.*

II. Origin of the Idea of God

1. *Possible Sources of the Idea.*—We here mean, not any mere notion of God without respect to its truth, or as it might exist in the thought of an atheist, but the idea as a conviction of the divine existence. How may the mind come into the possession of this idea?

There are faculties of mind which determine the modes of our ideas. Some we obtain through sense-perception. Sense-experience underlies all such perception. We cannot in this mode reach the idea of God. Many of our ideas are obtained through the logical reason. They are warranted inferences from verified facts or deductions from self-evident principles. Through the same faculty we receive many ideas, with a conviction of their truth, on the ground of human testimony. There are also intuitive truths, immediate cognitions of the primary reason. The conviction of truth in these ideas comes with their intuitive cognition. Through what mode may the idea of God be obtained? Not through sense-perception, as previously stated. Beyond this it is not necessarily limited to any one mental mode: not to the intuitive faculty, because it may be a product of the logical reason or a communication or revelation—to the logical reason; nor to this mode, because it may be an immediate truth of the primary reason.

If the existence of God is an immediate cognition of the reason, will it admit the support and affirmation of logical proof? We have assumed that it will. Yet we fully recognize the profound distinction in the several modes of our ideas. The logical and intuitive faculties have their respective functions, and neither can fulfill those of the other. Further, intuitive truths are regarded as self-evident, and as above logical proof. Yet many theists, learned in psychology and skilled in logic, while holding the existence of God to be an intuitive truth, none the less maintain this truth by logical proofs. We may mistake the intuitive content of a primary truth and assume that to be intuitive which is not really so. Many a child learns that two and three are five before the intuitive faculty begins its activity, particularly in this sphere. The knowledge so acquired is not intuitive. Yet that two and three are five is an intuitive truth. But wherein? Not in the simple knowledge which a child acquires, but in the necessity of this truth which the reason affirms, in the cognition that it is, and must be, a truth in all worlds and for all minds. That things equal to the same thing, or weights equal to the same weight, are equal to one another is an axiomatic truth; but it is its necessary truth that is an intuitive cognition, while a practical knowledge of the simple fact of equality may be acquired in an experimental mode. The point made is that some truths, while intuitional in some of their content, may yet be acquired in an experimental or logical mode. So, while the existence of God may be an immediate datum of the moral and religious consciousness, it may also be a legitimate subject for logical proofs. It is a truth in the affirmation of which the intuitive reason and the logical reason combine. Hence in holding the existence of God to be an immediate cognition of the mind we are not dismissing it from the sphere of logical proofs. . . .

Sufficiency of the Atonement

The substitution of Christ in suffering answers for an atonement through a revelation of such moral truths as give the highest ruling power to the divine law. It must, therefore, embody such facts as will make the necessary revelation. Only thus can the atonement have sufficiency. It is proper, therefore, that we specially note some of these facts of atoning value. Authors differ somewhat respecting them. This may arise, at least in part, from a difference in the doctrine. The vital facts are clear in the light of Scripture.

101

I. The Holiness of Christ

1. *A Necessary Element.*—A criminal cannot be a proper mediator. Whoever dishonors himself and the law by his own transgression is thereby disqualified for the office of mediation in behalf of a criminal. If human government does not require moral perfection for such office, still, the mediator must not be amenable to penalty on his own account. And the higher his personal righteousness and moral worth, the more valuable will be his mediation as the ground of forgiveness. As a mediation, so accepted, must inculcate respect for law and enforce obedience to its requirements, so, much depends upon the moral worth of the mediator. And Christ, in the atonement, must be without sin and clear of all its penal liabilities. He must be personally holy. . . .

II. His Greatness

1. *An Element of Atoning Value.*—Whoever needs the service of a mediator is concerned to find one of the highest character and rank attainable. The minister of the law vested with the pardoning power is officially concerned therein. For the value of the mediation is not in its personal influence with him, but from its rectoral relations. He may already be personally disposed to clemency, but lacks a proper ground for its exercise, so that law shall not suffer in its honor and authority. Such ground is furnished in the greatness and rank of the mediator. And the higher these qualities, the more complete is the ground of forgiveness, or the more effective the support of law in all its rectoral offices. There is a philosophy in these facts, as manifest in our previous discussions. Beyond this, the case may be appealed to the common judgment. . . .

III. His Voluntariness

1. *A Necessary Fact.*—The injustice of a coerced substitution of one in place of another would deprive it of all benefit in atonement for sin. But when the sacrifice is in the free choice of the substitute, its voluntariness not only gives full place to every other element of atoning value, but is itself such an element.

2. *Christ a Voluntary Substitute.*—On this fact the Scriptures leave us no reason for any question. And the frequency and fullness of their utterances respecting the freedom of Christ in the work of redemption give to that freedom all the certainty and significance which its truth requires. It

is true that the Father gave the Son; that he sent him to be the Saviour of the world; that he spared him not, but delivered him up for us all; that he prepared for him a body for his priestly sacrifice in atonement for sin: but it is none the less true that in all this the mind of the Son was at one with the mind of the Father; that he freely and gladly chose the incarnation in order to our redemption; that he loved us and gave himself for us, an offering and a sacrifice to God; that, with full power over his own life, he freely surrendered it in our redemption. And the fact of this freedom is carried back of his incarnation and atoning suffering to the Son in his essential divinity and in his glory with the Father.

3. *The Atoning Value.*—The voluntariness of Christ crowns with its grace all the marvelous facts of his redeeming work. His atoning sacrifice, while in the purest free-willing, was at once in an infinite beneficence toward us, and in an infinite filial love and obedience toward his Father. And the will of the Father, in obedience to which the sacrifice is made, so far from limiting its atoning worth, provides for its highest sufficiency by opening such a sphere for the beneficence and filial obedience of the Son. Both have infinite worth with the Father. So he regards them, not in any commercial valuation, but as intrinsically good. Now forgiveness on such a ground is granted only on account of what is most precious with God, and therefore a vindication of his justice and holiness, of his rectoral honor and authority, in the salvation of repenting souls.

IV. His Divine Sonship

1. *Sense of Atoning Value.*—The nearer a mediator stands in the relations of friendship to an offended person the more persuasive will his intercession be. But this is a matter of more personal influence, not of rectoral service. The person offended is regarded simply in his personal disposition, not as a minister of the law, with the obligations of his office; and, so far, the case has more affinity with the satisfaction theory than with the governmental. According to this theory God needs no vicarious sacrifice for his personal propitiation. His need is for some provision which will render the forgiveness of sin consistent with his own honor and authority as moral Ruler, and with the good of his subjects. Hence, while we find an element of atoning value in the divine Sonship of Christ, we find it not in a matter of personal influence with the Father, but on a principle of rectoral service. This value lies in the moral worth which the Sonship of Christ gives to his redeeming work in the appreciation of the Father. The nature of it will further appear under the next heading.

2. *Measure of Value.*—The divine filiation of the Redeemer furnishes an element of great value in the atonement. This may be illustrated in connection with two facts of his Sonship.

The divine filiation of the Redeemer is original and singular. It is such as to be the ground of the Father's infinite love to his Son. On nothing are the Scriptures more explicit than on the fact of this love. Therein we have the ground of the Father's infinite appreciation of the redeeming work of the Son. And the truth returns, that forgiveness is granted only on the ground of what is most precious with the Father. By all this preciousness, as revealed in the light of the Father's love to the Son, his redemptive mediation, as the only and necessary ground of forgiveness, gives utterance to the authority of the divine law, and the obligation of its maintenance; to the sacredness of moral rights and interests, and the imperative requirement of their protection; to the evil of sin, and the urgency of its restriction. These are the very facts which give the highest and best ruling power to the divine law. And thus we have an element of sufficiency in the atonement.

The redeeming love of God toward us is most clearly seen in the light of his love for his own Son. Only in this view do we read the meaning of its divine utterances. Why did the Father sacrifice the Son of his love in our redemption? It could not have been from any need of personal propitiation toward us. The redeeming sacrifice, itself the fruit of his love to us, is proof to the contrary. He gave his Son to die for us that he might reach us in the grace of forgiveness and salvation. Why then did he so sacrifice the Son of his love? The only reason lies in the moral interests concerned, and which, in the case of forgiveness, required an atonement in their protection. But for his regard for these rights and interests, and, therefore, for the sacredness and authority of his law as the necessary means of their protection, he might have satisfied the yearnings of his compassion toward us in a mere administrative forgiveness. This he could not do consistently with either his goodness or his rectoral obligation. And rather than surrender the interests which his law must protect he delivers up his own Son to suffering and death. Therefore, in this great sacrifice—infinitely great because of his love for his Son, and therein so revealed—in this great sacrifice, and with all the emphasis of its greatness, God makes declaration of an infinite regard for the interests and ends of his moral government, and of an immutable purpose to maintain them. This declaration, in all the force of its divine verities, goes to the support of his government, and gives the highest honor and ruling power to his law, while forgiveness is granted to repenting sinners.

V. His Human Brotherhood

1. *Mediation Must Express an Interest.*—A stranger to a condemned person, and without reason for any special interest in his case, could not be accepted as a mediator in his behalf. A pardon granted on such ground would, in respect of all ends of government, be the same as one granted on mere sovereignty. The case is clearly different when, on account of intimate relations of friendship, or other special reasons of interest, the mediation is an expression of profound sympathy. Forgiveness on such an intercession is granted, not for any thing trivial or indifferent, and so evincing an indifference to the law, but only for what is regarded as real, and a sufficient justification of the forgiveness. This gives support to law. It loses nothing of respect in the common judgment, nothing of its ruling force. And the profounder the sympathy of the mediator, the greater is the rectoral service of his mediation as the ground of forgiveness.

2. *The Principle in Atonement.*—Christ appropriates the principle by putting himself into the most intimate relation with us. In the incarnation he clothes himself in our nature, partakes of our flesh and blood, and enters into brotherhood with us. Herein is the reality and the revelation of a profound interest in his mediation. The love and sympathy of this brotherhood he carries into the work of atonement. They are voiced in his tears and sorrows, in the soul agonies of Gethsemane, in the bitter outcryings of Calvary, and are still voiced in his intercessory prayers in heaven. Men and angels, in a spontaneous moral judgment, pronounce such a mediation a sufficient ground of forgiveness, and vindicate the rectitude. The divine law suffers no dishonor nor loss of ruling power. Thus the human brotherhood of Christ gives sufficiency to his atonement.

Hugh Price Hughes

Hugh Price Hughes (1847–1902) was a local Methodist minister, a political reformer, an influential editor of a church paper, and a writer on theology and ethics. Combining passion and compassion, intellectual effort with practical service, and evangelism with social reform, he became a leader of Free Church interests in England. Spokesman and leader, Hughes set directions for much that has followed. The chapter selected for inclusion in this sourcebook is from *Social Christianity* (London: Hodder and Stoughton, 1890), pp. 3-15 (preached at St. James' Hall, Sunday afternoon, October 30, 1887).

Jesus Christ and the Masses

"When He saw the multitudes, He was moved with compassion for them."—St. Matt. ix. 36.

Our subject this afternoon is "Jesus Christ and the Masses: what He thought of the Masses of the People." Jesus Christ was essentially a man of the People—a working man. He spent all His days among the poor; and after His public life had begun He almost lived in the crowd. He was constantly surrounded by the crowd. Nothing is more characteristic of Jesus Christ than the familiar saying that "The common people heard Him gladly." Therefore when we come across anybody whom the common people do not hear gladly, he may be a very estimable man, but we know that he is not like Jesus Christ. I was very much struck by a remark I heard in Scotland about an undoubted Christian. Some one said of him:

106

"He is a very good man, but he does not remind me of Jesus Christ." How many good men there are who are really very good men, but who do not remind us of Jesus! No man can really remind us of the Jesus of the Gospel unless he loves the people, and is loved by the people. I admit the truth of Tennyson's awful impeachment that "the Churches have kill'd their Christ," and that we have presented to the masses of the European peoples all sorts of false Christs, caricatures of Christ. But the real Christ is one who, when seen, attracts the crowd everywhere. Wherever Jesus went He was surrounded by the multitude.

It is only within the last few years that I have noticed the beautiful and significant fact that in nearly every instance in which we find Jesus Christ face to face with the multitude, the Evangelist tells us that He was "moved with compassion." When Jesus Christ saw a crowd His heart yearned over them. He pitied them. When you saw the crowd on Lord Mayor's Day, what was your feeling? When you saw the crowd on Jubilee Day, what was your feeling? If Christ had been in the window of some house in Trafalgar Square, His feeling would have been one of pity. When Jesus Christ saw a great crowd, He was moved with compassion. Mark it well—not with hatred; not with fear. It is the invariable tendency of heathenism, both ancient and modern, to hate and to fear the people. Horace was a fine old Roman gentleman, and a worthy representative of many a fine English gentleman of the present day. Not a few of those who are found in the West-end clubs of this very city would feel very much at home in the society of Horace. His views and theirs are remarkably alike. Horace honestly enough begins one of his best-known odes with these words: "I hate the vulgar crowd, and keep them at a distance." The illustrious Frenchman, Ernest Rénan, who has a passionate and almost idolatrous admiration for the old Greek civilization, and who, in a memorable passage, bitterly regrets that Paul ever went to Athens to destroy it, acknowledges, in a work now passing through the press, that the Greek civilization, with all its refinement and culture, utterly failed in this: that the thinkers and statesmen of Greece had no compassion for the multitude. Their policy was alternately to bribe and to massacre the masses of the people. Heathen statesmanship had no better method then, and it has no better method now.

The best excuse we can offer for politicians of all classes, and of all sections and positions in society, who either hate or fear the masses of the people, is that they do not know the people. One of the greatest calamities of the existing social condition of this country is that between us—who I suppose all belong to the privileged and fortunate classes—

and the masses of the suffering poor there is too often a great gulf fixed. We know very little of them, and they know very little of us. As one has well said: "Beneath the sea there is another sea." You may be a large employer of labour, but what do you know about the men and women you employ? Between you and them there exists too frequently only what Carlyle, in his grim, vivid way, calls a "cash-nexus." They come on Friday or Saturday for their wages. They get so much money for so many hours' work, paid through a hole in the office window. If you do not want them any longer, you give them notice to quit; and, in the same way, if they do not wish to remain with you, they give you notice.

That is the beginning and that is the end of too much of the existing social relation between Capital and Labour.

And as regards the different sections of English society, in some respects the situation is getting worse and worse; for the strong tendency to-day is for those who are in a better social position to leave the crowded centres and go and live in pleasant suburban villas, where they can have a garden. I do not blame them. It is more healthy. It is an advantage to their wives and children, but it is a very calamitous thing. In London at this moment the poorer districts are growing poorer and poorer, and those who ought to mingle with the less privileged are several miles off. The Bible says: *"The rich and the poor meet together"*; but they do so no longer. As one has wittily said, in the present day we put the yeast into one pan and the dough into another, and then expect the dough to rise. I am profoundly convinced that this must be altered, and Christians of the privileged class must, in the Spirit of Christ, come back from the suburbs and live among the masses of the people. There is one Christ-like man in the East-end—Mr. Barnett, the Vicar of Whitechapel—who is promoting this. He told me some time ago that several gentlemen of position, who could choose their own residences in wealthy quarters, have, in the most Christ-like spirit, resolved to go down to Whitechapel, to live among the poor. I heard the other day of a shrewd solicitor in Bristol, who came to the conclusion that he was demoralizing his own children by living in Clifton, where they had nothing to do, nothing to resist their natural selfishness, nothing to draw out real sympathy with their less privileged fellow-citizens; and positively for the sake of his own sons and daughters he went back to live in the very centre of crowded Bristol, that they might be taught to be unselfish and Christ-like. And it may be the duty of some of you who hear me now to come back from your suburban residences to live here with us in the midst of the people and to promote their happiness.

I am quite sure the suspicion and dread which rise in many minds with respect to the masses of the people would disappear if we knew them better. Victor Hugo is right when he says: "Mix with the people and love them, and you will trust them." Do not be afraid of the roaring and advancing tide of democracy. Rush into the midst of it, take a header into it—to use the phrase Mr. Spurgeon employed in this place the other day. Mix freely with the people. It will help to purify you of your innate selfishness, and you will come out of the crowd glowing with the enthusiasm of humanity. This at any rate is true: when Jesus Christ saw the people He had compassion on them. When He looked at Jerusalem He wept over it. Why? Why did the masses of the people excite in the heart of Jesus Christ not hatred, not fear, but deep pity? St. Matthew tells us that when He saw the multitude He was moved with compassion because they were "distressed and scattered"; or, as it is rendered by other scholars, because they were "harassed and neglected."

And that is more true to-day than it was then. The masses of the people even in London are harassed and neglected. They are harassed by the dogs of hell, who take advantage of their poverty and of their helplessness. Oh, the anguish of the starving poor! It seems to them as though every man's hand was against them. While they are worried, badgered, and harassed by those whom they too frequently meet, they are neglected by you—the wise and the good! Oh, how ignorant they are! how helpless! how miserable! and how often may they truly say in the bitterness of their hearts: "No man careth for our souls"! It is almost impossible for some of us, even by the most desperate effort of the imagination, to enter into the feelings of the suffering and starving poor. I shall never forget the revealing word which my friend, Mr. Henry Broadhurst, uttered to me two years ago. Looking at me as I sat on the other side of his fire-place at Brixton, he said: "Why, you don't know what hunger is. You have never been hungry in your life"; and as I reflected I felt it was true. I had been what we call hungry, but the hunger of the starving poor, who go for days without bread, I had never felt; and I should like to know how many persons there are in this hall to-day who have ever experienced the gnawings of an unendurable hunger. Alas! alas! that in this great London there should be so many thousands whose whole life is absorbed in a desperate attempt to keep their heads just above water. Oh, the sufferings of the respectable poor, of those of whom you never hear!

I am reminded at this moment of a terrible instance which came under my notice some time ago. A girl who had been a superior servant in a gentleman's house, and had enjoyed comfort and even luxury there, married an artisan in every way worthy of her. In the terrible depression of trade and prolonged distress he was for many months out of work, and gradually all their savings disappeared. They owed many pounds to their landlady, their butcher, and their baker. Nearly all their clothes were pawned, and they shivered in the winter cold. At last came the day when the baker called and said he could not afford to give them any more bread on trust. I know not for how many weeks they owed him then, and it was to his credit that he had given them so much. Yet for the three weeks which preceded that day the whole family had nothing but bread and water. And, oh, my God! that young woman was expecting to be a mother every day, and she knew not what to do. In the most extraordinary manner, doubtless by the intervention of God, my wife was directed to her house, and the case was relieved. But think of the anguish of that poor woman with her starving children! When we saw the man he was half-starved; and he had wandered miles every day looking for work. Who could enter into the feelings of that poor woman in her time of anguish? She had suffered through no fault of her own; neither was her husband a drunkard. Here was the case of a man seeing his wife and children dying under his eyes. Some people will say, "Why did they not go to the workhouse?" What! Break up their home and have upon them the brand of the pauper?

And what shall we say of these poor girls in London, who are making a living—or, as Miss Rye rightly names it, "a starving"—by earning five shillings a week, and that at the cost of stitching for twelve or fourteen hours every day? I entirely agree with the opinion expressed by my friend, Mark Guy Pearse, this morning, when he said that if this was Christianity, the sooner we got rid of Christianity the better. We may attend prayer-meetings and sing psalms until we are black in the face, but if we do not deal with such social evils we are neglecting our duty. We have too long overlooked the misery of the suffering and starving poor. Who can enter into the feeling of some poor orphan girl of the class to which I have referred? . . .

And we may add that the man who professes to be a child of that God, but does not "care for all," is deceiving his own soul. He is not the brother of Jesus Christ, who

> ". . . into His heart, with large embrace, has taken
> The universal sorrow of mankind."

So much depends upon occupying Christ's standpoint. If you are at the standpoint of some doctrinaire political economist, or of some thoughtless writer who has never known what hunger means, you may pour forth column after column of heartless folly. But if you know the suffering of the poor as Christ knows it, you will pity them. Have you ever thought of the tender and charitable meaning of that oft-quoted passage in the book of the prophet Isaiah, where God puts this confession into our lips: "All we like sheep have gone astray"? Like sheep, not like wolves. We are accused of ignorance, of stupidity, of heedlessness, rather than of *malice prepense,* or of downright and deliberate wickedness. There is a great deal more of the sheep than of the wolf in sinners; especially in those who, humanly speaking, have never had a chance; who have been the victims from the very first of unfavourable circumstances; who, in the terrible language of Charles Kingsley, have been "damned from their birth." And, my dear friend, do not flatter yourself too much if you are better than they. You might have been in their position. That was a wise saying of good John Newton's when he saw a handcuffed man walking along in charge of a constable: "There, but for the grace of God, goes John Newton." If I had to watch my wife and children starving under my eyes, I do not know what I should say in Trafalgar Square. Let us not take too much credit to ourselves for the position we occupy. We owe a great deal more to our circumstances, to our social privileges and safeguards, than we sometimes imagine. The teaching of this Book commends itself to every good man's reason.

We—society at large—must take a big share of the blame for the sin and folly of those who break the law. There was a good old Saxon rule in this country many years ago: when anybody did something wrong in a parish, every parishioner was fined for it—a most excellent rule, founded upon profound reasons. I should like to have it reinforced. As Mark Guy Pearse said this morning, how can you expect virtue and morality from people living in one room? Have you done your best to put the right men in the Vestry and on the Board of Guardians? All our hearts were moved to-day when Mr. Pearse gave us a touching description of the awful circumstances of thousands of people in London who have to herd together in one room, where common decency is impossible. It can never be "a home." The Vestries will not move in these matters. Too many vestrymen are elected to represent selfish interests. Not a few Christians think that if they attend prayer-meetings they are doing their duty. But let me remind you that you are partially responsible for every unsanitary dwelling in the place where you live. A part of

111

true religion consists in securing laws which will absolutely prohibit such buildings; and in electing to positions of authority men who will not permit them to remain a dead letter.

There are only two alternatives before us to-day—Christianity or revolution. What can we do? A thousand things. If you will come here on Sunday afternoons, I will tell you a few of those things in plain English. At any rate, let us do this one thing. *Let us place ourselves at the right point of view.* Let us look at the masses of the people through compassionate eyes of Jesus Christ. I felt humiliated a few years ago when I read that it was the duty of every Buddhist priest in Asia to spend some time each day in contemplating the misery of mankind, in order that his sympathy might be aroused. It occurred to me that I should do well to imitate the Buddhist priest in that. Let us reserve some sacred moments every day to contemplate, through Christ's compassionate eyes, the sin and the misery of mankind. When our hearts are moved we shall soon discover some method, great or small, of relieving that misery and that sin. Then assuredly, as we were reminded by the Lesson, an hour will come when the voice of Christ will say: "Inasmuch as ye did it unto one of the homeless poor in Trafalgar Square, or unto one of the down-trodden harlots in Piccadilly, ye did it unto Me."

Part III

Changing Direction

The turn of the twentieth century brought a new era in Methodist thought. Protestant liberal emphases became characteristic of Methodist theology. The most important person in this transition was Borden Parker Bowne, who provided a philosophical foundation for theological construction. Bowne also represented a heightened sensitivity to contemporary culture. He developed his thought in relation to reigning cultural themes such as personality, process, and moral character. Albert C. Knudson's article on Henry C. Sheldon describes some of the important alterations that were taking place. Independent from, but congenial to Bowne's interests, John Scott Lidgett in England and Wilbur Fisk Tillett in the United States pursued specific aspects of liberal concern. Edgar Sheffield Brightman continued Personalism's philosophical enterprise and Georgia Harkness explored practical aspects of this tradition. These thinkers combined a rational defense of Christian faith with devotion to Christian service.

Borden Parker Bowne

Borden Parker Bowne (1847–1910) was the most influential Methodist Episcopal theologian at the beginning of the twentieth century. Born into a pious Methodist home in New Jersey, he possessed unusual intellectual ability and graduated as valedictorian of his class at New York University. He stayed on to earn a master's degree then entered the parish ministry. He continued his education through two years of study in Germany and France. In Germany he was primarily influenced by Rudolf H. Lotze and Hermann Ulrici upon whose foundations he developed his philosophical position of personal idealism, or, as he designated it, *personalism*. Bowne always remained a layman. In 1876 he joined the faculty at Boston University and established the most interdisciplinary, inclusive, and important school of Methodist theology in North America. Among his more important books are *The Philosophy of Herbert Spencer* (1874) and *Studies in Theism* (1879).

Bowne attempted to mediate between his Methodist inheritance and his cultural context. He responded positively to critical study in Bible, history, and philosophy; he held an optimistic view of human nature and stressed the themes of God's immanence and moral character. He also followed a vision of service to God's earthly kingdom and the goal of moral achievement among human beings. From these perspectives he reinterpreted Methodist theology and set it upon a new course of development. "The Immanence of God" is from *The Immanence of God*

114

(Boston and New York: Houghton, Mifflin and Co., 1905), pp. 1-4, 116-28, 139-53.

The Immanence of God

The progress of thought is slow, but there is progress nevertheless. In every field of life men have had painfully to find their way. In religion man has always had some sense, more or less dim, of an alliance with the unseen and the eternal, but it has taken ages to organize and clarify it and bring it to clear apprehension and rational expression. As men begin on the plane of the senses, this unseen existence has been mainly conceived in sense terms, and hence has always been exposed to destructive criticism from the side of philosophy. The crude anthropomorphism of early thought invited and compelled the criticism. Again, this vague sense of the unseen has always been confronted by the apparent realities and finalities of the outer world; and in comparison with them it has often seemed unreal and fictitious. Matter we know and things we know; but God and spirit, what and where are they? When thus skeptically accosted by the senses, they sometimes fade away. Hence religious faith has always had a double difficulty to combat, arising from its alliance with sense forms, on the one hand, and from sense dogmatism, on the other. The alliance was perpetually plunging religion into destructive anthropomorphism; and the sense dogmatism led to a frequent rejection of religion as baseless, because spiritual realities lie beyond seeing and hearing. But we are slowly outgrowing this. Religious thought is gradually casting off its coarse anthropomorphism; and philosophic criticism is fast discrediting the shallow dogmatism of sense thinking, with its implication of mechanical and materialistic naturalism. Thus religious thought is progressing; and the result to which all lines of reflection are fast converging is the ancient word of inspiration, that in God we live and move and have our being. This is at once the clear indication of thought and the assured conviction of faith. In this conclusion, moreover, both religion and philosophy find their only sure foundation.

This doctrine we call the divine immanence; by which we mean that God is the omnipresent ground of all finite existence and activity. The world, alike of things and of spirits, is nothing existing and acting on its own account, while God is away in some extra-sidereal region, but it continually depends upon and is ever upheld by the ever-living, ever-present, ever-working God.

115

This divine immanence has important bearings on both speculative and religious problems, and contains the solution of many traditional difficulties. To trace this doctrine into its implications is the aim of the discussion. The thought will centre on four leading points,—God and Nature, God and History, God and the Bible, and God and Religion. On each of these points naturalistic and deistic dogmatism has long wrought confusion and mischief.

Thus far we have considered the bearing of the divine immanence upon our thought of nature, history, and the Bible. We have seen that it discharges the false or "bald" naturalism of popular thought, and dispels the fears of naturalism which haunt so much religious discussion. Instead of a self-sufficient mechanical nature, it gives us a supernatural natural, that is, a natural which forever depends on the divine will and purpose, and a natural supernatural, that is, a divine causality which proceeds according to orderly methods in the realization of its aims. We have now to consider the significance of this doctrine for the religious life.

And here, too, popular thought has been confused greatly by the traditional misconception of the natural. As God was supposed to be in nature and history only, or at least mainly, in the form of signs and wonders, so he was supposed to be in the soul only, or at least mainly, in the form of manifestations of a somewhat anarchic and prodigy-working type. And as the familiar laws of nature were supposed to represent no divine purpose, but only a mere determination of a blind and unpurposed mechanism, so the familiar laws of life and mind, and all the normal workings of human nature, were supposed to be unrelated to any divine purpose, and were dismissed as "merely natural." Of course, in both cases, by the logic of the situation it was necessary to look for the divine in the extraordinary and anomalous. And the dealers in such things verily thought that they were defending religion, and never suspected that they were really the victims of a shallow philosophy. The uproar over Dr. Bushnell's "Christian Nurture" fifty years ago is a good illustration. Many ark-savers experienced the severest alarms at what seemed to them an ignoring of the supernatural.

Now here again the divine immanence helps us. We are in our Father's house and Father's hands; and though we may not be able always to trace his presence or interpret every feature of his work, yet his will is being done. And this is really what faith seeks for in this matter. The soul longs to find God, to believe that it has not fallen into life headlong, to feel that it is in the hands of him that made it, and that he

116

is ever near. The religious soul fears naturalism because nature seems to be a barrier between God and itself, and to thrust him into a past so distant as to make him doubtful and to put him beyond any real, living, present interest in us. And a naturalism of that sort is to be feared, as in its presence high faith is sure to wither, or cry out in mortal anguish. It is not nature or law that the soul fears, but nature or law without God in it. It is not the burdens and distresses of life that oppress and depress us, but burdens and distresses that spring from nothing and lead to nothing. If they are appointed by our Father for our discipline and development, we can bear them with good courage and unrepining hearts; we break down only when we view them as the blind raging of a storm. Now from this distress the belief in the divine immanence saves us. He is in the darkness as well as in the light, in failure and sorrow as well as in success and joy, in death as well as in life. He is the God of all things, and is God over all things, and is blessed forevermore. This view, we repeat, is what religious thought really desires to reach in its opposition to naturalism and its emphasis on the supernatural. Its real aim is to find God, not prodigies; but it errs and strays from the way because of the crude philosophy which banishes God from the natural and finds him only in the strange, the anomalous, the chaotic. And this illiteracy culminates in the fancy that this is the only religious view.

But after we had driven off false naturalism from the philosophy of nature and history, we found a place for a true naturalism. Similarly here, after we have driven off false naturalism from the spiritual life, we find a place for a true naturalism. In other words, the conviction that we live and move and have our being in God does not decide the form and mode of God's work in us; and to learn this, we must fall back on experience.

The great error of religious thought in this matter is the same as its error at the corresponding point in its thought of God in nature. It has sought to walk by sight rather than by thought and faith. Hence the conception has been almost exclusively thaumaturgic. A changed life, a clean heart, a strengthened will, a deeper moral insight, and a purer devotion would be very poor marks of a divine indwelling in comparison with some psychological exaltation which, by its strangeness or excess, might impress persons of wonder-loving mental habit. Hence, again, there has been a very general tendency in the history of the church to look upon emotional ebulliencies, anarchic raptures, anomalous and spectacular experiences, as the truly classical manifestations of religion, while the interaction of religious feeling, intellect, and moral will has been viewed as a falling away from the highest and only classical form. To guard against this error, we must analyze our problem somewhat at length.

And first of all we must bear in mind that it is not a question of the reality and necessity of God's work in the soul in order that we may attain unto the life of the spirit. Upon occasion we should steadfastly deny any Pelagian self-sufficiency of the human will, and that for both philosophical and religious reasons. It is simply a question respecting the form of this divine co-working. Is it natural or supernatural?

This question at once reveals the fact that these terms have peculiar meanings in religious speech. Natural is often used to mean the sensuous in distinction from the spiritual, as in the text, "That was not first which is spiritual, but that which is natural." Sometimes it means that which is possible to man's unaided powers; and the affirmation of a supernatural means a power from above which reinforces our weakness. And sometimes natural means that in which an order of law can be observed and traced. It is in this last sense that we use it here. We are far enough from affirming that man is sufficient unto himself in the spiritual life. Such a view is a mark of gross philosophic and religious illiteracy. The professional defender of the faith seldom discriminates these widely differing meanings, and thus begins, continues, and ends in confusion.

God's work in nature and history, we have seen, is not against law, but through law. The thaumaturgic element, in any case, is a vanishing factor in comparison. A moment's reflection convinces us that the same must be true of God's work in the soul. It is not against the laws of mind, but through them, that God realizes his purposes in us. This is an absolute condition of our mental and moral sanity. If we are to lead a moral and rational life of any sort, there must be an order of life on which we can depend. If religion is not to be an excuse for indolence, we must work out our own salvation. It is indeed God who worketh in us, but he works according to law, and in such a way as to call for all our effort. He gives us spiritual bread as he gives us daily bread. In the latter case the bread supply does not come by any celestial express, but through the springing corn and the ripening harvest; yet it is from God after all. In like manner spiritual blessing is not conferred in any scenic and unmediated fashion, but by power moving along the lines of normal life, and manifesting itself in its products rather than its abnormal methods. And in the case of both physical and spiritual bread, we have to work for it.

The religious life is the last realm to be brought under the notion of law. Law is now a matter of course in physics, astronomy, meteorology, medicine, hygiene, education, but it is very imperfectly apprehended in its religious bearing. In all those subjects we see that there are conditions to which we must conform if we would accomplish our ends. No one would expect to get a harvest by prayer alone, while neglecting to plow and sow. No one would expect to become educated without appropriate labor. But in religion we have not yet learned this lesson. We expect God to work in the spiritual realm immediately and without reference to law. We are simply to ask and receive. To speak of law is to thrust a barrier between the soul and God. To suggest conditions is an act of unfaith. To work for spiritual blessing through the laws God has made is to lean to our own understanding and have confidence in the flesh. Education is the work of man; as for the work of the Spirit, we cannot tell whence it cometh nor whither it goeth. In all this the false naturalism and false supernaturalism of untrained thought are manifest. God's action is supposed to be above and apart from law, rather than through it, or in accordance with it; and religion is supposed to be something apart from living interests, a thing of frames and retreats and special exercises, rather than a spiritual principle for all living, the abiding inspiration of all work.

Religious thought cannot too soon unlearn this false supernaturalism and learn the lesson of law. We must lay to heart and remember that the fact that God worketh in us in no way vacates the rule that we must work out our own salvation. The wise man proceeds in spiritual things as in physical things. In the latter case, he inquires for the laws which rule and adjusts himself to them. In the former case, he asks for the laws of successful and developing life and adjusts himself to them. He avails himself of all his knowledge and of every means of influence in both cases. This we must all do. We must study the order of life, and avail ourselves of all the normal means of influence for developing character and of all the great institutions evolved by humanity on its upward way. We must look upon the family, the school, the social order, the great industrial and commercial activities, as ordinances of God, or as instruments through which he works as certainly as through the church and formal religious exercises. Pray upon the family, the school, the social order, the great industrial and commercial activities, as ordinances of God, or as instruments through which he works as certainly as through the church and formal religious exercises. Prayer and meditation of course will always have their place and function, but they are by no means the only way of reaching God and securing his aid. We must discern the divine presence and agency in life as a whole, and work with him along the natural lines which he has established, in the full faith that thus we are co-workers with God, and that results thus reached are as divine as they would be if reached by some miraculous fiat. The undivineness of the natural is the great heresy of popular religious thought, and a great source of the weakness of the religious life. Good intentions, zeal, and deep religious desire often come to nought from being left to lose themselves in formless religiosity, instead of being directed into normal lines of effort in accordance with human needs and human nature. And there will be no lasting reform in religion until we return to a true naturalism in this matter, recognizing that only God can give the increase, and also that God will give no increase unless we plant and water, and further recognizing the natural order of things as a part of the divine appointment for our spiritual training, and as the field for our life's work. . . .

In his work, "The Varieties of Religious Experience," p. 200, Professor William James gives an interesting passage from Jonathan Edwards which shows that Edwards already understood the influence that suggestion, expectation, and imitation often have in moulding experience. Edwards says:—

> A rule received and established by common consent has a very great, though to many persons an insensible influence in forming their notions of the process of their own experience. I know very well how they proceed as to this matter, for I have had frequent opportunities of observing their conduct. Very often their experience at first appears like a confused chaos, but then those parts are selected which bear the nearest resemblance to such particular steps as are insisted on; and these are dwelt upon in their thoughts and spoken of from time to time, till they grow more and more conspicuous in their view, and other parts which are neglected grow more and more obscure. Thus what they have experienced is insensibly strained so as to bring it to an exact conformity to the scheme already established in their minds. And it becomes natural also for ministers who have to deal with those who insist upon distinctness and clearness of method, to do so too.—"Treatise on Religious Affections."

Edwards had not the language of modern psychology, but he had recognized the fact of suggestibility and the influence of expectation in the religious field with all clearness. In his works written after the "Great Awakening," one clearly sees a growing conviction on his part that "manifestations" are very uncertain tests of a work of grace. And the only way out of all these confusions is never to aim at "experience," but to aim at righteousness, and find the essential and only sure mark of the divine presence, in a religious sense, in the fruits of the Spirit. And along with the marked and sudden transitions of character which may occur in mature persons of strenuous type, we must make place for a gradual training of the will under the divine education of life, or for quiet, unreflective growth into the kingdom of heaven. Here too the divine immanence helps us. We are no longer compelled to set nature and grace, the secular and the religious, the human and the divine, in mutually exclusive antithesis; but rather find them in mutual penetration.

If some days were ushered in with a mighty bang, and other days came with the quiet of the dawn, we might conceivably have an astronomical school of bangers and one of anti-bangers; and they might so confine their attention to the bang as to forget that the only point of any real importance is to have the day come, with or without a bang. Compared with this, the bang question is insignificant. We have these schools in religious experience, emphasizing the bang or the non-bang and overlooking the only matter of importance,—the dawn of the spiritual day.

This false supernaturalism in the inner religious life of the subject has led to corresponding error in determining religious duty. The result has often been an abstract religiosity and other-worldliness, which has sometimes made sad work of the life that now is. Submission to the will of God is indeed the central thing in religion, and its importance cannot be overestimated. Hence religious thought has occupied itself largely with securing this harmony without inquiring what that will is in its positive contents. The result has been a body of determinations, largely negative, and for the rest mainly concerned with the securing of tempers, dispositions, and aspirations supposed to be peculiarly spiritual. When this result is combined with the disastrous separation of the secular from the religious, it leads straight toward asceticism and monasticism. In the Protestant bodies it has led to fixing attention too exclusively on sin and salvation, abstractly conceived, as the matters of supreme importance in religion.

Now this may be good as far as it goes, but it certainly does not go very far. To be sure, submission to the divine will must be secured, if it be wanting; but what is that will for men? After man has returned from his willful wanderings, he is only at the beginning, not the end. Now he must begin to work the will of God. As worldliness consists less in what is done than in the spirit of the doing, so religion consists less in what is done than in the spirit of the doing. Both the worldling and the Christian have to do largely the same things. But the worldling loses himself in the outward and sense life, and fails to relate it to any divine meaning and purpose. The Christian, on the other hand, is in the same sense life, but he relates it to a divine order, and seeks to glorify that life by filling it with courage and devotion. Religion conceived as a specialty, as a matter of prayers and rites and ceremonies, is a minor matter, and one of no great importance; but religion conceived as a principle which knows no distinction of secular and religious, but pervades all life, and perpetually offers unto God in living sacrifice as its continual spiritual worship the daily round with all its interests and activities sanctified by the filial spirit,—this is the ideal of humanity. So long as we form any lower conception of religion than this, so long will religion be only one interest among many, and life will lack its true unity.

This I conceive to be the deepest aim of Christianity. The forgiveness of sins is essential, but it is only introductory. The forms of worship and the practices of piety are important, but they are only instrumental. They are not the thing, and their significance consists entirely in what they help us to. The thing, the central thing, is the recognition of the divine will in all life, and the loyal, loving effort to make that will prevail in all life: first of all in the hidden life of the spirit, and then in family life, in social life, in political life, in trade, in art, in literature, in every field of human interest and activity. Only thus can religion be saved from unwholesome and baneful subjectivities. Only thus can it gain the healthy objectivity needed to keep it sane and sweet. The religious spirit must have all fields for its own; and at the same time we must remember that all that is normal to man and demanded by his life has its place in the divine purpose and its justifying function in the divine training of men. To think otherwise is atheism.

One of the good signs of the religious times is the growing recognition of this fact. We are outgrowing the conception of religion as a thing of rites and ceremonies, of cloisters and retreats, of holy days and holy places, and are coming to view it as the divine principle for all living, whatever the day or the place or the work. We are coming to deny the distinction between secular and religious work, and to adopt into holy places all the normal and necessary work of the world. All of this is a divine ordinance, and expresses God's will concerning us. Men are tiring of the cloister and the smell of incense. They are tiring equally of the barren inspection of their spiritual states, and of churning up artificial emotions. They need to be taken out of themselves and given some worthy task to perform under some worthy inspiration; and this they find in the realization of the kingdom of God upon earth, and the doing of his will here under the stars as it is done in heaven. It is under the unconscious influence of these impulses, which are really strivings after God, the present God, the immanent God, that men grow dissatisfied with the formal and barren exercises of traditional religion.

The need of the divine help in order to live the life of the spirit is as manifest as it ever was. The sense of a divine presence in our lives is not dying out, but it is taking on a new form in accordance with a more careful psychology and a greater precision of thought. Instead of being something sensuously presentable or emotionally definable, it is rather the assurance of faith and the sense of reality which comes in spiritual living. Along with this has come the insight that it is preeminently in the conscience, the pure heart, the surrendered will, and holy activities that God makes his abode with us. From this we may expect great gain to religion. We shall lay aside our irrational fear of naturalism and also our crude supernaturalism. We shall find God everywhere, not merely in unmediated and miraculous manifestations, but also in the world he has made, in the laws he has ordained, in the great forms of life and society which he has appointed, and in the multitudinous activities which life necessitates. We shall come into communion with God in prayer and meditation, and also in work of all kinds, as we seek to build up his kingdom in the earth. We shall work more definitely along lines of training, culture, education, the improvement of all the conditions of human life in accordance with the laws of our being, yet without closing the spirit to direct contact with the Divine. In so doing we shall manifest ourselves as wise sons of God, and the divine manifestation will correspond. Indeed, there is no telling what God would do for a community thoroughly bent on doing his will and using all the means of influence in their power. Nature is no closed system, but forever becomes that which God wills it to be. Along with a moralized humanity might well go new heavens and a new earth. To them that have shall be given. At this point I more than suspect that I am what Professor James calls himself, "a crass supernaturalist." My "crassitude" is limited, not by any respect for nature as something having metaphysical existence and rights of its own, but solely by the insight into the necessity of an order of experience on which we can depend. Without that, we should be equally at sea in both mind and morals. We must, then, learn the lesson of law and self-help. For some time, at least, the keynote of religious progress must be found, not in vague and illiterate utterances about the supernatural, but rather in the divineness of the natural and the naturalness of the divine. This term supernatural has so many misleading associations, and is still the subject of so many misunderstandings, that we would do well to abandon it altogether and in its place write God; and then, in the assured faith that we are in his world and his hands, resolutely set about our Father's business, looking not for signs and wonders, but for the coming of the kingdom of God in the form of higher and holier living.

Thus we see the deep significance of the divine immanence for religious thought. It dispels that great cloud of difficulties, born of crude naturalistic thinking, that haunt popular religion. This is largely a negative service, but it is important nevertheless. It recalls God from the infinite distance in space and time to which sense thought must banish him, and where we so often lose him, and makes him the omnipresent power by which all things exist and on which all things continually depend. This metaphysical presence does not indeed secure spiritual sympathy and fellowship on our part, but it removes the speculative obstacles thereto that exist in many minds, and thus makes room for the spiritual life of communion and sonship. This life itself can be secured only in devout and faithful living by each for himself, but it is something to have the speculative intimidations removed that sometimes, like Bunyan's lions, frighten pilgrims from the way. It is something to know that this world, however mysterious and even sinister in many of its aspects, is after all God's world; that we are not standing helpless and hopeless in the midst of Strauss's "enormous machine" world with its pitiless wheels and thundering hammers, but we are in a personal world, a moral world, where character is being wrought out and a kingdom of righteousness is being set up. In such a world it is permitted to see visions and dream dreams, and devote ourselves to the service of the highest and best, in the sure faith that they are also the truest and most real, the abiding and essential stuff of the universe.

But we also see the necessity of uniting this thought of the divine immanence with the thought of law. All is law; all is God. All is God; all is law. We read it either way, according to the emphasis demanded by the times and circumstances. For those who have not learned the lesson of law, who are seeking short cuts, and who are not availing themselves of the natural means of growth and influence, we say, All is law. For those, on the other hand, who have lost God in the law, and who have fallen into the paralyzing notion of a self sufficient mechanism, we say, All is God. In both cases alike we say with the apostle: Work out your own salvation with fear and trembling; for it is God who worketh in you, both to will and to work for his good pleasure. For in him we live and move and have our being.

Albert C. Knudson

Initially as a professor of Old Testament and then as a systematic theologian, Albert C. Knudson (1873–1953) became a prominent Boston personalist. Knudson was born into a parsonage family in Grand Meadow, Minnesota, and received his education at the University of Minnesota. He attended Boston University for graduate work and joined its faculty in 1905. Knudson lived through and was keenly aware of the changes taking place in Methodist Episcopal theology at the turn of the century. Knudson used his article on his predecessor on the Boston faculty, Henry Clay Sheldon (1845–1928), as an occasion for discussing the transition in Methodist theology and revealed as much about himself as about Sheldon. Knudson's most important theological books are *The Doctrine of God* (1930) and *The Doctrine of Redemption* (1933). He also made significant contributions with his *Philosophy of Personalism* (1927) and *The Validity of Religious Experience* (1937). The selection chosen for inclusion in these readings reflects Knudson's understanding of the alterations in Methodist theology at the turn of the century. While it overstates the failures of Sheldon's predecessors, it accurately describes the Protestant liberal theology which characterized much Methodist Episcopal theology of the first half of the twentieth century. "Henry Clay Sheldon—Theologian" is chosen from *Methodist Review* (March 1925), vol. CVIII, 5th series, vol. XLI, pp. 175-92.

Henry Clay Sheldon—Theologian

This article is not a personal eulogy; it is an historical study. Its occasion is the eightieth birthday of Methodism's most learned and most influential theologian.

Dr. Henry Clay Sheldon was born in Martinsburg, N.Y., March 12, 1845. He graduated from Yale University in 1867 and from Boston University School of Theology in 1871. During the year 1871–72 he served as supply at the Methodist church in Saint Johnsbury, Vt., and in 1872–74 was pastor at Brunswick, Maine. He was admitted into the Maine Conference on trial and also was ordained deacon in 1873, and in 1876 was ordained elder and received into full connection. In 1874–75 he studied at the University of Leipzig. On his return from Germany he became professor of historical theology in Boston University School of Theology, and held that chair for twenty years (1875–1895). He then transferred to the department of systematic theology, and occupied that position until he was granted the *emeritus* relation in 1921. For forty-six consecutive years he was thus actively engaged as a teacher of theology. This is a record unequaled by any other Methodist theological teacher with the exception of Dr. William Fairfield Warren, who, however, during most of his long career as an educator was able to devote only part of his time to the actual work of teaching because of his heavy administrative duties as Dean and President.

In its outward aspects Doctor Sheldon's life has been a comparatively uneventful one. He has not participated to any marked extent in the councils of the church. He has not figured in the sessions of the Annual and General Conferences. With extraordinary steadiness of purpose he has devoted himself to the office of a teacher in the church. No ecclesiastical ambition has seduced him from the path of scholarly research. The lure of administrative position has made no appeal to him. Not even the excitement incident to a charge of heresy has fallen to his lot. To a very unusual degree he has escaped that curse of the scholar's life, the doing of "other things," and has been permitted to keep the even tenor of his way. . . .

But it is not simply the extent of his learning, his productivity and the general soundness and sobriety of his judgment that give to Doctor Sheldon's work its importance. What makes his work of historic significance to the church is that it marks the change from the older to the newer type of Methodist theology. No one who knows Doctor Sheldon would accuse him of being a radical. Not even the crudest theological reactionaries in our church have, so far as I know, assailed his ortho-doxy. And yet it is he more than any other systematic theologian in our church who has given to our theology the stamp of what may be called "modernity." The change he introduced had no doubt been prepared for by others. His "theology" when it appeared, did not impress the church as a novelty. But it did stand in sharp contrast with all the earlier sys-tematic treatises, so much so that Doctor Sheldon himself apparently had no idea that it would receive the kind of official recognition that has been accorded it. In 1897, when his class lectures on theology appeared in typewritten form, I urged their publication, but he met the suggestion by saying that it would be fifty years before the Methodist Episcopal Church would be ready to accept his standpoint. It turned out, how-ever, that eleven years from that time not only was there no serious objection in the church to his theological position, but those very lec-tures were adopted as the textbook of theology in our Conference Course of Study. This fact might perhaps impugn any claim that Doctor Sheldon might make to being a prophet—as he himself facetiously remarked when he was reminded of it—but it does not imply that he was mistaken in the view he held in 1897 of the marked contrast between his own type of theology and that current in the church up to that time. It is no exaggeration to say that he introduced into Methodist theology an abrupt change.

That this change did not cause any particular stir was due to a num-ber of reasons, three of which may be briefly mentioned.

First, the earlier Methodist theology did not express the real genius of Methodism. It was not in the proper sense of the term a native growth; it was rather an exotic, transplanted from other spiritual climes. In the theological field early Methodism was not creative. It took most of its theology second-hand from others, and in it it had no immediate and profound interest. It was, for instance, over eighty years after Methodism was organized before its first "Systematic Theology" was written; and not until fifty years later was the next work of any conse-quence in the field published. The *Theological Institutes*, by Richard Watson, appeared in 1821–29, and the first edition of William Burr Pope's *Compendium of Christian Theology* in 1875. Both of these works display considerable learning, especially that by Pope, and both were in some respects remarkable productions. But it can hardly be said that the type of theology which they represent, and which held the field throughout the nineteenth century, stood organically related to the life and thought of the Methodist movement. Much of it was traditional in

127

character, and sustained a purely adventitious relation to that vital experience of religion which was the basal emphasis in Methodism. Hence a change in theology did not affect the Methodist Church so seriously as it did some of the other communions.

Second, the Methodist works on systematic theology, written during the twenty-five years preceding the publication of Sheldon's *System of Christian Doctrine,* failed in a marked degree to adjust themselves to the new developments in the field of biblical criticism and of science in general. They distinctly did not keep pace with the times. This is true of Miner Raymond's *Systematic Theology* (1877), of John Miley's *Systematic Theology* (1892, 1894), and of the colossal work, entitled *Studies in Theology,* projected by Randolph S. Foster in his old age and carried through six volumes (1889–99). Of these six volumes Bowne once said in all kindness that the pathetic thing about them was that they were obsolete before they came from the press. And the same might be said to a large extent of Raymond's and Miley's works. These scholars made no real advance beyond the theological method of Watson and Pope, and they fell noticeably behind the scientific and theological thought of their own day. They thus suffered from a double handicap. Their theology stood in no vital relation to the Methodist emphasis on religious experience, and it was out of accord with modern science. The result was that it became a burden to faith instead of a help; and hence it was with a measure of relief that the church laid it aside, as one would an outworn garment that never had been a fit, and accepted in its stead a more modern type of theology.

A third reason why the transition from Miley to Sheldon was effected with so little difficulty is found in Doctor Sheldon himself, his profound acquaintance and sympathy with historic Christianity. As professor of historical theology he had for twenty years immersed himself in the life and thought of the church. When he came, therefore, to his task as a systematic theologian, it was with a mind and heart rooted deep in Christian history. For him a disturbing radicalism was impossible. However modern he might be, he felt himself at one with the faith of the past. This feeling pervades his entire *System of Christian Doctrine.* The work is ballasted with such a profound knowledge and reverence for history that only the most recalcitrant obscurantist could have any serious doubt as to its safeness. It is this fact especially, a fact manifest in the temper as well as the content of the book, that has saved it to such a large extent from adverse criticism.

Thus far I have spoken of the transition from the older to the newer type of Methodist theology, introduced by Sheldon, without defining the nature of the change. The question now arises as to what the change consisted in. In what respects does Sheldon's theology differ from that of his Methodist predecessors? A detailed answer to this question would call for a small volume. Here I can deal with only a few of the outstanding differences.

The first and most striking difference is found in the field of apologetics, in the method of grounding the Christian faith. The Methodist theologians from Watson to Miley and Foster were authoritarian rationalists. They based the Christian faith on the divine authority of Scripture, and this authority they believed could be established by purely rational considerations. The argument appears in its purest form in Watson, but in its substance it is repeated by the others. Watson distinguishes between "external" and "internal" evidence. The former he regards as primary and fundamental. It consists in an appeal to the fact of miracle and of prophecy. "Miracles," he says, "must be considered as the leading and absolute evidence of a revelation from God" (*Theol. Inst.*, one vol. ed., p. 55). The internal evidence, which has to do with the essential rationality and intrinsic excellence of the biblical revelation, is in itself altogether inadequate. "The reason for this," he says, "is evident. A mere impression of truth on the understanding could not by itself be distinguished from a discovery made by the human intellect, and could have no authority, as a declaration of the will of a superior, with the person receiving it; and as to others, it could only pass for the opinion of the individual who might promulge it. An authentication of a system of truth, which professes to be the will, the law of Him who, having made, has the right to command us, *external* to the matter of the doctrine itself, is therefore necessary to give it authority, and to create the obligation of obedience" (p. 41). A distinction is thus made by Watson between the truth of Scripture and its authority, and between what he elsewhere calls "rational" and "authenticating" evidence. "Rational evidence," as Raymond says, "shows reasons why the proposition is true, or why it must be true. Authenticating evidence shows reasons why we should believe it is true" (*Syst. Theol.*, I, 119). The latter type of evidence can only be found in miracle. Apart from miracles the teachings of Scripture might, says Watson, "be true, but they are not attested to be divine. We have no guaranty of their infallible truth, because our own rational powers are not infallible, nor those of the most gifted mind" (p. 56). Hence "though the rational evidence of a doctrine lies in the doctrine itself, the rational proof of the divine authority of a doctrine must be external to the doctrine" (p. 58). But although "external to the doctrine" the authenticating evidence is rational in character. It is an appeal to the intellect. A religious teacher, says Raymond, "claims that what he says, God says; and as evidence that his claim is valid he proposed to do, and does do, what no man can do except God be with him" (I, 48). That is, he performs a miracle, and the miracle is convincing evidence of the truth and divine authority of his message. The inference from miracle to truth and authority is assumed to be logically irresistible; the human reason by its very nature acknowledges its cogency. The whole argument for Christianity thus takes the form of authoritarian rationalism.

Pope, Raymond, and Miley, it is true, gave a larger place than did Watson to the self-evidencing power of faith or religious experience. But they did not make this idea an organizing principle in their theology. It remained external to their system; it did not form a structural part of it. While they conceded a certain apologetic value to religious experience, their own standpoint remained essentially rationalistic. Take, for instance, Miley's argument against the view that the Christian consciousness is a source of theology. "To assume," he says, "the religious feelings as first in order, and then to find in them the central truths of theology, is to reverse the logical and necessary order of the facts. Clearly a knowledge of the central truths of Christianity conditions the Christian consciousness and must be first in order. . . . As the Christian consciousness is thus conditioned by the possession of the central truths of Christian theology, it is impossible to deduce these truths from that consciousness. Back of these truths there is no Christian consciousness to begin with" (*Syst. Theol.* I, 21). In these statements an intellectualistic view of religion is manifestly implied. Christianity is represented as a body of doctrines rather than a unique form of experience. At least, experience is secondary; the doctrines come first, and so express the essential nature of the Christian religion.

These doctrines, it is true, are thought of as supernaturally communicated. They did not originate in the human reason, nor do they even necessarily commend themselves to man's reason. In the latter respect a distinction was made between different doctrines of Scripture. Some of them were regarded as standing on the plane of "natural religion" and as having an adequate rational basis. To this group, according to Raymond, "belong the doctrines of the being and attributes of God, moral distinctions, the free agency, moral responsibility, and immortality of man, the fact of sin and need of salvation, probation in the life that now is, and retribution in the life to come" (I, 124). As distinguished from these doctrines, however, there are others that were regarded as the peculiar property of "revealed religion" and as completely transcending human reason. To these, says Raymond, "belong the doctrines of the trinity, divinity of Christ, the hypostatic unity, the personality and divinity of the Holy Ghost, the atonement, justification by faith only, supernatural agency in the regeneration and sanctification of the believer, the witness of the Spirit to adoption and heirship, and the resurrection of the dead" (I, 124f.). Substantially the same list appears also in Watson, except that he puts the atonement in the first group. Of the truth of the doctrines in the second group "we have," says Watson, "no evidence whatsoever" (p. 118). They are to be accepted wholly on the authority of Scripture. But this does not mean that they are in and of themselves irrational, or that it is irrational on our part to accept them. There are, we are told, adequate grounds for believing that the Bible is the Word of God; and, if it is such, its contents, no matter how much they transcend human reason, are in the very nature of the case rational. An irrational divine revelation is unthinkable. "Nothing," says Miley, "is accepted with higher reason of its truth than that which God has spoken" (I, 47). The standpoint of the earlier Methodist theologians was thus clearly and explicitly rationalistic. Their ultimate appeal was made to the theoretical reason, not to Christian experience. They thought that religious truth could be presented in the form of assent-compelling knowledge, so that even the non-religious mind would be forced to admit its logical cogency. This was the motive of the so-called "authenticating evidence," the appeal to miracle and prophecy, as well as that of the so-called "rational evidence." Miracle was regarded as an adequate rational ground for accepting the super-rational teaching of Scripture. The entire apologetic structure thus in the last analysis rested on the non-religious reason; and in this sense the whole theological system of the earlier Methodist theologians was, as I have termed it, an authoritarian rationalism, or, what amounts to the same thing, a rationalistic authoritarianism.

When we now turn to Sheldon, we find all this changed. There is no polemic against the older view, but it is quietly set aside. We hear no more about "authenticating" as distinguished from "rational" evidence. Miracle recedes into the background. It is, we are told, "most appropriately regarded as a part of the rounded whole of revelation. Whatever it may have been to the contemporary generation, for us it is adapted to establish conviction in the biblical system only as it fulfills a function of revelation, only as it is harmoniously connected with the process of

131

sacred history, and serves to disclose the character of God or to illustrate his redemptive purpose. Outside of this relation and office, it does not generate faith in the Bible, but rather needs an already existing faith to provide for its acceptance" (p. 118f.). Miracle thus becomes a deduction from faith rather than the ground of it. And with the adoption of this standpoint the "external evidence" of the older apologetics completely collapses. The "internal evidence" takes its place. "The proof for the Bible," says Sheldon, "lies in its contents—that is, in the spiritual wealth of the factors which it contains, and in their harmonious relation to each other—rather than in any form of external attestation" (p. 118). There is, therefore, no basis for the old distinction between the truth of Scripture and its divine authority. Apart from the convincing and convicting power of the truth it expresses, the Bible has no authority. Its authority consists in its truth. It is the truth of Scripture that proves its inspiration, not the reverse.

Such is the position adopted by Sheldon; and with it we are introduced to a new type of Methodist theology. The old rationalistic authoritarianism, with its assumption of biblical infallibility, is at an end. In its stead we have a theology that is at once more empirical and more rational, truer to the genius of Methodism and more in accord with modern science.

It is more empirical in two respects. First, unlike the older theology it constructs its theory of inspiration in harmony with the facts instead of with an abstract ideal of perfection, and so rules out the notion of biblical inerrancy. Second, unlike the older theology it holds that revelation not only finds its ultimate attestation in religious experience, but is also determined in its scope by its power of appeal to the human heart. Revelation is not, then, an objective entity, unrelated to experience. It is conditioned both in its nature and range by faith.

The newer theology, represented by Sheldon, is also more rational than the older in that it tends to limit revelation to the religious realm and denies to it a coercive power over the human reason. It allows to science its full rights and does not attempt in the name of religion to impose upon the modern man the imperfect scientific notions found in the Bible. Thus without being rationalistic it avoids a conflict with the theoretical reason. It does this chiefly by its freer attitude toward Scripture. The older theology was vitiated to an almost incredible degree by a false biblicism. It was led to take up irrelevant issues, wasted its strength in futile attempts to harmonize the Bible with modern science, and as a result failed to bring out, as it ought to have done, the distinctive character and true ground of the Christian faith. Faith stands in its own right; it has a reason of its own. In this sense we may, if we wish, speak of a new religious rationalism, a rationalism based on the autonomous validity of our religious nature instead of on the theoretical reason. Such a rationalism is founded on experience, and furnishes an incomparably firmer basis for the Christian faith than did the older authoritarian rationalism. Indeed, the latter has lost practically all value. It has been rendered obsolete by biblical criticism. The only fundamental and adequate apologetic is to be found in the self-evidencing power of faith. This I have sought to show at some length in my *Present Tendencies in Religious Thought*, recently published; and in developing this idea I have simply brought out the new point of view introduced into Methodist theology by Sheldon's *System of Christian Doctrine.*

A second difference between Sheldon and the earlier Methodist theologians appears in their treatment of the doctrines of the trinity and the subject of christology. The point of special interest in this connection is the divinity of Christ. In his presentation of the evidence in support of this doctrine Sheldon marks a decided advance beyond his Methodist predecessors. The latter made a very uncritical use of Scripture, failing to discriminate between the different strata in it and citing the Old Testament almost as freely as the New. They also laid chief stress on the biblical ascription to Christ of such divine attributes as eternity, omniscience, omnipotence, omnipresence, and immutability. It was his miracle-working power and his participation in the work of creation and providence rather than the ethical and spiritual quality of his life that in their opinion stamped him as divine. In Sheldon, on the other hand, the tendency is to emphasize the ideal character of Christ, his consciousness of oneness with God, his triumph over the world, his fidelity to his divine vocation, and his spiritual lordship over men. It is these qualities that stand out in the Gospel picture, and that make of Christ the true revealer of the Father and the Redeemer of the world. This line of evidence, however, does not lead Sheldon to deny value to the christological theories and affirmations that appear in the New Testament writings. He cites them and apparently accepts them as valid; but the stress falls on the facts of Christ's inner life rather than on speculations concerning his person, no matter how early they may be.

In his construction of the doctrine of the trinity Sheldon concedes a certain value to such analogies as those drawn from the different forms of mental activity, from the social implications of the ethical life, and especially from the idea of the divine immanence in us. In this respect

133

he differs from the earlier Methodist theologians who denied all value to such analogies, and relegated "the trinity and its cognate doctrines" to the realm of absolute mystery. But while holding this view they were certain that "a Person in the Godhead continues his personality in the human nature, which is therefore of necessity itself impersonal or without any personal existence independent of the Divine" (Pope, II, 115). This is also the position taken by Olin A. Curtis, and taken with the utmost emphasis. "All the personality," he says, "of our Lord he brought with him into human existence. He takes on an addition, a human addition, to his individuality, that is all. The mankind is ever impersonal, never anything but a lower coefficient for the abiding person of the Son of God" (*The Christian Faith*, p. 235).

In Sheldon, however, we find a different emphasis. He lays no special stress on the full personality of the preexistent Son, nor does he sacrifice the human to the divine element in Christ. He recognizes both, but if anything makes the human factor primary. He represents "the finite psychical nature in Christ" as mediating "the divine content in more or less of a partitive and successive fashion," and speaks of "the divine as fulfilling . . . the function of an oversoul uniquely related to the humanity of Christ and uniquely contributory to its furnishing for an unexampled mission" (p. 356). In these statements we manifestly have a step in the direction of an anthropocentric as distinguished from a theocentric christology, but only a step. Sheldon abides by the traditional recognition of the two natures, but he does so with so much moderation and metaphysical restraint that he may be regarded as leaving the door open to those who feel constrained to move further in the anthropocentric direction than he himself does. . . .

There are two other important developments in Sheldon's theology that call for consideration, but space will permit only a brief reference to them. One appears in his treatment of the atonement, and the other in his idea of the divine immanence.

The older Methodist theologians leaned either to the "satisfaction" or the "governmental" theory of the atonement. Watson and Pope were not satisfied with either, but expressed a preference for the former. Raymond rejected the "satisfaction" theory, and expressed dissatisfaction with the "purely governmental" theory, but his own "declarative" theory was apparently only a modified form of the latter. Miley was a champion of the governmental theory, and contended that this is the true Methodist theory. Sheldon, however, rejects it, at least in the form represented by Miley. He criticizes Miley for distinguishing too sharply between God as Person and as Ruler. "There is," he says, "in truth no occasion for a disjunction between the personal and the governmental in him. In his absolute self-consistency he stands in the same identical plane as Moral Ruler and as Divine Person" (p. 400). But while rejecting the traditional governmental as well as the satisfaction theory Sheldon seems reluctant to adopt the Abelardian or moral-influence theory, which sees in the death of Christ the supreme revelation of the love of God. He contends for "an objective element, or Godward bearing, in Christ's work"; but inasmuch as it "in no wise implies a change of attitude in time on the part of God toward the race," and as it consists simply in the demonstration "that the love which is outpoured so lavishly is still *holy* love," I cannot see that his view differs in any essential regard from the "moral theory" advocated by Bowne. It is this theory, if such it may be called, which is rapidly gaining headway in current religious thought; and Sheldon's treatment of the subject really marks the transition to it in Methodist theology.

The idea of the divine immanence, together with the personalistic idealism associated with it, stands opposed to the natural realism held by the earlier Methodist theologians. Realism affirms the extra-mental existence of the material world. However the world originated, it at present is an independent and self-running mechanism. There are thus, from the realistic standpoint, two kinds of being, one spiritual and personal, the other material and impersonal. This dualistic view of the world did not form a specific item in the older theology, but it constituted its background and virtually determined its conclusions on a number of important points. It was this realistic and dualistic philosophy that made the idea of miracle so fundamental and dominant in the older theology. For in an independent and self-running world of nature it is only through miracle that God can make himself directly known and felt; the genuineness of the biblical revelation and the validity of Christian experience imply miracle. A sharp antithesis is thus established between the natural and supernatural; and how on this assumption to think of the divine providence, of answers to prayer, and of the relation of divine grace to human experience becomes an insoluble riddle. Confusion and obscurity in one's fundamental thinking result, and the whole theological situation is bedeviled, so that Curtis was hardly exaggerating when he referred to the crude philosophical realism of Wesley as an "unspeakable curse." Yet it was this type of thought that formed the philosophical background of all the earlier Methodist theologians. Not even Foster transcended it. It was Sheldon who first intro-

135

duced into Methodist systematic theology the idealistic viewpoint with its conception of the divine immanence. This carried with it a new conception of miracle, of the natural and supernatural, of revelation and inspiration, of Christian experience, and of the general relation of God to the world, and in so doing removed to a large extent the intellectual scandal involved in the old conflict between science and theology. In this philosophical background of his thinking is to be found perhaps as important an aspect of Sheldon's theology as any, though it does not obtrude itself in the pages of his *System of Christian Doctrine. . . .*

Methodism in the past has been too much inclined to look upon theology as a kind of ecclesiastical accessory, necessary perhaps as an adjunct to church activity, but not an essential part of it. The result has been that she has not made adequate provision for the theological training of her ministers, nor has she given adequate encouragement to thorough and original investigation in the field of theology. We have been too complacent in our attitude to our own theology; we have prided ourselves on its being "preachable" or we have tacitly expressed ourselves as being contented with it by taking an indifferent attitude toward theology in general. We have not as a church come to grips with the theological problem as we ought and as we must do, if we are to fulfill our mission in this day and particularly in the day to come. We have been too passive in matters theological, we have accepted too readily leadership from without. For this there no doubt have been historical and perhaps adequate reasons. But a new responsibility for educational work now rests upon our church, a responsibility that she dare not and, I believe, will not shirk. We need to be more creative than we have been in the field of religious thought, we need to construct our theology more in harmony with the distinctive nature and major emphases of the religious movement that we represent. But this we can do only as we throw more of our resources and more of our energy into theological education. We need to make provision for a larger number of such careers as that of Doctor Sheldon. He stands out today as a shining example of the immense service that can be rendered the church by a lifetime of devotion to theological scholarship.

John Scott Lidgett

John Scott Lidgett (1854–1953) was the leader of Methodist theology in Great Britain at the turn of the twentieth century. He lived a long, fruitful life of service, leading a church center in London and consistently writing on theological topics. He represented well the emphases of the era: the Fatherhood of God and the Brotherhood of Man. These themes he related to his Methodist heritage and set them within European and British theological discussion. Consequently, the doctrine of atonement was a focal concern. The section of his writing included here is from *The Christian Religion* (London: Robert C. Culley, 1907), pp. 101-17.

The Content of the Christian Religion

What is the content of the Christian Religion? This is the first question to be asked and answered in dealing with the problem of Christian Evidences. These, like every other subject of human inquiry, must begin with some datum. There is something, that is to say, which they take for granted, and have to explain and justify. What is it which in the case of Christian Evidences is given to be explained? The only satisfactory answer is, that this is Christ—His place and influence in the world, and what is made manifest thereby. This includes, on the one hand, the explanation of Christ in the world, and on the other, the explanation of the world with Christ in it. Thus the question becomes: What is revealed as to the nature of the whole universe of reality by the presence and

137

place of Christ within it? The two elements must be kept well in view. But, first of all, there is Christ Himself, as He is revealed in His own personal history, in His direct influence upon the life and progress, upon the spirit and experience of men, in the measure and meaning of His affinity with the characteristic faiths and strivings of mankind. Anything less than the whole, which includes all these elements, comes short at some vital point of the Christianity which has to be explained. The Person, His influence, His relation to what is fundamental in human nature—these are the three elements of the complete manifestation of what Christ is. To leave out of consideration any one of these is to omit something that is essential. To examine any part of this whole simply in the form of a theoretic doctrine is to weaken its force by abstracting from the spiritual experience of mankind wrought out in history, out of which the formal doctrine proceeds.

The first step, therefore, in a satisfactory presentation of Christian Evidences, is carefully to ascertain what is distinctive of Christ Himself. This means, above all, the determination of the content of His own spiritual consciousness, as it is presented to us in the records which have come down to us; establishing, so far as is necessary for this purpose, their authenticity. It involves, further, the establishment and explanation of certain facts about Him, without which His own consciousness could not have created His influence in the world. It includes, further, the investigation of that influence in order to seize upon what is characteristic of it, and to interpret the doctrines about Him and His work which were developed in order to describe and explain the characteristic influence He exerted. It necessitates one additional step; namely, the inquiry as to how the influence of Christ, thus set forth in doctrines about Him, stands related to the general texture of human consciousness, and to the deliverances of the human spirit working in apparent independence of the history and the Spirit of Christ.

In modern times, at least, no satisfactory beginning of Christian Evidences can be made from any other starting-point than this. It is the great service rendered by the Ritschlian school that, with certain grave defects in their treatment of Christ and Christianity, as well as of the relation of both to the world, its teachers have emphasized the cardinal necessity of founding the truth of Christianity upon the relation of Christ to the Christian consciousness, and through it to the general spiritual life of mankind.

This starting-point, proper in itself, will be felt to be the more necessary in proportion as the unique place of Christ in the evolution and history of religion is realized, and also the unique nature of the bond which unites believers to Him. How unique that bond is such thinkers as Martineau recognize as expressly as do the more orthodox. In his earlier days he wrote, "Whoever sees in Christ, not an original source of truth and goodness, but only a product of something else, is destitute of the attitude of mind constituting religious discipleship; which implies, not that we have been convinced by the reasoning of an equal, but that we have been subdued by the authority, and possessed by the intuitions of a higher mind."[1] In later years he wrote, "Supreme in the hierarchy of inspiration, standing unique at its culminating point, identical in filial will with the Infinite Father's perfection, is Jesus Christ, the moral incarnation of the love of God."[2] Still later he declared, "I have no faith in a religious future for those who renounce their allegiance to that personality, whether to try a philosophic Theism or a bare Ethical Ideal without him."[3]

The first question is, therefore, that of the nature of the religion which Christ embodies and conveys. What is it? How does He convey it?

I. In the first place, Christ gives a final theology to the world as the expression of a perfect religion. That His theology is final, that His religion is perfect, may be taken as generally agreed. If either is abandoned, it is not in order to find a better, but because religion is pronounced an illusion and theological conclusions are declared to be beyond the reach of human faculties properly exercised. The next point is equally important, namely, that it is by means of the perfect religion that Christ announces the final theology. The whole of His theological teaching is expressed through a religious realization of, a response to, a manifestation of, certain divine relationships which He describes. His teaching, His outward life, His inner spiritual experience, constitute an indissoluble unity, to which the inner experience is the key. In every other case there is some disparity between the two sides. Religious instincts may find little consistent expression in doctrine, may even diverge widely in substance from the dogmatic forms in which they are expressed. Still more may theological teaching become theoretic and abstract; derived from the exercise of the logical understanding rather than from the deeper spiritual and moral sources of the heart. The fact that theological science has so often broken away from such sources, and even neglected to correct itself by their help, has frequently rendered it artificial and unsatisfying. But in Christ the unity of religion, life, and teaching is

---

1. *Rationale*, 3rd ed. (1845).
2. Letter to R. H. Hutton (1885), *Life*, vol. ii., p. 80.
3. Written in 1888, *Life*, vol. ii., p. 218.

complete. Each element contributes a consenting voice to the others. The teaching is reflected in the life; teaching and life proceed from experience; the experience carrying within itself a direct and immediate assurance of its own truth, and being verified by its power to inspire the spirit and conduct by which the life is carried to a satisfying and triumphant close. Hence there is in Christ a unique combination of conscious union with God, and also with man; of intensest devotion with the total absence of any sense of sin. The first step towards understanding Christianity is to ascertain the nature of this harmonious union of religion and theology in a completely consistent life.

1. If inquiry as to the nature of this union be made, it will be found that the religion expressed through the theology our Lord's consciousness of the Fatherhood of God, realized in and through a consciousness of Sonship in complete correspondence with that Fatherhood. The Father is made known to, and is made manifest by, the Son. The consciousness of perfect correspondence with the Father pervades His life. The saying, "I do always the things that are pleasing to Him" (John viii. 29), sums it up.

First and foremost is the consciousness of perfect spiritual and moral affinity between Himself and the Father. In that consciousness lies at once His own knowledge of the Father, and His power to reveal Him to men. What the Father is, what God therefore is—for the Father is simply God revealed in the one supreme relationship of Love and Life—is manifest to and in the spiritual and moral qualities of the Son. These are directly derived from the Father. Therefore the Father is what the Son manifests Him as being in the perfect life of Sonship.

This relationship between the Father and the Son is unique. Christ is the Son as none else is, or can be. This consciousness of distinction is present throughout our Lord's consciousness and teaching.

Yet the very peculiarity of His Sonship contributes the basis of a unity between Him and mankind, and lays down the nature of His office for mankind. "No [one] knoweth the Father but the Son, and he to whomsoever the Son willeth to reveal Him" (Matt. xi. 27). The life of Christ, therefore, as He is conscious of it, is a manifestation of the Father: "I have glorified Thee on the earth" (John xvii. 4), is His own summing-up of both the nature and the completeness of His life at the end.

The Fatherhood manifest in the Sonship shapes His course throughout. Every power which He possesses is derived from it. Every temptation which He withstands is an incitement to depart from the perfectly filial spirit by way of some form of disloyalty. Throughout His life, this direct, personal, all-determining and unique experience of relationship to the Father is the key to our Lord's life.[4] . . .

The whole of this doctrine of God is, as has been said, revealed in the life of Sonship as a religious and life-ordering experience. In the directness and completeness of that experience is shown the unique peculiarity of the Son, as distinguished from all other men. The metaphysical nature of His Sonship is revealed in and through this spiritual and moral experience. Apart from the spiritual splendour of Jesus Christ, the dogmatic propositions about His nature would be incredible. Just as the so-called natural attributes of God are made manifest in His spiritual revelation, so the metaphysical relationship of the Son to the Father is manifest in and through the unique spiritual and moral relationships in which He stands to Him, as shown in a life that is permeated by the Father's presence and power. The more this spiritual consciousness of Christ is considered, the stronger becomes the impression of its unique nature; by reason alike of its directness and intimacy, of its fullness and certainty of knowledge, and of its perfect spiritual response. Yet, although this unique relationship removes Christ, not only in degree but in kind, from the ranks of all other men, it is, notwithstanding, the complete fulfilment of the promise made in human nature.

Our Lord's consciousness of being the Son of God is all-important for the understanding of His life and work in the world. Of the two conceptions by which Christ is explained—His divine Sonship and His Messiahship—His Sonship is the more important; for it was by this consciousness of Sonship that He interpreted the meaning of His Messianic office for mankind. It is usually said that our Lord spiritualized the Messianic ideal current in His time, and substituted a spiritual and inward kingdom for the outward and miraculous conception of the Jews. That He did this was entirely due to His consciousness of Sonship and to His realization of what that Sonship meant as to the nature and purposes of God, the nature of man, and the way of salvation. It has been argued that our Lord came gradually and comparatively late to a distinct consciousness that He was the Christ; it is not open to question that His first and original consciousness of Himself was that He was the Son of God.

2. But if our Lord's first and all-determining consciousness was that He was the Son of God, coupled with and growing out of that consciousness was the consciousness of being the Son of Man. That title is Messianic in its origin; it rests upon the vision of "one like unto a Son of

---

4. See further on this the author's *The Fatherhood of God in Christian Truth and Life*, pp. 13, 14. Also, *The Spiritual Principle of the Atonement, chap. ii.*

Man coming in the clouds of heaven" contained in Dan. vii. 13, 14. While this vision represents a miraculous advent, yet the whole quality of the Messiah thus revealed is spiritual and moral. It is as the complete embodiment of a perfect humanity coming forth from God, upheld by God, and serving God, that the Son of Man introduces an everlasting kingdom of abiding humanity, before which the successive kingdoms of the wild beasts pass away. Thus, when the whole context of Daniel is taken into account, the title, "the Son of Man," lends itself perfectly to our Lord's consciousness of being the Son of God. It was in this direct relationship to His Father that His authority, the certainty and permanence of His kingdom, were grounded. It was in His complete consciousness of Sonship that His perfect embodiment of the ideal of human nature was contained, as being at once free, reasonable, and loyal, in contrast to all that is typical, not of man, but of the wild beast.

Hence, it is not surprising that in the mind of Christ the spiritual and moral elements of the title, "the Son of Man," became supreme. It was used by Him to set forth His typical humanity, His breadth of human sympathy, and even, with a reminiscence of its ordinary prophetic use,[5] His human frailty and apparent insignificance. Christ came "not to destroy, but to fulfil."[6] If this was true of His relationship to the law, it was true, above all, of His relationship to the human nature, which underlies all law and makes law possible. To fulfil the law involves fulfilling the human nature, which is subject to, embodies, and responds to the law. This was our Lord's office as the Son of Man—an office which He could so fulfil only because of His life through, in, and to the Father as His Son. This consciousness that He completely realizes human nature in such wise that He is united with, and not separated from mankind, is vital to the understanding of our Lord's teaching as to His life and work.

3. Our Lord is conscious of being the Christ. It has been alleged, on very insufficient evidence, nay, by distorting the evidence that is produced, that Jesus never claimed to be the Christ, and that such statements of His Messiahship as are to be found in the New Testament are the invention of His disciples. Taking all the conditions into account, it would, on the other hand, appear almost inconceivable that He could claim to fill so unique a position towards the spiritual life of Israel and of the world, without having the consciousness that He was the Christ. Both the titles, which were frequently on His lips, the Son of God and the Son of Man, carried with them the suggestion of Messiahship. We

---

5. See Ezekiel.
6. Matt. v.

have seen that this was the case with the latter. But as to the former, it will be remembered that Jehovah said of Solomon, "I will be to him a Father, and he shall be to Me a son" (1 Chron. xxi. 10); while of Israel He said, "Out of Egypt have I called My son" (Hosea xi. 1). The perfection of Divine Sonship, therefore, suggested to any one acquainted with the Old Testament the position of Messianic authority and power. . . .

From all this it follows that the personal relationship in which men as individuals are to stand to Christ is everywhere emphasized. Discipleship, not merely as the means of acquaintance with His truth, but as the condition of entering into inward and outward fellowship with His life, is the way by which His kingdom is set up in the hearts of men.

This fellowship by the way of discipleship is not only the satisfaction of human need, but brings salvation from sin. Everywhere behind and with inhuman need Christ sees the presence of sin as its cause. This fact is so familiar, and the evidence of it is so manifest throughout the Gospels, that it is needless to enlarge upon or to establish it. For the present purpose it may be taken for granted. A study of the gospels will show that Christ's ministry as Redeemer from sin has three aspects, which were naturally developed at a later stage into the doctrine of His three offices—the Prophetic, the Priestly, and the Kingly. First in order comes His work as the Revealer of the Father in grace and truth; the imparting of a knowledge, which He alone possesses, to men whose spiritual nature is in such need of it as to be unfulfilled without it, but who can apprehend it only in Him, as His words become to them "spirit and life." Secondly, there is His Priestly office, not so clearly outlined in the Gospels as the Prophetic, yet to be found there, and emphasized in the closing scenes of His life, especially according to the Gospel of St. John. Thirdly, there is the Kingly aspect of His work, resting upon spiritual foundations, and spiritual in its nature. Its essential feature is that all the teaching of Christ becomes an authoritative command over the life, unfolding a law of life and love to be received by faith, and to be embodied in action. "Ye call me Master and Lord: and ye say well; for so I am."[7] Master and Lord, not by virtue of a merely external authority, but by virtue of dominion over the hearts and lives of men, who are constituted for faith in the Son of God.

These three offices, or aspects of Christ's work, are bound together in the closest unity. Each is co-extensive with the whole of His teaching, doing, and suffering. Every element of His life belongs to a complete unity, which is, according to the point of view from which it is regarded, entirely

---

7. John xiii. 13.

prophetic, entirely priestly, and entirely kingly. Into that unity the death of Christ is brought, not as an unforeseen, a meaningless, incident, but as a vital part, even *the* vital part, of His Messianic work. He gives "His life a ransom for many."[8] Upon the cross His identification with man becomes complete; His taking over the burden of their sin and sorrow is perfected in a great act of vicarious suffering; His obedience to the Father attains its consummation. By a final act of revelation, of self-surrender, and of love for men, He enters into the fullness of His Christly office through the sacrifice of Himself. . . .

4. Our Lord's filial consciousness, and the conception of His work as Christ, which was consequent on it, involved His transformation of the accepted doctrine of the kingdom of God.

The conception of the kingdom of God was accepted by Christ, and formed the basis of His teaching. No phrase is so frequently on His lips as that of "the kingdom of God," or "the kingdom of heaven." The form is Jewish; representing the theocratic conception which was embodied in their state, and formed the substance of their expectation of the future. But while in form the conception lent itself to those external and mechanical views which, with their childish imagery and their nationalist ideals, characterized Messianic hopes in our Lord's days, yet in substance the doctrine of the kingdom of God was an attempt to give expression to the underlying consciousness—essential to all true religion—of the absoluteness of God, of His complete control over all human life and over the world. It represented also, though in inadequate form, the faith, also essential to the highest spiritual life, that God, who is absolute in His sovereignty, exercises His sovereignty to secure adequate, spiritual, and moral ends, bringing with them satisfaction to human hearts and heirship of the world to men of faith. That the conception had become impoverished was due to the lack of adequate depth, breadth, and content in the spiritual and ethical ideals of those who held it. It needed the uplifting and enlargement of those ideals in order to make it satisfactory.

Our Lord adopted this conception, and made it the basis of His teaching, not only because it was the connecting-link with the past, but because it did thus express certain elements which are vital to a living spiritual faith. A kingdom entering into human life from above, representing the absolute sway of God exercised for supreme spiritual ends, and adjusting the universe to those ends as they are wrought out,—this was the starting-point of our Lord's teaching.

---

8. Matt. xx. 28; Mark x. 45.

Three great changes in the conception, however, were brought about by the filial consciousness of our Lord. In the first place, the absolute God, whose will controls all things and brings about their consummation, is the Father. Hence a new graciousness, spiritual depth and breadth, and even geniality, are brought to the ideal of His kingdom. The sovereignty of God in His sovereignty for the accomplishment of fatherly ends by fatherly means. His Kingship is the authority and executive power of His love and grace.

Secondly, entrance into the kingdom of God is conditioned, not by external peculiarities or advantages, but by the reception of the filial spirit, which responds to the Father's love, and which creates and maintains righteousness, purity, and love upon earth.

Hence, thirdly, the conception of the kingdom as affecting the community and embracing the material universe shares in this spiritual transformation. It no longer represents the external supremacy of bare will, as though God were a Supreme Other and Outsider, imposing His kingdom by an omnipotent decree upon the refractory material of the earth. In perfect balance, the kingdom of God is represented as both transcendent and immanent, as a gift from above and a growth from within, as a divine event, and as a natural process depending on spiritual forces. Hence the breadth of God's providence, which includes the sparrow and the lily. Hence the inwardness of the kingdom, which is not Here or There, but is within man. Hence its expansive growth as the mustard-seed and the leaven; although in its manifestation it encounters opposition and falls like seed upon all kinds of ground to take its chance. In this process it works judgement on those who will not receive it. Within its comprehensiveness these great spiritual and moral issues are clearly recognized. Personality is so emphasized in God and freedom in man, that the doctrine of immanence is guarded at all points against Pantheism. God's presence in man is not due to the fact that man is a part of nature. On the contrary, the presence of God throughout nature is due to the fact that nature is a province and an instrument of the spiritual life, which becomes manifest in the dealings of God with men.

Wilbur Fisk Tillett

Wilbur Fisk Tillett (1854–1936) was a theologian in the Methodist Episcopal Church, South. Professor of Systematic Theology and Dean of the Divinity School at Vanderbilt University, Tillett attempted to speak to his own time with an eye to the scholarly developments in the study of religion. Convinced of the importance and openness of his Methodist tradition, he engaged the issues of the religious nature of human beings and the shared search for God found in the world's religions. The selection below is from his book *Paths That Lead to God* (New York: George H. Doran, 1924), pp. 25–42.

A Knowledge of God Man's Greatest Need

There is nothing more needed in the world to-day, or in any day, than for men to have a deep conviction of the existence of a living God. Some objects of knowledge are possible only to the few—to the wise and learned. A knowledge of God is possible to all men. A true conception of God is foremost in importance among all the objects of human knowledge that is possible to all men. Until a man orients himself rightly with reference to God, it is impossible for him to give that direction to his life which can alone insure his reaching that goal which is the only aim and end that can satisfy the soul of a rational and immortal being. There is no preparation for large and efficient life-service that is so primary and fundamental as that awakening and inspiration which results from a vision of God and an experience of his presence and power in

146

one's life. The Christian worker above all men is dependent upon his knowledge of God and a right relationship to him for that spiritual equipment and guidance without which there can be no real success in Christian service and no real happiness in Christian experience. It was the revelation and vision of God which Moses received at the burning bush in the Arabian desert that was not only the beginning of his life of service, but it was in the truest sense his enduement with the knowledge and power that enabled him to found and organise the greatest nation in moral achievement in the ancient world. The vision which Paul received of his divine Lord was in like manner the turning point in his career and the beginning of his life of unequalled service in spreading the Christian religion throughout the world.

I. Man's Search for God

Not only is it true that a knowledge of God is man's first and greatest need, but it is also true that men are at all times and everywhere seeking God. The deep-thinking philosopher and the unthinking peasant travel along different roads in their search for God, but both alike are seeking Him who alone can explain their problems and meet their respective needs. Whether men are conscious of it or not, and whether they acknowledge it to themselves or not, they are all, with varying degrees of intelligence and sincerity, seeking God. Many of these seekers after God need guidance and counsel that they may not miss the way. There are many misleading guideposts and sign-boards along the way, saying, "Lo, God is here," or "Lo, God is there"; but, following them, men find him not. There are no paths that human beings tread that need to be made plain and kept open so truly as the paths that lead to God. He who would help men to find God must interpret him in terms of thought and speech adapted to the intellectual and religious conditions and states of mind characteristic of the age. In meeting these needs in any age the religious perplexities and obstacles to faith incident to that age have to be considered. Hence books on Theism and the Philosophy of Religion, on Apologetics and the Evidences of Christianity, must be written afresh for each generation. For the world to be content from generation to generation with one and the same text book on Theism or Apologetics would indicate that it was intellectually static and spiritually stagnant. For a book, even a good book, to become obsolete is often a sign and proof of healthful religious activity and progress.

Practical Divinity

1. *The Causes and Occasions for Present-Day*
Doubts and Inquiries Concerning God

Each new generation has its own causes and occasions for fresh inquiry concerning the nature and character of God—inquiries which, however indicative they may be on the surface of doubt, are more deeply indicative of faith in the personality and power and in the wisdom and goodness of the Divine Being who created, sustains and governs the universe. There are some forms of doubt and unrest in religion that are signs of healthful thought and progress, and others that are indications of unhealthful and perilous tendencies in the moral and religious life of men and nations. It is important to distinguish the one from the other. The former may be safely let alone; the latter needs to be carefully considered as to its causes and its cure.

Much of the religious unrest and doubt of our day is expressing itself in questions that bear on the existence and character of God to an extent which, some think, has rarely if ever been equalled before in the history of human thought. Some of the causes for these questions about God are manifest and easily named. Four or five of these need only to be named in order to be recognised at once as provoking causes of doubt and inquiry in our day.

First and most immediate in our day is the recent great World War and the ills that have followed it, involving the sufferings not of the guilty alone, but even more of innocent people to such an extent and to a degree so appalling as to cause men to ask how God could be possessed of infinite power, infinite knowledge and infinite goodness and allow such wrongs and sufferings to take place. If he could prevent so great an evil, but would not, they have asked—repeating the age-old question raised in the book of Job—how can we regard him as infinitely good? If he would have prevented it, but could not, can we regard him as infinite in power? If God is infinite both in power and in goodness, do not such unspeakable evils as this World War and the suffering of innocent men, women and children involved in it, prove that things like these are outside the sphere of his operation and control? Who then, or what, is God anyway? And where? Thus men have been led to question his goodness, his power and his wisdom, and even his existence. Is there no answer to such questions?

A second subtle cause of unrest has been at work. Men's ideas and ideals of governments and their rulers have changed from that of an arbitrary, imperial and absolute monarchy where the ruler's will was the one and only law, from which there was no appeal, to a commonwealth and government of and over free beings whose interests are so identified with those of their ruler as to make him the embodiment of a democratic ideal of lordship, which means, or should mean, that love and beneficence control the will and direct the power of the ruler. The God of traditional Calvinistic theology with his sovereign and absolute will deciding the destiny of men before they are born, and the course of their lives after they are born, no longer satisfies the minds and consciences of modern thinking men who demand that God's sovereignty shall be interpreted in terms of a divine and social democracy which they believe is the divine ideal of government for God as well as for earthly rulers and governments. This means that God is the Ruler of free beings who may defy as well as obey, his will; and his government of men and nations involves overruling the rebellious as well as ruling the righteous and obedient.

Again, the rise of the doctrine of evolution and its acceptance in the scientific world has been so pronounced and widespread as to create not only unrest but alarm on the part of those who have believed that creation was an instantaneous act of God accomplished in six days; and these disturbed believers have interpreted the doctrine of evolution as getting rid of God in the realm of nature and as deifying and enthroning natural law and physical force.

Coupled with this cause, and more or less identified with it, is the fact that ours is pre-eminently an age of science, and science presupposes and is based on faith in the absolute regularity and uniformity of the operation of nature's laws; and so deeply does this conviction as to natural law possess the modern mind that there is a growing tendency to call in question the accuracy of any statements as to the past which represent certain events as having been brought about by a divine interruption of nature's laws. There is therefore a manifest and outspoken tendency not only to retire miracles from the foreground to the background of modern Apologetics, but to drop them entirely as an argument unconvincing to the modern scientific mind. This appears to many as being tantamount to eliminating everything supernatural from the Christian religion.

In like manner, modern scholars by reinterpreting the Bible in keeping with the principles of literary and historical criticism applied to all other types and realms of ancient literature, have made it to appear that the human element in the Scriptures is a source of possible error in the sacred record and interpretation of events and facts, some of which affect more or less seriously the character of God, especially the God of the Old Testament. In so doing the modern scholars have seemed to believers in the traditional doctrine of Biblical inspiration and inerrancy to take God out of the Bible, as evolutionists have seemed to them to take him out of nature as its Creator and Preserver.

Yet a fifth cause for theological unrest and for questions about God should be mentioned. A change has come about in men's attitude towards the heathen religions of the world. Most of the traditional types of theology prevalent in the past have interpreted these religions as false, as more satanic than divine in their origin and form of manifestation, and have regarded the heathen, because of these false religions, as children of the devil and as such necessarily without God and without hope in the world. The modern science of Comparative Religions has, on the contrary, more and more interpreted these religions as a proof of men's search for God and as an honest and sincere expression of their faith in God, regarding them as something inadequate, erroneous and unsatisfying rather than as something false, sinful and satanic in origin and form. Many have found it difficult and confusing to adjust this new attitude towards the heathen religions of the world to the fact that our conception of God and our Christian faith constitute the one and only true and saving religion in the world.

Now it may be that these five things which I have mentioned—the unspeakable atrocities of the World War, the incoming of modern democratic ideals of government and sovereignty, the scientific doctrine of evolution, the modern scholar's view of the human element in the Bible as the source of possible error, and the new science of Comparative Religions—should not, and would not if properly interpreted, raise doubts as to the existence or the beneficent activity of God, or in any way dethrone him or impeach his character as an absolutely perfect Being. But, as a matter of fact, it is quite certain that all five of the facts named have caused, and are causing, questions about God's existence and character that need to be answered. Nor do these by any means exhaust the causes of religious unrest and of the inquiries concerning God and his Providence that are characteristic of our day.

And it may turn out that the only satisfactory answer to these questions will involve or result in a reinterpretation of God in terms of modern thought and faith and in a restatement of the Christian doctrine of God in different language from that found in the historic creeds of Christendom. If so, what shall the reinterpretation be? Where will the new emphasis be placed?

But, after all, these inquiries about God, even though they may seem to be critical of the Church and her creeds, and to imply doubts as to the very existence of an omnipotent, omnipresent and omniscient Being of infinite goodness, are a proof of the prevalent, widespread and undying interest of men in religion. Men are "incurably religious," and they cannot rest without a satisfying conception of God. To doubt at the right time and the right place and to give expression in the right manner to this doubt may be the best cure for doubt and the best evidence of an irrepressible faith. Honest doubt concerning God and matters of religion may save faith from superstition and lead to a faith that is at once intelligent, sane and satisfying, and mark a forward movement in the progress of religious thought and Christian faith.

2. Need for Reinterpreting God and Restating the Grounds of Theistic and Christian Faith in Our Day

A recent thoughtful and illuminating volume by Bishop Charles Gore of Oxford, England, titled "Belief in God," has attracted wide attention among scholars and theologians by its able discussion of the fundamentals of Theistic faith. He considers especially the question as to how our conception and interpretation of God have been affected by the results of modern scientific research and biblical scholarship. A second volume, titled "Belief in Christ," does for God incarnate, the divine-human Person of Christian faith, what the first volume undertook to do for faith in God. The first chapter in Bishop Gore's "Belief in God" is titled "The Breakdown of Tradition" and begins with this sentence: "The world in which we live to-day can only be described as chaotic in the matter of religious beliefs."

"If I read our times aright," says Sir Henry Jones, in beginning his lectures on the Gifford Foundation at the University of Glasgow, Scotland, "there are thousands of thoughtful men in this country whose interest in religion is sincere, but who can neither accept the ordinary teaching of the Church nor subject themselves to its dogmatic ways. I would fain demonstrate to these men, both by example and precept, that the enquiry which makes the fullest use of the severe intellectual methods, supports those beliefs upon which a religion worth having rests. Let man seek God by the way of pure reason and he will find him." The Church is here to stay; but its "dogmatic ways"—and this phrase, interpreted etymologically, simply means its "ways of teaching fundamental truth"—are not only subject to change, but should be changed from time to time if they are to be made most effective in each succeeding generation.

151

Each generation has its own special religious needs; but the need for a fresh study of God, for a new realisation of his presence and power, and a new interpretation of him in terms of the living thought of the faith of the day, is an ever-present need of every generation of men. Some things are subjects of occasional thought. God is the one supreme subject that is always the foremost object of thought among men. As rational beings we cannot think and reason without taking into our thought and into our reasoning Him in whom we live and move and have our being.

The cure of theological and religious unrest that may characterise our own or any other age can only come through serious and honest thinking, with open, truth-seeking minds and truth-loving hearts bent on not only finding out who God is and where he is, but on getting acquainted with him and knowing him,—bent on knowing his will not for the purpose of idly speculating about it, and correcting the opinions of others, but for the purpose of doing that will in and through self-forgetful and sacrificial service for others. These are the pilgrims for whose guidance we are making inquiries concerning "the paths that lead to God."

II. A Survey of the Paths That Lead to God

1. The Spiritual Interpretation and Use of Nature

The first path that we shall take we designate "Through Nature to God." To reason from nature, physical nature, up to nature's God is to follow a stream of thought that always empties itself into that boundless ocean whose depths no man can fathom. Science is the careful and comprehensive study of nature in all its phases in order to discover and register its laws; and when it is recognised that all laws are but the methods and means by and through which some personal will acts, every devout and observant student of science will find that to study science is to travel through nature to a God whose personal power can alone explain the laws of nature. Whether we study nature extensively or intensively, whether we look through the telescope at the unnumbered worlds of light that constitute our universe, or through the microscope at the elementary substances and ingredients that enter into mineral, chemical and biological forms of existence that are called atoms and electrons, we are driven alike along each and every one of these highways and byways of thought to the irresistible conclusion that Nature as we know it is inexplicable without a personal God.

152

One of John Fiske's famous volumes bears the title "Through Nature to God." It is chiefly interesting in that it shows how profoundly convinced an ardent evolutionist and student of science can be that nature rightly interpreted furnishes irresistible and overwhelming proof that there is a God, which proof he considers confirmed in and through human nature by "the everlasting reality of religion."

2. Man's Nature a Revelation of God

From physical nature we pass to another pathway which we may designate as "Through Man to God." However valuable may be the material which physical nature furnishes for the study of the nature and attributes of the Divine Being, human nature furnishes material yet more valuable and trustworthy. Seeing that man was made in the image of God, and continues to bear his image, to reason from man's nature back to God, and up to God, should prove a sure and satisfying pathway to a knowledge of the Creator. This will suggest various subsidiary lines of approach that might bear designations such as "Through psychology to God," "Through conscience to God," "Through philosophy to God," which phrases at once suggest man's intellectual, emotional and volitional nature, and point to the fact that he is possessed of a conscience and of moral free agency. Human nature, therefore, as well as, and even more than, physical nature, when carefully studied furnishes to the mind of man arguments which, when logically combined, not only make irresistible the conclusion that there is a God, but prove much as to the essential character of the Divine Being.

As the mind of man thinks, as the heart feels and loves, as the will chooses among different alternatives and as by its volitions a man becomes a conscious cause of certain definite and desired effects, so, from these subjective psychological facts and experiences, he infers, and cannot escape the conviction, that, back of and over and above himself and all nature, there must be a supreme Being possessed of these functions and powers without which nature and finite personality would be inexplicable. And it is not easy to see how man could carry in his wonderfully complex nature a stronger and more convincing proof that the Creator and Governor of the world must be a moral Being than is furnished by the universal presence in man of a conscience, a moral consciousness, a sense of right and wrong and responsibility that proclaims the existence of a moral law and moral government which absolutely require a moral God to explain them.

153

John Locke, the well-known English philosopher, in his famous "Essay concerning the Human Understanding," gives expression to a profound conviction in these words: "I presume I may say that we more certainly know that there is a God than that there is anything else without us." We do not wonder therefore to find that this eminent philosopher followed this volume with another titled, "The Reasonableness of Christianity."

Some intuitive philosophers contend that the idea of God is innate, that it is born with us and in us, that it is an intuitive truth and involved in our very consciousness, and is therefore a condition of thought and not something demanding a process of reason and to be reached only as a conclusion. The knowledge of God, say they, is an instinct of the soul; and while it may be confirmed by reason, it does not need reason to account for its existence. If this be true, then every man has in his own self-consciousness the God whom he seeks, and all his studies of nature and human nature will simply mean an increase and enlargement of his knowledge of One whom he already knows in part.

When Helen Keller, deaf, dumb and blind from early childhood, had been so educated that others were able to communicate with her, and find out her thoughts, and convey thoughts to her, they arranged it so that Phillips Brooks should first talk to her concerning God. And when he told her concerning the Creator and Heavenly Father she burst into the utmost rapture that she was capable of manifesting and responded through her interpreter that she had long had thoughts about him and had so much wanted some one to talk to her about him. Possibly no instance could be taken from actual human life more favourable to the view that the idea of God is innate than this of Helen Keller, who, it was discovered, had had a knowledge of God and an experience with him, long before any communication concerning him had come to her from the outside world.

"Through Philosophy to God" is thus a phrase that points to a method of approaching the infinite and eternal Person through a process of thought and reason that sustains the same relation to the human mind and its laws that science sustains to physical nature and its laws. Science has to deal with the facts and phenomena of nature; philosophy and metaphysics deal with the fundamental ideas of the mind and the causes of things, with the underlying but invisible principles at the foundation of things in so far as they are objects of thought and knowledge. But if theism is true the fundamental and ultimate fact of all being is God. All theistic philosophy is theology in that it finds the

154

explanation of all things, the reason why they are what they are, in God.

To study God's revelation of himself in the history of the human race ought to be a pathway to God as truly as that which leads through nature and science. The fact that free agents so often, whether acting separately as individuals or collectively in groups and as nations, oppose and thwart the purposes of God concerning them, makes it more difficult to trace the footprints of the Governor of men in history than it is to trace the footprints of the Creator in physical nature. And yet, rightly interpreted, history is a revelation of God's nature and of his providential government of men. The philosophy of the Christian Religion is a study not only of the dominant and all pervasive influence of religion in history, but to some extent of the moral philosophy of history, of the hand of God, as seen in the life of men and nations, especially as influenced by their religions and their conceptions of God.

3. God's Best Revealer—the Divine-Human Christ

But there is a plainer and surer path to God than either physical nature or human nature—it is through Him who alone of all earthly beings possessed not only a complete human nature, but a divine-human nature. "Through Christ to God" will, therefore, furnish our best approach to an understanding and knowledge of the nature and attributes of God. The first path (nature) will lead us to God the Creator; the second (human nature) will lead us to discover God not only as Creator, but as the moral Governor of those free moral beings whom he created in his own image. This third path, the divine-human Christ, will bring us to a knowledge of God as not only a Creator and Governor, but as our loving heavenly Father—and if perchance one has forfeited through wilful and persistent sin his right to be called a child of God, Christ reveals himself as one who can restore the prodigal son to his Father's household. If we start upon this path with Christ, looking upon Him as a mere man, as did the disciples of old, before we have reached the end of the journey our fellowship with him will convince us that he was more than a man—that he who called himself the Son of Man was really the Son of God even more truly than he was the Son of Man.

While God could and did reveal something of himself in and through physical nature, and still more of himself in and through human nature, it was only when he had a divine-human Nature in whom and through whom to reveal himself that his revelation could be adequate and complete. "He that hath seen me hath seen the father," said Christ, and this

155

he said, not so much to tell us that he himself was like God as that God the Father was like himself, the Son. The incarnate Christ revealed God not only in the words he spoke concerning him, and in the God-like deeds with which his life was crowded and crowned, but, being the divine Son and the express image of the Father, in his person also he revealed and glorified him. It is impossible to exaggerate, or even adequately to express, the value of the revelation of God which the incarnate divine-human Christ brought to men.

But we cannot think of God in Christ as the Saviour without thinking of man as a sinner. "Through Sin to God" seems on first thought to be an expression that involves a contradiction, an ethical impossibility; and yet rightly interpreted the phrase indicates that man may be driven to God as well as drawn to him. The deep and awful helplessness and misery of the human soul in the experience of sin and guilt compel the sinner, through very anguish and wretchedness of spirit, to realise the need of a God who can forgive and blot out sin and deliver him from its awful bondage. "Who can forgive sins but God only?" A blessed day for the sinner is it when he is driven to exclaim and cry out in his anguish of soul, "Oh, wretched man that I am! who shall deliver me from this body of death?" The best thing that sin can do for a man is to make him feel the need of a divine Saviour from sin, and thus drive him to God.

4. The Divine-Human Book

"Through the Bible to God" is perhaps the most familiar of all the paths that lead to the divine Being; and yet if the Bible be not read thoughtfully and interpreted truly, it may, taken in its entirety, lead to confused and contradictory ideas of God. Read with discrimination and interpreted as a progressive revelation of God extending over hundreds or even thousands of years, and completed only in and by Christ, who was the one and only absolutely perfect revealer of God, it becomes the best of all guide-books for pilgrims who are in search of God. It has long been common to designate this path to God as that of divine revelation in contrast to that of nature and human reason—the supernatural as distinct from the natural and human. As Christ is a divine-human person, so may we regard the Bible as a divine-human book in a sense that is not true of any other book in the literature of the world. No interpretation of the Bible can be true to the facts which fails to recognise both the human and the divine elements that enter into its composition. The writers are as genuinely human as any writers in all literature; and to rob them of their human limitations and imperfections is not to add to, but to detract from, the value of their writings; and yet there is a something in their writings, an element of moral and spiritual truth in their messages, that is so much above what is found in other religious writings, that it has justified the claim that the writers of this most remarkable and influential of all books were divinely inspired.

This divine-human book, moreover, contains a record of certain events which are so far above and beyond anything which nature or man, as we know them, can bring about that they are called miracles or supernatural events; and these have to be most carefully studied and interpreted if they are to be helps and not hindrances to faith in our day. There are also certain predictions of future events, especially concerning the coming in the fulness of time of one who is called the Messiah, which are so far beyond the ordinary powers of the human mind to foresee and foretell that they have been interpreted as divine revelations possible only to omniscience. The most outstanding characteristic of the Hebrew Scriptures is its monotheistic conception and definition of God in terms of spirituality, personality, unity and holiness, in marked contrast with the materialistic, pantheistic, and polytheistic conceptions of God found in other ancient religions; while the revelation of God in terms of Fatherhood and love is, in like manner, the most notable contribution made by the New Testament to the religious thought and life of mankind.

The books of the Old Testament have been well designated as "the divine library." The first book in this "Library" begins with the words "In the beginning God created the heavens and the earth." Among the last, and possibly the very last, of all the inspired books in date of composition is St. John's Gospel, and it begins with a sentence no less majestic and noble than the first words in Genesis: "In the beginning was the Word; and the Word was with God, and the Word was God." The Bible begins, continues and ends with God as does no other book in all literature.

5. The Church a Witness for God

The Church is composed of those who know God in and through a personal experience and are organised to bring those who know him not into that saving knowledge which they enjoy. It is only in and through experience that any one can attain unto a satisfactory knowledge of God. One may get an intellectual conception of God from others, and learn something about God from creeds and from books of theology; he may have pointed out to him all these pathways to God that we have noted, and which other men have travelled and are still travelling; but not until he himself has a vitalising experience with God will he really know him. To be told that God hears and answers prayer, that he forgives the sin of every truly penitent soul that humbly seeks pardon, that he can break the bondage of sinful habit and remove the sense of guilt from the conscience of contrite sinners who turn from their wicked ways; that he can put a new love in one's heart and a new song in one's mouth—one may hear and assent to all this, and still be a stranger to God. But let him put all these matters to the test of experience, and find out for himself that God is a prayer-hearing and prayer-answering God; let him know in his own heart the joy of sins forgiven and feel the expulsive power of a new and divine affection—and from that moment he will know God, and find him wherever he goes, and every path he travels will become to him a pathway to God—indeed God will reveal himself and be in close communion with him all along the way and not simply at the end of his pilgrimage. This does not mean that everything will be from this time on exactly as he would have it—that trials and tribulations will be at an end in his life—far from it. But it does mean that he will have found in the grace of God and in the power and presence of the Holy Spirit that which will not only sustain in every trial, but even turn his very trials into spiritual blessings and make his life more effective in service to others. Of all the proofs that there is a God, the crowning evidence is that of personal experience.

Not, then, until men have an experience of God can there be a Church, a divine-human institution composed of those who know God, an organised body of true believers whose one great and divine mission is to lead men to God. Only those who know God by experience are prepared to seek and find those who know him not, and lead them into a saving knowledge of him. As in the study of the divine-human Person and of the divine-human Book, so in the study of the divine-human Institution as a path that leads to God, it is all important for us to recognise both the divine and the human elements that enter into it. After making all due allowance for its errors and shortcomings, no one can deny that the Church is the greatest agency in the world for guiding men to a saving knowledge of God. It is the mission of the Church, working as a corporate body and in its individual members, to use all possible means and methods of leading a lost world to God. To be lost is to be away from God; to find God and to know him aright is the goal of human thought and the end of life. Heaven is, whatever else it may or may not be, the place where we shall know God even as we are known by him. To help men find and know God here on earth, and to find and know him in the final and more perfect fellowship of heaven— that is the great mission of the Church militant until it becomes the Church triumphant.

6. The Revelation of God Through Suffering and Death

It is only through suffering that some men are ever brought to a sense of their need of God, and when we recall that those who already know God are brought to a fuller and deeper knowledge of him oftener perhaps through suffering of one kind and another than through any other agency, we recognise in the discipline of suffering an instrument which divine grace transforms into a beneficent pathway to God. And when suffering has done its worst, when one comes to tread the winepress alone, or when the cup of sorrow is being drunk and drained to its very dregs as one sees a life that he loves better than his own go out in the darkness of death, then one's first thought may be, and indeed often is with the light-minded and light-hearted, "There is no God—there can be no God—or such suffering and sorrow could never be." But, on second thought, more deep-minded and deep-hearted, the suffering soul finds that God in the deeps of sorrow whom he never cared to find on the surface of a self-centred life.

When a man buries his loved one there comes to him not only new and deeper thoughts about a future life and a profounder realisation of the necessity of it in order to satisfy the deepest desires of the soul, but he realises that there can be no future and eternal life unless there be a God—and unless there be suffering and death. And when one approaches death himself, his heart cries out for a living God. No argument for a God is more potent than that which comes from a new-made grave. Then it is that He who alone brings life and immortality to light is welcomed as an abiding guest. It is through death that we learn of deathlessness; and it is only in and through death that we can enter into that life where alone it is possible for God fully to reveal himself to those who bear his image.

7. The Use of Reason in Finding God

Reason arrays all these facts into arguments and transforms them into a faith that hath foundations. It is only as intelligent and rational beings that we can travel along these pathways of thought that spread out before us in our search for God. "Through Reason to God" is a phrase which indicates that a satisfactory knowledge of God may be arrived at through a process of reason; that the world and human life abound in facts and experiences which furnish to the mind of man the arguments which, when logically combined, not only make irresistible the conclusion that there is a God, but prove much as to the essential character of the Divine Being whose existence is thus proved. It is probably true that few if any intelligent human beings have ever lived who did not find themselves at times driven by reason to faith in the existence of a Divine Being—times when the conviction came to them and pressed itself upon them that the denial of a personal Creator and Ruler of the universe is more unreasonable than the assumption of such a Being. All these paths that we are to travel are paths of reason, paths of thought involving rational processes and leading to rational conclusions. We may say, and say truly, that most men come "through the heart to God"—through the feelings, through love, through a longing for companionship with the Infinite, and All-loving—and this may seem to be an approach to God through a pathway quite different from that of reason; but the moment we think about it and construct it into an argument, it becomes a rational process and takes its place in theology and philosophy.

With this general survey of the paths that we are to travel we pause to consider more definitely, before entering upon our pilgrimage along these great highways of truth, who it is that we are seeking to find and to know. There are gods many and lords many. Surely there is some One among them all, if we can only find him, in whom dwelleth all the fulness of the Godhead bodily. To know him aright will secure personal and spiritual fellowship with him in a life that is eternal. We inquire, therefore, concerning God—Who is he? What is he? Where is he?

Edgar Sheffield Brightman

Edgar Sheffield Brightman (1884–1953) was born in Holbrook, Massachusetts. He attended Brown and Boston Universities and then taught at Nebraska Wesleyan University and at Boston University as the Borden Parker Bowne Professor of Philosophy. He developed the historical and contemporary connections of Bowne's philosophy, especially in his own concentration on the metaphysical statement of personality. Brightman was the most eminent philosophical theologian in the Boston Personalist school after Bowne. He wrote on a full range of issues in philosophy of religion but was especially influential for his discussion of the problem of evil and his idea of God as limited. Among his more important books are *An Introduction to Philosophy* (1925) and *Finding of God* (1932). He also wrote on biblical topics and the spiritual life. Brightman built his philosophy upon the basis of experience and intended to construct an empirically defined philosophy. His position is acknowledgedly Christian in perspective, and his effort to explore the nature and power of God was germane to his total work. Religious experience, he argues, leads to an understanding of God as finite, as a Person limited by givens that contain principles of delay and suffering. These dimensions of his thought are discussed in the selection which follows: "The Resultant Idea of God" is taken from *The Problem of God* (New York: Cokesbury, 1930), pp. 107-38.

The Resultant Idea of God

We have found that the tendency of history, accentuated by many aspects of modern thought, is toward a broadening and enlargement of the idea of God. We have seen that the broadening in one direction usually also involves a narrowing in another. This, in many instances, is a logically necessary result. On the other hand, the broadening involves a loss in meaning. There is some danger that our ideas may become so broad as to be meaningless. Thus we seem to move back and forth between an expanded and a contracted idea of God without finding a resting place.

A cynically minded conservative might be tempted to comment that, if for every plus that is added to our conception of God a corresponding minus must be subtracted, we always have the same quantity on our hands with which we started, and we therefore retain the traditional idea of God unchanged. But such a view is hopelessly wooden. Surely none of our ideas can escape change as the race advances. Even the simplest and most certain facts, the observations made by sense or the elementary processes of arithmetic, come to acquire a new meaning when seen in the light of the advancing interpretations of science. Red always looks red to the normal eye; but it conveys vastly different meanings to the railroad man, the socialist, and the physicist. Eight plus eight will always be sixteen in the sphere of arithmetical integers; but the moral law and the beauty of holiness can never be understood by a mere process of counting. Thus our thought must always move on to a fuller and more complete understanding and even to a transformation of the meaning of the most commonplace and apparently obvious facts of life. Otherwise we become dogmatists, life stagnates, self-content renders further growth impossible. In every field stagnation and smug self-satisfaction are deadly, but nowhere more so than in the field of religion. When religion reaches the stage where it says to itself, "I now know all that I need to know. I am perfectly right, and I expect no further light either from man or from God," then religion needs no foes from among the ranks of skeptics or atheists to attack it; it has already poisoned itself from within. Dogmatic self-complacency is the suicide of religion.

It is one of the anomalies of history that anyone who has believed in God could have been satisfied that his belief was in need of no essential improvement or revision. Since the idea of God is the idea of a being supremely good and just, it would naturally follow that such a being would not leave the human race without any clew to his purposes.

162

Hence many have supposed that there has been revealed in Scripture a complete and adequate idea of God. Yet this seems to be a radically mistaken view. God is, indeed, revealed in his world, in human experience everywhere, in the life of all genuine religions, and especially in the development of Judaism and Christianity. But there are two contrasting views of how a God might reveal himself. Revelation, whatever form it takes, may be regarded as a stopping place for thought and life, a point of rest; or it may be regarded as a stimulus to further thought and life, a starting point of motion. On the former view, revelation is dogmatic; it imparts fixed and unchangeable truths. On the latter view, it is teleological or functional; it serves the purpose of leading men to move nearer the real God, and this may be accomplished even when the ideas believed to be true are not wholly correct. If we accept the second view, the most devout Christian believer will be as open-minded as the experimental scientist, and far more so than the dogmatic skeptic. He will not only welcome investigation, being aware that fear of investigation is a mark of the guilty rather than of the innocent, but he will also be among the first to perceive that no understanding of God which we have yet attained can come anywhere near to exhausting the whole truth about the divine nature. From every point of view, then, we must acknowledge both the need and the possibility of learning more about God, if there is any God at all. . . .

Sooner or later everyone who cares about honest dealings in religion comes to the point where he must state plainly his conception of God. If there is no other value in his statement, it will at least enable others to avoid his errors; and if there is any real truth in his idea, they may profit by it. It is in this spirit that I shall now formulate a definition of God in which I have come to believe as a result of my investigations. I shall state it at first, in a rather detailed way, as follows:

> God is a conscious Person of perfect good will. He is the source of all value and so is worthy of worship and devotion. He is the creator of all other persons and gives them the power of free choice. Therefore his purpose controls the outcome of the universe. His purpose and his nature must be inferred from the way in which experience reveals them, namely, as being gradually attained through effort, difficulty, and suffering. Hence there is in God's very nature something which makes the effort and pain of life necessary. There is within him, in addition to his reason and his active creative will, a passive element which enters into every one of his conscious states, as sensation, instinct, and impulse enter into ours, and constitutes a problem for him. This element we call The Given. The evils of life and the delays in the attainment of value, in so far as they come

163

from God and not from human freedom, are thus due to his nature, yet not wholly to his deliberate choice. His will and reason acting on The Given produce the world and achieve value in it.

This definition may be put more concisely in the following terms:

God is a Person supremely conscious, supremely valuable, and supremely creative, yet limited both by the free choices of other persons and by restrictions within his own nature.

This definition makes God much more limited than does traditional theism, yet much less limited than does any form of dualism which contrasts God with matter or with any being in the universe which originated independently of God. Let us now consider this definition in its background and development. . . .

One who asserts that God is a spiritual personality and who is conscious of the limitations of human reason is likely to be impressed by the counter assertion that God is suprapersonal. To say that God is personal sounds much like saying that God is human. Yet this is not intended. Of course the being that originates and controls the universe is far above the human plane, and must have powers and properties of which we know nothing. Yet, if we are not to talk nonsense, we must not ascribe to God any attributes which contradict the best we know. It is highly probable that the good, the true, and the beautiful for God are so far beyond the best truth and goodness and beauty of our experience that we may well be said to be playing on the shores of an infinite ocean of goodness, truth, and beauty. Nevertheless, if God is God, his truth cannot contradict any real truth we possess; likewise his goodness and beauty cannot contradict experienced truth and beauty. Hence, if we wish to call God suprapersonal, there is no objection to doing it, provided by suprapersonal we mean only superhuman. Who can deny that God's experiences transcend man's? But if we mean, as some do mean, to deny that God is a conscious spirit, then we are moving off into the dark. To deny that God is conscious is to assign to him a state of unconsciousness; it is to deny that he can love or know or will or purpose, for all of these are conscious processes. If there is a God at all, a being worthy of our worship, he must be conscious. A blind force might be feared, but could not be worshiped; an unconscious spirit might be pitied, but could not be adored. To be a God is to be conscious. To try to improve on consciousness is to go beyond the evidence of experience and the powers of imagination. If we seek for something which is not consciousness, we find only the unconscious. An unconscious being is not a being more than human; it is far less than human. In this sense, the suprapersonal turns into the subpersonal. But there remains the truth in the idea of the suprapersonal that there is always more to learn about God. Yet as soon as we grant the possibility that more may turn out to be utterly irrational, so soon we have taken away the ground of all rational thought whatever.

We have been discussing the first trait of God in the concise definition given above, namely, that he is supremely conscious. Now let us turn to the second, namely, that he is supremely valuable. The goodness of God is his most essential attribute. We could feel much more religious in the presence of an impersonal and unconscious power that was making for goodness in the world than we could in the presence of a conscious person who was evil or indifferent to values. While this is abstractly true, it does not render the idea of an impersonal or unconscious God any more reasonable. Moreover, goodness and all other values are meaningless except as conscious experiences. If the universe has any value beyond man's enjoyment of value, it is because there is a cosmic consciousness that realizes that value. Goodness that is nobody's goodness is no goodness at all. A reason that is unconscious and impersonal is not reason until a mind understands it. Beauty which is no one's enjoyment is only a possibility of beauty, but not real beauty. Value does not belong to impersonal things; it dwells only in minds.

Religion has always been concerned with value. It has faced the evils of life with the confidence that there is a good power behind them, just as science has faced the unsolved problems of experience with the confidence that they have a cause. As Hoffding says, religion rests on the axiom of the conservation of value as science has rested on the axiom of the conservation of energy. The critics of religion have always made much of the facts of evil; but no more than has religion itself. Sin and suffering have been the central problem of most great religions. On the other hand, critics of religion have evaded the problem of good. By the problem of good I mean the explanation of how there comes to be any good at all in the universe. Evil is a problem only because there is some good which we are not now attaining and which the evil prevents our attaining. "Where did all this evil come from?" asks the doubter. "Where did all this good come from?" asks the believer. We need, it is true, a conception of God which will account for both good and evil in the world. However, almost any conception of God has the advantage over atheism of at least attempting a fundamental explanation of both good and evil; whereas atheism assumes that the whole range of value experience arises in man from a source that neither knows nor cares anything about value. In the next chapter we shall consider value experience as evidence for God. But whether this God of ours exists or not, the only reasonable way to conceive him, even as a possibility, is as supreme value.

This conception of God means that we think of him as the one who can bring good out of evil. If he is supreme value, he cannot allow any evil that will permanently frustrate his purpose. He may delay, but he cannot fail. Whatever the origin of evil may be, and however awful it may be, God is the one who is never baffled by any evil. It may be that many goods are possible only through a co-operation of God's will and man's will, and it may be that man may fail to co-operate. Yet, in any given situation, we may suppose, God can achieve certain goods through man's co-operation; if man does not co-operate, then different goods will have to be achieved by God in a different way. But no situation is finally evil. Beyond every obstacle there lies a possible achievement, out of every evil a possible good may grow. This is the meaning of faith in God.

The third point in our definition of God was that God is supremely creative. To speak of creativity is to mention God's most mysterious attribute. Yet this particular mystery is no product of religious thought; somehow, in some way, some power has originated the energy of the universe and has brought the worlds into being. The mystery of creation is inherent in the nature of things, and, strangely enough, this particular attribute of God is one that is most easily and most widely believed. Yet if anything were to justify us in regarding God as suprapersonal, it is his creative power. For God to create means for him to bring into being by an act of will. Human wills cannot create; they can only select from that which has already been created or combine factors in such a manner that powers beyond their control will create something new. Pure creation is indeed superhuman and mysterious. But mysterious as is the thought of creation, it is far less so than those theories which would account for the origin of all things apart from purpose and will and would try to explain all of the actual facts of purpose and will in the world as products of unconscious and impersonal forces. There must be some source of the vast cosmic energies: To regard that source as a will is to make creation less miraculous than to regard it as a mindless source of mind or an unconscious source of consciousness.

To call God creative involves several points. It means that the entire universe is dependent on his will for its existence. The idea that creation occurred at some one point in time, long ago, is untenable in the light of the expansion of the idea of God. The constant conservation of the energy of the universe points to a will that is eternally creating. Hence, creation implies the immanence of God in all things. In particular, it means that the law of evolution is God's method of creation. It is coming to be generally recognized that evolution is not merely a recombination of pre-existing elements, but is the scene of the arrival of new qualities which could not possibly be explained merely as forms of what had been there before. Consciousness, for example, when it arises in the course of evolution, is plainly no combination of atoms, no matter how subtle or complex the atoms are. It is a genuine novelty. Similarly, evolution could not progress at all unless novel variations were to occur which are fit to survive. Thus evolution reveals with especial vividness the creative activity of God, and, by its teaching of the relatedness of all life, adds much to the force of the argument for one divine creator. Furthermore, God is creative in a special sense when he produces other persons. There seems to be no reason for regarding physical nature as anything other than the conscious will of God in action. There is no ground, or very little ground, to suppose that physical nature has any inner life of its own apart from the God who controls it. The case is different with persons. We know by experience that a person has an inner life, or, rather, is an inner life; and we have seen in connection with our study of pantheism how unreasonable it is to suppose that any imperfect or incomplete person is literally a part of God. Therefore, when God creates persons, he wills that there shall be consciousness in the world other than his own; that there shall be wills which are self-determining; and so, in this supreme act of his creative power, he limits his control over the universe. Thus we have found that a supreme act of divine expansion produces a supreme contraction.

We have now reached the fourth and last of the elements in the definition, namely, that God is limited both by the free choices of other persons and by restrictions due to The Given within his own nature. That he is limited by the free choices of other persons is generally conceded by all who believe in God, in accordance with the point of view which we have just expressed. If we find God a problem, it is not impossible that he also finds us a problem. Supreme reason may find the strange uses we make of our freedom far less intelligible than human reason finds God. Yet the limitation due to human freedom is, in the last analysis, founded in the will of God, and so is not to be regarded as a serious threat to the traditional attribute of omnipotence.

167

The new part of my definition is the suggestion that there are real limitations within the divine nature. The idea seems at first abhorrent. But, as we have said before, the evidence for God lies in experience, and we must think God, if we are to think truly, in such manner as to make experience intelligible. At this point we have to consider the mass of evidence which pointed toward what we have called the contraction of God. On the one side is God, the glorious and expanded one, supreme in goodness and power; on the other, the facts of evil in the world. It may be that we can ascribe all sin to human wills; but we certainly cannot impute to man the blame for the slow and painful processes of life, or for the presence of earthquakes, cyclones, and disease germs in the world. It is difficult for the mind to refrain from two judgments on nature: that it is the work of a power which aims at ends and achieves them, and also that this power is working under great difficulties. Indeed, so great are the difficulties that some observers can see nothing but them. H. M. Kallen says that "a surd lurks under every law of nature, a flaw in every design of God," and General Smuts speaks of "the dark opaque character" of the universe—ethically and rationally. But our view frankly sees these dark factors as elements within the life of a good God.

Four main types of evidence have contributed to my conviction that God is limited. They are based respectively on the facts of evolution, the nature of consciousness, the principle of dialectic, and religious experience. Let us consider these separately.

In the long sweep of evolution, Mother Nature (a name we use when we wish to avoid saying God) seems to display prodigality and wastefulness. Many species die an untimely death, entire species perish and are known only through their fossil remains, many forms of life are seemingly trivial, and others, such as disease germs and parasites, are destructive and exclusively' harmful. In the light of these facts, it is impossible for me to say honestly that I can regard all this as the deliberate purpose of an all-powerful and good God. On the other hand, the law and the progress evident in evolution, the adaptations of life to environment and of environment to life, the origination of higher and higher forms, all make it evident that evolution is purposive. Putting these two aspects together, we are led to say that nature is the work of a power that is achieving its ends in the face of what seems to be opposition. There is evidence of design in nature; there is also evidence of frustration of design and of delay in its achievement.

There are at least three possible explanations of this situation, if we are to assume a God at all: first, that this element of opposition is a product of the creative will of God, chosen as the best means of attaining his ends (this is the view of traditional theism); secondly, that this element is something external to God (this is the view of Manicheism, Zoroastrianism, and some forms of modern dualism); and, thirdly, that it is due to factors within God himself, which are eternal aspects of his nature, but not products of his will or choice. The last-named view is the one which I have become convinced is nearest to the truth, and I shall undertake to show why I regard it as the best attainable idea of God at the present stage of thought. It holds that God is eternal reason and eternal will, dealing with what I have called The Given in his eternal experience. God's will is the creative aspect of the universe, but that will is limited by the laws of eternal reason and by the facts of The Eternally Given. That there is an eternal reason must be evident to anyone who has studied elementary mathematics or logic; Plato knew that God geometrizes. That there is eternal will follows from the purposive ongoing of things. That there is an eternal Given element in divine experience which is not a product of divine will is evident from the difficulties under which the divine will evidently labors in expressing perfection in the world. . . .

Another consideration growing out of evolution points to the idea of a finite God. Evolution plainly means that time and change are of fundamental importance in the universe. Now the traditional faith has laid great stress on the immutability of God, his absolute eternal unchangeability. Doubtless the universe must be guided by certain unchanging laws; but our whole experience is that of a world changing and evolving in time. Religion has sung of the day when "the trumpet of the Lord shall sound and time shall be no more"; but if there is such a day, thought cannot avoid asking about the day after that. In short, any view of God which elevates him entirely above time and process and renders him an eternal *nunc stans*—a standing present—pays tribute to his excellence without relating his being to the actual facts. The only God worth believing in, however, in the light of the evidence, is a God in living relation to the facts of cosmic and human history. He is a God into whose very being time enters; we need a temporalistic rather than a purely eternalistic view of God. God is one who works; one to whom the passage of time means something; to whom the events of a progressive creative evolution are significant; for whom change is profoundly important—such changes as occur in human character, as well as those more sublime changes in his revelation of himself to man in the course

169

of history. Indeed, taking evolution in the largest sense, it may be that the development of the entire physical universe as we know it is but an insignificant episode in the eternally active history of God. For to call God temporal is not to deny that he is eternal; it is only to deny he is timeless, or that he is not intimately related to and concerned with events in time. . . . Thus our finite God is not one of a finished perfection; his perfection and the perfection of his world consist in their perfectibility. This does not mean that God is ever ignorant or evil in his will; he always knows all that can be known and his will is always guided by perfect devotion to the ideal of love. Yet it does mean that he confronts within his own experience genuine difficulties, out of which arise the apparent defects of the physical world. On this view, God does not deliberately choose the cruelties of evolution and the sufferings of creation; they represent, rather, the necessary, outcome of his own eternal Given nature, out of which he is always bringing a higher good.

Evolution, the first type of evidence for the belief in a finite God, has been discussed. The second type, as we stated, is based on the nature of consciousness. Assuming, again, that there is a personal God, I wish to show from the nature of consciousness that he must be finite. It is true that some have used similar considerations to disprove God's existence, or at least his personality. I use them to disprove the conception of a God so infinite that he cannot be personal. We shall reflect on human freedom and its relation to the divine foreknowledge, on the relation between will and "nature," and on the presence of active and passive factors in consciousness.

First, then, let us examine the bearing of human freedom on our conception of God. That every human consciousness is largely determined by factors beyond its control is manifest. The past and the environment exercise an unescapable influence on us. One who holds to freedom does not deny these facts or belittle them. Freedom, indeed, can be rationally defined only by reference to them, for it consists in the choice or selection of elements from a total field of experience which is determined by a power beyond our control. The effects of our choice are beyond our direct control too, in a sense, although not beyond our powers of prediction and indirect control. If this is the nature of human freedom, it is not impossible that there is something analogous in the divine freedom, although only remotely so. With all the creative power of God there may be something Given in his nature as subject matter for his choice. I offer this particular argument very diffidently. More confidently I express the view that if man is truly free, God must be finite as regards his knowledge. At least, if our temporalistic view of God be true, and God is not utterly above and beyond all time, he cannot be thought of as knowing in advance what a free person will choose. This we have discussed already in another context. Man's freedom is an actual limitation on the foreknowledge of God. A thinker no less than John Locke said: "I cannot make freedom in man consistent with omnipotence and omniscience in God, though I am as fully persuaded of both as of any truths I most firmly assent to." We have here the calamitous consequences of the influence of a one-sided devotion to the expansion of God. Even when the expansive ideas lead to contradiction, they are held to tenaciously. Why not be consistent and acknowledge that God is limited in his foreknowledge? His power and wisdom would still be amply sufficient to bring good out of any situation that could arise.

Next, in our examination of consciousness, we note that there is an inseparable relation between the will and the nature of any conscious being. Every conscious being, or every being of any sort whatever, must have a nature; that is, it must have a definite structure, definite properties and qualities. In the nature of a conscious being it is possible for it to make choices; this fact we call its will. But its will is not a separate faculty or power; it is, rather, the act of a whole self possessing a specific nature. Traditionally God has been thought of as self-caused—(*causa sui*) and as pure actuality (*actus purus*)—a being completely self-determined with no potentiality for further development. These abstractions, an inheritance from the great Aristotle, have been entirely on the side of expansion and have blinded the eyes of theists to the empirical difficulties of the view. If God be regarded as a wholly self-caused will, we are brought into serious difficulties. Can God choose whether his nature shall be in time or not? Can he choose whether the laws of reason shall be true or not? The old questions haunt us: Can he make a round triangle, a two which multiplied by two will produce six, a time prior to his own existence? Manifestly not! Rather his eternal nature includes reason, never-ending activity in time, and the rich realm of The Given with which his will has to cope in the task of world building and development. His nature as a conscious being sets limits to his will; God must be finite. . . .

The third main argument for the finiteness of God may be stated briefly, although it may be taken as a surprising twist of thought. Hegel is the one thinker of all in the history of philosophy who would be most radically opposed to the finiteness of God. He believes that God is the infinite and absolute. Yet he developed an important principle of

171

thought which plays right into the hands of our conception, namely, the principle of dialectic. Stated simply, this means that all reality is full of opposition and contrast; everything that is stands in contrast with something else; every thesis implies some sort of antithesis. This means that the nature of God is to contain opposition and tension. But every opposition leads on to a higher level of life; every struggle points to a higher meaning or synthesis. Thus, for Hegel, as for our view, the divine life consists essentially of struggle and victory over opposition, a victory for which a price has always to be paid even by God himself. The traditional view almost inevitably engenders the idea that God's task is an easy one; that he stands apart from the struggle in spotless white. Our view sees him as the greatest sufferer in the universe and through this the greatest victor; his nature is not merely goodness but also dialectic struggle, or, rather, his goodness is not merely an abstract quality but the constant victory of constant effort.

The fourth main argument is derived from religious experience. Religious life demands that full weight be given to the contraction of God. Sometimes this demand is crude; God is thought of as having a human form, as being capricious and lawless, as feeling angry or as being opposed by devils and powers of darkness. But these beliefs are not the heart of religion; they are its excrescences. Some hold, indeed, that any finite God is of no worth. This is the view of McTaggart, who knew very little about religion, save as a body of beliefs; it is also the view of Hocking, who is one of the most sympathetic interpreters of religion in modern philosophy. Yet the testimony of most religious experience points to something like the finiteness we assert. It worships a God who is, on the one hand, reasonable and good, and, on the other, mysterious and above our comprehension. His ways are not our ways. He is one to whom the believer prays knowing that he will be heard justly and reasonably; yet he is also one who has hidden counsels which lead him often to answer in the negative. It seems to be the voice of religion that there is something above and beyond reason in the reasonable God. This is a hard saying, against which I have often rebelled. Yet I wonder whether it is not an intuitive recognition of the depths of the eternal divine experience, which our view has led us to recognize as Something Given, which his reason and will do not create, but with which they have to deal. Jakob Boehme speaks of a "bitter torment," a "fire of anger" within God; Rudolph Otto describes the irrational element in the divine nature as "the numinous." This dark aspect of religion points to a tragic reality in God. God is not simply a happy, loving Father; he is the struggle and the mysterious pain at the heart of life. He is indeed love; but a suffering love that redeems through a Cross.

It might seem that the resultant idea, as we have been describing it, surrenders too much of the expansion of God to his contraction. But this is not the case. Rather, we accept the expansion in so far as it refers to the divine goodness and the range of his experience, and assign the contraction to the divine power. The advance of modern thought has compelled us to modify our faith either in God's character or in his omnipotence. We believe that it is far more reasonable to deny the absolute omnipotence of the power manifesting itself in the world than to deny its goodness. On our view, God is perfect in will, but not in achievement; perfect in power to derive good from all situations, but not in power to determine in detail what those situations will be. It is not a question of the kind of God we should like to have. It is a question of the kind of God required by the facts.

Georgia Harkness

Georgia Harkness (1891–1974), a native of New York State, was educated at Cornell and Boston Universities. After teaching at Elmira and Mount Holyoke colleges, she taught at Garrett Biblical Institute and at the Pacific School of Religion for twenty-two years. Harkness was the first woman to become a major professional theologian in the United States in the twentieth century. She wrote some thirty-six books along with numerous articles, pamphlets, and occasional pieces. In both her personal life and social concern she impressively exemplified basic qualities of Christian character. Harkness' theology worked out themes derived from Boston personalism such as the Fatherhood of God, the Bible as witness to Christian experience, Jesus as Lord and example for Christian living, and the Holy Spirit as the sustaining presence of God. Among her most important publications are *Conflicts in Religious Thought* (1929, 1949), *Christian Ethics* (1957), *Foundations of Christian Knowledge* (1955), *Understanding the Christian Faith* (1947), and *Grace Abounding* (1969). "The Work of the Holy Spirit" excerpt continues the traditional Wesleyan emphasis on the role of the Holy Spirit in personal and corporate life. It is taken from *The Fellowship of the Holy Spirit* (Nashville/New York: Abingdon Press, 1966), pp. 82-99.

The Work of the Holy Spirit

In the preceding chapters, and particularly in the three devoted to a biblical survey, we have had occasion repeatedly to note the effects of

174

the Spirit in human life. There has been no systematic discussion of these effects, but it is impossible to consider properly what the Holy Spirit is without recognition of what the Spirit *does*. This is inevitable, for the Holy Spirit is no inert entity or metaphysical essence, but the living God himself as he imparts grace and power to the human spirit.

In the chapter which follows this one, we shall move into a difficult, but from a Christian standpoint an unavoidable, question, the doctrine of the Trinity. There we shall discover that the Trinity makes sense if it is grounded in Christian experience. If it is not, the problems multiply until irrationality breeds despair.

The present chapter, standing midway between the biblical survey and the theological issue soon to be examined, has a dual purpose. It aims to lay further groundwork for the declaration that the Trinity makes sense if it is rooted in Christian experience. Further than that, it aims to suggest from a biblical base how the works of the Spirit, manifold but discernible as certain continuing types, are vitally relevant to life at all times. Far from being simply an historical legacy from long ago, the Holy Spirit is still "God present and God acting."

Where shall we begin? As we saw in noting Paul's contributions, he recognized that the work of the Holy Spirit relates to the whole of life. The whole of life is many-sided, and thus every angle is related to every other. Yet there can be no system without a beginning somewhere, and this involves a selection of categories and their arrangement in a sequence.

The rubrics I shall adopt are historical and biblical, but they are also contemporary in meaning if not in terminology. Let us, then, think of the work of the Holy Spirit as the Life-giver, as Source of power, as Sanctifier, and as Revealer of truth.

In the Nicene Creed, repeated times without number in services of Christian worship since the end of the fourth century of our era, stand the words, "I believe in the Holy Ghost, the Lord, the giver of life." That the Holy Spirit is the Lord, even though not the only manifestation of the Lord, is clearly evident in the New Testament and especially in the words of both Paul and John. But what does it mean to say that he is also the giver of life?

To retrace some ground, though from a new perspective, even before the Old Testament and its people and times emerged, there was a belief in spirit as the giver of everything important. Whether as many spirits in animism, as *mana* in a semi-pantheistic monism, or personalized in some such fashion as in Longfellow's

175

> Gitche Manito, the mighty,
> The Great Spirit, the creator,

both nature and human life were more than themselves, and owed their existence to a Power beyond themselves. This mysterious Power—this "something more"—was spirit, not material substance, and Spirit was the life-giver.

This primitive faith was, of course, transcended in both Hebrew and Christian thought. It must be affirmed beyond possible misunderstanding that origins do not determine or define the subsequent stages of development. A higher stage was reached when in the words of the Jahwist writer (the "J" narrative of creation) we find in Genesis 2:7, "Then the Lord God formed man of dust from the ground, and breathed into his nostrils the breath of life; and man became a living being." Still later the author of the priestly, post-exilic story of creation suggests that the Spirit of God not only gives life to man but order to nature, "The earth was without form and void, and darkness was upon the face of the deep; and the Spirit of God was moving over the face of the waters" (Gen. 1:2).

It would not be profitable to restate here all that was said in chapter two about the work of the Spirit as it is found in the Old Testament. However, Ezekiel's vision of the revivification in the valley of dry bones is especially pertinent. Israel was alive biologically; it was almost dead spiritually. . . .

Not until the coming of Christ did this vision find fulfillment. Then it was not the nation, but individuals, that "came alive" with a great new faith and hope. This occurred again and again as Jesus brought healing, cleansing, and renewal of life to those whose lives he touched. We have seen that this was a major note in the coming of the Holy Spirit at Pentecost. Such new life in the Spirit is evidenced in the courage to witness to the faith and to spread the gospel to ever-widening areas that shines through the pages of the book of Acts and Paul's letters. For Paul such new life in the Spirit begins, continues, and ends in the living Christ, and his major message is its availability through God's grace to any who will claim it in penitence, faith, and love. . . .

Thus far, we have thought of the Holy Spirit as life-giver to the individual. This, indeed, is what the Bible for the most part does. Yet the work of the Spirit is by no means limited to solitary selves, or even to persons in their immediate, face-to-face relations.

The Church came into being through the life-giving work of the Holy

Spirit. That is what Pentecost is all about. Probably not all of the initial 120 Christians in that company, and certainly not all of the ensuing 3000, knew each other by face and name. Yet all were quickened to new life both individually and in their corporate relations, and the Church was born.

So it has remained to the present insofar as the Church has been Christ-centered, life-renewing in its service, and renewed in its own life as changes have taken place from age to age. There have been arid stretches, and as institutions took shape and form tended to replace spirit, the glow of Pentecost faded. Administrators replaced prophets, and the sacraments became functional elements in ecclesiastical control. Yet never wholly, and the institutions and sacraments may themselves be regarded as the vehicle of the Holy Spirit to the extent that they are genuine channels of grace. Without them the Church, if it continued to exist, would be much weakened in its endeavors for the glory of God and the service of the world. . . .

Some would stop at this point, and regard the life-giving work of the Holy Spirit as limited to the Christian experience of the individual believer and the corporate fellowship of the Church. Here we must be careful in our use of terms. We have seen that the Holy Spirit, as two words with one meaning, is found only in the New Testament, and as a designation for the living Christ still present in the lives of his followers, it is limited to a Christian context. Nevertheless, the Holy Spirit is the Spirit of God, and the divine Creator Spirit is not thus limited. The "living God who made the heaven and the earth and the sea and all that is in them . . . did not leave himself without witness" (Acts 14:15-17) among any people.

From this far-reaching fact it is legitimate to infer that the Spirit of God is present in the spiritual strivings, insights, and achievements of people who seek him through other paths than the Christian. Furthermore, he is present in the life-giving forces of nature. The passage just quoted continues with evidence of this, "For he did good and gave you from heaven rains and fruitful seasons, satisfying your hearts with food and gladness" (vs. 17). Need we hesitate to say that the Spirit is present and active in man's utilization of these gifts for human good? If we may, then the life-giving eternal Spirit is present also in man's eternal quest for goodness, truth, and beauty; for government "with liberty and justice for all"; for spiritual foundations in other high religions. This is not to say that any of these channels of the Spirit can be a substitute for the Christian way; it is to say that "God is greater than our hearts"

177

(I John 3:20), and it is unbecoming for us to fence in the life-giving work of his Spirit.

An ancient prayer, spoken in services of worship for many centuries and still in use in the more liturgical churches, is *"Veni, Creator Spiritus!"* *"Come, Creator Spirit!"* This may well be our prayer today.

If there is one thing that all persons may be said to possess, it is a desire for power. Even the ever-present fact of human sin is not more pervasive, for it is in the longing for or the exercise of power to be, to do, or to have what one wants, regardless of obligation to God or man, that the sinning lies.

There are, of course, many kinds of power. As power to survive, the instinctual urge to self-preservation is shared with man by the animal world, and to this is linked in varying degrees the power to possess and to dominate. It characterizes nations, races, economic, cultural, and even ecclesiastical groups as well as individuals. No society could exist without it, yet from this fact stem some of the greatest perversions of justice. Obviously, the Holy Spirit may not be regarded as the source of the manifold perversions of power which are visible to anyone who reads his newspaper or listens to the radio or television.

It is power of a different sort, centering in self-mastery, concern for others, and obedience to the divine will that the Holy Spirit imparts. It is epitomized in the power of love and the reconciliation of man to God and to one another through love. Yet the power of the Spirit is no vague emotion dignified with the name of love; it is a dynamic, energizing force.

To glance again at the biblical sources, wherever the Spirit of God appears in the Old Testament there is an imparting of power, whether of physical strength to Samson, ecstatic utterance to the early bands of prophets, inspiration to the great prophets, or revivification to Israel. In the Gospels the Holy Spirit is to come upon Mary by the power of the Most High (Luke 1:35); Jesus returns from the wilderness temptation in the power of the Spirit (Luke 4:14); he undertakes his life's mission in the conviction that the Spirit of the Lord is upon him (vs. 18). Nowhere in the Gospels is the relation between the Holy Spirit and the earthly ministry of Jesus more clearly stated than in Peter's words to Cornelius in the tenth chapter of Acts, "You know . . . how God anointed Jesus of Nazareth with the Holy Spirit and with power; how he went about doing good and healing all that were oppressed by the devil, for God was with him" (Acts 10:36-38).

It is, of course, in the book of Acts and in the letters that one sees the tremendous increments of power that came into the lives of ordinary persons when they were Spirit-filled and Spirit-led. It is significant that in the post-resurrection promise of the coming of the Holy Spirit as this is recorded in Acts, power is the one specific gift mentioned (Acts 1:8). This gift was bountifully imparted and gloriously used. The records of courage under difficulty, forthright and inspired witness in speech, and fidelity in Christian living under tremendous odds ought never to leave us unmoved. Further healings of the infirmities of the body are recorded, but most of all, the healing power of the Spirit. Like a cleansing wind—to revert to the original meaning of the term—the Holy Spirit blows away the mists and impurities of the human spirit to give new life and new power. . . .

It was this emancipation of spirit that Paul found in Christ through the Holy Spirit. Thereafter he did not feel himself a slave to other men or to old traditions, but to Christ alone. Obligations there still were, more binding than before, but they were obligations accepted with a new zest. They could be accepted seriously but joyously, by men who found themselves no longer slaves to legalism or to passion but sons of God. . . .

Familiar as we are today with the disorders that send people to psychiatrists and mental hospitals, with family quarrels terminating in broken homes, with bitter strife between racial, economic, and national groups, who can say that such counsel is irrelevant to the times? If such freedom is possible through ordered and disciplined living in the power of the Spirit, we had better find it!

Sanctification with its correlative term "holiness," as applied to Christian experience, is in bad odor today. Those of an older generation (and possibly not so old) who have heard those of the "holiness" sects talk about their "entire sanctification," claiming a self-righteous superiority in the victory over sin which others fail to see manifest in their living, will have no truck with either term. Recent theology with its stress on the holiness of God but the sinfulness and unworthiness of man moves in the same direction. If we add to "sanctification" and "holiness" a third term, "Christian perfection," the rout is apt to be complete.

With the rejection of what these terms are commonly taken to mean, I have great sympathy. However sincere the belief that one has reached the point of no return in his sinning, sin remains, and the Christian must fight an ongoing battle with it. To repent, to ask forgiveness of God and usually of the human person sinned against, and to go forward humbly by God's grace, is the continuing experience of the Christian.

Yet in a deeper sense, the Holy Spirit remains the Sanctifier that the Christian tradition has long conceived him to be. The Latin "sanctus" is the English "holy," and the Holy Spirit does impart what John Wesley called "scriptural holiness." God's design in raising up the people called Methodists, he said, was not to form a new sect but "to reform the nation, particularly the Church, and to spread scriptural holiness over the land." It need hardly be said that this task is not the exclusive prerogative of Methodists.

Such scriptural holiness with the Christian perfection which is its goal would arouse less confusion and dissent if it were understood to mean growth in Christian experience and in moral victory through Christ. It means, in short, "growing in grace," and there is no finer statement of its meaning than in the injunction found in II Peter 3:18, "But grow in the grace and knowledge of our Lord and Savior Jesus Christ. To him be the glory both now and to the day of eternity." The New English Bible further accents Christian maturity by suggesting an alternative reading, "But grow up, by the grace of our Lord and Savior Jesus Christ, and by knowing him."

John Wesley may have had more confidence in the possibility of Christian perfection, or of being "made perfect in love in this life," than do most Christians today. Yet what he was above all concerned about was the actual difference it makes to become a Christian and to continue going forward in the Christian way. And on this point, and on the work of the Holy Spirit in the daily demands of Christian living, the New Testament is completely clear. . . .

Since in traditional terminology a sharp distinction is sometimes drawn between justification and sanctification, a further word at this point may be in order. There is certainly a difference between the initial act of decision for Christ, which may be accompanied by a great emotional glow though it need not be, and the humdrum and difficult processes of daily Christian living. Yet there is no absolute line of demarcation. What the Holy Spirit does in bringing us to Christian commitment, whether suddenly or gradually, is also what the Holy Spirit does in the years of growth to greater Christian maturity. What is different is that "every one to whom much is given, of him will much be required" (Luke 12:48). As the gifts and the requirements increase, so does the sense of the undergirding presence and power of the Holy Spirit. There may be less of an ecstatic glow about it; what matters is that the light still shines and the fire burns.

The New Testament abounds in passages which indicate the difference the Holy Spirit makes in the life of the Christian. Perhaps the greatest, and certainly the most familiar, is "the more excellent way" set forth in I Corinthians 13. Yet for a summary of the gifts and graces imparted by the Spirit, nothing excels Galatians 5:22: "But the fruit of the Spirit is love, joy, peace, patience, kindness, goodness, faithfulness, gentleness, self-control; against such there is no law." Nor, we may add, is there any insuperable barrier to such fruit in those who will let the Spirit have his way within us.

One cannot read the account of the promise of the coming of the Holy Spirit as found in the Last Supper discourse in John's Gospel without discovering the prominence given to the work of the Holy Spirit as the revealer of truth. Yet it is truth projected forward from the revelation already given in Christ. In the words Jesus is quoted as speaking to his disciples the Counselor, the Holy Spirit, will "bring to your remembrance all that I have said to you" (14:26); the Counselor "will bear witness to me" (15:26); the Spirit of truth "will take what is mine and declare it to you" (16:14). It is clear that to the author of this Gospel the Spirit's revelation of truth was to be no independent witness dissociated from the truth already disclosed. Yet it is equally clear that the entire mood of these passages is open-ended and oriented toward the future. This is implied throughout but epitomized in the words, "I have yet many things to say to you, but you cannot bear them now. When the Spirit of truth comes, he will guide you into all the truth" (16:12-13). . . .

The term "inspiration" is often bandied about today, whether in reference to the Bible or to some kind of human experience which may or may not be religious. Without attempting to give an extended analysis of its meaning it may be pointed out that there is a direct connection between the Holy Spirit and a Christian understanding of inspiration. In the field of Christian faith and life, the possibility of new insights depends not only on long and rigorous search but on the illumination of the Spirit. In fact, the word inspiration means "inbreathing"—a cognate term to the original meaning of "spirit." This readily suggests that the breath of God continues to blow upon the human spirit from the supreme and decisive revelation in God's Son. . . .

The possibility of the discovery of new truth and a fresh understanding of the will of God amid changing circumstances is a great boon. Yet it is beset with perils. No communication is given except to and through human minds, and these are always susceptible to sin and error. Ever in the offing is the danger lest human presumption replace divine leading. That this can happen unconsciously even in sincere Christians, and per-

181

haps most often in persons of such inflexible conviction that a sense of dogmatic certainty replaces humble quest, should put us all on guard.

To know when we are hearing the voice of the Holy Spirit, and when we are listening to our own unhallowed subconscious impulses, is not an easy matter. There are indices and channels of discovery in an unbiased and comprehensive survey of the total situation, in corporate worship that is deep and genuine, in interchange of thought with other wise and well-grounded Christians, in prayer and commitment that carries with it a willingness to go where the Spirit leads. Yet there is one safeguard that is indispensable to all others. It is what Paul calls the mind of Christ. Whatever carries forward our understanding of God and of his will as this has been revealed to us in Jesus is the work of the Holy Spirit; all else is suspect.

Part IV
New Times

The middle of the twentieth century was a time of repositioning in Protestant theology. The impact of post–World War I European and North American theology was being sharply felt. Efforts to extend and challenge inherited theological assumptions was expressed by a number of Methodist thinkers.

Edwin Lewis reacted to the anthropology and Christology of liberal theology. Albert C. Outler led an effort to freshly explore and restate John Wesley's thought. Robert E. Cushman reflects the impact of neoorthodox assessments, and Daniel T. Niles carries these new emphases into another culture. With these figures, Methodism was responding to and helping to shape a new time.

Edwin Lewis

Edwin Lewis (1881–1959) was born in England, emigrated to Newfoundland, Canada, and then came to the United States. He was educated in Canada and the United States, completing his work at Drew University in 1918. He joined the faculty of Drew in 1920 and served there until his retirement. Originally an exponent of a liberal Protestant position in theology, he wrote several books of importance: *Jesus and the Human Quest* (1924), *A Manual of Christian Beliefs* (1927), and *God and Ourselves* (1931). He was co-editor of the *Abingdon Bible Commentary* (1929), and it was this work that precipitated a change. In the 1930s he shifted to a more traditional position and in *A Christian Manifesto* (1934) challenged the assumptions of liberalism and stated a case for a new appreciation of biblical authority, the two natures of Jesus Christ, and human sinfulness. Upon this new ground he built his mature theology as expressed in *The Faith We Declare* (1939), *A Philosophy of the Christian Revelation* (1940), and *The Creator and the Adversary* (1948). "A Christian Manifesto" comes from "The Fatal Apostasy of the Modern Church," *Religion in Life* (Autumn 1933), vol. II, no. 4, pp. 483-92.

A Christian Manifesto

Modern theological liberalism undoubtedly rendered the church an important service. It helped to break the strangle-hold of terms and phrases which had become in all too many cases merely empty shibbo-leths. It re-established, after the fashion of the thirteenth century, the rights of the intellect in the evaluation of the things of the spirit. It gar-nered for the use of the church the rich harvest of scholarship in many fields—biblical, historical, sociological, psychological. It served notice to a world too often skeptical that a man could believe in Jesus and at the same time be fully aware of all the amazing kaleidoscopic changes occurring in contemporary life. For such a service we cannot but be grateful. Nevertheless, all is not well with us. Liberalism has not brought us to the Promised Land. We may have gained a battle, but the campaign is still on, and there is more than a suspicion that the gain made at one point involved a serious loss elsewhere. We yielded posi-tions whose strategic significance is becoming more and more manifest. We so stressed the Bible as coming to us in "the words of men" that the sense in which it is also "the word of God" has become increasingly vague. We so freely allowed the influence of contemporary forces in the development of doctrine as to have endangered the continuity of that living core of truth and reality for which contemporary forces were but the *milieu*. We exposed all the delicate nuances of spiritual experience to the cold dispassionate gaze of psychology, until it has become a ques-tion whether psychology of religion is not in danger of destroying the very thing it lives by. And in particular we were so determined to recov-er for the church "the human Jesus" that we lost sight of the fact that the church is the creation of "the divine Christ," or at least of faith in Christ as divine. Have we sown the wind, and is the whirlwind now upon us?

The Gospels and the Church

The *Hibbert Journal* symposium of a generation ago, "Jesus, or Christ?" was a sign of the times. It showed very clearly the results of the "Jesus-study" of the latter part of the nineteenth century. It prophesied an increasing emphasis on "the religion of Jesus," a prophecy which has been abundantly fulfilled. In many quarters of the modern church it is now taken for granted that "the Jesus of the Gospels" is the primary datum for Christianity. This would not be disturbing if Jesus were given his complete significance, but before he can become a datum he must be passed through the alembic of critical investigation. By that time, he has become a hardly recognizable Figure, as Schweitzer himself—notwith-standing his own arbitrary construction—so vigorously contends. But such as he is, he is given to us. We are asked to suppose that one who may have been anything from the energetic "go-getter" of Bruce Barton to "the Man of Genius" in the Middleton Murry sense, is the adequate explanation—plus certain "tendencies" in the time—of the genesis of Christianity and of its historical growth. Let us therefore "return to Jesus." Let us eliminate from Christianity everything not agreeable to the "Portrait" we have had reconstructed for us. Let us be done with the majestic Figure of the Epistles. Let us admit that the Prologue of the Fourth Gospel, and the Kenosis passage in Philippians, and the daring flights of Colossians, and the introduction to Hebrews, represent simply so much mythologizing—understandable enough in the circumstances, but corresponding to nothing in the world of actual reality. Having thus arrived at "the essence of Christianity"—Harnack's familiar grouping, "the Fatherhood of God, the value of the soul, the righteousness of the heart, and the commandment of love"—let us "re-think" the whole Christian enterprise in the appropriate terms. Let us be realistic. Let us frankly change our direction. Let us abandon definitely and forever the whole concept of the supernatural; and as men who will tolerate no illusions, comforting and inspiring though they may be, let us set ourselves anew to the church's unfinished task. Which is—*what?*

But perhaps the case is not so simple as it seems. Say what we will, the stubborn fact remains that the Gospels are themselves the product of a community which already had "seated Christ at the right hand of God," and that, failing that audacious act of their mind and heart, we had had no Gospels at all. If the dangerous expression may be permitted, it was "Christ" who saved "Jesus" to us. That is to say, although Jesus was saved to posterity by "the Christian community," that community organized itself not around the fact that a man named Jesus had lived and taught and wrought and died, but around the belief that in that same Jesus had "dwelt all the fullness of the Godhead bodily." But for that belief, Jesus would have disappeared from human ken, for not one single unimpeachable reference to Jesus of any independent value do we possess from the first century outside of the Christian literature. We may object to the faith of that early community. We cannot but admit, however, that it is to this community that we owe the Synoptic Gospels. They produced for us and saved to us the very documents by which we propose to discredit their dynamic faith! They produced them, used them, loved them, circulated them, at the same time that they were integrating their Lord with the very being of the Godhead, saying of him that he is the Spirit, that he *is* the Ever-living One, that by him the invisible God is apprehended, and nowhere is there the least

186

evidence that they felt any incongruity in doing this. By the Gospels they accounted for their historical origin and justified their claims, but the community preceded the Gospels. There was a Church of the Living Christ before there was any attempt made to collate the traditions respecting Jesus. Apply to the Gospel Portrait all the historicism and psychologism you will: you cannot thereby get rid of that confident faith in a Redeemer-God which is the sole reason why we have the Portrait at all. Take the Synoptic Gospels, discriminate their sources, lay bare their inconsistencies and contradictions, explain away their mighty works, find the Rabbinic parallels of their teachings, "reduce" Jesus to what level you will—and you have not destroyed Christianity thereby, because Christianity was born not of these documents but of contact with the Personality whom the documents attempt to describe. And be it added that although in the order of *time* the contact with him was "in the flesh" first and "in the spirit" second, nevertheless the *fundamental* contact was the second because it was through that that the first came to its full understanding and appreciation. . . .

The Original Christian Message

The Christian "facts" are not to be limited to what fell between Bethlehem and Calvary. What was then said and done was but part of a larger whole—of a movement taking place within the very being of God. Men believed that this was implied in the indubitable historical and experiential facts. They therefore wrought out the idea of "pre-existence" as applied to their Lord, identified him as the permanently active occasion of that life of fellowship in which the church as they knew it was constituted, and from this were led on step by step to formulate finally the doctrine of the Trinity. It is easy enough to complain that this was to transform "the simple Gospel" into a *Weltanschauung,* yet we have no evidence that the so-called simple Gospel was ever preached, even at the beginning, apart from at least some of the elements of this philosophy. Not that unlettered apostles suddenly found themselves possessed of a full-blown philosophy that answered all questions in the world and out of it. But they were making affirmations of such an astounding character as that inevitably before long took to themselves coherence, and the original Christocentric religion became a Christocentric philosophy.

As to this, the New Testament is the evidence, and the New Testament reflects the life and faith of the primitive church. Here we read of a God

187

who had an eternal purpose respecting mankind, a purpose that had to do specifically with delivering men from the power of sin and bringing them to holiness. We read that such a deliverance could not be an arbitrary act upon the part of God, since in all that he does he must be true to the demand of his own holy nature. We read that God himself was so constituted that he could enter in the most intimate and personal way into the stream of human life both to experience all its limitations and struggles and to establish within the stream the principle of its purification, and that the point of this entry was the man Jesus, who would never have existed at all but for the eternal purpose of God. We read that the ensuing intimacy of relationship between the Eternal God and this human life was such that the experience of the man thereupon became the experience of God—which makes it actually true to say that the Infinite knows finitude, that the All-Holy knows moral trial, that the Creator knows creatureliness, that the Deathless knows death. We read that therefore something has "happened to" God which makes his relation to men different from what it would have been had this *not* "happened." And we read that henceforth in speaking of God men may speak of him as One who was in Christ reconciling the world unto himself: therefore the Christian God is God suffused with all the qualities men saw in Jesus, and a God so suffused and transformed is also that divine Christ who is the very source and center of the life of the redeemed.

What then is the object of Christian faith? Not a man who once lived and died, but a Contemporary Reality, a God whose awful holiness is "covered" by one who is both our representative and his, so that it is "our flesh that we see in the Godhead," that "flesh" which was historically Jesus of Nazareth but is eternally the divine Christ whose disclosure and apprehension Jesus lived and died to make possible. I do not deny for a single moment that this overwhelming conception lent itself to all sorts of crudities of expression, impossible analogies, and gross materialisms. But he is blind indeed who cannot see what the New Testament is trying to say. Though language were not adequate to the thought, we can see what the thought aimed to be. It was that thought that created and sustained the church, and the church languishes to-day because it has substituted that thought with one of lesser power as it is of lesser truth.

The Repudiation of Christianity

Many reasons are alleged for the modern turning away from Christianity as thus understood. Not one of these reasons can touch its intrinsic credibility. A philosophical view that precludes it is quite possible. A philosophical view that allows for it is equally possible. Why is the first view so generally accepted? Because Christianity, with the view of things it necessarily calls for, makes such a terrific onslaught upon human pride. We would fain be self-sufficient, and this means that we are not. We would fain be the masters of our fate and the captains of our souls, and this says that our fate is in another's hands and that our souls are not our own but have been bought with a price. We do not like Christianity, not because it is intrinsically incredible but because it is so vastly humiliating. We do not *want* it to be true that "the Son of Man came to give himself a ransom for many," and so we find "critical" reasons for doubting that the words were ever spoken—as though by proving that Jesus did not say them we should prove that they were not true! We do not *want* it to be true that "the Word became flesh and dwelt among us": therefore we get rid of one of the most profound, heart-searching, and revolutionary truths ever uttered—the truth which must always be the touch-stone of any proposed Christology—by the simple device of labeling it "Platonism." We do not *want* it to be true that "through one act of righteousness the free gift came unto all men to justification of life": this being so, we ask by what right Paul "distorted" the simple Gospel of brotherhood and service and good will by introducing into it misleading analogies from temple and law-court.

No; we do not like Christianity. We do not like its cosmic audacity. We do not like its moral pessimism. We do not like the way it smashes the beautiful orderliness of our metaphysical systems. We do not like its uncompromising insistence on the possibility of our being damned souls, whose only hope is in the sovereign grace of God—a God who voluntarily endured self-immolation as the cost of his own graciousness. We be *men*—men whose prerogative it is to stand before God, face him without a tremor, and *demand;* not slaves whose duty it is to kneel before him with covered face, humbly and reverently and gratefully to *accept*. Away with this doctrine of grace! Away with this whole mythology of Incarnation! Away with this outworn notion of Atonement! Make way for emancipated man!

The Plight of the Church

But in this pride lies our shame, our weakness, and our defeat. What has it done for us? What has it done for the church—at least, for evangelical Protestantism? How far have we gotten with our various substitutes? Look over our churches: they are full of people who, brought up on these substitutes, are strangers to those deeper experiences without which there had been no New Testament and no Church of Christ. Thousands of clergymen will go into their pulpits next Sunday morning, but not as prophets. There will be no burning fire shut up in their bones, by reason of which they cannot forbear to speak. Those who come to listen will not be brought face to face with eternal verities. Hungry sheep will look up, but will not be fed. Men harassed with a thousand problems and seeking not inexpert advice on how to solve them but the sense of another world in whose light they can see this one and find strength to cope with it and remold it nearer to the heart's desire, will go away as impotent as they came for anything the preacher has to say. Grievous is the hurt of the daughter of God's people, and slight is the proffered healing. They go to Gilead, and there is no balm. They go to the fountain of waters, and they find there a broken cistern. They cry for bread, and behold a stone.

And to a large extent, this plight of the church is traceable to a weakening of its dogmatic basis. Whether the phrase "humanitarian Christology" is defensible or not is a question. Unless Christ is conceived as one who "stands on the divine side of causality in effecting redemption," it is difficult to see why we need a doctrine of him at all. If Jesus is not specifically related to God's eternal purpose to enter sacrificially the stream of our humanity, to the end that he might thereby change its direction and set it flowing toward himself, then we no more need a doctrine of Jesus than we need a doctrine of Jeremiah or a doctrine of Paul. There is no permanent resting-place between *some form* of the Logos Christology and a "humanitarian Christology" (allowing the phrase) which in effect surrenders the whole idea of direct divine sacrificial saving activity. And what we mean theologically by a Logos Christology we mean practically by a Christ-centered religion rather than a "religion of Jesus." If the emulation of "the religion of Jesus" were presented as the possible end of a Christ-centered faith, that would be different. What we are actually doing, however, is supposing that unregenerate men can be "like Jesus"! Even a casual acquaintance with great sections of modern Protestantism makes it evident that it has departed very widely from the Christocentric emphasis. We must recover that emphasis, or perish. The divine Christ saved the human Jesus from disappearing, and if the human Jesus is to continue to mean for men all that he should, it must still be through the divine Christ. Christ must continue to save Jesus!

It is not that men cannot live "the good life" without faith in the divine Christ. It is not that there cannot be a profound appreciation of the character of Jesus without it. But Christianity does not consist simply in the good life and in moral appreciation and endeavor. It *is* this, of course. One of the incredible suppositions of our day is that the only persons who are interested in the wellbeing of their fellows are the so-called "humanists." No one who really knows what Christianity has done for the world could possibly make that supposition. . . .

Yes; Christocentric religion means human devotion carried to its ultimate issue—say a Damien with a crucifix on his breast the while he dresses the rotting stumps of a leper, a Damien who, as R. L. Stevenson says in his noble defense of the man, "shut to with his own hand the doors of his own sepulcher." But it means an "experience" as well—an experience falling within that "unleaguerable fortress" of the innermost soul "whose keys are at the cincture hung of God," and which is something one can better know for oneself than describe to another. And this experience, whence comes it? It comes of *belief*. If we are going to psychologize religion, well and good; but by what imaginable psychological process can there be "spiritual experience" completely independent of all intellectual assent? It were absurd to say that Christianity is *only* credal; to say that it is in no sense credal would be equally false. And to say that "it does not matter what one believes" so long as one "lives the good life" and "has a religious experience" reveals rather an amazing *naïveté* than any profound insight into the life-movement.

But what *does* the modern church believe? The church is becoming creedless as rapidly as the innovators can have their way. The "Confession of Faith"—what is happening to it? Or what about the "new" confessions that one sees and hears—suitable enough, one imagines, for, say, a fraternal order. And as for the Apostles' Creed—"our people will not say it any more": which means, apparently, that "our people," having some difficulties over the Virgin Birth and the resurrection of the body, have elected the easy way of believing in nothing at all—certainly not in "the Holy Catholic Church." So we are going to allow them to be satisfied with "The Social Creed of the Churches," quite forgetful of the fact that unless the church has a "religious" creed besides a "social" creed the church as such will cease to exist long before it has had time to make its "social" creed effective in the life of the world. "But the social creed *is* religious." Yes; but has its religion proved dynamic enough, impelling enough, to maintain itself at the high point—the Himalayanly high point—necessary to make its creed effective? The church has set itself to do more at the very time that it is lessening its power to do anything.

191

"What Must We Do to Be Saved?"

The church, especially the American evangelical churches, must re-enthrone Christ, the divine Christ, in the life and thought of the people, or cease to exist. Not that the church merely as an institution is the necessary desideratum. But the church in the high New Testament sense of "the body of Christ"—this *must* be saved for the sake of the world. Here is the world's one redeeming force because here is the world's one redeeming message—if the message be *complete.* It is that completeness whose lack is the secret of our impotence. Can we recover it? Nay rather, do we here highly resolve that we *will* recover it? Let us be done with compromise, and let us affirm—affirm magnificently, affirm audaciously. Let us affirm God—his unchanging love for men, his unchanging hatred of sin, his sacrificial presence in all the life and work of Jesus. Let us affirm Christ—Christ as the meaning of God, Christ as what God *is* in virtue of that mysterious "kenosis" by which he made himself one with a human life, and at the same time that he was doing the utmost he could do for men endured the worst—a Cross—that men could do against him. Let us affirm the Spirit—the divine concern to bring to bear upon the hearts and consciences of men the impact of what God in Christ has done and is forever doing on their behalf, to the end that they may be moved to repentance, to that faith which ensures forgiveness, to that love which brings moral empowerment, and to that surrender of the will which makes God's purposes their purposes. Let us affirm the church—the community of the redeemed, those who in all their life seek the regnancy of the spirit of Jesus, carrying on and extending the mystery of the Incarnation against that day when God, the Christ-God, shall be all and in all. Let us affirm the Kingdom—the Christianizing of life everywhere, children with straight backs and happy faces, women released from drudgery and set free for creative living, industry conducted for the good of all, war and kindred evils done away, racial antipathies lost in a universal brotherhood, the rich heritage of culture made available to the last man. O there is no limit to the affirmations, and, better still, no limit to the dynamic needful to make them effective, once we grasp the profound structural coherence of Christianity, the wide sweep of its thought, the absoluteness of its demands, the revolutionary results of its consistent application. "That in all things he, who is the image of the invisible God, might have the pre-eminence."

Albert C. Outler

Albert C. Outler (1908–1989), a native of Georgia, was educated at Wofford College, Emory and Yale Universities and taught at Duke and Yale Universities. The greater part of his career was spent on the faculty of the Perkins School of Theology at Southern Methodist University. A specialist in the history of doctrine and in the theology of John Wesley, Outler made significant contributions to the history of Christian thought and was a leader in contemporary ecumenical activities. Among his important works are *Tradition and the Unity We Seek* (1957), *That the World May Believe* (1966), *Who Trusts in God* (1968), and *Theology in the Wesleyan Spirit* (1975). In his writings Outler attempted to reinterpret the inner life of Wesley's theology in order to make a contemporary statement of the Christian gospel. Outler was the principal author of the statement on doctrine, which appeared in the 1972 *Discipline* and which continues to represent United Methodism's theological position. "Holiness of Heart and Life" is from *Theology in the Wesleyan Spirit*, pp. 65-78, 84-88.*

Holiness of Heart and Life

Most non-Methodists, and not a few Methodists, would be startled by some of the questions a Methodist ordinand is asked in the course of his "being received into full connection" (i.e., membership) in an Annual

*Copied with permission from *Theology in the Wesleyan Spirit* © 1975 by Discipleship Resources, Nashville, TN.

Conference. The present list is a curious conflation of various examinations that Wesley devised for "admitting" his own preachers into "connexion." When one recalls that these men were all laymen, it is obvious that these queries are also applicable, in principle, to any and all baptized/confirmed Christians. Their being reserved now for ordinands does not alter the fact that, for Wesley, they were appropriate clues for the examination (*self*-examination!) of all earnest Christians, to be asked and answered with unflinching seriousness.

The first one is commonplace enough. But then come three real "stickers," certainly for sensitive and knowledgeable young men and women nowadays—and for the generality of Christians of any age and station:

1. Have you faith in Christ?
2. Are you going on to perfection?
3. Do you expect to be made perfect in love in this life?
4. Are you earnestly striving after it?

The requisite answer, in each case, is affirmative!

All too often, in actual current circumstances (as Methodists will know from experience), these probes into the very heart of a person's Christian self-understanding are dealt with in a way that appeals to the individual interpretation of the several ordinands, few of whom have puzzled their way deeply enough into the Wesleyan doctrine of perfection to have clear and responsible commitments to what they are professing ritually. Nor is it always and altogether clear to their elders in the Conference!

There are at least two reasons for this pious confusion. The first, of course, is a widespread consensus in modern culture (instructed as we have been by depth psychology, together with an inbred cynicism) that rejects any notion of "perfection" simply out of hand and would, therefore, assess anybody's serious expectation of being "made perfect in love *in this life*" as symptomatic of a psychotic delusion. The second reason is historical and is related to the greatest tragedy in Methodist history: the nineteenth century conflicts that swirled around Wesley's emphasis upon "holiness of heart and life" and its alterations and distortions at the hands of men and women who were seeking to be faithful Wesleyans (on both sides!) without having experienced anything close to the theological and spiritual struggles out of which his own original synthesis had emerged. The ironic outcome of this process (especially in America) was that the keystone in the arch of Wesley's own theological "system" came to be a pebble in the shoes of standard-brand Methodists, even as a distorted version of Wesley's doctrine of sanctification (as "a second and separate work of grace *subsequent* to regeneration") was becoming a shibboleth of self-righteousness amongst a pious minority of Methodists who professed themselves holier than the rest. That conflict and its abrasions had the effect of leaving the average Methodist (and many much above that average) alienated even by the bare terms—"holiness," "Christian perfection," "sanctification"—not to speak of an aversion toward those persons who actually profess such spiritual attainments. . . .

But I take comfort and courage in such a venture from the undeniable fact that John Wesley believed and taught an explicit doctrine of "holiness" as the goal and crown of the Christian life, and if this gives you trouble, the burden of proof shifts over onto your side (if, that is, you profess to be a Wesleyan at all) to explain why you are prepared to reject or ignore what he regarded as not only essential but climactic. His irreducible minimum of Christian fundamentals were, as we have seen, three: (1) sin and repentance (i.e., self-knowledge), (2) justification and pardon (i.e., assurance) and (3) "holiness of heart and life." "Sanctification," "perfect love," "Christian perfection" were various synonyms, in his vocabulary, for "holiness," and he rang the changes on this theme throughout his whole evangelistic career, insisting that it was the special mission of the Methodists to hold "and to spread [this doctrine of] scriptural holiness over the land."

It is important, therefore, always to start with Wesley's first conversion (1725), a conversion to the ideal of holy living, and to remember that he never thereafter abandoned this ideal even when further conversions (and other experiences) complicated his interpretation of it by a good deal. The seed of the idea had been planted in his mind in the Epworth parsonage by Susanna, one of whose favorite devotional texts was Lorenzo Scupoli's (or, as was then thought, Juan de Castaniza's) *Spiritual Struggle*. The seed had flowered under the stimulus of Jeremy Taylor, Thomas à Kempis, William Law and others. But the idea of perfection as a dynamic *process* with a flying goal did not take its mature form until, finally, Wesley found his way back to the great devotional traditions of Eastern Orthodoxy—Clement of Alexandria, Gregory of Nyssa, Macarius of Egypt, and others. The first fruits of these discoveries may be seen in the only great sermon of his of which we have any record before 1738. This was "The Circumcision of the Heart" (written in December of 1732

195

and preached in St. Mary's on January 1, 1733 [which was not New Year's Day on the then current calendar]). Too little attention has been paid to the implications of the fact that Wesley never discarded this sermon or even recast it. It turns up, in its original text but out of its chronological order, as No. XIII in *Sermons on Several Occasions*, vol. II, 1748.

It is true, that in those years, 1725–1738, he consistently misplaced "holiness" (or pure intentions) *before* justification, as preparatory to it. Bishop George Bull and most other Anglicans from Bull to Tillotson had done the same thing—and Wesley would berate them for it later on. One of the decisive shifts in his 1738 transformation was the reversal of this order. Thereafter, justification always stands first, without any antecedent "holiness" or merit of any kind as a *necessary* precondition to human salvation. Our natural sinful state can be dealt with only by God's sheer gratuitous mercy, based upon Christ's freely offered medi-atorial merit. Then, and only then, can anything like new birth and Christian nurture *begin* to restore the power not to sin intentionally which may then be developed further in a nurturing process toward the goal of sanctification: "the mature man in Christ." This relation of justi-fication to sanctification was the critical issue that had first been raised for Wesley in his encounters with the Herrnhuters and Salzburgers in Georgia. It was the main issue that divided Wesley and Whitefield almost as soon as the Revival began. It was the issue on which Wesley and Count von Zinzendorf soon clashed and finally parted.

It is easy for us to miss the originality of this Wesleyan view of faith alone and holy living *held together.* Here was a great evangelist preach-ing up *sola fide* and, at the very same time, teaching his converts to go on to perfection and to expect it *in this life!* His critics were quick to notice this strange move and to seize upon it as proof of Wesley's incon-sistency. Actually, it was yet another of Wesley's characteristic "third alternatives"—maybe his most original one. In this view, the stages of the unfolding Christian life may be laid out in something like the following sequence (a psychological sequence which was more nearly concurrent than spaced out): (1) contrition and repentance (true self-knowledge); (2) justification by faith alone (with Christ's atonement as the *meritorious* but not the *formal* cause—for, remember, this was the crux of his quarrel with the Calvinists!); (3) regeneration ("new birth") issuing in (4) Christian nurture in intensive small encounter groups (with no carpets and no nonsense!); looking toward (5) maturation into "holiness," always in its twin dimensions ("internal holiness" [our *love of God* and neighbor] and "external holiness" [our love of God *and of neighbor!*]). All this was aimed at a climax (6) "perfect love" of God and neighbor as the Spirit's greatest *gift* (which means that, in Wesley's mind, sanctification *by faith alone* was as self-evident as justification ever was, never a moral achievement). And yet, as Wesley never ceased to insist, none of these "stages" is static, none of them so fully completed that one may not lapse from it by unbelief or willful sin—hence his rejection of "final perseverance." What mattered most was that "going on to perfection" has a consistent character and a clear end in view: (1) *love* (of God and neighbor), (2) *trust* (in Christ and the sufficiency of *his* grace) and (3) *joy* (joy upwelling in the heart from the "prevenience" of the indwelling Spirit). This *is* "holy living": to love God and neighbor with all your heart, to trust securely in Christ's merits, and to live joyously "in the Spirit"!

But this vital linkage between faith alone and holy living was forever being misconstrued and Wesley was forever being baffled by its misconstructions. Somehow, he could never grasp the fact that people formed by the traditions of Latin Christianity were bound to understand "perfection" as *perfectus* (perfec*ted*)—i.e., as a finished state of completed growth, *ne plus ultra!* For him, certainly since his own discoveries of the early fathers, "perfection" meant "perfecting" *(teleiosis)*, with further horizons of love and of participation in God always opening up *beyond* any given level of spiritual progress. This seemed so *obvious* to him that he allowed himself a swig of smug triumphalism:

> It has been frequently observed, that [in the Reformation time] very few were clear in their judgment both with regard to justification and sanctification. Many who have spoken and written admirably well concerning justification had no clear conception, nay, were totally ignorant of the doctrine of sanctification. Who has wrote more ably than Martin Luther on justification by faith alone? And who was more ignorant of the doctrine of sanctification, or more confused in his conceptions of it? . . . On the other hand, how many writers of the Romish Church (as Francis Sales and Juan de Castaniza) have wrote strongly and scripturally on sanctification, who, nevertheless, were entirely unacquainted with the nature of justification! insomuch that the whole body of their Divines at the Council of Trent totally confound sanctification and justification together. But it has pleased God to give the Methodists a full and clear knowledge of each, and the wide difference between them.

Regeneration ("new birth," "change of heart") is a concurrent effect alongside justification. The sense of God's unmerited favor prompts an inner transformation, a new disposition toward God and neighbor, a new self-understanding, a new outlook and hope. Even so, "this is only the threshold of sanctification. . . ." The Christian life goes on from here, in a dynamic process of nurture, piety, activity—and of *expectation:* that what is imputed in justification will be *imparted* in the Christian life and its fulfillment. *This* is "Christian perfection"—"to be made perfect in love in this life," even if only in the hour of death (which was Wesley's normal "calendar" for it).

> It is, then, a great blessing given to this people, that as they do not think or speak of justification so as to supersede sanctification, so neither do they think or speak of sanctification so as to supersede justification. They take care to keep each in its own place, laying equal stress on one and the other. They know God has joined these together, and it is not for man to put down asunder. Therefore, they maintain, with equal zeal and diligence, the doctrine of free, full, present justification, on the one hand, and of entire sanctification both of heart and life, on the other; being as tenacious of *inward* holiness as any mystic, and of *outward* [holiness] as any Pharisee.

Who then is a Christian, according to the light which God hath vouchsafed to this [Methodist] people? He that, being "justified by faith, hath peace with God through our Lord Jesus Christ," and, at the same time, is "born again," "born from above," "born of the Spirit"; inwardly changed from the image of the devil, to that "image of God wherein he was created"; he that finds the love of God shed abroad in his heart by the Holy Ghost which is given unto him, and whom this love sweetly constrains to love his neighbor (i.e., every man) as himself; he that has learned of his Lord to be meek and lowly in heart, and in every state to be content; he in whom is that whole mind, all those tempers, which are also in Christ Jesus; he that abstains from all appearance of evil in his actions, and that offends not with his tongue; he that walks in all the commandments of God, and in all his ordinances, blameless; he that, in all his intercourse with men, does to others as he would they should do to him; and in his whole life and conversation, whether he eats or drinks, or whatsoever he doeth, doeth all to the glory of God.

This is an important version of Wesley's doctrine of "holiness of heart and life" in his own words. Its development (apart from *this* statement) is marked out in a series of six landmark sermons over the six-decade span of his ministry. (1) "The Circumcision of the Heart" which, as we have already seen, was his first full definition of the holy-living tradition. (2) "Christian Perfection" is a sermonic essay never preached, but published first in 1741 with the express encouragement of Bishop

Edmund Gibson of London—who could tell an authentic version of the holy-living motif when he saw one. (3) "Sin in Believers" is something of an afterthought, added (in 1763) to correct mistaken interpretations of "Christian Perfection," as if it implied *sinless* perfection. It doesn't, and never did, for Wesley. (4) "The Lord Our Righteousness" (1765) marks the decisive parting of the ways between Wesley and the Calvinists—which is to say, a majority of the evangelicals in the Church of England and most Nonconformists, too. The issue, as we have seen, is between "formal cause" and "meritorious cause." This may sound like a quibble until you probe it more closely (like reading the debates at Trent and Bellarmine and Davenant!). Actually, it's the same issue as between imputation and impartation, between predestination and prevenience. "Formal cause" (to the Calvinists) implied predestination; "meritorious cause" implied God's prevenience and human synergism. The first is "protestant," the second is "catholic." And Wesley, after a full generation of evangelical preaching of justification, continues to insist that Christ's death is the *meritorious* cause of our justification but not the *formal* cause (which he takes to be God's primordial covenant that those who believe shall be saved and those who refuse shall not).

Sermon No. 5 would have to be "On Working Out Our Own Salvation" (1785), a remarkable statement of Wesley's "synergism" and, maybe, his most carefully nuanced exposition of "faith alone" and "holy living." Our last sermon (6), and a fitting climax for the series, is also the last sermon published in Wesley's lifetime. Its theme is "The Wedding Garment." I had never realized until recently (after all these years of poking around, too) that this particular parable had been a sort of shibboleth between the partisans of *sola fide* and of "holy living." What *does* "the wedding garment" signify? To the Calvinists it meant the spotless robe of Christ's righteousness flung as a cover over the "filthy rags" of our *un*righteousness. To the Anglicans generally it had signified holiness itself—i.e., that Christian moral character that is attained by God's *gift* of grace and his *demand* for holy living. With death only months away, Wesley restates his basic conviction, first fixed in 1725: that "the wedding garment signifies holiness, neither more nor less"—the holiness specified in Hebrews 12:14, "without which no man shall see the Lord." Have you ever preached on this parable or heard it preached on? Have you ever considered how much this issue matters to us *today?*

Holiness as a vision of the human potential is an easily distorted notion, and you can see Wesley struggling with its misunderstandings in his *Plain Account of Christian Perfection as Believed and Taught by the Rev.*

Mr. John Wesley from the Year 1725 to 1765 and thereafter (six editions from 1766 to 1789). There is also that wonderful little pamphlet of 1762 entitled *Cautions and Directions Given to the Greatest Professors in the Methodist Societies,* where the "professors" (i.e., of perfection) are given six highly relevant advices: (1) against pride and self-righteousness; (2) against pride's daughter, *enthusiasm* (defined as grasping for happiness without submitting oneself to its necessary preconditions); (3) against *antinomianism* (doing your own thing, regardless); (4) against sins of *omission* (getting tired and supposing that what you've already done is plenty—or at least enough); (5) against desiring anything above God, and (6) against *schism* (which, as Wesley saw it, was something like pious cantankerousness!). Obviously, these "cautions and directions" were timely—prompted by more than a few rare cases of self-righteousness and spiritual elitism. Indeed, it was just this syndrome of self-righteousness amongst the holiness people that led "mainstream" Methodists finally to throw the Wesleyan baby of true holiness out with the "second blessing" bath water! . . .

To love God is not merely a friendly feeling toward the ground of being, nor a mood of prayer and piety toward "The Man Upstairs." It is, rather, an awareness of our radical dependence upon God's grace and our gladness that this is the truth about our lives. It means a sense of Holy Presence and of security and warmth in that Presence. It means our recognition of God's upholding love and our gratitude for his love. It means serenity in the face of death because of our confidence that God's love cannot be conquered or cancelled by death. And, most of all, it means having no other gods of our own, since the *First* Commandment is also the *last!*

But overreaching humans cannot "obey" the command to love God as simple acts of choice or even as a life program aimed at self-salvation and happiness. This is why there's so much confusion nowadays about all these self-help programs, mystical exaltations ("religious highs" and things like that), as if this sort of thing could ever be equated with authentic Christian faith and love. This is why holy living is not, strictly speaking, a human achievement or any part of sinful humanity's "natural capacity" to initiate. It is not, at bottom, part of the human potential, save in the carefully guarded sense that God's prevenient grace stimulates and enables us to respond, positively and gratefully. "We love *him* because he first loved *us.*" It is God's *initiative* that makes possible our *response;* it is his *self*-presentation in Christ that frees us to accept his acceptance of us. It is his saving work in our justification that liberates us for valid ethical endeavor: in our personal maturations in grace and in our involvements in all effective transformations of society under the aegis of the Kingdom of God.

Thus "faith alone" remains as the threshold of all true holiness in heart and life—and of human happiness—here and hereafter. Wesley analyzes this in a remarkable trio of sermons on "The Law Established Through Faith." Faith stands first *(sola fide)* but not as an end in itself. Nor is it a meritorious *act*, as many fundamentalists seem to insist. Rather, faith is a means in order to *love* just as love is in order to *goodness*, just as goodness is in order to *happiness*—which is what God made us for, in this world—and the next. *This* is "holy living."

Likewise, our love of neighbor (if it ever becomes more than benevolent feeling) follows from our love of God. Love of neighbor is a function of our concern to hallow *all* of life, in all of its occasions, great and small. It is our part in answering the Lord's prayer, "Thy Kingdom come, thy will *be done on earth.* . . ." [Why *can't* we ever get that punctuation right? The comma belongs after *"on earth,"* not before!] In any case, I'd feel easier with my pietist friends if their neighborly love were not so self-selective of their own kind. I'd feel easier about my activist colleagues if their neighborly love weren't so often ruthless. The only love I've ever known that I've trusted and felt sustained by was *from* God, *through* men and women whose love was unselfish—i.e., people who have loved me gracefully. This indeed is what I *mean* by love—and all of us have been blessed by it, most of us far beyond our deservings or gratitude. It is grace-filled love that helps us become human and that nourishes our humanity.

This is why there was so much *joy* in Wesley (and in the best Wesleyan traditions of holiness of heart and life)—so much happiness in a man who had been taught from infancy to hold his emotions in check and whose temperament was remarkably cool (even amidst the violent emotions he managed to stir up). He was not an exuberant type and he deplored all flippancy and small talk. This is one reason why he has been easier for me to study than he would have been to live and work with. And yet, there is this strange, insistent reality of cheerfulness and high spirits that keeps breaking through this knit-browed earnestness. He was, I've come finally to realize, a happy man, in his own sense of "happiness": the human affects of loving God and serving others. And this joyousness of his (and of his brother Charles even more) was infectious. It became a part of the Methodist tradition, its hymnody, its distinctive lifestyle. Some of it still continues in our current tradition—sometimes trivialized, often faked. But what a wonder it would be if we could recover such a tradition's inner springs: viz., the grace of our Lord Jesus Christ who is the Father's redemptive love making life holy and happy, in and by the power of the Holy Spirit in our hearts! *Then*, we'd have no more trouble with those questions about going on to perfection, etc.! *Are* you? Yes, by God's grace! Then, right on! Praise the Lord!

Wesley died happy—singing and praying. The particular hymn that came to him on that last day was already a favorite with all those people in that little room in the house on City Road. It was by Isaac Watts—a sort of poetic comment on the "art of holy *dying*" that Wesley had so long taught his people as the converse of "the art of holy *living*." "I'll praise my Maker while I've breath. . . ." What we can see now, I hope, is that this was a reiteration, *in extremis*, of what Wesley had always said the breath of life is for—and what it had been for, for him, throughout his whole incredible career. God *has* made us for himself. Our first and last end *is* to love him, and to *enjoy him* forever. This *is* holiness of heart and life, and it was Wesley's witness in life *and* death. It was, therefore, a last reprise of the theme of that first conversion, long ago:

> I'll praise my Maker while I've breath
> And, when my voice is lost in death,
> Praise shall employ my *nobler* powers.
> My days of praise shall *ne'er* be past,
> While life *and* thought *and* being last,
> And immortality endures.
> Amen!

Robert E. Cushman

Robert E. Cushman (1913–1993)   was an American United Methodist minister, teacher, administrator, and theologian. Born to a Methodist parsonage family in Fall River, Massachusetts, he was educated at Wesleyan University, Connecticut, and Yale University. After teaching at Yale University and the University of Oregon, he became professor of systematic theology at the Divinity School, Duke University in 1945. From 1958 to 1971 he served as Dean of the Divinity School and then returned to teaching until his retirement. Involved in ecumenical activities, he was well-known for his writings, especially *Therapeia: Plato's Conception of Philosophy* (1958) and *Faith Seeking Understanding* (1980).

Cushman's theology carries on the reassessment of basic theological themes that was taking place in mid-twentieth-century North America. He was responsive to the revival of Wesleyan theology, to the renewed recognition of human sinfulness, and to the uniqueness of God's redemptive action in Jesus Christ. The article that is included in these readings sets forth his theological position in sharply defined contours. "The Shape of Christian Faith: A Platform" was published in *The Iliff Review* (March 1956), pp. 31-40. The author has added material to the end of the article to bring it up to date.

The Shape of Christian Faith: A Platform

If we are to talk about "the meaning of our religion," I would naturally suppose that the religion in question is none other than our

Christian religion. If this can be agreed upon without straining, then the question becomes somewhat more precise; namely, what is the meaning of our Christian faith? . . .

I premise as a beginning-point that our Christian faith is seated in and is responsible to a continuous living tradition. In this respect, it cannot be confused with a philosophy. A philosophy is prompted by a concern for intelligibility of the world. It undertakes to interpret reality in terms of some key-category of meaning which commends itself to a thinker or school of thinkers. The privileged category actually rests upon some acknowledged or unacknowledged criterion of meaningfulness, doubtless a judgment of value. Usually, however, the category is assumed to commend itself to all rational men universally. On the strength of this supposition, philosophy presumes to be independent of all tradition and to stand upon grounds of something called reason alone. This is what, in part, distinguishes philosophy fundamentally from the Christian faith and from any religious standpoint which defers to divine Grace in the attainment of religious knowledge. Religious faith is regularly convinced that man does not go it alone.

Christian faith neither can nor desires to claim this kind of independence and self-sufficiency. Christian faith neither was nor is thought out in the study by a cloistered and self-sufficient intellect. Such a conception of Christian faith would be fundamentally Pelagian. It would be human self-help directed to the end of attaining an intelligible world view. As such, it would be in essence an extension of scientific interest. It could be, as Aristotle long ago indicated that branch of "science" which comes after physics—that is, metaphysics, even though most practitioners of philosophy today prefer to call it ontology, if they concede its possibility at all. My own view is that metaphysics is a permissible and necessary undertaking but that it is never to be confounded with Christian faith and that it can, in no sense, exhaust or contain the meaning of our religion.

Return then to the statement that our Christian faith neither can claim nor desires to claim the independence that characterizes the method of philosophy. This is not because faith scorns human rationality as such. Such a notion is entirely mistaken. The fundamental reason is that Christian faith is not primarily a quest for intelligibility. It is, rather, a life which has already found integrity and redemption in and through the mediating power of a particular history (that of the people Israel), which culminated in and was climaxed by the ministry of Jesus Christ. Christian faith is not, in the first instance—though it may be in the end—an interpretation of reality. It is, rather, a doctrine of redemption. More exactly, Christian faith is not doctrine at all. It is a line of witness, a succession of witness, to restoration of life in Christ. Doctrine is the systematic representation of this witness, as well as interpretation and reapplication of it. This witness may properly be followed by an interpretation of all reality in terms of the key-category of meaning, namely Jesus Christ. Such an effort finds tentative beginnings in St. John's "Prologue" and in Philippians 2:5-11. . . .

Instead of trying to define it abstractly, I shall give you a signal instance of it in the history of our religion. I refer to Isaiah's classical account of his experience in the Temple. We are to recognize the symbolic nature of this account. Isaiah did not see the Lord high and lifted up within the precincts of the Temple, but he beheld the Lord. The seraphim did not literally cry out "Holy, Holy, Holy is the Lord of hosts, the whole earth is full of his glory." Isaiah was suddenly overwhelmed by the aweful majesty and absolute sanctity of the wholly Other by whose presence he was confronted. Here is, indeed, as Rudolph Otto long ago pointed out, something like the nouminous awareness of the Mysterium Tremendum. It is a kind of experience which stands in its own right. It is unique and sui generis like the consciousness of beauty. If you have no participation in it, no amount of argument will convince of its reality; but with it the Divine is given. And the human subject is precipitated into crisis.

What is the crisis? Again Isaiah supplies the answer: "Woe is me! For I am undone; because I am a man of unclean lips, and I dwell in the midst of a people of unclean lips; for mine eyes have seen the King, the Lord of Hosts."

To be in the presence of the wholly Other who is also the Holy Other is a fearful experience, because it is to be personally and totally called into question. The absolute sanctity of the Divine renders everything in its presence profane and unworthy. Hence, the prophet cries out, "Woe is me. I am undone." All pretentious righteousness is negated. The absolute contrast between the altogether Holy and human profaneness registers itself in the consciousness of sinfulness and alienation. Yet, the converse side of the same experience is absolute reverence. Reverence for the Holy One together with awareness of absolute responsibility toward the sacred righteousness disclosed—"Ye shall be Holy as I am Holy." Thus, the authentic moment of religious apprehension embraces two antithetical phases: On the one hand, man finds himself presently contrary in his whole being to the holiness of the Divine Presence. This is his profanity, his wrongness of being. On the other side, he is drawn to the Holy One in relation to whom he is presently the negation. Moreover, he knows himself as unconditionally obligated not to do, merely, but to be assimilated to the sacred righteousness of the Divine. The crisis is intense: Man is not only presently contrary to the Divine Presence, but also there is, as a result, a self-destroying cleavage within his own personal life. It is the contradiction between two inertias. Man at once is inclined away from and toward the Divine. He is divided in the middle, and is the battle ground of contrary powers. . . .

By way of summary and by way of drawing out the implications of the foregoing, certain generalizations offer themselves:

First, according to the Hebraic-Christian tradition, which is our heritage, religion is not man seeking God, fundamentally, but rather God having found and confronted man. This is to say that the religious situation is not one of questing but of having been found. Everything depends upon discovering that one is discovered.

Second, religion is human life in crisis calling for solution through reconciliation. It is the whole and entire man—intellect, affection, and volition—who is engaged and involved in the supremely significant moment of his existence.

Third, in the religious situation the primary desideratum is not the solution of an intellectual problem but the urgent problem of life in disruption. The issue is not what is the intelligible structure of the world, but "what must I do to be saved?"

Fourth, the "meaning and truth of our religion," using E. W. Lyman's phrase, cannot possibly be understood apart from participating personally in its two major moments, that of alienation and that of reconciliation.

Fifth, the problem of Christian apologetic is not that of vindicating the truth of theism or the reality of God, but that of discovering man's condition to himself, that is, his condition as he is approached by God. This was the method of Socrates, of the Prophets, of Augustine, of Pascal, of Luther, of Wesley, and many more.

Sixth, it is notoriously true that men may be blind to the fundamental nature of their plight. From Isaiah to Jesus there is the recurring complaint: "Ye have eyes but ye do not see." Religious blindness is a species of self-ignorance on account of which there is *eo ipso* blindness to God.

Seventh, the Christian faith testifies to the overwhelming of this blindness through the person and work of Jesus Christ in that, as St. Paul affirms, "God was in Christ reconciling the world unto himself."

The meaning of our Christian faith is that through the reconciling ministry of Jesus Christ our estrangement from God is overborne and the divisive self-disagreement within us is replaced by a new integrity of life. This manifests itself in having God as Father and men as brothers. This is justification and reconciliation on both dimensions of our existence.

. . . To come to the positive standpoint of this section, I revert to the implications of the first section. The implications were that religious faith is not prompted by the effort to solve an intellectual problem; neither does faith exist by being the solution of one, except incidentally. Religious faith does not rest upon a crisis of the understanding threatened with the unintelligibility of the world. It is precisely because this has been the prevailing problem and the prevailing perspective of a post-rationalistic epoch, that people find it so hard to participate in the actual standpoint in which the religious problem is engendered and finds its solution.

This standpoint is precisely that of the "prophetic consciousness" described above. While the prophetic consciousness was actually a minority consciousness in ancient Israel and encountered heavy going, nevertheless it was this consciousness which became the core and gave shape to the history of Israel, the history of rebellion and reconciliation.

The prophetic consciousness is not represented simply by ethical criticism which the prophets one and all leveled at iniquitous personal, social, political and ecclesiastical arrangements. This was only a by-product; and concentration upon it has obscured the deeper level. The prophetic consciousness is an overwhelming awareness of the aweful sanctity of the Holy Other whereby everything human is laid under judgment and called to accounting. The profanity of man is laid bare in the dazzling light of the Divine sanctity. Man is not confronted by titanic power of external dimension. He is confronted by power transcending or irrelevant to physical magnitude but qualified in such a way as to startle man, powerfully convict, and render him aghast at his unworthiness. . . .

From this comes a practical observation, namely, that Christian proclamation is essentially and always has been a vigorous effort to get men to examine themselves. It is based on the assurance that, as men see and concede the fundamental distortion in their total nature, they know themselves to be standing under a norm by which they are called to account. But the norm is not a principle; it is a claim of a claimant. That is why Jesus begins with the words: "Repent and believe!" Faith follows on repentance, for faith is reconciliation with God, and there can be no reconciliation without repentance. To treat the reality of God as something to be proved is to approach Divine Reality as if it were of the same order as all other objects. This is to step completely outside the circle of the true religious situation; for when a man is in the circle, he discerns that his first business is not demonstration but obedience.

How then do we commend God to men? Very much, I think, in the way we have described: by inducing them to see where they stand. "Blessed are they that mourn, for they shall be comforted."

The salvation we seek will depend on how we construe our plight. The plight of 20th century man is many-sided. The literature of diagnosis is vast, and proposed therapies are about as numerous. Every department of the social sciences as well as philosophy, religion and belles lettres has made contribution. So the testimony among the intellectuals is well-nigh universal that something is radically wrong with man and society. . . .

There is no panacea for this predicament. But our Christian faith is relevant to it and it to Christian faith; so at least we are not left speechless. In the first place, it is historic fact that great Christian faith, that of St. Paul, of Augustine, of Luther, and of Wesley was triumph out of despair. It was admittedly a different sort of despair because under different auspices. But there is an element of identity—man at the end of his rope. As Wesley himself frequently noted, man, totally disabused of his own capacities, is just fit for the kingdom of God. Salvation happens, if we may trust the Hebraic-Christian tradition, when man is so reduced in his own resources that he is shorn of the will longer to resist divine Grace. "Thus a man who is cast down by fear of the commandments of God, and so has reached knowledge of Him, is justified and exalted by faith in the divine word" (*The Reformation Writings of Martin Luther*, London: 1952, p. 375). If the Christian message is to have any relevance to the modern spiritual situation, it must cease caricaturing itself by exhorting men to godly works and recover *sola gratia* as its essential word of salvation. Man does not need to do something more, but to be something else. Pelagian Christianity may have sufficed for the 19th century; for the 20th it is trifling irrelevancy. When the children cry for bread, it is giving a stone. This is the first and more obvious point.

The second is more difficult to convey. I can only sketch it. Everything depends upon man's recovery of his sense of dignity and his escape from isolation.

Paradoxically, the common man of the West—and well into the 19th

Century—was in large part possessed of his sense of dignity in the measure that he shared with and in the Hebraic-Christian consciousness such a condition as the General Confession of the Liturgy gives voice to. He was, however haltingly, a self-acknowledged sinner inasmuch as he knew himself the subject of a Divine address that laid him under obligation more compelling than his immediate interests. In that variously acknowledged Divine mandate his status and dignity, as a responsible subject of the Divine notice, was conferred upon him. On the one hand, and in the overarching presence of the Holy Other, he was relieved of his isolation; on the other hand, he was discomfitted by "the infinite qualitative difference" between his culpable humanity and the Divine Sanctity. Thus, while, from time to time, he might be disquieted by awareness of dreadful estrangement from God, yet, in the same moment of consciousness, he was also aware of an exalting destiny in his call to be found faithful in the sight of that same Being. As he was laid under judgment before God, so also, was he aware of an injunction coupled with invitation to be conformed to the image of God and as a candidate for inclusion in the Kingdom. Because, meanwhile, secular man has become progressively unaware of himself in the sight of God, he has become proportionately unaware of himself as sinner, and conversely.

Thus is disclosed the paradox insuppressibly resonant in the prophetic consciousness of the Scriptures but muted and falling to near silence for modern sensibility. For the prophetic consciousness, two seeming incompatibles are inseparable: man's dignity and his awareness of the gap, the shameful disparity, between his *Is* and his *Ought-to-be* that, now and again, would sound in his confession of sin or acknowledged contrariety respecting an imperious mandate other than his own. For the consciousness of sin—according to Isaiah and colleagues—is the initial and insuppressible notice to humanity of the ultimate relationship in which it stands as human, namely, to God. Nevertheless, for the prophetic consciousness, the awareness of sin is not attended by simple negation, for, with it and at one time, we are, by our Maker, affirmed in and with the very negation. The vexing burden of indefectible obligation is man's ultimate privilege, his conferred dignity and pending Divine destiny. Luther's rediscovery in Romans 3:21 of the *justitia Dei* as the promise of God in the "righteousness of God" opened doors to a reformation of Christendom. His despair of estrangement is surmounted by the grace of God, it is true, "through Jesus Christ our Lord." But Luther found that we lay hold of the grace of God by faith, first, by conceding the existing alienation in which we stand after the manner of

Isaiah and, thereby discover our destiny manifest in Jesus Christ and, therewith, our conferred dignity as human beings *all* as a gift of divine grace.

From these things comes the judgment that the principal task of Christian teaching and proclamation today, as also yesterday and tomorrow, is—along with Isaiah and Jesus—the opening of willfully deaf ears and blinded eyes. Hope for our humanity is rightly to discern and distinguish between the seeming and the real causes of man's ageless disquiet, alienation from his Ground of Being, and its present-day agony verging on despair. Such teaching will include unabashed, tireless, candid, yet winsome, invitation to honest self-understanding before God—this under the aegis of the now age-old and ecumenical Christian experience of human redemption through Christ the Lord.

Wherever, and in the measure this nurture of the Spirit advances to some realization, there the *prime datum*, or first principle, for any authentic Christian interpretation of "the misery and possible glory of man" (Pascal) may emerge clearly enough to become self-authenticating to searching human understanding. As to that prime datum, I refer flatly to what St. Paul describes as "the light of the knowledge of the glory of God in the face of Christ" (2 Cor. 4:6). The onset of this traumatic insight is called "faith" in both Scripture and tradition. When it comes to pass, this same Jesus Christ, commends himself age by age, as the One in whom all alienation from the Holy Other is transcended by being overcome. Whence it is the witness of faith in all ages that, in this One and through Him, the righteousness of God (which terrified Luther, the honest man!) becomes, not God's just condemnation of the sinner, but, in Jesus Christ's victory over temptation, Abba, Father. So that St. John declares: "And from his fulness we have all received, grace upon grace" (Jn. 1:16. Cf. Rom. 5:15, 17).

It may be that faith awaits such honesty as that of the truly contrite heart which, may yet, be thunder-struck by the *given* historical mystery of Jesus Christ; for it is only at that given point in our human history that the standing and insuppressible paradox afflicting the prophetic consciousness is answered or is answerable. For it is answerable only *by the kind of actual human life that resolves it*. For the Apostolic church it was so resolved in that reconciliation of opposites which was, as Paul saw, Jesus Christ and his Cross. In this Jesus of history the implicit Divine *affirmation* of all humanity without limit (i.e., God's Grace) is actually mated with God's timeless and universal demand for obedience. Given, however, what we are, the latter leaves us all sinners before God, i.e., original sin. Whereas, by contrast, in the mystery of Jesus' historical presence, as Paul saw and said, the standing Divine-human alienation is resolved in a now restored fellowship *(koinonia)* of man with God and of God with man. With this, the kingdom of God is actualized in history. Here was the "new creation" for Paul, and a new humanity rooted in Christ becomes the expectancy of the whole New Testament.

What has been said must, here, suffice to indicate something of what is intended by the statement that Jesus Christ is the *primary datum* of the Christian religion and the first principle for all Christian reflection as faith moves always onwards toward understanding. Of that primary datum we may say, again, it is Jesus Christ because he is the actual occasion in our human history in whose word-deed the resident paradox of the prophetic consciousness of both Testaments finds its redemptive resolution.

Stated once more the paradox may be objectively described in this: that human beings, created to be conformed to the image of God, decline to espouse their given and exalted calling. Their dignity consists, however, in their call-declined which, at the same time, is their sinful disobedience. In a word, man is paradoxical in that he can be a sinner because he is called to be a son, that is, a "saint." His misery is at once his half-awareness of that fact while he often spares little to evade its acknowledgment. By contrast, Jesus Christ is first principle of Christian thought because in him the misery of man's self-alienation from God is resolved and, with it, estrangement of man from God and human beings from one another. This, in a word, is why and how the twofold Great Commandment of Mark 12:29-31 encompasses the twofold way of the Kingdom. As the entire love of God restores community as between humanity and God the Father, so from that restored fellowship shared derives alone the sufficient motivating and sustaining good will of any and all human community of persons with one another in this world. In the twofold Great Commandment we are advised by Jesus that, until we are at home with God in this world, we are ill-equipped to be at home with the neighbor, or he or she with us, that is, for long.

211

Daniel T. Niles

D. T. Niles (1908–1968) was from India and sustained his relation to his culture and his people. He was nurtured in Western
theology and spoke from this educational background. At the
same time he intended to appreciate, utilize, and speak to his
native cultural setting. A chief point of his witness was the importance of Jesus Christ. Niles was one of the earliest and clearest
voices to speak from a non-Western Christian community both to
his own culture and to the churches in the West. He taught many
to appreciate and respect points of both difference and common-
ality. The selection here is from his book *Who Is This Jesus?*
(Nashville/New York: Abingdon Press, 1960), pp. 13-18, 88-100.

Who Is This Jesus?

My wife was a teacher in a Christian girls' high school when I married her. Apart from teaching music and singing, she was also the guide
captain in the school. In many ways the guide captain served also as a
pastor, the person who dealt in a pastoral way with the girls' personal
problems and needs. One of the most talented pupils in the school, a
Hindu, was particularly close to my wife because she was a patrol
leader in the guide company. She was also a good violinist and, though
a Hindu, played the violin for the singing in the church. She was a very
likeable and alive person. During a crisis in the girl's life, my wife
prayed with her and for her and also found real opportunity to talk to
her about Jesus Christ. About the time that the girl was to leave school,

she was very close to the decision to become a Christian, but she did not. In the final conversation that she had with my wife on this subject, she said that she had pondered the whole question but could not persuade herself that it was worth giving up her own Hindu home and her immediate Hindu community in order to become a member of the Christian church. She had no intention of rejecting the claims of Jesus Christ on her own life, nor of pronouncing a judgment on the Christian community; but she felt that she could be true to him without adding to her decision all the burdens that would arise if she should choose to belong to the Christian community also. She said to my wife, "You will continue to love me still, but that is no reason why I should become a Christian."

Whenever I have thought about Jesus Christ and who he is, this particular incident has a way of intruding into my thinking. I myself was involved in this incident because I too prayed with this girl during the days of her decision. I have never been able to forget the fact that somehow Jesus was able to stand apart from the Christian community in the thinking and deciding of someone whom he had surely managed to find.

The Nature of the Question

I believe fully that a decision to follow Jesus Christ is inextricably linked with the decision to become a member of the Christian church. There is a very true sense in which the refusal to become a Christian constitutes also a refusal to belong to Christ. The story that I have related is not intended to question the theology of this connection between Jesus Christ and his church. It is related rather to show that, in spite of this connection, men and women do find themselves confronted by Jesus alone and, whatever their decision, it is on the distinctive question of who he is that that decision has turned.

Though in the story which I have related there was no intention to pronounce a judgment on the Christian community, sometimes the way in which the decision for or against Jesus Christ presents itself to a person makes a judgment on the Christian community also inevitable. After our marriage, my wife and I lived in the village where the school is at which my wife taught. A member of that village community met us one day and told us that he was being faced with the decision to become a Christian. He belonged to one of what we call the depressed class groups. "We are told," he said, "that if we become Christians, we can

213

have the help of the church and of the missionaries to provide for us economic and educational uplift." But, as he put it, his problem was that he could not bring himself to practice the dishonesties that were necessary if he were to find favor with the missionaries and with those in authority in the church. He decided to remain as he was.

This incident revealed to me something about the nature of the Christian church which I had not seen before. The Hindu community has no religious organization, nor has the Buddhist. They have religious institutions, but there is no organization that dispenses patronage and in which careerism is both a temptation and a necessity. The very nature of the church's task in the world has made the church a socio-religious organization. To have such an organization linked theologically to Jesus Christ produces a number of problems which are well-nigh insoluble. The Gospel records show how Jesus Christ came into conflict with the socio-religious organization of his own time and people. The crux of the matter lies in recognizing that such a conflict is not only inevitable, but also legitimate. The crucifixion was not a disaster which overtook Jesus. It was the only possible outcome of that conflict in which Jesus was involved: an outcome which is the source of the illumination, power, and authority which men have needed to give their own answers to this conflict, as they have faced it in every generation and in every varying situation. The particular person I have been talking about found himself unable to face the question, "Who is this Jesus?" by itself. He could not get it disentangled from a host of other questions in which it was enmeshed. All the more reason, then, that we look alone at the question of Jesus Christ. Who is he?

There is a third person I want to talk about. He is a personal friend of mine who is also our family doctor. He too is a Hindu. The apostle Paul speaks of the fruit of the Spirit as love, joy, peace, patience, kindness, goodness, faithfulness, gentleness, self-control (Gal. 5:22). By using the singular, the "fruit of the Spirit," Paul is not merely talking of these various virtues and qualities, but about the way in which they belong together and interpenetrate one another. (When he speaks of the works of the flesh, he talks in the plural.) Speaking quite deliberately, I would say that one of the best examples I know of the fruit of the Spirit, as Paul has defined it, is this doctor friend of mine. I am quite aware that we have a tendency to look at our fellow Christians under a microscope, whereas we look at other good men through a telescope. And yet I am prepared to stand by my statement. My object in making it, however, is not to state a comparison between Hindu and Christian, but to point to the fact itself that here in a Hindu is the fruit of the Spirit.

214

But why do I speak of a Hindu in Christian terms? Only because I cannot find in Hinduism itself a satisfying explanation of the source and vitality of true goodness. Only in Jesus Christ and the forgiveness wrought by him, and only in the Holy Spirit and the energy he bestows do I discern an adequate explanation of how man can be good.

Here we see from another angle the point of the question: Who is this Jesus? What is his relation to men, to all men, to each man? To think of Jesus as the founder of a religion and, therefore, to seek an answer to the question, "Who is Jesus?" by approaching it from within that religion seems to me to be quite misleading. The question, "Who is Jesus?" cannot be an important question unless it is also a question concerning every man.

Let what I have said so far serve to provide a glimpse into the kind of questioning I find myself grappling with as I seek to understand the true meaning of who Jesus is and the implications thereof. The particular twists and turns of the argument may otherwise be quite puzzling. Each man comes to the question, "Who is this Jesus?" by his own particular road. No one can avoid the junction where these roads meet, but the road by which each has arrived at the junction has its own interpretative significance.

The Man Jesus

To speak of the finality of Jesus Christ is to speak specifically of the man Jesus. It is to talk neither about the finality of the Christ-experience, nor about the finality of the Christ-revelation, but about Jesus Christ himself. The issue is not whether all true religious experience is an experience of God in Jesus Christ, nor whether Jesus Christ is the final and, therefore, determinative revelation of God; but whether it is true that God has set, in the world and among men, this man Jesus as final—him to whom they must hearken, him whom they must obey, him through whom they will live and by whom they will be judged. Is Paul right when he says, "For although . . . there are many 'gods' and many 'lords'—yet for us there is one God, the Father, from whom are all things and for whom we exist, and one Lord, Jesus Christ, through whom are all things and through whom we exist"? (I Cor. 8:5-6.)

Some time ago, at an international student conference of theological students, I had a strange experience. I found myself listening to a discussion about Jesus Christ, only to find that the Jesus Christ they were talking about was simply a historical point of reference around whom a

215

body of doctrine and ethics had been built. They kept on saying, this is the Jesus Christ whom through the centuries the church has believed in and proclaimed and whom Christians have experienced. But they denied that it was possible really to know what Jesus Christ was like or said or did when he walked the earth in the flesh. There was a bare skeleton of events which could be attested to with certainty. The rest was claimed to be "proclamation." It is not my intention to go into this question at this time. But I do want to say that, if our attempt thus far to get within hearing and seeing distance of the man Jesus has been a failure, then talk about the finality of Jesus Christ is simply futile. The crux of the finality issue is whether or not in Jesus Christ men confront and are confronted by the transcendent God whose will they cannot manipulate, by whose judgment they are bound, and with whose intractable presence in their midst they must reckon.

The Coordinates of Faith—the Universal and the Particular

As one lives and works with men of other faiths, one is made constantly aware not only of the fact that Christians have beliefs different from those who are not Christian, but also of the fact that they believe in a different way. The very act of faith is different. The basic reason for this is that the coordinates within which the graph of the Christian faith is plotted are quite different from the coordinates used in other religions and other systems of belief. It is not simply that the graphs themselves are different.

One basic difference is that whereas, in all other religions, the coordinates of faith are determined by the relation between the infinite and the finite, the eternal and the temporal, in Christianity they are determined by the relation between the universal and the particular. The scriptural testimony is not that Jesus Christ is a finite manifestation of the infinite, but that he is the universal become particular—the image of the invisible God (Col. 1:15). Jesus Christ is neither a darshana nor an avatar.

The point at issue is the difference between the various experiences of meeting God and the experience of the compulsive specific obedience which one has when one meets Jesus. Jesus of Nazareth, whenever he addressed men, addressed them with specific demands: leave your nets, take up your bed, sell what you have. He is still the same Jesus. The experience of meeting God which is known as the mystical experience, and which is testified to by the devotees in all religions, is best understood within the relation between the infinite and the finite. When one is talking about the finality of Jesus Christ, however, one is talking about how this mystical experience is pegged down to this earthly life. To paraphrase Paul, the particular consists "in the works he has prepared for us to walk in" (Eph. 2:10).

That which is being contended for is not the prestige of a particular place of meeting between God and man, but the peculiarity of what happens when men meet God in Jesus Christ. When Jesus announced that "the kingdom of God is at hand," and demanded of men that they "repent, and believe in the gospel" (Mark 1:15), he was asking not for some general response to the requirements of religion or morality, but for a specific commitment to a particular event and person. The religious man is one kind of man, a Christian disciple is another kind of man. There is no substitute for the "shattering" which takes place when men meet God at God's place and hour of appointment, and for the consequences in discipline and discipleship of that experience.

Attempts have been made, again and again, to change this axis around which the Christian faith rotates, to change these coordinates within which the graph of that faith is plotted. There have always been those who have desired to understand the Christian faith, not in terms of the relation between the universal and the particular, but in terms of the relation between the infinite and the finite, the eternal and the temporal. In this discussion, the crux of the argument has always been concerning the resurrection of Jesus Christ. The New Testament insistence on the decisive significance of the resurrection of Jesus Christ constitutes a denial of the view that Jesus is a temporal manifestation of the eternal God, a finite appearance of him who is infinite. The finite and the temporal are categories which apply to that which is repeatable. The resurrection faith, however, is concerned with the eternity and universality of Jesus Christ himself. What the New Testament is announcing is not that the Christ-experience cannot be destroyed by death, nor that in the Christ-revelation death is seen to be not final, but that Jesus himself rose from the dead. The testimony is not to the life of Jesus after death, but to his conquest of death. What the New Testament makes clear is that while the risen Christ offers himself only to the perception of faith, he is nevertheless to be proclaimed to all men as having risen from the dead. There is a happening apart from faith which is proclaimed, even though it is to faith that the proclamation is addressed. As Paul puts it, "God . . . has given assurance to all men by raising him from the dead" (Acts 17:31). When Peter says, "This Jesus, . . . you crucified and killed. . . . But God raised him up" (Acts 2:23-24), he means not something that had happened to the disciples, but something that had happened to Jesus.

Also, even as by its testimony to the resurrection of Jesus Christ the New Testament witnesses to the eternity of the specific man Jesus, even so by its testimony to the ascension of Jesus Christ the New Testament seeks to say that in Jesus the distinction between the infinite and the finite is an irrelevant distinction. "Seated at the right hand of God" is a way of saying that here is the operative reality, the whole is present at this point and in this person, this is both the infinite and the finite, he is what God is with respect to all things—their Sovereign and Savior, their Judgment and their Judge.

Now we can see how it is that, while the New Testament testimony is to a specific event which happened, it is able also to speak of this event in the present tense. For precisely in the fact that the New Testament faith concerning Jesus Christ is stated unambiguously in terms of the relation between the universal and the particular lies the ground for the New Testament witness that Jesus Christ is the same yesterday, today, and forever (Heb. 13:8). The finality that is asserted is not the finality of an event in the past or a person in the past, but the finality of him who is continuously and identifiably present. "He must reign until he has put all his enemies under his feet." (I Cor. 15:25.) "I am with you always, to the close of the age." (Matt. 28:20.)

When God revealed himself to Moses, he revealed himself as one who was recognized by being continuously present, and by being known by that presence alone (Exod. 3:14). Moses had to lead his people to follow a God who would never become past tense. The second commandment, "You shall not make yourself a graven image" (Exod. 20:4), is a commandment not to attempt to make God static. Indeed, no understanding of God which is delimited by a past tense is satisfactory. The attraction of thinking in terms of the infinite and the finite is that the finite can keep on repeating itself so that no past tense need be determinative. There is no finality because there is constant repetition. As the Bhagavad Gita has it, "Though unborn and immutable in essence, though Lord of Beings, yet governing Nature which is mine, I come into being by my delusive power. For whensoever right declines, O Bharata, and wrong uprises, then I create myself" (iv. 6-7).

The biblical faith has a different thrust. The finality which is affirmed about Jesus Christ is set within the context of an ongoing activity of God, whereby the past does not remain past but is continuously becoming present. In the Exodus passage to which reference has been made, it is the God of Abraham, Isaac, and Jacob who reveals himself to Moses as "I am." So also, the New Testament witness to the finality of Jesus

218

Christ is not simply to the finality of a past event, but of a present Savior. It is the same bush which is burning without being consumed. When the church confesses, "And I believe in Jesus Christ—born, suffered, crucified, died, and buried; who rose again and has ascended and will come," it is of the same Jesus that every item in this confession is made (Acts 1:11). It is he who is final; not that everything is over, but that he encompasses everything that takes place. In the closing words of the Bible, as Jesus speaks them, "I am the Alpha and the Omega, the first and the last, the beginning and the end" (Rev. 22:13).

The Coordinates of Faith—This World and This Life

This way of relating past tense to present tense takes the discussion from a consideration of the person of Christ to a consideration of his work. When Jesus declared that the kingdom of God had come, there was a double thrust in that declaration. The event of the coming was past tense. But the kingdom of God itself was present continuous tense. The finality of Jesus Christ is the finality of an ongoing work.

This indissoluble connection between the person of Jesus Christ and his work, when speaking of his finality, leads to a clarification of a second basis of difference between the coordinates of the Christian faith and those of other faiths and beliefs. The scriptures of other religions deal fundamentally either with the interior life or the life after death. The Christian scriptures, however, speak in the first instance about this present life in this world in all its concreteness and its particularities. Other religions hold that the important thing in the drama of life is what happens to the actors; while the Christian scriptures affirm that what happens to the actors is only a part of God's concern. His total concern encompasses the whole drama—men, women, and children, and all of nature, in their relationships to one another and in their several particularities of age and sex, of community and race, of nation and religion, and across the generations of time. It is this insistence on this world and this life which gives to the New Testament declaration that in Jesus God became man its true context.

When the name of Jesus is announced as "Emmanuel—God with us" (Matt. 1:23), the announcement affirms the "with-ness" of God on which human life depends. Man is made in the image of God (Gen. 1:27). This imaging relationship, in which man is perpetually placed before God, constitutes the meaning and responsibility of human life. The God-man relationship is a treble one. "In him we live and move and have our

219

being." (Acts 17:28.) But this God, in whom we are, is also the God who is within us (Col. 1:27). He is constantly in our lives and within our personalities seeking to evoke in us a true response to himself. In the third place, he to whom this response has to be made, and who is seeking this response, is also constantly present as the reality of God outside us, impinging on us, both in wrath and in mercy, both in judgment and in demand (Rev. 3:20). There is no way of simplifying the God-man relationship so that any one of these three relations—God's inclusiveness, his immanence, and his transcendence—is subsumed under the other two. When Scripture testifies to the finality of Jesus Christ, it is speaking of this fact of Jesus as Emmanuel, God with us, in the richness of this threefold relation, and in so doing, bears witness to the several aspects of the work of Christ.

1. The first strand in the biblical testimony to the work of Jesus Christ is that it is *he from whom all things proceed and receive their vocation*. Paul states this quite directly when he says, "All things were created through him and for him" (Col. 1:16). Scripture does not find it a logical burden to attribute to Jesus Christ the origin of things, because it sees clearly that their meaning is in him. All things were not only made through him, but nothing made is outside him (John 1:13). He is the one in whom all things are, and who is in all things. Their true nature and vocation is what he is in them and what they are in him.

The significance of what is being said here lies in the fact that, by this way of saying it, the Creator and his creation are shown as being bound together. "He through whom all things were created is also the first-born of all creation." (See Col. 1:15-16.) The whole of creation is invested with meaning because he is part of them. In him the "with-ness" of God is affirmed. All things are from him and he is of them.

2. The natural next step in the biblical testimony is to speak of Jesus Christ as *he in whom all things cohere and work together* (Col. 1:17). Everything keeps moving and changing, and yet the whole thing holds together. Things do not fly apart. Life remains a unity in spite of all its diversity. The mystery of evil too is held within the exercise of God's sovereign grace (II Thess. 2:7-8). An inclusive purpose binds everything together, a purpose which belongs to someone in ultimate authority. Men experience this ultimacy in personal life, as they see how he rules and overrules all things, "in everything [working] for good with all those who love him" (Rom. 8:28); while, in the life of society, this ultimacy is maintained and declared through a mission. "All authority in heaven and on earth," Jesus says, "has been given to me. Go therefore

and make disciples of all nations" (Matt. 28:18-19). The apostles are sent everywhere and to everyone, because everywhere and over everyone, Jesus is already in authority. No wonder Paul in his close-knit argument in his letter to the Romans makes Jesus Christ the key to the understanding of the whole of history. "No failure," he says, "is final. No betrayal or disobedience is ultimate. There is always a way out of what seems a blind alley. No one is outside the overarching purposes of God. O the depth of the riches and wisdom and knowledge of God! How unsearchable are his judgments, and how inscrutable his ways! For from him and through him and to him are all things." (Rom. 11:33, 36.)

This way of stating the finality of Jesus rests on the fact that, as he is part of creation and is himself involved in human history, that which happened to him must become the source of that which happens to all. He is the pioneer of our salvation (Heb. 2:10). So that even as it is possible to speak of the whole as being infected by sin, we can speak of the whole as being infected by salvation (I Cor. 15:21-22). The pioneer does not set an example to be followed; he opens up a highway by which men can now go to the land that has been won for them by him.

3. However, the teaching of Scripture is not that in Jesus all is now well, and well anyhow. Jesus is *he by whom all things are judged and brought to judgment*. His finality bears a consequence for all things.

As John puts it, the fact that God has sent his Son into the world sets before men a real choice—either to believe in him and so to share in eternal life, the life which he lives in the world; or to live apart from him and so to perish (John 3:16). That which has perished has no use. Just as a fruit which has perished is useless for eating, so he who has perished is of no use to Jesus Christ. And, conversely, to be of no use to Jesus Christ is to perish.

The point is that there is a determining reality in the world which is Jesus Christ at work in it. "In him was life, and the life was the light of men." (John 1:4.) This light has now come into the world (John 1:9). So that the life he lives in the world becomes the way by which all men must walk, as it also decides the way in which all men must work. As he himself explained it, only those who work with him gather, while the rest only scatter (Luke 11:23).

4. But this testimony to the activity of God in judgment, of which Jesus Christ is the judge because he is God's intervention in and God's decision for human life, is set within the context of the promise that Jesus is *he through whom all things fulfill their destiny*.

In the prophecy of Jeremiah, the new beginning is set out in these terms: "I will put my law within them, and I will write it upon their hearts; . . . for I will forgive their iniquity, and I will remember their sin no more" (Jer. 31:33-34). A great act of forgiveness is the matrix within which judgment is exercised; or, in New Testament terms, Christ's act of atonement is also the basis of the judgment he exercises.

The New Testament does not worry about the logical contradiction between its teaching that damnation is a possibility for men, so that this may be the judgment which is pronounced on some at the last, and its teaching that God's plan in Christ for the fullness of time is to unite all things in him (Eph. 1:10). Indeed, the New Testament shows that it is out of this very contradiction that there arises both the gospel which is proclaimed and the reason for proclaiming it. If salvation is by grace, damnation cannot be by works; so that the issue of faith and unfaith must be stringently understood in relation to the person and work of Jesus Christ.

This recapitulation, however, of all things in Jesus Christ at the end of the process of history is already taking place in the world. It is personal experience that when the entries in the book of men's lives are brought under the heading of Jesus Christ, many a transaction which seemed at the time to be gain will be seen really to have been loss, while others which seemed at the time to have been loss will be seen to be gain. Besides, because this life and activity of Jesus Christ is his life and activity in the world, it is meaningful to speak too of human cultures being recapitulated in him and through him. Thus, when an Indian thinker speaks of "wedding the Spirit of Christ with the spirit of India," he is asking that Christ's presence in India be discerned so that that which belongs to India may be brought into his obedience and into the service of his glory. "They shall bring into [Zion] the glory and the honor of the nations." (Rev. 21:26.)

5. The climax of the biblical testimony, therefore, to the finality of Jesus Christ is that it is *he unto whom all things go.* This is the natural climax to the affirmation that the finality of Jesus Christ is not simply the finality of himself as a person, but is also the finality of his work as the effective presence in the world of the kingdom and reign of God.

On the one hand, there is this reign as it impinges on human life through the exercise of Christ's Lordship and Saviorhood. On the other hand, there is the work of the Holy Spirit in the hearts and minds of men, evoking repentance and faith, and enabling the response of obedience and discipleship. The finality of Jesus Christ receives its full Trinitarian affirmation only as it takes seriously this New Testament witness to the work of the Holy Spirit. For apart from him, the gift of grace in Jesus Christ is not received. It is the Holy Spirit who teaches men to live by the Father's welcome, enabling each man to say, "Abba! Father!" It is also by him that they are led to inherit that which Jesus Christ has made their inheritance (Rom. 8:16-17).

This essential work of the Holy Spirit has as its hallmark the way in which things and persons are brought to participation in the crisis of Christ's death and resurrection. Individuals die with him in his death, and find that in losing themselves they save themselves. Also, every perception of truth and every system of moral behavior is brought to dissolution by him, when it is submitted to him, and then resurrected to new life within his obedience and in his service.

Part V

Contemporary Voices

As Methodism has moved into the late twentieth century, it is characterized by vigor and diversity. The tradition is not insular and has responded to new historical, philosophical, and sociological challenges. In many of these areas, Methodist theologians have provided leadership for the wider theological community.

James H. Cone initiated and has expanded black theology. José Míguez Bonino is a clear Protestant voice among Latin American liberation theologians. Schubert M. Ogden is a strong and creative philosophical theological voice. Rupert E. Davies discusses authority in order to speak to contemporary sensibility. Frances M. Young returns with fresh insight to a continuing interest. Geoffrey Wainwright contributes by looking both to the past and the future of Methodism and the Christian faith. Stanley M. Hauerwas has exposed issues and offers positions that have helped to focus much debate. Rebecca S. Chopp sets an agenda and contributes content to a feminist theology.

James H. Cone

James H. Cone (b. 1938) has had a distinguished career at Union Theological Seminary, New York. He was the first black theologian to gain attention from the wider North American Christian community and continues to participate in theological conversation. His sense of his own tradition and its values, as well as his awareness of the general theological arena, have made it possible for him to speak across the boundaries and to enrich both. The article chosen here is from chapter 4 of his most recent book, *For My People* (Orbis Books, 1984, pp. 78-98). In this selection, Cone reviews his own work and sets it within contemporary theological discussion.

Strengths and Weaknesses in the Early Development of Black Theology

Black theology is not an unsophisticated, anti-intellectual reaction to whatever is happening at any moment in time—a mixture of emotion and pious propaganda. It is, rather, a hardheaded, practical, and passionate reading of the signs of the times in the white community as well as the black. It is an elucidation of what we have understood God to be about in our history, particularly in the history of our struggle against racist oppression. . . . Black theology was formulated by Christian activists in response to events—events which had the unmistakable sign that God is saying and doing something about black people in white America.

Gayraud S. Wilmore

Every theology is limited by the social location of the ones who create it. This is true of black theologians and preachers who created black theology with the Bible in one hand and the newspaper in the other. Black theology, as Wilmore has put it, is "eventful theology"—that is, a theology that came into being through black theologians' response to the eventful happenings of their time. They believed that God was involved in the revolution that was erupting in America, and their task was that of identifying God's liberating presence in the events so they could announce the coming kingdom of freedom and participate in its implementation.

Because theology is limited by the place and time of its creation, it is important for theology to evaluate itself critically, identifying its strengths and weaknesses, so that it can build upon the former and, as much as possible, avoid the latter. If theology does not become self-critical, it will definitely lose its Christian identity by becoming nothing but an academic reflection of the self-interest of those who do it.

Black theologians have been particularly critical of white theology because of its lack of self-criticism in relation to racism. That criticism will continue to have credibility only to the degree that black theologians apply to themselves what they say is lacking in white theology.

As one of the early interpreters of black theology, I cannot claim to be perfectly objective in my evaluation. Despite this limitation, I shall attempt to be self-critical regarding black theology, realizing that my own personal involvement in it necessarily prevents me from seeing what may be some of its most obvious and serious limitations.

The Strengths of Nascent Black Theology

Faith and Struggle

The most original and lasting contribution of black theology has been its ability to relate creatively the Christian faith and the black freedom struggle in American society. Although black preachers, before and after the Civil War, had already made important contributions in this area, it was the NCBC [National Council of Black Churchmen] black clergy radicals who deepened the connection between the gospel and the struggle to the degree that it has acquired a permanent place in the theology and activity of the black church. Some conservative members of the black clergy tried to ignore the radical, political side of their heritage, but they found it increasingly more difficult to deny it when confronted with the persuasive historical analysis of Gayraud Wilmore's *Black Religion and Black Radicalism* and its contemporary manifestation in the writings and activities of the NCBC clergy.

The central question that gave birth to black theology was: "What has the gospel of Jesus to do with the oppressed black people's struggle for justice in American society?" The radical black NCBC clergy pursued a substantial examination of that question, which separated them from both white liberal and black conservative church persons. In the process of rereading the Bible in the light of black history, black clergy radicals concluded that both biblical and black histories revealed God's unqualified solidarity with the poor in their fight against injustice. This revelation disclosed *God's salvation* as being identical with *human liberation*. In the United States, black theologians were the first to identify liberation with salvation, and thus with the core of the Christian gospel. It was in this context that they began to refer to God as the liberator of the oppressed Hebrew slaves in Egypt and to Jesus as the new liberator whom God has anointed "to preach the good news to the poor, to proclaim release to the captives, and to set at liberty those who are oppressed" (Luke 4:18, 19, RSV).

White liberal and black conservative preachers distanced themselves from the radical NCBC interpretation of the gospel as liberation, and many openly claimed that the gospel could not be identified with the politics of the poor or the rich, black or white. White biblical and theological experts often looked with a condescending scholarly arrogance upon our biblical exegesis, saying in essence that anyone with appropriate theological training knows that the gospel cannot be identical with the black struggle for justice. But black theologians refused to retreat from their claim that the God of the Bible is the liberator of victims of oppression. If that theological claim has any merit, they concluded, then the God of Jesus must be identified with the politics of black liberation.

Subsequent to black theologians' identification of the gospel with liberation, this theme has been enlarged with their discovery of similar emphases in the writings of feminist and Third World theologians in Latin America, Africa, Asia, and the Caribbean. Even many white biblical scholars have begun to give lip service to the centrality of the liberation theme in the Bible. But it is significant that black theologians were the first in the United States to identify liberation as the heart of the gospel of Jesus.

228

Attack on Racism

Another contribution of black theology was its exposure of and attack on racism in the white church and its theology. Although blacks have always identified racist acts as un-Christian, they had seldom claimed that racism in white churches excluded them from the Christian community. Of course white theologians and preachers, with perhaps a few exceptions, have not defended racism (certainly not as openly and consistently as in South Africa). But it was the black NCBC clergy that exposed the existence of racism in white churches and condemned it for what it was: an un-Christian heresy. This prophetic denunciation of white racism also made members of the black clergy realize that an alternative theology was needed if they were going to develop an interpretation of the gospel that would empower blacks in their liberation struggle. . . .

Accent on Black History and African Heritage

The black clergy radicals' rereading of black history in the context of their attack on white racism led to a deeper appreciation of their cultural past, extending back through slavery to Africa. "Black" replaced "Negro" and Africa acquired a special importance as black theologians searched for the theological meaning of their historical roots. "What has Africa to do with African-Americans?" That was the question that inspired our theological imagination and made us realize that Western Christianity could not exhaust the theological meaning of our religious past. The NCBC "Message to the Churches from Oakland" stated:

> We black people are a religious people. From the earliest recorded time we have acknowledged a Supreme Being. With the fullness of our physical bodies and emotions we have unabashedly worshiped him with shouts of joy and in the tears of pain and anguish. We neither believe that God is dead, white, nor captive to some highly nationalistic and dogmatic formulations of the Christian faith which relate him exclusively to the canons of the Old and New Testaments.

It was Gayraud Wilmore who brought the theological significance of blackness and Africa into NCBC documents. His *Black Religion and Black Radicalism* analyzed black religion as defined by its African heritage. Looking back, Wilmore said that the NCBC "launched the first attempt since Garveyism to separate mainline black Christianity from the theology of the white churches and conceived liberation in the context of the legitimate use of ethnic consciousness and power."

Others who supported Wilmore and also made significant published contributions included Henry Mitchell, Leonard Barrett, Charles Long, Albert Raboteau, and Cecil Cone. The investigation of the relationship between Africa and black religion in the U.S.A. had a profound effect on the interpretations of black theology. The emphasis on Africa and ethnic consciousness, along with the liberation theme, separated black theology from the religion of white churches. With the accent on Africa, the theme of *survival* was combined with that of liberation—the latter being influenced most by biblical and black church histories, and the former derived from African religions and philosophy.

Due to my limited knowledge of the impact of Africa upon black religion in the U.S.A., black theologians were particularly critical of my inordinate dependence upon European theology and philosophy in my initial efforts to develop a black theology of liberation. If theology is to be black, must it not use the cultural resources in black and African history for an explication of its identity? Can theology be black if it uses European theological and philosophical concepts as the primary tools for its interpretation of human existence? Black theologians forced these questions upon me, making it impossible to do black theology apart from a serious encounter with black history and culture.

The idea of a black God and a black Christ began to acquire a deeper meaning than merely that of a reference to the political and economic liberation of blacks. It acquired a cultural meaning that was unique to blacks as defined by their slave and African past. Although black theologians need to do much more historical investigation in this area, we have called to the attention of the black Christian community the theological significance of its African heritage.

Challenge to Conservative Black Churches

Just as black theology attacked the racism in white churches, it also criticized the conservative posture of black churches that tolerated racism. Although the black church was born in slavery as a beacon of liberation for enslaved Africans, the black church of the 1960s seemed to have forgotten its liberating heritage. Many young blacks of the urban ghettoes dismissed the black church because they did not see any real distinction between its gospel and the religion of whites. Furthermore, most black church leaders seemed unconcerned about the black struggle for freedom in society and focused their emphasis on a heavenly freedom in the next world. NCBC radicals attacked the pie-in-the-sky religion of black churches as an imitation of white religion. In *Black Theology and Black Power* I wrote:

> So far, the black church has remained conspicuously silent, continuing its business as usual. The holding of conferences, the election of bishops, the fund-raising drive for a new building or air conditioner seem to be more important than the blacks who are shot because they want to be [human]. The black church, though spatially located in the community of the oppressed, has not responded to the needs of its people. It has, rather, drained the community, seeking to be more and more like the white church. Its ministers have condemned the hopeless and have mimicked the values of whites. For this reason most black power people bypass the church as irrelevant to their objectives. . . .

Accent on Black Ecumenism

With the rise of black theology, it became clear that the denominational identities that black churches derived from the white churches from which they separated were completely irrelevant in our struggle for freedom. As Malcolm X taught us:

> When we come together, we don't come together as Baptists or Methodists. You don't catch hell because you are a Baptist, and you don't catch hell because you are a Methodist . . . , you don't catch hell because you're a Democrat or a Republican, you don't catch hell because you are a Mason or an Elk, and you sure don't catch hell because you're an American; because if you were an American, you wouldn't catch hell. You catch hell because you're a black [person]. You catch hell, all of us catch hell for the same reason. . . .

A black ecumenism that was defined by a radical commitment to the black poor sounded new to most twentieth-century black church persons. Martin King's civil rights movement created a similar ecumenical spirit, but it was destroyed with the rise of black power. But NCBC radicals were determined to reestablish communications and solidarity with those radicals who had broken with King. Black clergy radicals wanted to convince secular black activists that one can be radically black and also Christian. For according to the NCBC, one's Christian identity is defined more by one's commitment to the liberation of the poor than by repeating a confession of faith in Jesus written by Europeans.

231

The Weaknesses of Nascent Black Theology

Because theology is a human undertaking, it reflects the limitations of those who do it. I wish to point out four interrelated weaknesses in the development of black theology by black theologians and preachers.

Negative Overreaction to White Racism

We allowed our definition of black theology to be too much a *reaction* to racism in the white churches and society. A new black theological consciousness began with the publication of the "Black Power Statement" on July 31, 1966. It was written primarily as a reaction to the white church establishment that assumed that its liberal and neoorthodox theologies provided the most appropriate answer to the issues raised by black power. Instead of rejecting black power as the sin of pride among blacks (as whites asserted), black clergy radicals endorsed it as an appropriate assertion of black dignity in the context of conscienceless white power. . . .

A similar weakness is found in my early texts on black theology, especially *Black Theology and Black Power* and *A Black Theology of Liberation*. It was as if the sole basis for black theology were racism among whites. But if so, and if racism were eliminated, then there would be no need for a theology based on the history and culture of blacks. I said:

> The appearance of black theology on the American scene then is due exclusively to the failure of white religionists to relate the gospel of Jesus to the pain of being black in a white racist society. It arises from the need of black people to liberate themselves from white oppressors.

Black theology, then, was being created out of a negative reaction to whites rather than as a positive reaction to the history and culture of blacks.

Lack of Social Analysis

The response of black theologians to white racism was based too much upon moral suasion and too little upon the tools of social analysis. The assumption of the black clergy radicals of the NCBC was that the racism of white members of the clergy could be eliminated through an appeal to their moral guilt and consciousness as Christians. Although the un-Christian behavior of whites caused us to question their Christian identity, we still assumed that if the contradiction between racism and Christianity were clearly pointed out to them, they would change and act in a Christian manner. We were naive, because our analysis of the problem was too superficial and did not take into consideration the links between racism, capitalism, and imperialism, on the one hand, and theology and the church on the other. The connection between theology and racism became clear to us only gradually, because we did not have the theological training that could offer a serious intellectual challenge to Euro-American theology. Though we were convinced that white theology was racist, we could not articulate this conviction conceptually. The inability to articulate the theological meaning of the relationship of Christianity to blackness created a theological ambiguity in the early NCBC documents. If we had used the tools of the social sciences and had given due recognition to the Christian doctrine of sin, then it is unlikely that we would have placed such inordinate dependence on the methodology of moral suasion.

No one has given a more creative critique of the early NCBC documents than Vincent Harding in his "No Turning Back?" It is required reading for all black church members who have a radical bent. He points out the integrationist slant of the 1966 "Black Power Statement," which speaks of "our beloved country, of basically American goals, and of the desire for participation 'at all levels of the life of our nation.'" There is no creative social analysis and thus no program for radical change. It seems that we thought that change would occur through rhetoric alone. There is no analysis of the depth of racism or capitalism.

One reason for this serious limitation is related to the middle-class origins of black theologians and preachers, as well as the ecclesiastical context of the documents. The NCBC was reacting almost exclusively to white churches, and there was not much dialogue outside the context defined by our reaction to whites. As Vincent Harding expressed it:

> The churchmen were essentially reactors, not initiating concepts or programs, but answering, interpreting the initiatives of others. They had been called together by crisis—like so many black protestors—and had not developed an ideology beyond blackness, or a set of prophetic directions for black struggle. So they were forced to be vague. Indeed, there were not even any significant specific initiatives proposed for a movement to integrate into American society. Somehow, as a group, they were unprepared to provide them, and it was this lack of its own clear thrust, its own initiating point of view, which crippled the NCBC position.

The appeal to the moral goodness of whites reflected the continued influence of Martin King rather than that of Malcolm X. The content of the NCBC message was still derived primarily from Martin King, but the militant spirit in which the black clergy expressed it suggested a definite movement toward Malcolm X. The emergence of black theology, then, is due to the attempt of black theologians to integrate a cleavage in black life: Martin and Malcolm, Christianity and blackness, Christian love and a militant defense of black dignity. This was the paradox that captivated us and demanded a theological resolution. It was also the paradox that revealed our most serious limitations.

When a people's response to a situation of oppression is defined exclusively by its feelings of moral outrage, an appeal to the morality of the oppressor usually follows. This method of change is found throughout black history, from Frederick Douglass to Martin Luther King, Jr. It is the typical response of integrationists, because they are firm believers in the American Dream as defined by the Declaration of Independence and the faith of American churches. The early interpreters of black theology fall within this tradition, even though we were moving toward the nationalist philosophy of Malcolm X. The assumption behind the choice of the method of moral suasion was that the oppressor was unaware of the depth of the evil of racism, and that if its demonic consequences were revealed and acknowledged, the oppressor would be morally embarrassed and stop being racist. . . .

Vincent Harding correctly analyzed our problem:

> The documents . . . remind us of how nearly impossible it has been for the radical rhetoric to be transformed into radical action. They remind us that the men who control the systems of American oppression have consistently found ways either to cajole, co-opt, threaten, or destroy a frighteningly large portion of those black leaders who move in such radical directions. They remind us that the system itself has managed to absorb just enough changes demanded to assuage the immediate hurts. . . . Perhaps most importantly, they remind us that rhetoric has not often been turned into action, because rhetoric did not become analysis and analysis did not develop program and program did not lead to insistent, careful organizing of our people to effect radical change.

Lack of Economic Analysis

Related to our failure to move beyond moral suasion to the development of radical programs for change based on social analysis was our avoidance of Marxism as a tool for economic analysis. The black church in particular and the black community generally have a long history of avoiding Marxism. . . . Avoidance is partly due to the mutual marginality of Marxists and the black community, as well as the sectarian nature of the former and the reformist attitudes of the latter. Therefore, it is understandable, though not to their best interests, that black churches have remained aloof from Marxism, especially because it has always been difficult to separate Marxism as a tool of social analysis from Marxism as an atheistic ideology. How could one expect barely literate black church members to embrace a sectarian philosophy such as Marxism while living in the belly of the beast of capitalism?

However, when one reflects upon the 1960s and '70s, it can be argued that black clergy radicals could have deepened their radicalism by using Marxism as an instrument (not ideology) for analyzing the institutions of racism. They had tried integration while following King and later moved toward Malcolm's nationalist philosophy. Both responses have a long history in the black community and neither has achieved alone or together our desired goal—liberation! That fact alone should open us up for new ideas so that we can move beyond the rhetoric of a moral appeal.

Because of the success of Marxism in the Third World and because Soviet Russia no longer defines its essential meaning, young black radicals of the black power era began to experiment with it. The Black Panthers of Oakland are well known for their Marxist bent. Others included the League of Revolutionary Black Workers and several black power advocates in the SNCC. In fact, the preamble to James Forman's *Black Manifesto* was defined by a neo-Marxist ideology. This provided an occasion for black clergy radicals to face head-on the question of Marxism as a tool for analysis. But to my knowledge, we did not even consider the issue seriously. In fact when the NCBC board of directors responded to the *Manifesto,* it did not even mention the Marxist analysis on which it was based, nor did Gayraud Wilmore deal seriously with Marxism in his theological response. The NCBC focused on the demands, not the philosophy. It was not until whites referred to the Marxist philosophy in the *Manifesto* as an excuse for rejecting the demands that the NCBC took up the issue. But even then, we did not really consider Marxism seriously. In our most radical posture (as in the "Message to the Churches from Oakland"), we avoided the issue:

> We do not shrink from the revolutionary, anticapitalistic implications of the *Manifesto.* While all of our members do not give unqualified endorsement of every strategy and tactic stated or implied in the original document issued in Detroit, the National Committee of Black Churchmen, as a

body, is committed to the essential spirit and meaning of the analysis and proposals, and will continue to press them upon the churches and synagogues of America. . . .

Black theologians also encountered Latin American liberation theologians at the TIA conference in Detroit in 1975. About twenty of us met together because of heated public discussions regarding the interrelatedness of racial and class oppression. The dialogue was even more intense in our private meeting, with many black theologians avidly promoting capitalism over socialism. It was at that time that it became clear to me that either black theology would incorporate class analysis into its perspective or it would become a justification of middle-class interests at the expense of black poor. Although claiming to speak for the poor, we actually speak for ourselves. . . .

Since the 1975 encounter with the Latin Americans, I have become convinced that economic analysis is not only an option but a necessity. . . . I am concerned about black theologians' silence on Marxism. How can we provide a genuine check against the self-interest of black theologians and preachers who merely use the language of liberation and the gospel in order to justify their professional advancement? Unless black theologians and preachers face the class issue, the integrity of our commitment to justice for the poor will remain suspect to other freedom fighters and to the poor we claim to represent. Again Frazier was right:

> Although the black bourgeoisie exercise considerable influence on the values of Negroes, they do not occupy a dignified position in the Negro community. The masses regard the black bourgeoisie as simply those who have been "lucky in getting money," which enables them to engage in conspicuous consumption. When this class pretends to represent the best manners or morals of the Negro, the masses regard such claims as hypocrisy. . . .

The reason why King was and still is more radical than the clergy of the NCBC and other interpreters of black theology was the integrity of his commitment and the depth of his analysis. Commitment without analysis leads to romanticism and eventually to despair. Analysis without commitment leads to opportunism and eventually to a betrayal of one's people. The black community needs black theologians who have both a commitment to their people's liberation and the intellectual expertise needed to analyze the nature of this oppression.

Lack of Sexual Analysis

Although I will discuss sexism in black theology and the black church in some detail later . . . , it is important to identify it as a serious weakness among the early interpreters of black theology. Like our failure to deal with classism, sexism blinded us to the depth of the problem of oppression in the black community, and it stifled the development of the human resources for fighting against it. I realize that it was not likely that we could have been progressive and prophetic enough to view sexism as a problem to be addressed in the black community and the society at large. But I believe that the gospel combined with social analysis provides Christians with insight into evil that others often overlook. That is what creates prophets: the gift of God's grace combined with critical interpretation. . . .

Black theologians and ministers, men and women, have major problems to face in the church and the society. Will we be able to face them adequately and thereby create structures in our churches and the community that are liberating? Do we have the *courage* to "tell it like it is," not only in relation to white racism but also in regard to sexism and classism in our churches and our community? Telling the truth can be a risky venture in a church that defines its life on the basis of the professional self-interest of its leaders. It is always much easier to tell the truth about others, and black theologians and preachers have done this task well. But the critical test of the gospel that we preach is whether we can tell the truth about ourselves. For I believe that the gospel of Jesus demands that we tell the truth about our churches that claim to be Christian but in fact have denied that faith with devilish deeds. In the remainder of this book, I will investigate the faithfulness of the black church in relation to urgent problems in our contemporary world in hope that we will face up to our responsibility to live in solidarity with those who are struggling for freedom.

José Míguez Bonino

A Methodist theologian from Argentina, José Míguez Bonino (b. 1924) has viewed Christian interpretation from within the cultural context of Latin America. He has been a leader in Protestant liberation theology and has sought to relate his theological position to critical practical concerns such as serving on the commission to find persons who disappeared in the political turmoil of his nation. Deeply aware of his Methodist tradition, he has sought ecumenical and political extensions. His achievement is to bring freshness to traditional doctrines. The selection included in this volume is from *Rethinking Wesley's Theology for Contemporary Methodism*, Kingswood Books, 1998, pp. 169-82.

Wesley in Latin America: A Theological and Historical Reflection

As a theologian shaped by both the Wesleyan tradition and Latin American Liberation Theology my consuming interest has always been in asking how theological resources might help address the practical realities of human life. On this occasion, in keeping with the trajectory of Ted Runyon's own recent work, I want to explore the relevance of the Wesleyan tradition for a theological understanding of contemporary Latin American religious and social conditions.

A question like this cannot be explored in the abstract. In particular, any appeal to the Wesleyan tradition in the current Latin American setting must take into account the history of how this tradition was introduced and has functioned in this setting. Therefore, I will organize my discussion in three sections: (1) a brief account of how the Wesleyan traditions were introduced into Latin America; (2) an analysis of the specific "readings" of Wesleyan theology that were brought along with these immigrating groups; and (3) a reflection on the relevance of Wesley's own theology for the present Latin American situation.

The Introduction of Wesley to Latin America

As far as I am aware, Wesley never walked south of the English-speaking areas of colonial America. Moreover, I have found no references in his writings to the Latin American countries—perhaps the indexes of the Bicentennial Edition of his works, when they appear, will uncover some unexpected word! Wesley had learned Spanish during his stay in Georgia, from a Sephardic Jewish colony that he visited on the border of Georgia and Florida. There are reminiscences of John of the Cross and Teresa of Avila in some of his writings, although the names are not identified. It seems that he came to know them (particularly Teresa) through brother Molinos of Avila, whom he includes in the *Christian Library* that he prepared for his Methodist people. We know also that he sharply criticized other Spanish (and French and German) mystics for what he saw as their "quietism."

Between 1840 and 1920 however, Wesley was introduced into Latin America through the missionary efforts of the churches that evolved out of the original Wesleyan revival. This immigration took place in three waves.

The first wave came from "mainline" British and North American Methodism, beginning at the opening of the nineteenth century. The earliest arrival was with British settlers (businessmen, ranch or plantation owners, and immigration groups) who obtained permission to practice their religion—naturally, only in the English language—in an otherwise closed Catholic territory. In the second decade of the century, the Methodist Episcopal Church (MEC) in the United States began to send missionaries. Their early efforts were somewhat tentative: to Haiti (1823), Dominican Republic (1834), Uruguay and Argentina (1835), Brazil (1836), and Mexico (1844–45). In the last quarter of the century the pace picked up: Cuba (1873), Panama and Chile (1877), Paraguay and Peru (1886), Bolivia

239

and Venezuela (1890), and Puerto Rico and Costa Rica (1900). By the end of the century the MEC or the (now independent) Methodist Episcopal Church South had established missions in practically all of Latin America.

These early arrivals had to struggle for religious liberty, together with Baptists, Presbyterians, and other mainline Protestant churches. In this effort, they found allies in the new intellectual liberal elites—freemasons, free-thinkers, and positivists. Some of the most outstanding missionaries developed a twofold ministry: an evangelistic mission among the poor (workers and marginal urban and rural populations, "the dust on the surface of society") and an educational and intellectual task among the intelligentsia. The Methodist churches pioneered in the educational task, creating both large, modern schools catering to the children of liberal elites and more modest parish schools serving the poor children of the *barrios*. Social work—hospitals, orphanages, and cooperatives—was also part of their regular program. One result of this educational and social involvement was a socioeconomic mobility that often elevated this first wave into modest middle-class churches. By the 1930s they were well organized and definitely part of the religious establishment.

Today, however, such mainline Methodism represents less than a third of the total Wesleyan family in Latin America. A significant portion of the remaining percentage trace their roots to a second distinct wave of immigration. This second wave was connected to the "holiness movement" that troubled North American Methodism in the second half of the nineteenth century. Out of the tensions created by this movement eventually emerged such holiness denominations as the Wesleyan Methodists, Free Methodists, Church of the Nazarene, Pilgrim Holiness, Church of God (Anderson), Salvation Army, Christian and Missionary Alliance, and several other small churches. Many of these holiness churches already had a missionary presence in Latin America by 1914 and participated in the great Missionary Congress in Panama in 1916. Their evangelistic commitment has helped them become a significant presence, and their theological influence permeates to some extent all Protestant Christianity in Latin America.

The third wave of Wesleyan-influenced churches impacting Latin America began in 1909 in the Methodist church of the port city of Valparaíso in Chile, where a Methodist missionary (Willis Hoover) and his wife received the news, through a missionary in India, about the

Pentecostal renewal that had begun three years before in Azusa Street, Los Angeles. Pentecostal manifestations soon appeared in their church. Two years later a baffled and "orderly" Methodist Church expelled the "rebellious" missionary and congregation on charges of being unbiblical, irrational, and decidedly un-Methodist! The resulting *Iglesia Metodista Pentecostal* (Pentecostal Methodist Church) and the closely related *Iglesia Evangélica Pentecostal* (Pentecostal Protestant Church) make up 75 percent of the total Protestant population of Chile today. Indeed, Pentecostalism now accounts for the majority of Protestants throughout Latin America. Woven through this Pentecostal presence is a major strand of Wesleyan influence, although mixed with several other strands.

It is not terribly important to assess the numerical force of Wesleyan churches in Latin America. Those that officially recognize their Wesleyan origin would probably represent 10 to 15 percent of the total Protestant population of the continent. But the influence of the Wesleyan awakenings has penetrated Latin American Protestantism much more broadly than this official presence suggests.

Which Wesley Was Introduced to Latin America?

With some sense of *how* Wesley was brought to Latin America, we are in position to ask *which* Wesley was brought to Latin America. That is, what influences beyond Wesley himself colored the theology, spirituality, social praxis, worship, and missionary zeal of these three waves of immigration? And how Wesleyan were the resulting churches that took root in Latin America? To answer these questions with any degree of precision would require a major ethnographic study, which has not yet been undertaken. Even so, a few general characterizations can be ventured.

To begin with, Latin America clearly received *a mediated Wesley.* It inherited much of the early Methodist evangelistic zeal. It reproduced some of the original organizational features (certainly a very positive stabilizing factor). In some churches it showed an active social concern reminiscent of Wesley. It also received elements of Methodism's original theological heritage. But all of this was *filtered through the American* (i.e., North American) *experience.* More precisely, the Methodism introduced into Latin America was that shaped by the North American "second

241

great awakening" and holiness movement. One of the clearest evidences of this is the typical hymnal of Wesleyan churches in Latin America. A cursory check will show that they are dominated by the "gospel hymns" of British and American revivalism, and rarely contain more than five or six Wesley hymns. (Given the formative influence of regular singing, this is an important indicator indeed!)

The tendencies of Anglo-American revivalism that were conveyed with the founding of Wesleyan traditions in Latin America continued to influence their development, even in Methodist churches who officially adhered to the classical confessional documents (the Articles of Religion, the General Rules, and Wesley's standard sermons). The polemical conditions in which these churches grew—struggling for their right to exist and to evangelize—reinforced the anti-sacramental and anti-liturgical tendencies already present in that revivalist heritage. One can also discern a strong influence on the self-understanding of Wesleyan-related churches in Latin America (perhaps with the exception of churches related to the MEC) of the polarization between evangelism and social concern that came to characterize American evangelicalism by the early twentieth century (in what Moberg has called "the great reversal"). To be sure, many churches were helping the poor at a local level, and some created and supported schools and orphanages. But this service was not integrated into their evangelistic and theological self-understanding.

The ability of Wesley's precedent to counter such tendencies was hampered by the fact that his story, his writings, and his theology have been largely absent from Latin American Wesleyanism. Only the fifty-two "standard" sermons and a few scattered writings have been translated into Spanish, and books on his life and thought numbered less than a dozen until very recently. In fact, one could say that Wesley has been sequestered—albeit probably unconsciously. This situation was ironically demonstrated at recent workshops that the Latin American Council of Churches (CLAI) organized in Peru, Bolivia, and Chile for ministers of churches of Wesleyan origin—including Methodists, Nazarenes, Pilgrim Holiness, Salvation Army, and Wesleyan Pentecostals. The pastors, many of them from rural and small village congregations, were introduced to a wide variety of Wesley's writings. Their interest in these works was intense. They felt a sense of familiarity with them, but it was a spontaneous response that did not come so much from their prior theological education as from the natural connection they found Wesley making with their own everyday pastoral experience.

As with all generalizations, there are some counter examples to the points that I have made so far. In fact, there is a great diversity in the Latin American Wesleyan family. In some cases the response to specific challenges has resulted in new initiatives that have a certain flavor of early Wesleyan practice (though the persons involved are typically unaware of the similarity). One example would be the Church of the Pilgrims in Peru which, under the crisis of poverty in the 1920s and 1930s and the crisis of violence in the 1970s and 1980s, developed local leadership in small towns and villages that is now widely recognized as the main religious and social reference point for the people of the area. Another example are the Chilean Wesleyan Pentecostal churches, who have strongly engaged their culture—in song, methods of expansion, language, and so on—while retaining the connexional organization, ministerial order, and the sacramental life (including infant baptism) of the Methodist tradition. And one could note how the Methodist church-es in Argentina, Brazil, Mexico, and Uruguay have joined efforts in CIEMAL (Latin American Council of Methodist Churches) to develop graduate and postgraduate Methodist or ecumenical seminaries, to launch publishing houses, to support urban ministry, and to articulate—in different ways and contexts—a theology of participation in public life, which they defend as part of their Wesleyan heritage.

On the whole, despite such scattered counter examples, Wesleyanism (and the broader Protestant community) in Latin America has suffered from the impact of Anglo-American revivalism. This is particularly true in the area of theology. What should be a Christological concentration has become instead a *reductionism* in which God the Father frequently appears only as a deistic starter of the world or as a character in an Anselmian-controlled drama of redemption. Christ the Logos, through whom all things were created, and Christ the Lord, the risen One who has defeated the powers and principalities, is given little role in inform-ing or broadening the understanding of what it means to "be saved." Christology is reduced to an individualistic soteriology, and the Holy Spirit is restricted to the subjective experience of conversion and indi-vidual (frequently moralistic) sanctification. To be sure, the life of Protestant Christians and churches is much richer than this picture—their love, service, evangelistic passion, and compassion far exceed the limitations of their theology. But this very fact introduces ambiguities and contradictions which are clearly visible, and which seriously impair their mission and testimony in these lands.

243

The Potential Contribution of Wesley's
Theology to Latin America Today

Given the way that the *mediated* forms of Wesleyanism contributed to creating these ambiguities and contradictions, one might expect little interest in turning to Wesley's theology and ministry for help in now overcoming them. Yet there has been noticeable new interest in Wesley in Latin America, not only by his ecclesial descendants, but in the broader Protestant community, and even among Roman Catholic theologians.[1] Somewhat paradoxically, participation in the ecumenical movement has been a positive factor in this development. We have already noticed that it was the ecumenical Latin American Council of Churches that took the initiative in bringing churches of Wesleyan origin together to look at their roots. Likewise, the process that resulted in the autonomy of Latin American Methodist churches in the 1970s, rather than weakening interest in their roots, has freed this interest from purely organizational and legislative concerns, strengthening the consideration of the theological and social richness of the Wesleyan inheritance.

It is in keeping with this new interest that I turn now to reflect on what contribution Wesley's own theology (as contrasted with the *mediated* form with which we are so familiar) might make for the present Latin American situation. But I need to delineate my focus at the outset. On the one hand, I am not interested here in trying to repristinate some real or imagined Wesleyan heritage, lay claim to some private confessional distinctive, or carve out a space in the annals of Latin American Christianity for Wesleyanism. On the other hand, I am not proposing to shape the agenda for Latin American theology by appeal to an eighteenth-century movement, however significant it may have been. That agenda will properly be forged by the testimony and thinking of Latin American Christians and churches as they wrestle with the questions, sufferings, and hopes of the Latin American peoples. If Latin American Protestants (*evangélicos*, as we are called and call ourselves) are to have a place in this agenda, it will be together with other Christians and with the whole of our people. It is precisely in relation to this common task

1. Signs of this interest include the growing participation of Latin Americans in the work of the Oxford Institute; the appearance of books like *La tradición protestante en la teología latinoamericana: Primer intento—lectura de la tradición metodista*, ed. José Duque (San José, Costa Rica: DEI, 1983) edited by an ecumenical center and with the participation of several non-Methodist authors; and the great interest and cooperation by Latin American theologians and ministers (not only Methodists!) in the Spanish translation of Wesley's works now in process.

244

that we can and *must* look at the shortcomings of our own action and thinking, and ponder whether there are any traits and forces in the history that has shaped our identity that might now enrich or correct our participation in this common mission.

This is the sense in which I am raising the question of the potential contribution of Wesley's theology to the present situation in Latin America. I will only be able to offer a few exploratory suggestions of traits in Wesley's theology that I believe hold promise for enriching or redirecting the self-understanding and ministry of Latin American Christians and churches.

A Trinitarian Understanding of Grace

One of the most common charges that critics have made about Latin American approaches to theology is that they are dangerously one-sided. While advocates of these approaches dispute this charge, they do not dispute that misunderstandings and distortions in faith and practice would result from truly one-sided approaches to theology. Indeed, the resolve to do justice to the full range of praxical, theoretical, and spiritual dimensions of human life is at the heart of the Latin American concern for salvation/liberation. The fact that this resolve has often been blunted or obscured in actual presentations of Latin American Liberation Theology has led to a quest for a theological paradigm that might more adequately convey the balance intended. Interestingly, this quest has led to a concentration on trinitarian reflection.

I would suggest that Wesley offers some help in developing this trinitarian paradigm, and bringing greater coherence and wholeness to Latin American theology, particularly in its Protestant forms. His specific contribution lies in his understanding of grace. In their rich and suggestive book on a Wesleyan approach to theology, Walter Klaiber and Manfred Marquardt have called attention to the fact that Wesley's emphasis on prevenient, justifying, and sanctifying grace follows a trinitarian logic.[2] They recognize that, as a whole, the doctrine of the Trinity has played a subordinate role in Methodism; however they argue that Wesley's understanding of God as active, self-giving love leads almost unavoidably to a trinitarian paradigm. They then note

---

2. Walter Klaiber and Manfred Marquardt, *Gelebte Gnade: Grundriss einer Theologie der Evangelisch-methodistischen Kirche* (Stuttgart: Christliches Verlagshaus, 1993), 223: "In a certain direction, these dimensions of grace correspond to the trinitarian revelation of God: prevenient grace to the work of God as Creator, redemptive grace to the redeeming action in Jesus Christ, and sanctifying grace to the work of the Holy Spirit."

how this trinitarian logic becomes more visible in John Wesley's later sermons, and even more apparent in Charles Wesley's hymns. Impetus for, and some guidance in developing, a notion of the trinitarian fullness of grace is a potential contribution of Wesley to contemporary Latin American theology.

Prevenient Grace as Integral to Redemption

The specific notion of prevenient grace is another area where consideration of Wesley may hold promise. This (originally) Augustinian doctrine has drawn the frequent attention of Latin American theologians like Juan Luis Segundo. For Wesley it serves—ironically—as a rebuttal to any interpretation of "total depravity" which seems to leave human beings deprived of all possibility of human freedom, of any spark of good will and human love. Wesley appears to sense that such a view of depravity neither represents human beings as they actually are, nor leaves them the possibility of even hearing God's self-communication. But, unlike other ways of referring to prevenient grace, Wesley wants to see it in the unity of God's loving self-giving to us. He therefore stresses the sometimes underplayed affirmation of the Council of Orange that prevenient grace is "the same grace of redemption," a universal benefit of Christ's atoning work, rather than some pause in original justice, or a piece of "natural goodness" saved from the Fall. I submit that this is not merely a theological trick but a theological way of underlining the necessary unity of God's triune work (*opera trinitatis*)—in which the love of the Father, the presence of "the Lamb slain from the foundation of the world," and the creative Spirit that hovered over the face of the chaos cannot be divided (*indivisa sunt*).

Wesley gives two interesting examples of his use of this doctrine. One is a somewhat romantic view of "the good savage," which experience forced him to correct. The second is his case against slavery, where a deeper insight appears. The rejection of slavery is presented as not merely an ethical question, it is (we would say today) a *status confessionis:* it touches the very heart of faith because slavery denies the freedom—and therefore the God-given possibility—of a human being to make a decision, to assume responsibility, in short to be a human being. When Gustavo Gutiérrez speaks of people who have been reduced to "non-persons" being the focus of God's liberating word, he is speaking the same language.

Wesley himself does not (to my knowledge) refer much to prevenient grace as serving to empower human beings to do the good, however imperfectly and ambiguously. It was the nineteenth-century British Methodist theologian, William B. Pope, who developed this line more coherently. In a carefully woven trinitarian argument (to be sure informed by a pre-Freudian psychology that we could hardly use today) he affirmed human responsibility, building on three theological bases: (1) while sin has distorted and utterly corrupted human existence, it could not reduce us to nonhuman, ethically irresponsible beings; (2) the Holy Spirit brings the universal free grace flowing from Christ's redeeming work (the Atonement) to every human being, restoring to us a sense of moral obligation and a freedom to crave for the good which enables us to act as moral agents; and (3) this "prevenient," "preventive," "initial," or "preliminary" grace tends forward to the realization of full humanity through the free acceptance of sanctifying grace.[3]

Sanctification as Restoration

Sanctification was undoubtedly at the heart of Wesley's entire theology and ministry. My own impression, however, has been that his theological development of the doctrine suffered from serious limitations. It seemed to me that it did not move beyond the area of individual or ecclesial life and, even there, was mostly concerned with individual behavior in everyday private life, as seen from the General Rules. Besides, the meaning of sanctification seemed so exclusively related to the personal soteriological domain that the wider trinitarian dimensions of sanctification in the historical, social, or cultural realm were left out. I was naturally aware that Wesley was deeply concerned with these areas of human life, as his writings abundantly prove. The question was whether he related these concerns to his whole theology, and particularly to his view of sanctification.

---

3. Pope's argument is developed in different sections of his three volume *Compendium of Christian Theology* (London: Wesleyan Conference Office, 1880). Two brief quotations may help to display the passion that lies behind the insistence on this theme: "Certainly, there is nothing in the condition of human nature that shuts out the possibility of redemption. Its depravity, taken at the worst, is not a total extinction of every element that grace might hold on: the voice of conscience speaking in every language under heaven, in the accents both of fear and of hope; the irrepressible yearnings after some great Deliverer . . . all proclaim that there may be redemption. . . ." (2:46). "The preliminary grace which we regard as the firstfruits of the Redeemer's intervention for the race explains the secret desire of man to be restored; *and thus lights up the whole sphere of ethics*" (3:158, emphasis added). The fuller development of the doctrine of prevenient grace will be found in 2:358-90. It is no wonder that William Townsend says that the emphasis on prevenient grace was perhaps Pope's most lasting contribution to Methodist theology, in *New History of Methodism* (London: Hodder & Stoughton, 1909), 1:25.

The recent work by Klaiber and Marquardt which I mentioned above and a new book by Ted Runyon seriously challenge my earlier interpretation.[4] Runyon in particular argues that Wesley's view of sanctification takes in the whole of "the great salvation" or "the new creation." That is, Runyon suggests that Wesley understood sanctification to include both the full restoration of humanity in the image of God (which involves the totality of human life—spiritual, moral, political, and more) and the restoration of the whole creation (which had been entrusted to human care and disrupted by human sin). On these terms Runyon is able to relate Wesley's emphasis on sanctification to his concrete concern for issues like human rights, poverty and the rights of the poor, the rights of women, environmental stewardship, and ecumenism. Such a reading would also allow Wesley (or later Wesleyans) to open the notion of sanctification to a trinitarian scope, in which creation and eschatology, or christology and pneumatology, could be seen both in their unity and particularity. Scholars will have to debate whether this interpretation of Wesley can be sustained or not. But from the perspective of our Latin American concerns there is no doubt that it offers a particularly fruitful insight.

Christian Obedience as Concrete Action

If indeed Wesley understood sanctification as restoration it would help explain another aspect of his ministry that provides warrant for rethinking some of the models of spirituality and Christian life that were mediated to Latin America. This aspect is Wesley's growing interest in bringing out into the open and denouncing the specific social, political, and even ideological conditions which were producing the contemporary social and economic problems that distorted and thwarted God's design. His interpretation of the causes and cure of poverty, his analysis of the consequences of the laws of enclosure, his discussion of the nature of the slave trade, his subtle denunciations of the causes of war, and even some curiosities like his interest in health and medicine, while limited or inadequate at many points, suggest *a respect for the autonomy of the different spheres of reality.*

Through his example Wesley shows that Christian love cannot remain at the level of generosity or good will when it faces the specific problems of a society; it has to tackle the underlying structural issues. Even the

---

4. Theodore H. Runyon, *The New Creation: John Wesley's Theology Today* (Nashville: Abingdon Press, 1998).

altruistic activities of the Methodist societies needed to be structured and organized in such a way that they did not merely satisfy immediate needs but opened more permanent possibilities and conditions for the beneficiaries of their charity. Similarly, when Latin American theology demands an organic place for social and human sciences in the theological enterprise, it is not merely using an instrument—an "auxiliary discipline" as they used to be called. It is trying to understand the structure of a reality in which God's creation and human sin have intertwined in mechanisms, causalities, possibilities, and impossibilities through which, in the power of the Spirit, Christians and other people can work to restore the design of the Creator, the final goal of the Redeemer.

Christian Life as Synergistic Love

Wesleyan scholarship on the concepts of holiness and perfection has made quite clear that the core of these doctrines was "God's love . . . poured into our hearts through the Holy Spirit that has been given to us." The full recreation of God's image is, in the last resort, for Wesley, nothing but the total control of human intention, purpose, and action by God's love. It is the work of the Holy Spirit and (whether it happens progressively, or suddenly, or both) it is the culmination and perfection of God's redemptive action. "Perfection" is not so much a measure to be filled as a fullness that has no limits. The insistence on "social holiness" or "social Christianity," rather than a sociological conception, is but a way of underlining the centrality of love.

This centrality of love is also at the heart of Latin American Liberation Theology. The "option for the poor" is simply the concrete sign of the universality and intentionality of love. Juan Luis Segundo has made of it what amounts to a confession of faith in the expression: "no action of love is lost in God's world." It is the center of Gutiérrez' spirituality as expressed in *We Drink From Our Own Wells, The Power of the Poor in History,* or *On Job: God-talk and the Suffering of the Innocent.* Even a "hard" theologian like Hugo Assmann will not hesitate to characterize the central concept of faith as praxis as "the personal need to love and to be loved, the giving of one's life for the brothers [and sisters], seen in the wide context of the historical process," or "the new dimension of love in a socialized world."

If sanctification is to be understood as "love poured out into our hearts through the Holy Spirit," i.e., as the very presence of the Holy Spirit (the same Spirit that is active in all of human life as prevenient grace), then human life and action have a "Spirit dimension."

Obviously, we have here the old and debated question of synergism. I see little doubt that an assumption of the "incorporation" of the creature in God's acts of liberation—both in the evangelistic call to repentance and conversion and in the liberating acts of justice for the sake of the poor—which is clearly present in Latin American theology, is also central to the Wesleyan perspective. In his article on "Methodism's Theological Heritage," Albert Outler speaks of Wesley's undeniable synergism, which he characterizes as a "covenantal synergism . . . in which both prevenient *and* saving grace are recognized as coordinate providential activities of the one true God of love who, in his love, makes and keeps covenant with faithful [persons]." In a recent dissertation on Liberation Theology, Guillermo Hansen, a young Lutheran theologian, affirms the same point in a very sharply formulated fashion:

> It is in this manner . . . that we reach our final point, namely, that precisely in the enhypostatic nature of Christian praxis, the event of the divine-human "cooperation" coheres, not as a reality pertaining to two causal agential entities involved in a reciprocal-conditional exchange, but as the relationship existing between the hypostatic termini posited by God's decision to be God not without the creatural—i.e. to be triune.

Certainly, this affirmation of synergism needs to be carefully protected by the eschatological proviso: we are not yet at the point where "God is all in all," but in an intermediate time where the human actor still maintains, as Hansen himself says, "the characteristics and constraints of any human witness and praxis (thus always subject to the judgment of God)."

Reclaiming the Christological Balance in Defining Love

The final area where I would suggest that dialogue with Wesley might be fruitful for Latin American Liberation Theology is on the issue of how appeal to Christ serves to define the nature of love. In this case the potential benefit would come in the form of the balance that can derive from dialogue with a contrasting one-sided position. Analyses of Wesley's Christology have generally concurred that the concrete humanity of Christ—the earthly Jesus, as we would put it today—does not play a significant role. One result is that there is little appeal to the earthly Jesus in Wesley's clarifications of the nature of love.

By contrast, in Latin American theology the earthly ministry of Jesus is the paradigm on which both Christology and praxeology (to use Jon

Sobrino's expression) are built. For them, love is defined specifically by appeal to Jesus' proclamation and embodiment of the Reign of God—liberating the poor, the oppressed, prisoners, and wounded. On this christological interpretation of love the struggle for justice for the poor is not something secondary to faith and salvation (as a mere consequence of saving faith) but already has, so to speak, "soteriological density."[5]

But the Latin American approach is prone to the opposite weakness of Wesley's Christology. In the justified effort to avoid a dichotomy between faith and social praxis, sacred history and human history, love of God and love of neighbor, they run the risk of blurring the specificity of the Incarnation, the *ephapax* nature of God's intervention in Jesus Christ.

If we treat love simply as an anthropological category, do we not run the danger of losing sight of how God's love incarnate in Jesus Christ serves to define and measure true love? If the emphasis on one single history is not critically confronted with the uniqueness of the Christ event, do not the story of Jesus, the Cross, and the Resurrection become mere models of service, suffering, and hope to be reproduced, rather than a once-for-all event into which we can enter eschatologically through the power of the Spirit? And turning to eschatology, does not the conflictive character of God's action in history tend to be reduced to the progressive—though conflictive—overcoming of structures of injustice and oppression, obscuring the radical nature of "the mystery of evil" to which the apocalyptic tradition bears witness?

Finally, consider the missionary/evangelizing consequences of this imbalance. The one-sided focus on the earthly Jesus has tended to weaken the radicality of the call to conversion: instead of a "turning" or a "new birth," it becomes a growth, a new awareness, or a greater commitment. The specificity of the "personal encounter with Christ"—to use typically evangelical language—is liable to be totally equated with a commitment to the poor and the struggle for justice, with serious loss both for the life of faith and service of the individual Christian and for the community.

Certainly, this criticism does not evacuate the significance of the fundamental affirmation of Liberation Theology concerning the unity of

---

5. This last point might raise the vexed debate on *sola gratia-sola fides*. Wesley has not infrequently been questioned as to his Protestant purity in this respect. It seems to me that, placed in these terms, the discussion is not too fruitful. It is the result of the absolutization of an "extrincesism" of grace—the classical *extra nos*—which had a necessary polemical function in the struggle against "works righteousness" but which, out of that context, and used as the theological touchstone to understand the operation of grace, risks issuing in the "cheap grace" that Bonhoeffer denounced.

God's action in the world and the understanding of historical liberation as a necessary dimension of salvation. Nor can we forget Gutiérrez' careful qualitative distinction between human achievement and the transcendence of grace. The very life of the thousands of faith communities throughout the continent witnesses to the depth of this spirituality.

But it is important to seek a theological framework in which this foundational element of liberation theology is freed from misunderstanding and deeply rooted in God's self-revelation. A trinitarian basis like that hinted at in Wesley is, in my view, the best protection in this respect.

Schubert M. Ogden

Schubert M. Ogden (b. 1928) is an Emeritus Distinguished Professor at the Perkins School of Theology, Southern Methodist University. Ogden has been an intellectual leader among North American Process thinkers. Rooted in the philosophy of A. N. Whitehead and Charles Hartshorne, he has extended the work of these philosophers and has made important theological contributions. From his vantage point he has engaged philosophers of religion, liberation theologians, and biblical scholars. His statement used in this sourcebook represents his basic position and can be found in *The Reality of God* (Harper & Row, 1964), pp. 1-20.

The Problem of God Today

One of the obvious conclusions to be drawn from the latest developments in Protestant theology is that the reality of God has now become the central theological problem. This statement may seem odd, since, as popularly understood, theology is nothing if not, in Richard Hooker's words, "the science of things divine,"[1] and therefore an unending struggle with just this problem. The fact remains that for much of the theology of the first half of our century the reality of God was not its one great theme.

---

1. *Works*, Vol. I, ed. John Keble, Oxford: Clarendon Press, 7th ed., 1888, p. 374.

For a complex of reasons that need not be gone into here, the most influential Protestant theologians of the last generation focused their thinking on other themes. There were, of course, exceptions, and I do not wish to imply that the theological work of this period was either lacking in express treatments of the problem of God or is without significant bearing on its eventual solution. Neither implication could be supported by the evidence, and I should question in principle whether any thinking about the distinctive meaning of faith in Jesus Christ (with Karl Barth) or about the nature and destiny of man (with Reinhold Niebuhr) could fail to be relevant to this central problem of theology. Rightly understood, the problem of God is not one problem among several others; it is the only problem there is. Hence all our thinking, on whatever theme and whether properly theological or not, is of some, at least indirect, relevance to clarifying and solving it. Even so, the reality of God need not become directly thematic in our reflections, and even when it does, it may not be their one pre-eminent and all-determining theme. This is evident from the Protestant theology between the two world wars, when pronounced tendencies toward either christological or anthropological concentration removed the problem of God from the center of theological thinking.

Lately, however, the scene has shifted, and this problem is now very much to the fore. At once symbolizing and, to an extent, summarizing this change is one of the most remarkable books produced by the Protestant theology of the present generation: John A. T. Robinson's *Honest to God*.[2] Although the argument of this book bears on almost all the basic issues of Christian theology, its one all-controlling concern is with the possibility and meaning of an honest faith in God in our time. This became evident immediately from the responses that greeted the book and is fully documented by the summary of the whole discussion since made available in the follow-up volume, *The Honest to God Debate*.[3] Yet, significantly, Robinson expressly disavows that his proposals are in any way original and offers his little book as simply "an attempt at communication."[4] That his disavowal is more than false modesty is at once apparent from the content and character of his proposals themselves. *Honest to God* stands squarely in the main movement in Protestant theology since World War II, and there is ample reason for its constant

2. London: SCM Press Ltd., 1963. For a discussion of the significance of this book for our present problem, see my article, "Beyond Supernaturalism," *Religion in Life*, Winter, 1963–64, pp. 7-18.

3. Ed. John A. T. Robinson and David L. Edwards, London: SCM Press Ltd., 1963.

4. *Honest to God*, p. 21.

appeals to the work of Dietrich Bonhoeffer, Rudolf Bultmann, and Paul Tillich. Indeed, the main importance of Robinson's book lies in clearly focusing the one demand on which the contributions of these three thinkers all converge and in popularizing a program of theological reconstruction such as is necessary to respond to their demand.

And this brings us directly to the initial task of the present essay. If we are to deal with the problem of God responsibly, we must first of all understand the problem in its current form. A promising way to achieve such understanding is simply to ask why the reality of God has now become of central theological concern. Given a clear answer to this question, we should also be able to discern the present shape of the problem of God itself and thus be in a position to take the next steps toward its possible solution. Accordingly, we must now inquire as to the reasons for the recent change in Protestant theology just described.

The first of these reasons we already touched on in what was said about the importance of *Honest to God*. Robinson, I suggested, has rightly sensed that the three theologians whose influence has recently become determinative—Bonhoeffer, Bultmann, and Tillich—all agree in making one basic demand on contemporary theology. If we ask now as to the exact content of this demand, one reply is the insistence common to these thinkers that theology today must be in the strict sense postliberal. This reply, naturally, requires clarification, because the word "postliberal," like other words of its type, admits of diverse interpretations. But, since such labels are certain to be used, theological responsibility can never consist in eschewing them, but only in so clarifying their meaning that they serve rather than hinder a fuller understanding of the issues.

It is commonly recognized that the driving concern of the representative liberal theologians of the nineteenth century was with the meaning and truth of historic Christian faith, given the changed conditions of a distinctively modern cultural situation. Sensing that the Protestant orthodoxy of the previous two centuries had been decisively challenged by the criticisms of the Enlightenment, they undertook a comprehensive theological reappraisal directed toward assimilating the legitimate motives in these criticisms, while yet making possible an appropriate formulation of Christian faith. For a long time, the historiography of this period tended to disregard the second element in the liberals' concerns, presenting their work as simply the expression in the area of religion of the general liberalizing movement typical of the nineteenth century. But recent studies, benefiting from greater perspective and more inclined to be sympathetic, have succeeded in exposing the one-sidedness of such presentations.[5] They have made clear that liberal theology was, in fact, an authentic expression of the Christian faith, an eloquent testimony that the word which God has addressed to mankind in Jesus Christ should and can be heard even by the modern man who fully affirms his modernity. No less evident is that there was a distinctively Protestant inspiration behind the decision and outlook of the liberal theologians. In affirming, as they did, the proper autonomy and validity of secular methods of knowledge (thereby insisting, for example, that historical-critical research be applied even to Scripture), they but reaffirmed in their own situation the fundamental decision of the Protestant Reformers as expressed in the watchword, *sola gratis—sola fide.*[6]

The difficulty, however—and about this there is also general agreement—is that the liberals were on the whole unsuccessful in implementing their concern. In seeking a formulation of the Christian faith which would respect all that was valid in modern man's understanding of himself and his world, they too often proceeded uncritically and thus failed also to respect the distinctive claims of faith itself. In many instances, to be sure, the trouble lay in their perforce having to make use of conceptualities that obscured their real intentions. Recall, for example, Schleiermacher's definition of religion in terms of "feeling" *(Gefuhl)* or the attempt by Wilhelm Hermann and others to conceptualize the existential understanding of faith as "experience" *(Erlebnis).* Yet, important as it is to recognize this, it by no means accounts for the splendid failure that was liberal theology. (It remains true that the liberals' courageous pursuit of an inescapable theological task led to a certain compromising of essential Christian truth.)

That we today clearly recognize this is perhaps our principal debt to the creative theological movement of the first half of our century, which reacted so sharply against liberal theology. This movement has led to a fresh sense for the authentic witness of Holy Scripture and of the Reformers, and has impressed upon us that this witness can no more be brought into an easy harmony with the modern age than it can be assimilated to any other. Furthermore, it is impossible to dismiss the theologians responsible for these insights as if they were concerned merely to restore the status quo ante liberal theology of the seventeenth and eigh-

---

5. See, e.g., Christoph Senft, *Wahrhaftigkeit und Wahrheit, Die Theologie des 19. Jahrhunderts zwischen Orthodoxie und Aufklarung,* Tubingen: J. C. B. Mohr, 1956; and, for the later liberal development in America, Kenneth Cauthen, *The Impact of American Religious Liberalism,* New York: Harper & Row, 1962.

6. Bern G. A. Baschlin, 1919; 2d ed., 1922.

teenth centuries. One must never forget that the movement convention-
ally spoken of today as "neo-orthodoxy" was, in its beginnings, an
attempt at self-criticism from within the ranks of liberal theology. From
its first great expressions—Karl Barth's *Römerbrief* [7] and, in America,
Reinhold Niebuhr's *Moral Man and Immoral Society* [8]—the old orthodoxy
could derive but scant encouragement, because of their tacit acceptance
of much that the liberal theologians had sought to achieve. At the same
time, the new movement was not lacking in certain reactionary tendencies, and, as it developed, the liberals' characteristic concern with
the meaning and truth of Christianity in a modern setting was more and
more displaced by another interest. Especially through the influence of
Barth's later work in *Die kirchliche Dogmatik*,[9] the theological task came
to be viewed as entailing a radical separation of Christian faith and
modern culture, and many Protestant theologians once again assumed
a deliberately dogmatic stance.

Thus, although the main theological development between the two
world wars was in a sense postliberal, it was so only in a rather loose
sense. The new movement definitely succeeded in breaking the hold of
liberal theology. But this it did, at least in some of its representatives,
less by providing a more adequate solution to the problem with which
the liberals had struggled than by exposing the inadequacy of their
achievements and disregarding the seriousness of the problem itself.
The result was that, while some of the distinctive claims of Christian
faith were rediscovered and reasserted, the question of the meaning and
truth of these claims for men living in a modern secular world was for
the most part not even clearly posed, much less effectively answered.

Since the Second World War, however, the tendencies toward reaction
in Protestant theology have been arrested, and a new direction has
become increasingly evident. With the emergence into prominence of
Tillich in America and Bultmann and Bonhoeffer on the Continent, the
question of the meaning and truth of theological assertions, given a
modern situation, is once again being recognized as a serious question.
Hence the original concern of Protestant liberalism is finding renewed
expression; and, because this is so, the theology these three thinkers
have projected as the task of our generation is in the exact sense a
postliberal theology.

7. Cf. Gerhard Ebeling, *Word and Faith*, trans. J. W. Leitch, Philadelphia: Fortress Press,
1963, pp. 17-61, especially p. 55.
8. New York: Charles Scribner's Sons, 1932.
9. Zollikon-Zurich: Evangelischer Verlag, 1932–59.

Another way of characterizing this change is to say that, primarily through the work of these men, Protestant theologians today have once more been made aware of their inescapable apologetic task. Here, too, there are dangers of misunderstanding, since the word "apologetic" is likewise ambiguous. Moreover, while Tillich expressly designates his theology as "apologetic," Bultmann generally resists the designation and understands the word only in a pejorative sense. Yet, despite this obvious difference, both thinkers, together with Bonhoeffer, so conceive the theologian's responsibility as to include the task for which "apologetic" would still appear to be the best word. They insist that the terms of theological adequacy are always set not only by the faith which the theologian must seek to express appropriately, but also by the existence of man himself, to whom the theologian must try to express that faith understandably. This insistence assumes that Christian faith is not utterly alien to man, whatever his historical situation, but rather is his own most proper possibility of existence, which can and should be understandable to him, provided it is so expressed as to take his situation into account. I should say it is this assumption which, in some form or other, provides the minimal condition for all properly apologetic theology. If this is so, the use of the word "apologetic" in the present context is easily defended. Whether we use the word or not, this assumption, along with the conception of theological responsibility following from it, is just what is now being reasserted by the leading figures in Protestant theology.

This fact by itself, however, hardly explains why it is the problem of God, instead of any number of other problems, that has now emerged as of crucial importance. Therefore, we must press our inquiry still further and consider a second reason for this development. That reason, too, as we shall see, has to do with a certain alteration in our more recent history; only now the fact to be observed is not an immanent shift within Protestant theology itself, but a fundamental change that has become ever more apparent in our larger cultural situation.

The most succinct way to describe this change is to say that, when contemporary Western man is judged by some of his more creative self-expressions, his outlook no longer seems merely secular, but appears to have become increasingly secularistic. In saying this, one must, of course, depend on a distinction usually obscured in our ordinary language. We commonly use the adjectives "secular" and "secularistic," like the nouns "secularity" and "secularism," interchangeably, without observing any difference of meaning between them. Yet, for some time, it has been fairly common among theological students of the historical process known as "secularization" to insist that our ordinary usage at this point has to be refined if it is not to trap us in serious misunderstandings.[10] Thus Friedrich Gogarten, for example, holds that we must distinguish between "two fundamentally different kinds of secularization," for only one of which we should use the term "secularism."[11] Since I, too, believe that accurate analysis demands some such distinction, I venture to speak of the change we must now try to understand as one from a secular to a secularistic outlook—or, as we may also say, from secularity to secularism. I should perhaps add that the following discussion is in no way intended as an exhaustive analysis of this important change. My sole purpose is to illustrate its essential character sufficiently to provide what is necessary for the argument of this essay.

It is now a commonplace that the outlook of most men today who have been shaped by modern Western culture is more or less deeply determined by the scientific picture of the world. Ever since the seventeenth century, science and technology have been effecting such a radical transformation in our understanding of ourselves and our environment that even contemporary common sense includes an at least tacit acceptance of the world picture correlative with the scientific method.[12] Whenever, then, modern men have become reflectively self-conscious, they have for generations typically affirmed this method and picture as defining the horizon within which knowledge of the world and its phenomena must be obtained. Thus the pursuit of such knowledge has long since become, in the sense of the word intended here, a wholly "secular" affair. Any attempt by religious or ecclesiastical authorities to control the pursuit by imposing heteronomous criteria of truth has been consistently repudiated in the name of the autonomy of scientific method throughout the whole field to which it properly applies. Furthermore, all assertions which ostensibly have reference to this field, from whatever source and however long accepted, have been referred to this method and judged to be true only when they have met the criteria implicit in it.

10. See C. H. Ratschow's article in *Religion in Geschichte und Gegenwart*, Vol. V, ed. Kurt Galling, Tubingen: J. C. B. Mohr, 3d ed., 1961, pp. 1288-96.

11. *Verhangnis und Hoffnung der Neuzeit, die Sakularisierung als theologisches Problem*, Stuttgart: Friedrich Vorwerk Verlag, 2n ed., 1958 pp. 142f. Cf. also Gabriel Vahanian, *The Death of God: The Culture of Our Post-Christian Era*, New York: George Braziller, 1961, pp. 60-78.

12. See the discussion of so-called "common sense" in Stephen Toulmin and June Goodfield, *The Fabric of the Heavens*, London: Hutchinson & Co. Ltd., 1961, pp. 15-22.

Herein, of course, is the reason for "the warfare of science with theology" which entered its decisive phase a century ago.[13] Because so many traditional theological assertions have at least appeared to make scientific claims—and have been interpreted accordingly by both their defenders and their attackers—they have naturally been subjected to scientific criticism, only to prove unacceptable when judged by these criteria. Hence theologians have been forced to make such distinctions as that between "history" and "myth," which has gradually come to be regarded as necessary if theology is still to be a responsible undertaking. Even today, it is true, there are theologians who fail to take this distinction seriously, and, as Bultmann points out, it is a *testimonium paupertatis* for our theological situation that the demand for demythologizing has yet to meet with universal acceptance.[14] But, if anything seems certain, it is that this state of affairs cannot continue. The scientific world picture is here to stay and will assert its rights against any theology, however imposing, that conflicts with it. So far as his knowledge of the world is concerned, modern man long ago opted for the method of science and therewith decided irrevocably for secularity.

Accompanying this decision, however, was always another possibility, which was occasionally realized throughout the whole modern period, only to emerge more recently as the option apparently favored by ever larger numbers of Western men. For many cultured persons today, the general scientific method is not only the sole means for obtaining knowledge about the world disclosed by our senses, but this kind of knowledge is the only knowledge there is. The classic expression of this outlook in reflective philosophical terms is the position generally known as logical positivism, with its dogmatic claim that there are but two kinds of significant statements.[15] Aptly named "Hume's fork," since it goes back to a famous passage in David Hume's *Enquiry Concerning Human Understanding*,[16] this claim holds that all meaningful assertions are divided between either the tautologies of formal logic and mathematics or putative statements of fact that can be falsified by ordinary sense experience. The force of the claim, therefore, is to restrict all

13. See Andrew D. White, *A History of the Warfare of Science with Theology in Christendom*, New York: D. Appleton & Co., 1896.

14. H. W. Bartsch (ed.), *Kerygma und Mythos*, Vol. I, Hamburg: Herbert Reich-Evangelischer Verlag, 2d ed., 1951, pp. 23f. (English translation by R. H. Fuller in H. W. Bartsch [ed.], *Kerygma and Myth*, New York: Harper & Row, 2d ed., 1961, p. 12).

15. See especially Alfred Jules Ayer, *Language, Truth and Logic*, London: Victor Gollancz Ltd., 1936; 2d ed., 1946.

16. *Enquiries Concerning the Human Understanding and Concerning the Principles of Morals*, ed. L. A. Selby-Bigge, Oxford: Clarendon Press, 2d ed., 1902, p. 165.

knowledge of "how things are" to the general type of knowledge of which modern science is the refined and fully developed form. Since its original promulgation, this positivistic dogma has been extensively criticized and reformulated, and most philosophers who currently invoke it exhibit a keener sense for our different uses of language than did its first proponents. At the same time, the dogma is still widely accepted, and, even where efforts are made to limit its force, it has a curious way of reasserting itself.[17]

More important is that the basic standpoint for which this dogma is but the conceptually precise formulation has come to be shared by many persons who are by no means professional philosophers. For them, exactly as for their more reflective spokesmen, the issue is no longer whether the theologian can make assertions that conflict with science, but whether he can make any meaningful assertions at all. They reason that, if the kind of knowledge represented by science is the only knowledge there is, then the putative assertions of theology, so far as empirically unverifiable, can hardly make good their claim to cognitive meaning. Such reasoning, it seems to me, can no longer be considered merely secular, but must be distinguished by the different adjective "secularistic." It is one thing to affirm the validity of the scientific method and to insist on its complete autonomy within the field where it alone logically applies. But it is clearly something different to affirm that this method is the only valid means to knowledge we have, because it circumscribes the limits of the whole cognitive sphere. The first affirmation, I hold, is entirely of a piece with the legitimate secularity of modern culture. The second, on the other hand, is an integral element in that secularism which appears to have become ever more widely prevalent among contemporary Western men.

The shift from a secular to a secularistic outlook with respect to knowledge provides one illustration of the second important change that has led to our present situation. It would be easy to trace the same change in the other spheres of culture where parallel shifts have also become apparent. But, for the present, it will be sufficient briefly to note how morality, too, has become for many persons today utterly secularistic.

---

17. A perfect illustration of this is the argument of W. H. Walsh, *Metaphysics*, London: Hutchinson & Co. Ltd., 1963. Although Walsh effectively blunts Hume's fork by adducing the distinct logical class of "categorical principles" (pp. 154-60), his denial that these principles have any but a "prescriptive," noninformative character, and hence his further denial of "ontology," clearly presuppose Hume's distinction.

Practical Divinity

Throughout most of Western history, man's action, like his knowledge, was kept within definite bounds by religious or ecclesiastical authority. The official standards of moral conduct were either set or sanctioned by the will of God as interpreted in the teachings of the church. By the seventeenth century, however, the process of secularization had led to several attempts to develop a wholly secular ethic. As with so many other ventures toward secularity, these first attempts reached a rich culmination in the philosophical work of Immanuel Kant.

Indeed, nothing was more important to Kant than "the autonomy of the will as the supreme principle of morality."[18] By this he meant that man as a moral agent is bound to reject any effort to subject his action to moral laws or maxims which are not his own legislation as rational will. What makes any course of action morally obligatory is not that it is grounded, say, in the will of God, but that it is demanded by the "categorical imperative" implicit in man's own practical reason. Therefore, Kant sharply repudiated the views of "theological moralists" as a form of "heteronomy," which is "opposed to the principle of duty and to the morality of the will."[19] In doing so, however, he had no intention of affirming a morality without religious faith. On the contrary, he was convinced that it is just when one grasps the autonomy of moral action that the essential function of religion can be rightly understood. We can give an adequate account of our moral experience only by appealing to certain basic presuppositions or "postulates," which together make up the content of a "rational faith." Thus Kant held that we must not only presuppose our own freedom and responsibility as moral agents, but also postulate our subjective survival of death and the reality of God as the ultimate ground and guarantor of a morally reasonable world.

It is only by comparison with a secular moral philosophy such as Kant's that one can mark the fundamental difference in moral outlook that has become increasingly apparent in our own century. Kant's deep conviction that morality, while wholly autonomous, nevertheless "leads ineluctably to religion"[20] now strikes many a person as hopelessly unconvincing. In its place, one more and more encounters the claim not only that the sole standards of conduct are those implicit in human action itself, but that such action realizes no will to good beyond the

18. *Critique of Practical Reason and Other Writings in Moral Philosophy*, ed. and trans. Lewis W. Beck, Chicago: The University of Chicago Press, 1949, p. 97 (Foundations of the Metaphysics of Morals, Sec II).

19. Ibid., p. 144; cf. pp. 146-52 (*Critique of Practical Reason*, I,1,i).

20. *Religion Within the Limits of Reason Alone*, trans. T. H. Green and H. H. Hudson, New York: Harper & Row, 2d ed., 1960, p. 5.

merely human and neither requires nor admits of any transcendent justification.

It is true that contemporary discussions of morality often reveal a deeper and more discriminating understanding of man's nature than was possible for even as tempered a rationalism as Kant's. Especially through the writings of existentialist philosophers, we have recovered the insight that man is, first of all, an existing self or person, whose primary moral task is the realization in himself and others of an authentic personal existence. We now recognize that what we do is in a sense less important than how we do it and that "existential norms" like freedom, openness, and love are finally regulative of such traditional virtues as wisdom, prudence, and justice.[21] Hence the educated man of today is almost certain to be concerned with more than the earlier secular causes of disseminating knowledge and advancing men's social and economic well-being. He is also typically interested in the new task of preserving a measure of personal authenticity against the pressures toward conformity of a technological civilization. In fact, this whole development in our ethical perspective and, more generally, in our view of man's nature and destiny is so significant that it seems justified to speak of a distinctively postmodern phase in the over-all evolution of modern culture.

But, significant as this development is, it is neither the only nor the most far-reaching change in contemporary morality. This is evidenced by the fact that the very postmodern deepening of our moral understanding has as often as not found explicitly secularistic expression. Some of its most eloquent and influential statements, indeed, are those of avowedly atheistic writers such as Jean-Paul Sartre and Albert Camus. The thought of these men is clearly informed by a view of human conduct and of the human condition which, in its realism and tragic sense, cannot but recall many of the basic insights of classical Christian anthropology. And yet, in every case, these insights are present in their writings in a completely secularistic form, so that faith and sin, say, are the wholly immanent possibilities of man's self-understanding which Sartre designates respectively as "good faith" and "bad faith." Also significant in this connection is the way recent theological analyses of the nature of man and of moral action are frequently appropriated by persons who quite reject the theistic framework in which theologians present them. Thus, for instance, Reinhold Niebuhr's profound

21. Cf. John Wild, *The Challenge of Existentialism*, Bloomington, Ind.: Indiana University Press, 1955, pp. 250-72, especially pp. 258ff.

anthropological and ethical reflections have been extremely influential on historians, political theorists, and practical statesmen, as well as on Protestant theologians. But who would deny that many who have assimilated these reflections are still far from in any way sharing Niebuhr's own robust version of historical Christian faith?[22]

For these and other reasons, one is led to see the most fundamental change in contemporary thinking about morality, not in a certain postmodern deepening of ethical insight, but in an ever-growing secularism in moral outlook. In their understanding of action, as in the view of knowledge, numbers of men today are no longer content merely to affirm the autonomy and importance of their life in the world, but deny unequivocally that this world in any way points beyond itself.[23]

By now it should be evident that it is this secularistic denial in its several different forms which explains why the problem of God in particular has become central for Protestant theology. Such a denial is by its very nature the negation of God's reality, the claim, in Nietzsche's words, that "God is dead."[24] Therefore, because the denial is now so often heard, any theologian made newly sensitive to his apologetic task cannot but find his whole endeavor concentrated on a single point. His hearers have become concerned primarily with one question, to which they expect him and his colleagues to give a forthright reply: whether, if the word "God" as Christians use it has any meaning at all, the sentences in which it occurs somehow express assertions capable of being true.

If this conclusion is correct, our inquiry has indeed led us beyond an answer to our initial question. Not only have we discovered why the problem of God has now become of central importance, but, true to our expectation, we have also learned how this problem presents itself to us today. We have learned, in short, that our age, as Gerhard Ebeling has

22. Cf. Morton White's remarks about those who he calls, tellingly "atheists for Niebuhr" (*Religion, Politics, and the Higher Learning,* Cambridge: Harvard University Press, 1959, pp. 117f.). It is only fair to add that, if Niebuhr's anthropological concentration has proved to have its dangers, the same is true of the "christological concentration" of Karl Barth. This is well brought out by the title under which a book by one of Barth's students, Paul M. Van Buren's *Secular Meaning of the Gospel* (New York: The Macmillan Co., 1963), was reviewed in the *Christian Century* (October 2, 1963, pp. 1208f.): "There Is No God and Jesus Is His Son"!

23. The *Vorgeschichte* of this change, especially as regards morality, in the metaphysical rebellion of the nineteenth century is traced with unusual insight by Henri de Lubac, *The Drama of Atheist Humanism,* trans. E. M. Riley, New York: Sheed & Ward, Inc., 1951.

24. *The Joyful Wisdom,* trans. Thomas Common, London: George Allen & Unwin Ltd., 1910, p. 168.

said, is "the age of atheism"[25]—that, if the reality of God is still to be affirmed, this must now be done in a situation in which, on an unprecedented scale, that reality is expressly denied.

The question, then, is whether there can be another formulation of our problem that does not utterly exclude its possible solution. I believe one can formulate the problem differently and that other recent developments in philosophy as well as theology support this conviction. The clue to such a formulation lies in the lesson we all should have long since learned from the outcome of the original liberal theology. We noted above that the liberal theologians too often proceeded uncritically in appropriating the insights of their contemporary culture. Failing to discriminate between the legitimate motives in these insights and other motives that have subsequently been superseded, they foreclosed certain options for defining, and thus solving, their problem. But this is the very danger that also threatens our work today, as is evident from the procedure of those who would base Christian theology on the secularistic premise that God is dead. Their assessment of our cultural situation is completely undiscriminating in simply assuming that secularism is an essentially unified and internally consistent outlook. It is possible, naturally, that an analysis of secularism might show this assumption to be justified. But, as I shall now try to indicate, there are good reasons for doubting this, and it is important that these reasons be carefully examined. If the secularistic outlook of our day is so self-consistent that we must simply accept or reject it, then the prospects for theology are dim indeed.

We saw earlier that secularism differs from secularity solely at the point of its negations. The typical secularist not only affirms himself and the world in their significance and proper autonomy, but also denies any transcendent reality in which the secular order has its ultimate ground and end. Thus, with respect to knowledge, for example, the secularist is sure to be either a lay or a professional positivist. Not content to assert the validity of scientific statements, he goes on to deny that, with the exception of the purely analytic truths of logic and mathematics, any other kind of statements can make good on their cognitive claims.

Interestingly, however, this denial seems wholly unjustified in terms of the only criteria it itself admits as possible. It is certainly not a statement of fact that could ever be empirically falsified; nor can one plausi-

---

25. "The Message of God to the Age of Atheism," *Oberlin College Bulletin*, January, 1964, pp. 3-14.

bly contend that it is an analytic statement with a logical or mathematical kind of truth. If, on the other hand, one treats it simply as a postulate, as some positivists have tried to do, he must then deal with substantial objections to accepting it. Some of the best work by contemporary philosophers of ordinary language makes clear that restriction of the scope of knowledge exclusively to the empirically falsifiable derives no support whatever from our actual usage.[26] This by itself, of course, hardly establishes the validity of the metaphysical and theological knowledge that positivists wish to deny. Yet it does expose the basis of their denial to be arbitrary, and so dispels the notion that positivism has any self-evident logical force.

Most of us today, even if we are secularists, are determined in our thinking about God by a common intellectual tradition that has served throughout Western history for the conception of his reality. Broadly speaking, this tradition is that usually referred to as the *philosophia perennis* or "Christian philosophy," whose crowning achievement is a supernaturalistic theism uniquely combining elements of classical Greek philosophy with religious insights derived from the Hebraic-Christian Scriptures. For centuries, this traditional theism has been in the process of breaking down under the cumulative weight of experiences and reflections that run counter to its basic premises. Yet, remarkably enough, even where these premises are denied, they continue to exert an influence scarcely less profound than where they are still affirmed. Indeed, their atheistic critics commonly pay them the supreme tribute of being the only theistic premises there are, since to overcome them is supposed to be sufficient to "overcome theism" altogether. Because the defenders of the premises, for their part, suppose the very same thing, the unqualified claim of the attackers is bound to seem plausible, even if it is actually an arbitrary and highly debatable assumption.

This is all the more so because there is, in fact, an irreconcilable opposition between the premises of this supernaturalistic theism and the whole direction of our experience and reflection as secular men. Thus, for one thing, commitment to secularity entails acceptance of logical self-consistency as one of the necessary conditions for the truth of any assertion. And yet, as some three hundred years of careful criticism have shown, the main assertions of classical theists are utterly incapable of satisfying this condition. This is evident, for example, from traditional theological discussions of the creation of the world. Theologians

26. See especially Stephen Toulmin, *The Uses of Argument*, Cambridge: Cambridge University Press, 1958; cf. also below, pp. 88f., 110ff.

usually tell us that God creates the world freely, as the contingent or nonnecessary world our experience discloses it to be. This assertion is also made necessary because it offers the only really credible construction of the account of creation in Holy Scripture. At the same time, because of their fixed commitment to the assumptions of classical metaphysics, theologians also tell us that God's act of creation is one with his own eternal essence, which is in every respect necessary, exclusive of all contingency. Hence, if we take them at their own word, giving full weight to both of their assertions, we at once find ourselves in the hopeless contradiction of a wholly necessary creation of a wholly contingent world.

In a similar way, supernaturalists have traditionally maintained that the end of man is to serve or glorify God through obedience to his will and commandments. And yet the God whom we are thus summoned to serve is, in the last analysis, so conceived that he can be as little affected by our best actions as by our worst. As *actus purus,* and thus a statically complete perfection incapable in any respect of further self-realization, God can be neither increased nor diminished by what we do, and our action, like our suffering, must be in the strictest sense wholly indifferent to him.

This second antinomy may serve to indicate that it is by no means its theoretical incoherence alone that explains why traditional theism is unacceptable to secular men. There is the even more important consideration of its existential repugnance.[27] If what we do and suffer as men in the world is from God's perspective wholly indifferent, that perspective is at most irrelevant to our actual existence. It can provide no motive for action, no cause to serve, and no comfort in our distress beyond the motives, causes, and comforts already supplied by our various secular undertakings. But, more than that, to involve ourselves in these undertakings and to affirm their ultimate significance is implicitly

---

27. This existential motive in contemporary atheism is rightly emphasized by Henri de Lubac (*op. cit.,* pp. 3-7, 27-35, 61-73) and other Roman Catholic students of the matter like John Courtney Murray (*The Problem of God: Yesterday and Today,* New Haven: Yale University Press, 1964, pp. 77-121, especially p. 95). The weakness in their analyses, however, is that they never really free themselves from the assumption that Christian faith in God and supernaturalistic theism are indissolubly connected, and thus fail to do justice both to atheism's theoretical motives (as is particularly true of Murray) and to what is legitimate in the existential motive itself. De Lubac does concede that "the principle which inspired [the great systems of rebellion—namely, the assertion of man's dignity and freedom] was not devoid of nobility" (*op. cit.,* p. 34). But he nowhere seems to realize just what this principle implies nor does he anywhere so much as question whether a truly Christian affirmation of the greatness of man can ever be reconciled with the premises of classical theism.

to deny the God who is himself finally conceived as the denial of our life in the world. Small wonder that countless men have concluded with Ludwig Feuerbach that "the question of the existence or non-existence of God is the question of the non-existence or existence of man."[28] True, classical theists' statements about God do not add up to a consistent negation of our secular involvements. They generally contend not only that God is the metaphysical Absolute, whose only relation to the world is wholly external, but that he is also the loving heavenly Father revealed in Jesus, who freely creates the world and guides it toward its fulfillments with tender care. The difficulty, however, as we noted above, is the obvious incoherence of these two contentions, which both deny and affirm that God's relation to the world is real and that he is relevant to its life because it is relevant to his. Thus, even at best, supernaturalism offers but uncertain support for our affirmation as modern men of the importance of the secular; and, at worst, it so undercuts this affirmation that many of us have no choice but to reject it once we have clearly grasped its implications.

But here we may profitably remind ourselves that no theistic scheme, however adequate, can alone be sufficient to solve this problem. The only way any conception of God can be made more than a mere idea having nothing to do with reality is to exhibit it as the most adequate reflective account we can give of certain experiences in which we all inescapably share. This, too, it seems to me, is a conclusion that forces itself upon us out of our modern situation. We have slowly learned through our actual history that no assertions are to be judged true, unless, in addition to being locally consistent, they are somehow warranted by our experience, broadly and fairly understood. But one thing, it would appear, in which almost all of us today share is just our experience as modern, secular men: our affirmation of life here and now in the world in all its aspects and in its proper autonomy and significance. My conviction is that it is in this secular affirmation that we must discover the reality of God in our time. The adequate response to secularistic negations will not be made by a supernaturalism that is no longer tenable or by a naturalism that uncritically accepts the same negations. It will be made, rather, by an integral secularity—a secularity which has become fully self-conscious and which therefore makes explicit the faith in God already implied in what it itself affirms.

28. Quoted by Henri de Lubac, *op. cit.*, p. 27.

Rupert E. Davies

Rupert Davies (1909–1994) was a British Methodist theologian. He had particular interest in John Wesley and in the continuing Methodist tradition. He wrote an introduction entitled *Methodism* (Penguin, 1963) and *What Methodists Believe* (Mowbray, 1976). A leader in the ecumenical interests of British Christian churches he maintained a vision of church reunion. Fundamental to his theological construction was his interest in religious authority and the way it underpins both personal and communal life. The chapter chosen for this book is from his book *Religious Authority in an Age of Doubt* (London: Epworth, 1968, pp. 210-22).

Only One Way Forward

It must surely now be clear that the gift of infallibility in matters of religious truth is granted to no one and nothing—no book, no person or group of persons, no institution. There is in religion no such thing as infallibility; it is a concept which has no equivalent in reality. In answer to the challenge of Schleiermacher, consciously or unconsciously recognized as highly dangerous to all forms of authoritative religion, many theologians have made attempts, some of which are described in this book, to defend a doctrine of infallibility; and Churches, in their understandable, if not always laudable, desire to counteract the erosions of modern scepticism and secularism, have made great efforts to build guarantees of inerrancy—as, for instance, the argument that God *must* have made provision for an infallible guide, or else mankind would have been left in total darkness—into their theological systems. But the attempts and efforts have all failed; and their very frequency and variety, the continuing disputes among infallibilities as to *where* infallibility is to be found, and the shifts to which they have sometimes been reduced in order to render plausible the notion that human beings can in some circumstances be lifted above error, are eloquent testimonies to their failure. Infallibility is disproved theologically, since it implies a doctrine of God and man which is anti-Biblical and inconsistent with the rest of Christian faith; it is disproved empirically, since no claimant to infallibility has appeared who can stand up to the attacks of Biblical, historical and philosophical critics or to the counter-claims of his rivals.

And, even if, for the sake of argument, we were to agree that it is theoretically possible that there is somewhere an infallible authority, we should still never be able to identify it, unless we were ourselves gifted with infallibility. We might, of course, have a strong personal opinion that infallible authority is to be found in the Bible, or in the Papacy, or elsewhere; but since strong personal opinions are often, as all agree, mistaken, we should never know whether the pronouncements of the body or book or person whom we had elected to regard as infallible were in fact infallible. Roman Catholic writers, from Newman to Bishop B. C. Butler, have tried to circumvent this difficulty by distinguishing certitude (or certainty) from infallibility—certainty being limited to the occasion when we accept the Roman Church as infallible, infallibility being a permanent gift granted to the Roman Church and its head. But this does not really help their case very much, for, on this view, certainty is a kind of temporary infallibility, and temporary infallibility is, if anything, more difficult to locate than the permanent sort. Moreover, it is even more open to objection than the permanent infallibility of the Church; an individual, deciding whether to become a member of the Roman Catholic Church, is surely even less likely to be exempt from error than the majestic Roman Church, with all its history, wisdom and experience.[1]

So infallibility is out. The claim to possess it, and the belief in its existence, are seen to be attempts to short-circuit the endless questionings which arise within the human mind and soul about the nature and purpose of existence, by the assertion, itself claimed to be infallible, that *here* is the place where all doubts are laid to rest. All doctrines of infallibility are psychological, nor theological or logical; as such they may be highly successful in achieving the end for which they were in fact created—widespread peace of mind. But we cannot in our time be content with

1. I have argued this point at somewhat greater length in *Why I Am a Protestant*, pp. 56-61.

any doctrine which achieves this but is otherwise untenable: nor, perhaps, will it much longer achieve even this.

But are we not in a much better position if we withdraw the claim to infallibility, wherever it has been made, and say that a measure of authority which is sufficient for the spiritual and intellectual needs of the Church and its members is to be found in the Catholic Creeds, or the Roman Catholic Church, or the Pope, or the Bible, or in human conscience, or in human reason? By "a measure of authority which is sufficient for the spiritual and intellectual needs of the Church and its members" we should perhaps mean something like this: Granted that we cannot know the truth of the Christian religion *for certain*, or the truth of any particular doctrine *for certain*, we can be enough convinced of their truth to live by them without awareness of any contradiction between them and the rest of what we believe to be true: and an "authority" which can convince us in this way and to this extent is "sufficient."

This conception of "sufficient authority" is, as we shall perhaps see in a few minutes, a useful one. But can we ascribe this authority to the Pope, or to the Creeds, or to the consensus of the Church Catholic, or to reason, or to the spiritual insight or Inner Light of the individual Christian, or to Christian experience, or to conscience, or even to Scripture? The conclusion to be drawn from the preceding chapters is that we cannot. By "the Pope" we of course mean "the Pope speaking *ex cathedra*," or, since Vatican II, "the Pope speaking with the bishops of the Roman Church." "The Pope," in this sense, lacks "sufficient authority," not because he is not to be trusted at all as an exponent of Christian truth—no Christian would wish to deny that *ex cathedra* pronouncements can faithfully expound Christian truth—but because among *ex cathedra* pronouncements there are some, for instance the one on the Immaculate Conception of the Virgin Mary, which have no chance of obtaining the consent of the whole of Christendom and are thought by many Christians to be contrary to the Christian Gospel as they have accepted it. The Creeds are nearer than "the Pope" to possessing "sufficient authority," and there are few sections of Christendom which would entirely deny a measure of authority at least to the Apostles' and Nicene Creeds. But the measure is not "sufficient," because at certain points—not many, it is true—they state dogmatically what must be regarded as still open to inquiry—the Virgin Birth, for instance, and the Descent into Hades. And the Nicene Creed suffers from the additional disqualification in that it is said in two versions in different parts of the Church, one containing the *filioque*, and other not. Nor can we ascribe "sufficient authority" to the consensus of the Church Catholic, for although the consensus of the ancient Church is to some extent, as we have seen, available in the Creeds, the divisions of the Church have made it impossible for the consensus of the Church through all the ages and in all places to be ascertained.

The claims of reason, conscience, spiritual insight and the Inner Light are on a different level, but equally unacceptable. The chief objection to them is, of course, their individualistic character. One man's reason is another man's irrationality; one man's Inner Light is another man's darkness. One man's spiritual insight is another man's misguided prejudice. And within the Church—indeed within individual communions—consciences differ and conflict most profoundly. But even when reason, conscience and the rest can free themselves of their individualistic taint, we must still ask: What is the reason or conscience or insight, even of a large number of people agreeing together, to set itself up against the accumulated wisdom and experience of the Church at large (for this is what they are venturing to do if they claim "sufficient authority")?

The case of the Bible is different. Here, surely, is a source of authority by which all communions of Christendom, and almost all individual Christians, profess themselves willing to test their doctrines and their practices. Surely here, at least, we have "sufficient authority"? But even here the claim cannot be conceded. The historical and scientific errors of the Biblical writers do not matter at this point (they are important only if the alleged *infallibility* of Scripture is being discussed). But the Old Testament conflicts at many points with the New Testament, and the New Testament at some (not many) points conflicts with itself. These discrepancies cannot be resolved from within the Bible itself, despite the efforts of theologians since the very beginning of Christian history, and especially since the Reformation, to resolve them. To attempt such a resolution involves preference of one passage above another, and who shall determine the preference? And, much more seriously, as the Roman Church has clearly and consistently taught, the Bible needs an interpreter; it does not bear its plain meaning on its face. There are in existence many hundreds of interpretations of the Bible, several of them claiming to be infallible. A book which is at some points in conflict with itself, and is patient of many conflicting interpretations, cannot be said to possess "sufficient authority." And if the Bible does not possess it, the last and most promising candidate has fallen out of the race.

To some readers the contention made in the last few pages will seem, if true, to be a sentence of death on the Christian Faith. If we have no infallible guide, if we have not even any person or body of persons, or any collection of writings, or any gift within ourselves, by whose prescriptions and pronouncements we can live without contradiction or serious doubt, they will perhaps say, how can we be expected, or expect others, to accept the Christian Faith? If we cannot know that we are right when we recite the Creeds or believe the Bible or submit to the Church, we are, far more than those who "for this life only . . . have hoped in Christ," of all men most miserable. Christianity is not able to deliver the goods which it advertises, and we must turn elsewhere. And there seems nowhere else to turn.

But in fact, what seems to be a sentence of death is a charter of life and renewal and unity. Up till recently Christians have believed that there is a source of authority to which it is the duty of all to submit. Those who have been sure that the authority recognized in their own communion is the correct one have anathematized, persecuted and despised the subjects of other authorities. And those who have taken seriously the Lord's refusal to call down fire from heaven, at the suggestion of his disciples, on the Samaritan village which rejected him, have been puzzled and distressed by the Babel of authorities and by Christians' mutual destructiveness, and they have sought to mitigate in practice the rigours of the doctrine to which they have been committed.

But now we know that there is not, and never has been, an infallible guide, and that there is not, and never has been, one authoritative source of truth. At last, the real truth about our human situation is revealed, and we are free from the compulsions and constraints of the past. Immediately, of course, we are called to repent of our intolerance, our aggressiveness and defensiveness; and, although we may hope that God will wink at the times of our ignorance, to be conscious of the enormity of our offences against charity and humility. But at the same time we are enabled to approach the whole question from an entirely new position, without presuppositions and presumptions, and, although so ancient a problem will not be quickly solved, we can hope that a new beginning will lead to more rapid progress than has ever been possible before.

We can indicate the way forward in the simplest possible terms. A man becomes a conscious Christian when he commits himself to Jesus Christ. The nature of this commitment is that, with all his faculties in full possession and use, and in full awareness of the other theories of the world and the other patterns of life which have been propounded to him, he accepts for himself Jesus Christ as the meaning of the world and of human existence. That is, he recognizes God as Father, and he recognizes the principle, which can briefly be called the principle of love, asserted by Jesus in life and teaching, in death and resurrection, to be the principle on which the universe is created and sustained, as being in fact the principle which underlies all things; and, at one and the same time, he declares his intention of living by the same principle, so far as it lies within his power and at any cost. If we wish, as many of us probably will, to put this in more religious terms, we shall say that to become a Christian means to accept Jesus Christ as Lord, Master, Saviour, the Son and Word of God, and the supreme authority for thought and life.

This self-commitment is an act of faith, not an assertion of knowledge. Indeed, by making this act of self-commitment, a man forgoes and forswears the claim to *knowledge* about God and the universe and human life. He says, in effect, that in a world in which certainty on ultimate questions is impossible, and knowledge is confined to the vast but limited area of science, he is prepared, because he is aware of powerful reasons which appeal to his total personality (though they stop short of demonstration), and of no objections strong enough to counterbalance them, to put his personal trust in Jesus Christ and to live the life which is involved by that trust right through to the end. He can be said, from one point of view, to have accepted the most probable hypothesis, and to have adopted (as Bishop Joseph Butler recommended) probability as the guide to life; from another point of view, he deliberately lives by faith, and not by knowledge.

At this point a linguistic philosopher who happens on these pages may object that a Christian, in this case, is one who confuses his categories. For he has taken note of the life and teaching of a historical personage, and attached to them ontological significance and an ethical evaluation. These, according to many linguistic philosophers, are highly illegitimate things to do. Historical events and personages belong to one universe of discourse; attributions of ontological significance, if indeed they are allowable at all, belong to another, and ethical valuations to yet another. It is not possible to argue from a statement in one universe of discourse to a conclusion in another.

It must at once be conceded that the a-scription of meaning to Jesus Christ—which is what we maintain that a Christian makes—combines in one assertion what the objector claims to be two, or even three, universes of discourse. If this is illegitimate, then all religious statements are illegitimate, as in fact the logical positivists have alleged. To answer the objection satisfactorily would require a total defence of religion, for which this is not the place. Here it can only be pointed out that the illegitimacy of the "combination of universes" is not by any means undisputed among philosophers. But it can be added that what we have here

274

in mind, when we speak of the faith of a Christian, is not a proposition about God, man and the universe, but the declaration of a "policy of life"; and as such it is not vulnerable to the objection of the linguistic philosopher above set out. The theological statements to which we shall shortly come may be open to it, but the basic faith of a Christian is not.

Historians may come up with a further objection. A Christian, they point out, has now been defined as a man who has committed himself to a personage who, whatever else is asserted of him, is admitted on all sides to be historical. No one nowadays doubts his historical existence, but there is very considerable uncertainty about the course and details of his life as they are narrated in the Gospels, and very little certain knowledge of his actual words. Is what is known about him enough to justify self-commitment to him? The answer to this must be that, although we should very much have liked to know more about Jesus' historical career, we do know enough for the purpose. Historical research into the Gospels, which has been carried out in a more radical spirit than in virtually any other area of history, has left us at least with the outlines of the life and the central elements in the teaching of Jesus, it has verified in general the Gospel account of his death, and although it has certainly not removed the doubt which hangs over the personal resurrection of Jesus from the dead, it can be said quite definitely to have vindicated the historicity of the disciples' "resurrection experience." Moreover, it has left it open to less radical schools of historians to accept the historicity of a good deal more than we have just given, and to do so without loss of their academic respectability. We have enough for faith, though not enough to satisfy our legitimate curiosity.

But at this point, and on the same general theme, a theological objection may be raised. Is not the Christian, as we have described him above, putting himself far too much at the mercy of historical contingency? After all, it might one day be demonstrated that the whole Gospel is legendary; although this mode of attack has for the time being been dropped, perhaps some new historical discoveries or doubts may bring it to life again; and then where would our Christian faith be? If Christianity is to be asserted as true, there must be some guarantee of its truth outside history—the Holy, Catholic church, for instance, whose existence not even the most hardened sceptic can deny. We have seen already that no guarantees can, in fact, be available. And to the main burden of the objection we can reply that when the Christian commits himself to a historical person, he knows, or should know, exactly what he is doing. He is committing himself precisely to one who, on his own showing, although he was uniquely related to

275

God, has deliberately chosen to enter the realm of historical contingency, and has thus put himself at the mercy of any historian who claims to have proved his non-existence. God, as Jesus speaks of him, is exactly of such a character as to put himself and his revelation, in his desire to respect the freedom of human beings, at such a risk as this. To deny the submission of Christ to historical contingency is to deny the Incarnation, and turns Christianity into a kind of Gnosticism, according to which historical events are interesting but can be dispensed with by the intelligentsia.

The act of faith which is self-commitment to Christ has two immediate and lifelong consequences. The first is that by such commitment a Christian is incorporated into the Church, which is the historical fellowship of those who are thus committed. The second is that he is involved in working out the implications for life and thought of his commitment. The implications for thought make up what is called Christian theology, and take the form of doctrines and doctrinal teachings. The Christian works these out, assisted and guided (though not infallibly) by the Holy Spirit (as he firmly believes), by the use of his reason, by his spiritual insight (which is the best name for the Inner Light, since it does not imply, though it does not deny, that there is something of God in every man) and by his conscience. He does this in the context of worshipping and teaching life of the Church, and thus enters into its agelong heritage of theological thought and controversy.

At an early stage in this process, perhaps when he first stumbles on the fact that Christians dispute about many articles of the faith, there arises in his mind the problem of authority. Granted that reason and conscience and insight, and the teaching of the Church to which he belongs, point in a certain direction of thought, but granted also that teachers of another Church, or other teachers in his own Church, point in a different direction, how is he to know what to believe? And once the problem of authority has arisen for him, it is likely to remain his constant companion until he comes to terms with it. We have discarded several ineffective ways of dealing with it. What is there left? And here we must urge the replacement of the word "authority" by the word "witness." In the first part of this chapter we found a certain usefulness in the conception of "a measure of authority sufficient for faith." But now we can plainly say that the word "witness" corresponds much more accurately to the functions which we are now about to describe, and to the basic assertion, already made, but now made more explicitly and definitively, that for the Christian the supreme authority is Christ himself, to whom he has committed himself in faith.

The assertion of the supreme authority of Christ is essential to the position which this book represents. It means that there is no going behind Christ for further information about God, that in Christ is everything, implicitly or explicitly, that we need to be told about God and his purposes for the world and for us; it means also that we depend on faith just as much in the realm of authority as in any other part of the Christian religion. For we cannot know (the word is here used in the Pauline sense) Christ except by faith.[2]

This is the authority of Christ, in whom we trust. But our trust in him requires us to find out as much as we can about him and to work out as much as we can of the implications of trust in him for faith and life, as we have already said. And for this we require, not unimpeachable *authorities*, but trustworthy *witnesses*. And trustworthy witnesses are what we in fact have. Before all others, the Bible—which first of all is the record of the preparation for the coming of Christ in the history of Israel, its leaders and its prophets, and in its second part is the testimony of the only eye-witnesses to Jesus that we can ever have, set down by themselves or by those on whom they relied to do the task for them. After the Bible comes the undivided Church, which formulated in the Creeds what it clearly understood, after much argument, to be the main content of Scriptural teaching. The Bible and the creeds make up the major and the minor part of the Tradition which is the whole Church's most valuable possession. Then come the great liturgies of the great Churches of Christendom, the writings of the Fathers of the Early Church, and of the Fathers of the Middle Ages and of the Reformation and of later times. And then the "traditions" of the various communions into which the Catholic Church has been divided. And finally, but only just over the horizon of the future, is the prospect, held out by the Ecumenical Movement, of the reunion of Christendom and the reassertion and re-formulation of Christian truth by the once-again undivided Church.

The testimony of these witnesses needs to be adjudged and evaluated by the individual believer as he lives in and with the Church, and applies his reason, his conscience, his insight and his experience to it. These faculties and capacities of the believer are not witnesses in their own right, to be compared with the witnesses already mentioned and sometimes set over against them, and even preferred to them. Rather they are the means by which the witnesses are tested before they are accepted. They are the preparation for faith. Faith does not require indisputable evidence, nor is such evidence available; but it does require conviction that no contradic-

---

2. The fact that the commitment is in faith and claims no certainty helps us to avoid the awkward logical problem raised by all assertions of absolute authority.

tion of what is already believed or approved on good evidence is involved in the act of faith; and this conviction is provided by our human capacities as they are quickened by the Holy Spirit. For of course the acceptance of the witnesses is still an act of faith, however well-grounded in reason, conscience, insight and experience that act of faith may be and should be.

The order in which the witnesses have been mentioned is, as will have been seen, an order of priority. Yet no single witness, as we have also already seen, has a "sufficient measure of authority" in and by itself—not even the Bible or the consensus of the reunited Church. But in convergence and combination this measure of authority *can* be claimed for them. Not in *any* convergence and combination, for it is impossible that any witness who gives the lie to the Bible, even in harmony with another witness, should be believed, for the Bible is and must always remain the primary witness to the truths of the faith, for the simple reason that nothing else provides a first-hand account. But God is a God of order and coherence, and we may suppose therefore that when all the witnesses concur the authority which they possess will be as high as any authority we shall find anywhere in this world. This authority belongs to the future, not the present, since the Churches are not yet reunited. Meanwhile the concurrence of the others has very high authority indeed, the concurrence of the two parts of the Tradition an authority almost as high. But when the witnesses are in conflict, the authority of each of them (unless one of them is Scripture, and its testimony is absolutely clear) is in suspense until further light is granted to the Church. When only one witness offers testimony—unless that witness be Scripture—then the testimony can only be tentative until confirmation comes from another quarter; in the case of Scripture, its testimony can, if necessary, stand alone, with a strong claim upon our faith.

This gradation of our witnesses is certainly not free from difficulties; but the very difficulties serve to emphasize the essential features of our Christian existence. We are committed to Christ, and we live by faith in him. As we grow in the knowledge of him, we explore more and more deeply the truth as truth is in him. In our exploration we are assisted by many witnesses, not one of which either alone or in concert with the rest relieves us of the responsibility of thinking and deciding for ourselves, or puts us out of the reach of doubt or perplexity, but all of which help us to see the truth for ourselves. Sometimes the witnesses are in harmony, and we advance rapidly in understanding; sometimes they are in conflict, or seem to us to be, and we are impeded and puzzled. But we go forward in the same faith as that in which we started the journey, surely trusting, because we believe that Christ holds the meaning of all life, that, if not to us on earth, at least to the Church after us, will be granted unity in the truth. For the promise that the Holy Spirit will guide us into all the truth is the promise, not of a Spirit-proved inerrancy, but of a Spirit-guided exploration of the unsearchable riches of Christ.

Frances M. Young

1939

Frances Young (b. 1930) is a contemporary English Methodist theologian at the University of Birmingham. Although her interests range widely both historically and thematically, she has had a basic interest in interpreting the atonement, which is a persistent issue for Methodism. Utilizing both historical scholarship and insightful contemporary sensitivity, she explores fresh interpretation of this doctrine. The selection printed here is an article from the *Epworth Review*, vol. 18, no. 2, 1991, pp. 60-65, and is one of a twelve-part series on the doctrine of atonement.

Atonement

"For the life of the flesh is in the blood: and I have given it for you upon the altar to make atonement for your souls: for it is the blood that makes atonement, by reason of the life" (Lev. 17:11).

Such a statement is virtually meaningless to most of our contemporaries. They may be English speakers, they may even have some links with a church, but meaning does not rest in abstract ideas. Meaning relates to a shared culture, to a set of assumptions built into the normal patterns of social interaction, and the necessary set of assumptions for understanding these words seems no longer to exist. In an earlier generation, these words were related to a set of assumptions arising from what has been called the "introspective conscience of the West"[1] and the need for salvation from guilt, a need thought to have

---

1. Krister Stendahl, *Paul among Jews and Gentiles*, SCM 1977.

been anticipated in the sacrificial rituals of the Jewish scriptures and met through the blood of Christ. True, scholars sought to go behind these assumptions to the original meaning of the Hebrew words in Ancient Near Eastern culture, but they were largely modifying, not revolutionising, the assumptions they shared with everyone else; and they were not much heard, since what they claimed depended on too much specialist knowledge and too great a leap of the historical imagination for most people. The scholarly distinction between propitiation and expiation was hardly an issue of everyday life!

And now? Some are guilty about the guilt-producing preaching of the past. Furthermore, the thrust of most serious theological writing lies elsewhere; the problem of suffering, or current issues like ecology, feminism, liberation, etc., have replaced atonement, even salvation. Yet this is the so-called Decade of Evangelism, and the "simple Gospel" is still heard in Black churches and Gospel Halls. Growth is reported in churches which still sing about the blood of Christ and create a shared set of cultural assumptions in which that seems to make sense, largely by appealing to its authoritative givenness in scripture. Is all this language simply an albatross round our necks? If not, how can it make sense?

That very question implies abandoning the kind of approach to biblical interpretation that has dominated the last couple of centuries, and fuelled the debates between so-called liberals and those who claim to be fundamentalist or evangelical. The issue is not simply a matter of "getting back to the original," or "taking the text literally." We may or may not be able to do the historical reconstruction depending on the adequacy of the evidence: such reconstruction may or may not be illuminating when it comes to trying to appropriate the ideas in a different cultural setting; but if we cannot bring a text of the past into meaningful relation with the social realities of the present, then eventually no-one will behave as if it is of any significance, except those who artificially idolise it. Good preachers have always known that "the Word" has to be "applied."

Let's begin with a list of words commonly regarded as biblical and associated with the "work of Christ"; atonement, justification, propitiation, expiation, reconciliation, redemption, revelation, salvation, sanctification. How might we define them?

The important thing to recognise is that despite appearances they mostly are or derive from "ordinary" words used in daily life. Apart from religious connotations, Chambers dictionary suggests the following:

atonement: the act of atoning, originally making-at-one, or reconciliation; or giving satisfaction or making reparation. (We might add making amends, or paying compensation.)

justification: the act of justifying, and to justify is to prove or show to be just or right. (We might add that to justify oneself is to make excuses.)

propitiation: the act of propitiating, and to propitiate is to render favourable or appease, from the Latin *propitius* meaning well-disposed. (We might add that this implies making up to someone, often offering a gift or paying compensation.)

expiation: the act of expiating, which is defined as making atonement, or the means by which atonement is made (see above).

reconciliation: the act or means of reconciling, and to reconcile is to restore or bring back friendship or union; to bring to agreement or contentment; to pacify or conciliate.

redemption: the act of redeeming, and to redeem is to buy back, to recover or free by payment, to ransom or rescue.

revelation: the act of revealing, and to reveal is to make known, disclose, from Latin to unveil.

salvation: act of saving, and to save is to bring safe out of evil, rescue, protect.

sanctification: (the exception which proves the rule) the act of sanctifying, and to sanctify is to make, declare, regard as or show to be sacred or holy (which is the only specifically religious act in this list).

The list of definitions shows that the key words are almost all to do with restoring broken relationships. This kind of thing is not remote from our culture or society! It may help to consider the following episodes and situations.

Episode 1: A boy comes home from school with a friend. They disappear down the garden. Next thing we know is that they are throwing stones at a window in an old barn next door. True, it looks like a dilapidated building, but it has in fact been converted into a pleasant flat and is occupied by an old couple, who not only find their lounge window shattered, but are faced with the hazard of flying stones bouncing across their floor. An event has happened to shatter peace between neighbours, however remote their relationship. What has to happen to make it possible for them to live side by side without endless recrimination?

Is apology enough? Scarcely!

Is a box of chocolates and a bunch of flowers enough? Hardly!

282

Both are necessary, but only as an adjunct to compensation, to the repair of the damaged window.

Atonement implies that the offender satisfies the offended party by offering reparation, making amends by putting things to rights and going further to demonstrate sincere repentance and to offer a token of future goodwill.

But the boy cannot afford it. So who carries the can? His parents, of course. But that does not absolve the boy from the shame and embarrassment of personally apologising and offering the bunch of flowers and box of chocolates.

Situation 1: Israel's existence is some compensation for the Holocaust.

Situation 2: Whites have to make amends for the years of apartheid.

Episode 2: Two girls are running along a canal bank. It's in need of repair. One slips and ends up in the lethal filth of an urban waterway, the other panics. Can she save herself? It's more likely that her life will depend on someone being around to pull her out with a lifebelt or something else that happens to be at hand.

Salvation means rescue, and its "content" is related to the mess someone is in. Usually it depends on receiving assistance from someone else, and that may mean giving up the struggle and collaborating with instructions.

A youth cycles by, but ignores the situation. His parents justify his indifference on the grounds that he was too young to do anything—they are relieved he didn't get involved and run risks himself. The inquest determined that if he had used his bike to alert a policeman on a nearby bridge, help could have arrived in time. His irresponsibility was not justifiable.

Situation 3: Records reveal that the British authorities ignored information about Auschwitz because it was simply incredible.

Situation 4: Agreement is reached on the ransom to be paid for the release of the hostages.

Situation 5: If the Birmingham 6 are innocent, nothing can absolve British justice. Their punishment is nothing other than a gross miscarriage of justice.

I do not propose to comment on these "illustrations." They are intended to show that the language used in discussion of the doctrine of atonement does relate to social realities in our culture, in situations both individual and corporate. The discerning reader will undoubtedly make significant connections, pointers to which have been incorporated in the material, and not simply where the vocabulary used is explicitly reminiscent of the words defined to begin with. But what about the language of sacrifice? Here we are in greater difficulties. In a culture which does not generally recognise the existence of powers to be propitiated, spirits and ancestors with whom fellowship is important, the language of sacrifice has been debased. African Christians know it is not primarily about "giving up" but rather "offering" and "feasting." It is still part of the culture within which they live.

But wait: offering gifts is also part of our social interchange. Our culture disapproves of bare-faced bribes, but Heads of State and negotiating industrialists still exchange gifts as marks of mutual interest, and entertain one another to banquets. We celebrate birthdays, with gifts and parties. We say "thank you" or "sorry" by offering gifts. We honour someone by holding a dinner, or making a presentation, perhaps to mark retirement.

The social experiences necessary for understanding are there. What is missing is the sense of a divine society or divine being to which similar activities might relate. Hence "sacrifice" and "sanctification" no longer create their old associations, and propitiation (or expiation) have acquired purely secular meanings despite their originally religious connotations.

We cannot, therefore, rest content with the narrow vision of the dominant social and cultural world in which we live. The challenge of that "alien" world of the Bible must be allowed to bear upon our assumptions. For it speaks authoritatively of a people and a culture which grasped things our culture in general no longer understands. The "two-way" process of hermeneutics, recognising that the world of the Bible is different from ours, and yet a view of the same world to which attention might fruitfully be paid, has to be faced.

If salvation is rescue, what do we need to be rescued from? The answer we think of as traditional is guilt and sin. Since the Reformation, individual guilt has fuelled the evangelical message. Psychologists tell us there is still much guilt around, but we are now encouraged to think a lot of it is inappropriate, and for most "decent" Church people, it is only artificially put at the centre: we really are "not so bad" after all. (This is not to suggest that it is not important for some individuals, or appropriate in some contexts, e.g. prison ministry.)

What is emerging in recent scholarship is an appreciation of the fact that individual guilt was not the dominant concern in the Bible. Scholars used to think that Ezekiel was a great advance on earlier ideas, precisely because here the individual is supposed to take responsibility for personal wrong acts. What has become clear is that Ezekiel is really addressing his contemporaries, a generation which claimed that they were suffering exile because of the sins of past generations. As in the rest of the Bible, sin primarily relates to corporate social realities.

But surely that is not true of the New Testament, you may retort, especially Paul with his troubled conscience and his dramatic conversion. But perhaps we have been reading Paul too much in the light of Luther. Such is the challenge of Krister Stendahl[2] and E. P. Sanders.[3] After all Paul claims to have been a Pharisee of the Pharisees, *blameless according to the Law* (Phil. 3:6). Suppose Paul did not move from plight to solution, but from solution to plight. Suppose Paul only realised the impossibility of living a pure life in the light of Christ. And what about Bruce Malina's look at *The New Testament World* [4] through the eyes of a cultural anthropologist? He at least asks us to consider the possibility that ancient culture was not individualist but ancient societies had "dyadic personalities" so that identity related to social role, and conscience to the shame of flouting social expectations rather than some psychologically experienced guilt.

The idea of sin, even when not simply equated with sex, has been individualised and moralised in our religious culture, and so has the idea of salvation. We find the notion of corporate (or Original?) sin problematic. Or do we? Consider the following, the outcome of a dream I had one holiday.

Gadara 1945

Over the crest of the hill, the thunder of trotters
The thunder of trotters pursued by a cloud of dust,
The thunder of thousands stampeding down and down.

Over the edge of the crag, the thunder of waters,
The thunder of waters, deep in abysmal depths,
The thunder of bodies, cascading down to drown.

---

2. Op cit.

3. E. P. Sanders, *Paul and Palestinian Judaism*, SCM 1977; cf. *Paul, the Law and the Jewish People*, Fortress 1983, and *Paul*, Past Masters series, OUP, 1991.

4. Bruce Malina, *The New Testament World*, Insights from cultural anthropology, SCM 1983.

Practical Divinity

If only the thunder would drown the demons of war,
Of pogroms, oppression and concentration camps,
Apartheid, the Gulag and famine and greed and fear.

But among the tombs humanity sits and cries,
Indulging in self-abuse, cutting its flesh,
Cutting its flesh with stones till blood appear.

Among the tombs insanity sits, released
From every restraint—frustration has fractured the chains,
The fetters are frayed by friction and violence—we're free,

Yet demon-possessed can't enjoy our liberty.
Among the tombs we sit cutting our flesh,
Disturbed in our insecure security.

"Don't disturb us, leave us alone," we cry distraught,
Distraught we cry out, "Have you come to torment? Don't
    disturb!
We're free, we've broken our chains; so leave us in peace."

The dread demand's already come: "Your name?"
"We're the army of occupation," is our reply.
"We're the Legion detailed to act as security police

To ensure that the truth never gets out and here
Humanity sits tormented and crying out:
We're free, we've broken our chains; so leave us alone."

Demonic delusion like this cannot be suppressed
Or sublimated, controlled or banished or solved
By denial, self-knowledge or human will on its own.

Could transference to innocent victims—indeed
Their sacrifice in the boiling abyss of hell—
Ever free humanity's mind from Legion's power?

Permission was given—and over the crest of the hill
The thunder of horrors, pursued by a mushroom cloud,
The thunder of thousands meeting destiny's hour.

> To come to its senses, humanity must see
> That only the chains of love can set us free,
> That divine grace is essential for liberty.

Where's the "rub" if it is not individual guilt? It is the desperate anxiety produced by the "gonewrongness" of the world, the power of human aggression and oppression, the sense of helplessness to do anything about it, even in a democracy, the feeling of being trapped by one's social or ethnic position, the problem of suffering on a scale almost unimaginable, the approach of nuclear or ecological disaster. . . . Corporate sin is a reality.

The dynamic for Paul, I suggest, was a transformation beginning with the revelation of the exalted Christ (see Segal)[5], understood through a fresh reading of the scriptures, especially Jeremiah. His vocation to the Gentiles (nations) was perceived in terms of Jeremiah's call-vision (Jer. 1:4-10; cf. Gal. 1:15-16, 1 Cor. 1:27, 31, 2:6, 10, 2 Cor. 10:8-18, etc.); his message in terms of the new covenant of Jer. 31:31ff. (2 Cor. 3 *et al. loc.*).[6] Atonement was the process whereby the corporate human failure (Romans 1–3) was transformed into new creation (2 Cor. 5:17). The new humanity in Christ revealed the corruptness of the old. Paul moved, not from personal guilt to individual salvation, but from a vision of Christ the new creation to discernment of humanity's tragedy—from solution to plight.

Atonement embraces the whole creation, and therefore certainly includes the individual. The traditional post-Reformation "simple Gospel," and indeed the traditional post-mediaeval "theories" of atonement all express part of what it is about. It is impossible to explore here the many facets which years of research and thinking have uncovered for me. Let me outline some principles and insights in these concluding paragraphs.

Principle 1. Sin and suffering are not two separate issues, but are linked with one another, often not in terms of individual responsibility—it is not right to blame someone for their illness—but in terms of corporate human responsibility, e.g. the Ethiopian earthquake, the slaughter on the roads, etc.

---

5. Alan F. Segal, *Paul the Convert*, The Apostasy and Apostolate of Saul the Pharisee, YUP 1990.

6. See further "The Biblical Roots of Paul's Perceptions," in Frances Young and David Ford, *Meaning and Truth in 2 Corinthians*, SPCK 1987; and "Understanding Romans in the light of 2 Corinthians," SJT (forthcoming).

Principle 2. There must be coherence between the doctrine of creation and the doctrine of atonement. (Different traditions tend to give one or the other priority, and this results in very different stances towards the world.)

Principle 3. The Cross is about God taking responsibility for the "gone wrongness" of God's world—even if you believe in a devil, God remains ultimately responsible (unless you think the devil is eternal rather than a fallen creature of the one God, in which case you are not within the monotheistic Judaeo-Christian tradition). In other words, in Christian theology the only proper theodicy is the act of atonement revealed in Christ.

Insight 1. Simone Weil suggested that the act of creation is an act of abandonment—the only way that the infinite God could create was by withdrawal, allowing space for something to exist other than God's self. This necessarily involved risk—indeed a kind of alienation or the absence of God. The presence of God in creation is a constant waiting, a struggle to bring order out of chaos without violating the freedom of the "other" God has permitted to be. The best parable is that of a loving parent with a recalcitrant teenager, though the intention is to speak of the whole created universe, not simply of individual relationships with God, which mirror the cosmic dynamic.[7]

Insight 2. The doctrinal development of the first few centuries of Christian history is the story of people learning to do justice to the reality of the salvation revealed in the scriptures and experienced in the liturgy of the Church. They exploited a vast range of language, symbol and imagery, with the result that scholarly studies of atonement have found in the literature whatever "theory" they wished to emphasise. Fundamental to patristic thinking, however, was the notion of atonement as re-integration, or as the "marriage" between God and his creation. This was expressed in many different philosophical and doctrinal forms, but in the end the doctrine of incarnation was integral to this thinking.[8]

Conclusion

This article is not meant to spell out answers but to open doors—it is after all the introduction to a series. But let's return to the initial problematic text. Hearts and blood may seem to have been de-mystified by

---

7. See further Frances Young, *Can These Dry Bones Live?* SCM 1982.
8. See further Frances Young, *The Making of the Creeds*, SCM 1991.

transplants, but television drama suggests otherwise. There is something instinctive about blood being sacred, for it is the life. The important thing about the Leviticus text is that God is the subject of the sentence, as also in Rom. 3:25: the biblical claim is that God has taken action to supply what is necessary for the healing of God's own broken world, and like a responsible parent has undertaken the payment of compensation for the damage of human sin.

Geoffrey Wainwright

Minister - 1964
missionary teacher + pastor w. Africa
1967-73

2nd half of 20th cent.

Geoffrey Wainwright (b. 1939) is a British Methodist theologian who has taught in Africa, England, and the United States. He is currently the Robert E. Cushman Professor of Christian Theology at Duke Divinity School. He was trained at Cambridge University and in British Methodist schools, and holds a doctorate from the Ecumenical Institute in Bossey, Switzerland. With broad ecumenical interests, he is knowledgeable about Roman Catholic and Eastern Orthodox thought, and has played a strong role in recent and continuing ecumenical discussions representing world Methodism. The selection included is from *For Our Salvation: Two Approaches to the Work of Christ*, pp. 172-86.*

The Threefold Office in Prospect

To speak of a theological or practical prospect for the threefold office [of Jesus Christ] is something of a wager. Many perhaps would consider that the categories of prophet, priest, and king belonged already to a bygone age. Certainly there are few *kings* left in the world; yet the perdurance of an occasional monarchy, and the fascination which a royal family can still hold, especially for foreigners, suggests that the "divinity that doth hedge a king" may not quite have vanished from the face of the earth. The very term *priestcraft* as a synonym, and worse, for superstition and obscurantism may have practically disappeared from our "enlightened" world; yet a certain mystery attaches to science and technology as they discover and master the secrets of the universe. There may be few *prophets* for stoning, but gurus attract followers searching for deep wisdom. If we were to grant, however, that the terms *prophet*, *priest*, and *king* were relatively unfamiliar to the modern world, it might well be that therein resides precisely their chance. Perhaps the rather archaic quality they now possess would precisely allow them to function as archetypes. Let us examine what would be the necessary conditions for that to happen, and what its value might be.

In his interesting and influential book entitled *The Nature of Doctrine*, George Lindbeck has proposed to understand Christianity as a cultural and linguistic tradition.[1] While it would be a mistake to bracket the ontological reference of doctrines in favor of reducing them to a set of speech-rules (as many saw Lindbeck doing), his fundamental insight is valid that Christianity entails a complex of language-use interwoven with perceptions, habits, and skills which can only be appropriated by disciplined participation; membership in the ecclesial community requires learning one's way into the verbal and practical tradition. There is no reason to expect that its content and forms should be immediately accessible to the outsider. There is therefore nothing untoward about our maintenance—or, if it has been forgotten, retrieval—of the language of prophet, priest, and king, provided three conditions are met. First: the reference of prophet, priest, and king should have some relevance to the human condition. While the "cult of relevance" is deplorable, it would be a betrayal to think that the gospel were *irrele*-vant to human needs and possibilities, properly understood. Second: prophet, priest, and king would need to suit the person and work of the Savior and the nature of the salvation experienced in him. Here it is necessary to test whether our triad matches other scriptural and traditional ways of describing Christ and Christian existence. Third: prophet, priest, and king would have to retain or regain a living context in the devotional and liturgical life of the church, for it is in image and rite that archetypes dwell, persist, and exercise their power.

1. Knowledge, Power, and Redemptive Mediation

As to the first requirement, the relevance of our triad to the human condition: I will recall the way each of the previous chapters ended.

1. George A. Lindbeck, *The Nature of Doctrine: Religion and Theology in a Postliberal Age* (Philadelphia: Westminster, 1984).

First I invoked John Henry Newman on "the three principal conditions of mankind," namely, "suffering," "work," and "study," which were for him matched by the priestly, regal, and prophetic offices of Christ respectively. In the three subsequent chapters, I found my own equivalents. The prophetic office of Christ addresses the human questions of knowledge and meaning. The priestly office of Christ deals with human alienation and estrangement by providing a divine reconciliation and atonement. The royal office of Christ addresses the human questions of power and authority. What remains is briefly to indicate the connections among these themes of knowledge, power, and redemptive mediation.

Proverbially, knowledge is power; and some late-twentieth-century epistemologists have called attention to the reverse dynamic: rather benignly, J. Habermas has pointed to the "interests" which guide our acquisition of knowledge; in more sinister fashion, M. Foucault sought to show that power holders control what counts as knowledge. Without knowledge, power would be blind; without power, knowledge would be ineffective. Combined, knowledge and power give opportunity for good or for ill. In the fallen condition of humankind, wisdom can (apparently) be overpowered; and legitimate authority can (apparently) be ignored. Even worse, power and knowledge together can be used to express, produce, or maintain alienations between the possessors and the deprived in every sphere of human existence. Into this situation, Jesus Christ comes redemptively. Grounded in the reality of divine wisdom and sovereignty, Christ offers the vision and the possibility of a relationship between knowledge and power that is characterized by love. Freely undertaken at cost to self and for the good of all, Christ's sacrificial service bears the moral authority to invite human beings to enter in repentance and faith, through the liberating spirit, into that life of communion which God purposes for his creatures. There, knowledge comes through love of the other; and love of the other informs the exercise of power. And because the God revealed in Christ is the creator of all things and their redeemer, there is the real prospect that they will finally find their consummation in him. "To crown all," said John Wesley in harmony with the classic Christian Tradition, "there will be a deep, an intimate, an uninterrupted union with God; a constant communion with the Father and his Son Jesus Christ, through the Spirit; a continual enjoyment of the Three-One God, and of all the creatures in Him."[2]

---

2. Sermon 64, "The New Creation," in *The Works of John Wesley*, vol. 2, ed. Albert C. Outler (Nashville: Abingdon, 1985), pp. 500-510 (here p. 510).

2. The Savior and the Salvation

Let us move on to the second set of conditions: Does the threefold office touch all bases as a description of the Savior and his work? On its own terms, it avoids the inadequacy of taking any one of its facets singly. W. A. Visser 't Hooft put the dangers of the respective unilateralisms this way:

> A one-sided emphasis on the prophetic ministry leads inevitably to moralism and rationalism: Christ becomes a great teacher of ideas and principles, but his work, past, present and future, disappears from the horizon. An exclusive emphasis on the priestly function leads to pietism and mysticism: Christ is the Lamb of God, but his piercing word and his victory over sin and death are not taken seriously. The full concentration on the kingship of Christ leads to utopianism and apocalypticism: Christ is the glorious King, but it is forgotten that his victory is the invisible victory of the word and that in this world the road to glory is the way of the cross.[3]

Positively, it must be tested whether the threefold office appropriately covers the same area as is described by other intentionally comprehensive formulae for salvation in Christ. Not all triads are theologically significant. "Three strikes, you're out" is not necessarily of divine inspiration, nor even the three stumps that make up a wicket. But let us try out our triad in relation to two other familiar tripartite formulations. Jesus said: "I am the way, and the truth, and the life" (John 14:6). For Saint Paul, the three abiding graces were "faith, hope, love" (1 Cor. 13:13). For bringing these two other triads into comparison with our own, I am indebted to suggestions by the Roman Catholic Walter Kasper in the first case, and the Presbyterian George Stroup in the second.[4]

The Way, the Truth, and the Life

In calling himself "the way, the truth, and the life," the Johannine Christ was describing his own saving work in relation to humankind. He is the way to be followed; he is the revealer of truth; he is the source of abundant life.

First, truth. The revelation of truth belongs to the prophet and teacher. "The question of truth," says Kasper, "is a radical human question." It

---

3. W. A. Visser 't Hooft, *The Kingship of Christ* (New York: Harper, 1948), p. 17.

4. Walter Kasper, *Jesus the Christ*, trans. V. Green (New York: Paulist Press, 1976), in particular pp. 259-66; George W. Stroup, *Jesus Christ for Today* (Philadelphia: Westminster, 1982), in particular pp. 88-106.

was also Pilate's question: "What is truth?" (John 18:38). The truth of Christ is a key category of the Fourth Gospel. Truth is the removal of a veil, *a-lētheia*, letting reality be seen as it is in God's eyes. Only so can one get one's bearing and live authentically. "Light," says Kasper, "is therefore a symbol of salvation. But where is there a dependable light among the many will-o'-the-wisps and the deceitful glitter of the world?" The Old Testament speaks of the Lord himself as light (Ps. 27:1; Isa. 60:19); his law is a lamp to the feet and a light to the path (Ps. 119:105). The Fourth Gospel calls Christ "the light of the world" (John 8:12; cf. 1:9; 12:46). He opposed lies and darkness, which are the consequence of sin (John 1:5; 3:19; 8:44; cf. 1 John 3:8). At Christmas and Epiphany we celebrate Christ as the *sol invictus,* "the unconquered sun." In the Easter Vigil we hail "the light of Christ," the *lumen Christi.* These are traditionally seasons of baptism, the sacrament of faith, which the early church called "enlightenment."[5]

Second, life. The giving of life belongs to the priestly office. "Life," says Kasper, "is always more than the purely biological; life includes man and his question about life, about authentic, fulfilled, true life. Life longs for the light of life, and that light is an essential factor in life itself. But since life is constantly threatened by decay and death, the question of true life includes the question of abiding, eternal life." In the Old Testament, God is the fount and lord of life (1 Sam. 2:6; Job 12:9f.; Deut. 32:39; Ps. 104:29). God's life has appeared in Jesus Christ (John 1:4; 5:26; 11:25; 1 John 1:1; 5:11). Christ is sent to bring life to the world (John 3:15f.; 10:10). Christ sealed the gift of life by loving "his own . . . to the end" (John 13:1) and making his redemptive passover on the cross (John 19:28-37; 1 Cor. 5:7). "By giving his life, his self-sacrifice, Jesus is both sacrificial victim and sacrificing priest" (Kasper). Only then is his flesh given for the life of the world (John 6:51c); and "he who eats my flesh and drinks my blood has eternal life, and I will raise him up at the last day" (John 6:54). The Eucharist becomes the bread of life to the believer. By the rite which Christ instituted on Maundy Thursday, we commemorate the unrepeatable sacrifice of Good Friday, in continuing dependence on the heavenly intercession upon which Christ entered at his ascension.

Third, the way. The way of truth and life is a royal road; and direction belongs to the king, guidance to the shepherd. In the Old Testament, the Lord is Israel's king (Exod. 15:18; Pss. 95-99; 145; 146) and shepherd

---

5. So already Justin Martyr, *First Apology,* 61 and 65 (Migne, *Patrologia Graeca* 6:421 and 428; hereafter cited as *PG*).

(Gen. 49:24; Ps. 23:1). In the Fourth Gospel, Jesus is "the good shepherd," who "lays down his life for the sheep" (John 10:11-18); he is "the King of the Jews," who "bear[s] witness to the truth" (John 18:33-37). As the "pioneer of [our] salvation" (Heb. 2:10; 12:2; cf. Acts 3:15; 5:31), he has gone ahead to prepare a place for his followers, that where he is, there they may be also (John 14:2f.). Lifted up, he is drawing all people to himself (John 12:32). One theme of Ascension Day is the theme of the sovereignty of Christ, celebrated in the liturgical application of Psalm 47 to him. In 1925, Pope Pius XI instituted the feast of Christ the King, in order to reaffirm the universal rule of Christ in an increasingly secular age. Now moved from the last Sunday in October to the Sunday before Advent, it has been adopted into the calendar of many other churches also.

Faith, Hope, and Love

According to the apostle Paul, faith, hope, and love are the three gifts of God that last throughout the course of human salvation. Each of the triad rests upon the person and work of Christ.

First, faith. Jesus Christ is "the faithful prophet" (G. Stroup). Toward the God he calls "Abba," his trust is unreserved, and his obedience complete. Prefaced by "Amen" ("Verily, verily . . ."), his teaching testifies to the faithfulness (*'emeth*) of God. Indeed, he himself is the Amen of all the promises of God, and "that is why we [in turn] utter the Amen through him, to the glory of God" (2 Cor. 1:20). And that Amen of ours is the prayerful expression of all the trust and obedience that faith includes.

Second, love. What Stroup calls "the priest's cross" is grounded in the love of God. However inadequate the so-called Abelardian theory may be when it views Christ and his cross solely in terms of a "moral example and influence," no other account of the atonement—whether military, satisfactory, or penal—can claim to capture an aspect of the redemption unless it begins and ends, as Abelard did, in God's love. The human expression of that love was Christ's "having loved his own . . . to the end" (John 13:1). Christ's self-sacrifice invites his disciples to "take up [their] cross" (Matt. 16:24). To confess Jesus Christ in the flesh is inseparable, says the First Letter of John, from "love of the brethren," which itself is a test of love toward God.

Third, hope. If Christ is "the source of hope," says Stroup, it is because "Jesus reigns . . . [and] is also yet to reign." Death could not hold him, and the "last enemy" is therefore radically defeated.

Through Christ "we are more than conquerors": Nothing "in all creation, will be able to separate us from the love of God in Christ Jesus our Lord" (Rom. 8:37-39).

The way, the truth, and the life; faith, hope, and love: the brevity of my remarks may have left an impression of artificiality; but I hope I have done enough at least to suggest the correspondence in substance and pattern between the threefold office of Christ and those other two triads that the Christian Tradition has also sensed to be comprehensive statements of the person and work of the Savior and the nature of the salvation experienced in him. The third and final condition for prophet, priest, and king to continue as an archetypical triad was that it should retain or regain a vital place in the church's worship. . . .

4. Christology: Doxology and Dogma

To speak of Christ in terms of the threefold office has the value of uniting doxology and dogma in his regard.

The title Prophet is, at first sight, perhaps the most modest of the three, yet it gets filled with the majesty of God: the man from Nazareth is the eternal Word of God incarnate, the transcendent Wisdom of God in human expression. The title King is the grandest of the three, yet the Lord became a servant, so that finally we might share in his reign: "For you know the grace of our Lord Jesus Christ, that though he was rich, yet for your sake he became poor, so that by his poverty you might become rich" (2 Cor. 8:9). The title Priest captures the heart of Christ's mediatorial role, which in the face of human sin needed to be redemptive; in him, God reconciled the world to himself and restores humankind to the divine image.

From the earliest days, it appears that Christians have also *worshiped* the One who *mediates* God to us and our access to God, and who is himself the *pattern* of our communion with the Father.[6] This doxological practice constituted for the early church a basis and context for dogmatic reflection. Against Arianism, Athanasius established the godhead of the Son on the twin grounds that Christ received worship and that only God could reveal God and save humankind, our reception of revelation and salvation in him being precisely what motivates our worship of him.[7] Against Apollinarianism, Gregory Nazianzen established

---

6. See G. Wainwright, *Doxology: The Praise of God in Worship, Doctrine, and Life* (New York: Oxford University Press, 1980), pp. 45-86.

7. Athanasius, *Letter to Adelphius*, 3f. (Migne, *PG* 26:1074-77); *Letters to Serapion* I.29f. (Migne, *PG* 26:597-600).

the full humanity of Christ on the ground that "what had not been assumed would not have been healed,"[8] and it was left to Cyril of Alexandria, as T. F. Torrance has shown, to bring out the necessary role of the human mind of Christ if we are to bring our "reasonable worship" *(logikē latreia)* to God.[9] The Council of Chalcedon recognized that both the divine and the human natures of Christ are grounded in the one *hypostasis* of God the Son. One way the Council expressed that was to say that the Son, now and forever incarnate, receives "a single worship" *(mia latreia)*.

Within that dogmatically established regulative framework, to speak of Christ as Prophet, Priest, and King is to take a step in the direction of that more pictorial and affective language which is appropriate to doxology and kerygma. It was, in the first place, the practice of the church in proclamation and worship that helped the Councils of Nicea, Ephesus, and Chalcedon to the dogmatic recognition of Christ's deity and the unity of his Person in the two natures of divinity and humanity. That dogma itself is meant as a permanent service to worship and preaching.

Having briefly shown the suitability to christology of the combination of prophet, priest, and king, I want now to show the value for ecclesiology of the threefold office in and under the one Christ. . . .

5. Ecclesiology: Before God and in the World

The *manus triplex* in its threefold unity can assist the church's self-understanding and practice both in its eternal life and in its mission for the sake of the world.

Down the years, John Henry Newman, with a continual ringing of the changes in terminology and perhaps with some development in this thought, drew on the threefold office in order to expound the nature and structures of the church. Christianity, he said, for instance, is "at once a philosophy, a political power, and a religious rite." Or again, it is a "passion" (the priestly office), a "fellowship" (the royal office), and a "science" (the prophetic office). Or yet again: "Christianity is dogmatical [the prophetic office], devotional [the priestly], practical [the royal] all at once." . . . The health of the church depends on these three functions being kept in proper balance. Their upsetting allows one to deduce from

---

8. Gregory Nazianzen, *Epistle* 101 (Migne, *PG* 37:181).

9. T. F. Torrance, "The Mind of Christ in Worship: The Problem of Apollinarianism in the Liturgy," in his *Theology of Reconciliation* (London: Chapman, 1975), pp. 139-214.

Newman what Maurice Nédoncelle has called "a theology of the abuses of the Church."[10] Positively put, "the prophetical, priestly and royal offices constitute," in the words of Nicholas Lash, "a 'triangle of forces' that is in principle . . . an *equilateral* triangle." At least, each of the three offices is "reshaped by its coincidence with the others." Each qualifies, and is qualified by, the others; and so all together are transformed. The equilibrium is precarious, because, as Newman recognizes, "in man as he is, reasoning tends to rationalism; devotion, to superstition; and power, to ambition and tyranny." So, says Lash, with the state of the Roman Catholic Church after Vatican II in view: "Theological rationalism [needs to be] held in check by the theologian's engagement in and sensitivity to the particular circumstances, experience and suffering of the worshipping community to which he belongs. . . . The theologian's work requires the corrective influence not only of the context of worship but also of what I have called 'the operation of catholicity,' expressed (in part) through the practical instruments of the Church's administration." Similarly: "The characteristic tendency of church authorities prematurely to 'order' the life of the Church through the exercise of power requires corrective pressure both from the exigencies of worship and life in particular places, and also from the requirements of sound scholarship and good argument." Other churches might conduct a similar exercise of self-examination. Lash recognizes, of course, that "the ultimate ground and guarantee of [the] equilibrium, which is not under our control, is the abiding presence of the Spirit of the risen Christ."

Turning now to the place and role of the church in the world and before God, it is possible to sketch the interlocking functions of the *munus triplex* in terms of a triad that has found much favor in the modern ecumenical movement: *leitourgia, martyria,* and *diakonia*.

First, *leitourgia*. With Karl Barth and the Swiss Reformed theologian of worship Jean-Jacques von Allmen, we can see Christian worship as also a "public service" (corresponding to the Greek etymology of liturgy), which the church offers to God on behalf of a world that is *not yet* willing or able to render praise and prayer.[11] The church in Christ intercedes for the conversion of the world and the needs of humankind—grounded in the redemption which God has wrought and the church now celebrates.

10. M. G. Nédoncelle, "Newman, théologien des abus de l'Église," in *Oecumenica: An Annual Symposium of Ecumenical Research, 1967,* ed. F. W. Katzenbusch and V. Vajta (Minneapolis: Augsburg, 1967), pp. 116-32.

11. Jean-Jacques von Allmen, *Worship: Its Theology and Practice,* trans. H. Knight and W. F. Fleet (New York: Oxford University Press, 1965), e.g., pp. 16, 70; cf. Karl Barth, *Church Dogmatics* IV/2, trans. G. W. Bromiley (Edinburgh: T. & T. Clark, 1958), pp. 638-41, 695-710, and IV/3 (1962), pp. 865f., 883f.

Second, *martyria*. By its proclamation, the church testifies to the wonderful works of God and so seeks to bring the world also into God's marvelous light (cf. 1 Pet. 2:9), where spiritual sacrifices may be offered—both of praise and of doing good (cf. Heb. 13:15f.).

Third, *diakonia*. Although, for instance, in almsgiving, our left hand should not know what our right hand is doing, yet the witness of our good works should bring the world to the worship of God: "Let your light so shine before men, that they may see your good works and give glory to your Father who is in heaven" (Matt. 5:16).

Once again, the proportion and combination is important: *leitourgia, martyria, diakonia;* worship, witness, ministry; the threefold office of priesthood, prophecy, and royal service.

And now the end is in sight, and not only of these chapters; for "salvation is nearer to us now than when we first believed" (Rom. 13:11).

6. The Eschatological Outlook

The entire exercise of the threefold office has been geared toward the end. As Prophet, Christ reveals the will and pleasure of God, which includes for humankind a salvation in which we attain our "chief end," namely, "to glorify God and enjoy him for ever" (to speak with the Westminster Catechism). As Priest, Christ removes the guilt of fallen humanity and restores our access to God, which is the condition of our salvation. As King, Christ preserves believers in our salutary communion with God by helping us to overcome the power of sin and bestowing on us the riches of his grace. The church is the company of those who already receive the benefits of Christ's threefold mediation and actively share, in Christ, in its further extension to the dimensions God has in view.

For a glimpse into the end, we may turn to the book of Revelation, where the historic offices of Christ and our participation in them are not forgotten but eternally transfigured.

In the end, as envisioned in the book of Revelation, the prophetic scroll is unsealed, and proclamation turns to sheer praise of the Savior and the glorification of God:

> And between the throne and the four living creatures and among the elders, I saw a Lamb standing, as though it had been slain . . . ; and he went and took the scroll from the right hand of him who was seated on the throne. And when he had taken the scroll, the four living creatures and the twenty-four elders fell down before the Lamb, each holding a harp, and with gold-

en bowls full of incense, which are the prayers of the saints; and they sang a new song, saying,

> "Worthy art thou to take the scroll and to open its seals,
> for thou wast slain and by thy blood didst ransom
> men for God
> from every tribe and tongue and people and nation,
> and hast made them a kingdom and priests to our
> God. . . ."
>
> (Rev. 5:6-10)

Amen! Blessing and glory and wisdom and thanksgiving and honor and power and might be to our God for ever and ever! Amen.
(Rev. 7:12)

In the end, as envisioned in the book of Revelation, the priestly sacrifice has prepared the wedding banquet, in which the blessed rejoice with the Savior and find enjoyment in God:

Then I heard what seemed to be the voice of a great multitude, like the sound of many waters and like the sound of many thunderpeals, crying, "Hallelujah! For the Lord our God the Almighty reigns.
Let us rejoice and exult and give him the glory,
for the marriage of the Lamb has come,
and his Bride has made herself ready;
it was granted her to be clothed with fine linen, bright and pure"—for the fine linen is the righteous deeds of the saints.
And the angel said to me, "Write this: Blessed are those who are invited to the marriage supper of the Lamb." And he said to me, "These are true words of God." (Rev. 19:6-9)

In the end, as envisioned in the book of Revelation, the royal glory of "him who sits upon the throne" is shared by the Lamb; and his faithful servants who bear his name will reign with him:

Then I looked, and I heard around the throne and the living creatures and the elders the voice of many angels, numbering myriads of myriads and thousands of thousands, saying with a loud voice, "Worthy is the Lamb who was slain, to receive power and wealth and wisdom and might and honor and glory and blessing!" And I heard every creature in heaven and on earth and under the earth and in the sea, and all therein saying, "To him who sits upon the throne and to the Lamb be blessing and honor and glory and might for ever and ever!" And the four liv-

300

ing creatures said, "Amen!" and the elders fell down and worshiped. (Rev. 5:11-14)

The throne of God and of the Lamb shall be in [the city], and his servants shall worship him; they shall see his face, and his name shall be on their foreheads. And night shall be no more; they need no light of lamp or sun, for the Lord God will be their light, and they shall reign for ever and ever. (Rev. 22:3-5)

And as the Handelian choruses of "Hallelujah" and "Amen" resound, we can meanwhile only say, "Come, Lord Jesus!" (Rev. 22:20).

Stanley M. Hauerwas

Stanley Hauerwas (b. 1940), a Methodist theologian, holds the Gilbert T. Rowe Chair in Theological Ethics at Duke Divinity School. He has challenged dominant liberal convictions of modern Western culture, including theological, philosophical, economic, and political assumptions. In contrast, he argues for a return to Christian distinctiveness. In so doing, he combines direct, challenging, provocative critique with forceful constructive energy. Chosen here is an abridged form of the Introduction to his book *Wilderness Wanderings*, pp. 1-32.* Through staking out a position in relation to that of other theologians and philosophers, he builds a framework for much contemporary discussion.

Introduction

1. Speaking Theologically

Theology is best done without apology. I therefore have no intention of apologizing for the unapologetic character of this book.[1]

That I refuse to offer such an apology puts me at odds with much of modern theology, which has adopted as its task to "explain"—either to

---

1. William Placher has illumined these matters in his *Unapologetic Theology: A Christian Voice in a Pluralistic Conversation* (Louisville: Westminster/John Knox Press, 1989). I have no reason to deny the possibility of what some, following Hans Frei, call ad-hoc apologetics. I remain convinced, however, that theology is most compelling when it is done with confidence.

our cultural despisers or, to what is a growing and more characteristic population, the indifferent—what Christians believe. This explanatory enterprise is undertaken on the presumption that theologians, like Christians in general, will be more or less tolerated if they underwrite views on which general agreement prevails. The current sparsity of agreements about agreements, however, renders such a position extremely problematic. For one thing, theologians who adopt such an "explanatory" task often find themselves quickly "out of date," having sided with "agreements" that often become the site of further disagreements. Accordingly, the status of theology is further undermined because of the concomitant impression that theology (and thus those who do theology) lacks integrity.

The situation of the theologian mirrors the sociology of the church in social orders like that of the United States. Churches are thought to be a "good thing"—both by those in and without the church—to the extent that churches support what we care about most as a society or nation. This presumption is true for those on the political left and right. Those on the left want the churches to be for economic justice, while those on the right want the churches to be good for the family. As a result, churches find themselves in a difficult bind, particularly at the national level: they struggle to find ways to be "inclusive" without at the same time forgoing their distinctive "prophetic" calling to speak out or take positions on this or that issue.

That churches and theologians occupy a space that by its very nature is compromised should come as no surprise. I have no interest in blaming anyone for the hard reality that as Christians we presently find ourselves in such a doubtful, ambivalent position. Rather, in this book I try only to locate a central challenge facing those of us who care about theology; namely, how theology in our time might reclaim a voice that speaks with authority, a voice whose power compels without coercion and persuades without denigration. Accomplishing such a feat requires, at the very least, a competence to write and speak in such a manner that our language as Christians actually does some work. By "doing work" I mean the ability of our language to become not simply a means of "saying what everyone already knows," but an ability to deploy and engender linguistic practices which simultaneously enable Christians to discover and bear witness to a reality that we (and all that is) are God's good creation. In short, theological language which "does work" consists of those discourse practices which truly make a difference. (Language which "makes" a difference, of course, is so precisely because it also "reveals" important differences.)

303

. . . I have repeatedly argued that the central theological task is to render the world intelligible to Christians. For me the question is not, "How can Christians (and theologians) make Christianity intelligible in the modern world?" but "How can Christians (and theologians) make sense of the world given the way we Christians are taught to speak in and through our worship of God?" I therefore have very little sympathy with attempts to translate Christian speech into terms that are assumed to be generally available. I resist that project not because I think there is some unchanging "core" of Christian convictions which must be protected come hell or high water,[2] but because I have a number of theological and philosophical misgivings about the very idea of translation. The notion that Christian speech can and/or must be translated if it is to be acceptable to "modern people" too often embodies simplistic views regarding the nature of language. For instance, such views of the linguistic character of the theological task fail to understand the necessity of being trained as an adequate, skillful speaker of a language. From my perspective, if Christian theological claims no longer are doing any work, they are best given up rather than subjecting them to a re-surfacing operation (a "face lift") which tries to show that they really mean something else. . . .

The book begins with a response to John Cobb's published essay, "The Christian Reason For Being Progressive."[3] I know I am asking much of readers by having them begin with my reply to an essay many of them will not have read. I think, however, that the reader can gather from my response a sufficient understanding of Cobb's position to make my criticisms intelligible. Commencing with a chapter on Professor Cobb is important because it signals the ways in which he has helped me understand how it is that Protestant liberalism bequeaths to Christians a

---

2. The very notion of a "core" of beliefs that allegedly constitutes "what Christianity is all about" is one of the most dangerous assumptions in theology. Protestant liberal theology went to ruin trying to find an "essence." This search for a core I take to be the continuing legacy of the Reformation that gave Christians the misguided notion that they could freely range over Christian tradition deciding what we like and do not like. At the risk (albeit small) of exaggeration, that attitude which most characterizes Protestants is: "How much of all the past stuff that Christians used to believe do I need to continue believing in order to still think of myself as a Christian?" In contrast, Catholics tend to think: "Goodness, look at all the great stuff we get to believe!" Catholics rightly understand that they do not have to "believe" X or Y *as an individual believer*, since that is the function of the whole church. What matters is not what I may believe, but what the church believes.

3. Cobb's essay, along with my response, was originally given as the Shaffer/Mars Lecture at Northwestern University. Each essay was subsequently published in *Theology Today*, 51, 8 (January, 1995), pp. 548-562 and pp. 563-569 respectively. I also commend to the interested reader John Cobb's gracious response to my response, "Ally or Opponent? A Response to Stanley Hauerwas," pp. 570-573.

misguided sense that they actually know where they are. Liberals are convinced that particular knowledges are certain in a manner that Christian orthodoxy cannot be. By representing the faith in a manner that will appear both intellectually respectable and politically responsible, liberal Protestants try to help the rest of us "fit in." I share Professor Cobb's presumption that theology cannot be divorced from political and economic questions, but I obviously embrace quite a different theology and politics.

The chapters on Reinhold Niebuhr ("History as Fate: How Justification By Faith Became Anthropology [and History] in America" and "The Irony of Reinhold Niebuhr") exemplify the interrelation between theological and political questions begun in my discussion of Cobb. At first glance, Niebuhr and Cobb may seem to be unlikely allies. But closer scrutiny reveals that they share a critical attitude toward the Christian tradition, all the while seeking to justify Christian support for liberal causes. Particularly important is how they both understand the relation between liberal theology and their respective support of liberal political arrangements. They exemplify the project of social Christianity in America, albeit in quite different ways.[4] I am aware that some may still find it strange to treat Niebuhr as a theological liberal, but he certainly understood himself as such and thought his liberal theological views as essential for his support of political liberalism. . . .

The chapter on the work of James Gustafson ("God as Participant: Time and History in the Work of James Gustafson") was for me an essay in discovery. Gustafson was my teacher and is my friend. But it was precisely this friendship which impelled me to understand how it has happened that I find myself at such a different place than Gustafson, all the while conceding that that difference is partly due to what I have learned from him. In his spirited reply to those of us who contributed essays on his work in *The Journal of Religious Ethics*, Gustafson observes that his work, beginning with *Treasures in Earthen Vessels*, has been motivated by a desire to force Christian theologians to modify or correct their exaggerated claims about the "Spirit" or the "Church," particularly when

---

4. See for example Gary Dorrien's compelling account of this tradition in his *Soul in Society: The Making and Renewal of Social Christianity* (Minneapolis: Fortress Press, 1995). Dorrien rightly sees Cobb's economic views as a challenge to Niebuhr's acceptance of the capitalist market, but in many ways the kind of perspective Cobb assumes that Christians should adopt in modernity was first made possible by Reinhold Niebuhr. For an appreciative review of Dorrien's book see my review in *Modern Theology* (forthcoming).

those claims are tacitly empirical ones.[5] Accordingly, he characterizes his constructive suggestions in *Christ and the Moral Life*, as well as *Can Ethics Be Christian?* as "very naturalistic."

I am extremely sympathetic with Gustafson's "empiricism," if he means by that attention to the work that theological claims do. But I am not at all convinced that that requires those same claims be construed "naturalistically." For example, Gustafson takes me to task when, in my effort to differentiate myself from him, I say, "I remain stuck with the claim that through Jesus' resurrection God decisively changed our history. Therefore I believe we must continue to begin with the 'particular,' with the historical, not because there is no other place to begin but because that is where God begins." Gustafson expresses uncertainty regarding who might be included and excluded from the pronominal "our" in that opening sentence; the second sentence he simply finds "ludicrous." He says, "I can only infer that nature is of no theological significance, and that God was absent, or something, until Jesus's resurrection. God is not sovereign over nature, I take it. Nature is also, then, of no ethical significance as a source of direction in Hauerwas's ethics. Hauerwas becomes a twentieth-century version of Marcion."[6]

Gustafson further challenges what he takes to be my "radical historicism," which I use to try to force him to choose between being a historicist or a universalist. He rightly points out that Ernst Troeltsch's and H. Richard Niebuhr's basis for being "historicist" was philosophically grounded, as they rightly saw that one cannot sustain a claim for a radically historicist perspective on strictly historical grounds. Challenging further my Christology and ecclesiology, Gustafson concludes that "Hauerwas's is an intellectual and moral sectarianism of the most extreme sort; thus he keeps a clear distinction between Christianity and the rest of life alive but forecloses apologetics of any kind and limits the range of the ethical. Hauerwas's God becomes the tribal God of a minority of the earth's population. I could argue cogently, I believe, that it is very unbiblical in many respects."[7]

5. James M. Gustafson, "A Response to Critics," *Journal of Religious Ethics*, 13, 2 (Fall, 1985), pp. 185-209 appeared in the previous issue of the *Journal of Religious Ethics*, 13, 1 (Spring, 1985) edited by James Childress and Stanley Hauerwas. Though we meant the issue to honor Gustafson's work, he was, as we say in Texas, "none too pleased" by most of the essays. The specific page Gustafson makes this observation about his work is p. 198.

6. Gustafson, "A Response to Critics," p. 191.

7. Gustafson, "A Response to Critics," p. 196.

I have recounted Gustafson's response to my article not only because I think it fair to do so, but because I also think it helps locate the argument I am trying to make. I agree that little hangs on whether or not one is a "historicist," given the lack of clarity surrounding that designation. Nor does much hang on the alternative between particularism or universalism. Rather, the issue is fundamentally theological and Gustafson is right to focus on the question of creation or, more exactly, the character of our existence as determined by a God who freely creates. The claim Gustafson finds "ludicrous" concerns my remark about the God who creates as the only God worth considering, a God who is found not only in the cross and resurrection of Christ but in the continuing working of the Spirit.

The doctrine of creation only makes Christian sense as part of the doctrine of the Trinity. For Christians, the doctrine of the Trinity is necessary if we are to make sense of the world as we find it and as we hope it will be. Such a claim is "empirical," not in the sense of being verifiable, but in the sense that it requires a traditioned-determined community to narrate the way the world is and, given the way the world is, how Christians must be in such a world. As I will discuss in Chapter 12 ("Creation, Contingency, and Truthful Non-Violence: A Milbankian Reflection"), such a narrative may be "totalizing" in a manner Gustafson fears. However, Gustafson's fears are unfounded because the *content* of that narrative should, if understood rightly, prevent those who are shaped by it from forcing others into living as we do. All Christians seek to be is witnesses of that hope. But it is a witness whose very possibility and efficacy resides in the certain "uncertainty" of hope. In other words, Christians are able to witness to that hope, not because they know beforehand the direction of history, but precisely because they do not.

On Gustafson's account, God gets to be a participant. Similarly, we too get to participate in the historical (and natural) processes in which we find ourselves. Unfortunately, this is neither a theology nor a politics that holds out hope of radical change. For "participation" tends to be the language of the liberal manager and bureaucrat, those who assume that the way things are is about as much as one can expect. Just as Stoicism represented great wisdom for the Romans and for those who would rule Rome, so I think Gustafson's ethic represents great wisdom for the bureaucrats and the growing managerial class that rule liberal social orders. Were Christianity false, then clearly some form of stoicism would be the best alternative. Yet Christians cannot be stoics. For the God Christians worship creates and redeems, thereby making possible (but also imperative) that we live in a manner fully consistent with the anticipation of God's kingdom. Somehow the language of "participation," at least as it is used in liberal social orders, represents too pale an image of the Christian God, and subsequently of the people God has called to be his own. Hence, Christians rightly believe that God requires justice and hope rather than bureaucratic "participation," which is why the poor find the proclamation of the gospel such good news.

The next three chapters ("Can Aristotle be a Liberal: Nussbaum on Luck"; "Flight From Foundationalism, or Things Aren't As Bad As They Seem"; and "Not All Peace is Peace: Why Christians Cannot Make Peace with Engelhardt's Peace") are not about theologians, but philosophers. I have included them not only because I admire the work of Nussbaum, Stout, and Engelhardt but because I believe each in quite different ways has helped Christians begin to imagine what our world looks like in God's eclipse. Nussbaum and Stout are serious thinkers seeking to show us how to go on in God's absence. The Nussbaum essay was written soon after the publication of *The Fragility of Goodness*. I have included it in part because in it I anticipated her increasing sympathy with Kantian modes of moral analysis and her correlative support of liberal political arrangements; but more importantly, the continued relevance of the essay concerns the way in which it articulates perhaps the central issue in liberal moral and political theory—luck.

Liberalism is the moral passion which seeks to free our lives from the determination of bad luck, "accidents of our birth," and all other vicissitudes of history. History, from a liberal perspective, is the study of the past in order to render the past impotent for the ongoing determinations of our lives. In short, it becomes the way to put the wrongs of the past truly and irrevocably in the past through a kind of forgetfulness. The political arrangements of liberalism seek to free us from history by creating social orders in which "we can be what we want to be." Yet the means necessary to secure such "freedom" in an egalitarian manner creates societies that make our lives all the more determined by powers we do not recognize as powers.

Nussbaum, therefore, makes candid some of the ontological and political commitments that I began to suggest, in the essays on Niebuhr and even more on Gustafson, were inherent in Protestant liberalism; namely, a reconfiguration of Christianity in stoic terms. These themes are extended and deepened in the chapters on Milbank and Martin Luther King, Jr. In brief, my essay on Milbank is an attempt to suggest an alternative ontology required by the Christian doctrine of the Trinity.

Even more important, as I am sure Milbank would agree, is the witness of redeemed memory—as exemplified in the life and work and witness of Martin Luther King, Jr., a man who refused to forget. His refusal to forget derives, of course, from the conviction that our world is constituted by a God who makes forgiveness and, thus, hope possible.

Jeff Stout and Tris Engelhardt in different ways represent attempts to sustain liberal results without the epistemological conceits of liberalism (Chapters 6 and 7). I admire Stout's attempt at *bricolage* as well as his quite sympathetic acknowledgment of those of us who persist in trying to remain Christian. However, I must confess that I am as sympathetic with his project as I am doubtful of its possibility. He is right, of course, in using whatever moral resources that happen to be at hand; but I remain unconvinced that such resources can be made fully intelligible given that they remain abstracted from communities of memory necessary to form people of virtue. Stout would no doubt agree about the importance of such communities. Baseball and medicine are two important resources; but in the absence of a community (or communities) with a more determinative narrative, I do not see how they can resist distortion in the liberal market.

The chapter on Engelhardt provides an opportunity to explore the question whether or not the practice of medicine as the unqualified care of the sick can be sustained given current liberal political arrangements. Engelhardt, like Stout, seeks no "foundation" that might ensure him a place to stand outside history. Rather, like his fellow Texan, Lyndon Johnson, he only asks that we "reason together," assuming that we will prefer peace to conflict. Yet I fear that the sort of peace he has in view is bought with too heavy a price; for it asks us to equate peace with the absence of violence. I doubt any society built on such an illusion can long keep more overt forms of violence at bay.

I have followed the chapter on Engelhardt with an account of Paul Ramsey, "How Christian Ethics Become Medical Ethics: The Case of Paul Ramsey." I do so not only because this continues the focus on medicine, but more importantly because Ramsey helpfully returns us to the presuppositions (or at least the practice) of Protestant liberal theology. Ramsey would be shocked to be counted among the Protestant liberals, since he thought of himself as more theologically and politically conservative than anyone in that tradition. But it was Ramsey who also made the mistake of assuming that Reinhold Niebuhr believed what Ramsey believed. As a result, he thought he could "use" Niebuhr's realism without reproducing Niebuhr's Christology (or lack thereof). Just to the extent that Ramsey accepted the role of the "ethicist," he could not help but make his theological convictions appear as an after-thought.

The title of Chapter 9, "How To Go On When You Know You Are Going To Be Misunderstood, or How Paul Holmer Ruined My Life," is an obvious allusion to the title of the book. As I indicated above, the essay on Holmer represents something of a turn in the plot of the book. It is not so much a plot reversal as an attempt to say more explicitly and constructively what I think by directing attention to those who have taught me both what to think and how to think. The essay on Holmer in particular makes explicit the Wittgensteinian resonances that some may have already noted in this "Introduction" and, if they are discerning readers, in all that I have written. I do not pretend that this chapter is anything more than a gesture needing more adequate defense, but I hope the reader will nonetheless find it a helpful gesture. For if the position I have tried to argue in this book is close to being right, the only "adequate defense" is precisely the kind of display each of the chapter essays in this book hopefully represents.

The chapter on Iris Murdoch, "Murdochian Muddles: Can We Get Through Them If God Does Not Exist?" may at first seem to believe my claim that the rest of the chapters in the book are about thinkers with whom I am in general agreement. Yet I hope my immense debt to Murdoch is apparent even as I disagree with her "theology." Indeed, one of the things I find most fascinating about Murdoch is her willingness to believe almost everything Protestant liberals would want her to believe, yet she does so without seeing any reason why that would entail believing in God, let alone a God who creates. At the very least, my engagement with her work has forced me to be much more candid about the metaphysical entailments required by the Christian conviction that all that is is created.

The essay on James McClendon's work hopefully will not only give the reader a sense of what my kind of "systematic theology" might look like, but it also extends the material convictions that inform the perspective of this book. For example, McClendon's claim that war and its violence turn out to be anti-historical is exactly the kind of redescriptive work Christian speech must perform if it is to command the serious attention of Christians and non-Christians alike. Of course, such a claim invites and requires much "explanation," which turns out to be the kind of work theologians are supposed to be about. That McClendon works so patiently and well to that end is why I find his work so compelling, an important beacon in our time.

By the time readers come to the chapter on John Milbank, "Creation, Contingency, and Truthful Non-Violence: A Milbankian Reflection," they may well feel it is superfluous, since frequent reference to and use of his work appears throughout the previous chapters. In a singular way, Milbank has charted a new direction for theology for which in many ways this book is only a footnote. To be sure, Milbank's attack on the social sciences as providing theodical legitimations for the violence of liberal social orders can initially be off-putting because of its uncompromising character. Exposing the invisibility of the liberal narrative and practices (which are invisible exactly because they are now more or less identified with "the way the world is"), cannot help but appear as a violent exercise. But I would contend that the violence unveiled characterizes more the subject matter than either the one doing the exposing or the methods of unconcealment. My only difficulty with Milbank is the fear that in dismantling the master's house too many of the master's tools may have been used.

Nevertheless, Milbank is surely correct in claiming that finally all one can do is provide a better narrative. I remain agnostic whether "a better narrative" requires that we "out-narrate" all comers, but there can be no question that we must learn again how to do Christian history. Indeed, *Theology and Social Theory* may well be the closest thing we have in modern theology to Augustine's *City of God*. Such a comparison is obviously not fair to Milbank, but at least it suggests the genre within which I think his work is properly judged.

The title of this book came to me while rereading the essay describing Oliver O'Donovan's work, "Remaining in Babylon: O'Donovan's Defense of Christendom." O'Donovan has done what my criticism of Protestant liberalism suggests we must do. He has not sought to reach an accommodation with liberal culture, but to show why it is unintelligible without the God we Christians worship. His is a Constantinian project on the grandest scale before which I can only stand in awe. Not only do I stand in awe of what he has attempted, but I also stand in much agreement. He and I concur, of course, in our assessment of liberalism and its antithetical character to Christianity. But our agreements go deeper just to the extent that he too seeks no "transcendental" point that might free us from our obligation to be faithful to biblically narrated history. The crucial difficulty with O'Donovan's narrative, however, is that it attempts to help Christians recover the home we thought God had made for us in "the West." In contrast, I assume that one of the most important duties of Christians is to continually resist amnesia; that is, we must not forget the sense in which our

311

earthly journey invariably passes through wilderness places. For a people who live between the times, it should come as no surprise that we should find ourselves, more often than not, still in the wilderness.

The book closes with a chapter on Martin Luther King, Jr.—a good Protestant liberal. At least he was a good Protestant liberal when he came to write his theology. King's liberalism no doubt contributed to his power, which surely is an indication that much good remains in liberal theology. Yet as I suggested above, King's life and work were shaped by a people who knew they could not forget their ancestry or their history. They could not forget those who had gone before and whose past sufferings make present memories (and identities) possible. By remembering Martin Luther King, Jr., those of us who are not African-Americans are presented with a crucially important opportunity to become engrafted into a practice that makes us part of a history that, through God's grace, we might learn to acknowledge as our own. King did not and could not lead us out of the wilderness, but without him, and others like him, we would not have enough hope to sustain our wandering.

Such is this book's plot. There are subplots within the main plot that I trust some readers will find of interest. Indeed, the plot I have provided is only one way that these essays can be read and thus I am confident that some readers will find more interesting ways to plot the book. Certainly my hope is that my outline will not inhibit, obstruct, or prevent such readings—or, worst of all, tempt some readers away from reading the book altogether. Perhaps one should not worry oneself overly much about things concerning which one has little, if any, control. Nonetheless, I would be dishonest if I did not confess that central to my aspirations for this book is that it might suggest to some readers how wonderful it is to serve a God who has more interesting things for us to do than to make our world safe. . . .

Rebecca S. Chopp

Rebecca Chopp (b. 1952) is concerned to enlarge inherited theology beyond the limits of previous points of view. Writing from deep Christian commitment, she gives voice to dimensions of women's experience and to cries for justice and transformation in our society. She is at Emory University where she provides educational and intellectual leadership. The article chosen comes from her book *Saving Work*, pp. 97-115.* In discussing theological education, Chopp lifts up themes which reveal her vision and permeate her work.

A Particular Vision: New Ways of Thinking About Theological Education

It is time to evaluate my argument concerning feminist practices of theological education. I began this book with a wager that in order to address the specificity of feminist practices of theological education I would need to detour from the present conversation on theological education, which concentrates on the ideal aim of theological studies. Because, at least thus far, the current conversation about theological education has not focused on the students (who, quite literally, are the subjects of theological education), the social context in which students act, or the symbolic realm of Christian faith, I have had to focus on feminist *practices* of theological education. . . .

This particular vision arises at least in part because feminist practices of theological education, like feminism in general, can be explained neither as a correction to a Christian essence in terms of demanding equal rights nor as a supplementation to a Christian essence by lifting up the special gifts of women. As we have already seen, feminist Christianity represents a new type of Christianity, one which requires its own terms of understanding. Different forms of Christianity take on different emphases and shapes of piety and prayer, of worship and service, of education and morality, and of understanding and language. The pietist movement emphasized that heart-felt experience required a theological understanding of the subjectivity of feeling and intention, a well-developed discourse of the heart, so to speak. The language of real presence in medieval Christianity makes sense when one understands the liturgical and aesthetic practices of that time. Contemporary feminist Christianity requires understanding within its own practices.

It is only by standing within feminist liberationist Christianity that a particular vision emerges from the blending or perhaps weaving of all three practices in order to disclose the values, purposes, and themes that constitute the internal goods of the practices of feminist theological education. This weaving can occur through a recollection of the practices we have covered. The activity of recollection is not a mere literal remembering but a collecting together again in new ways that may well enable new understandings and visions of theological education.

The first practice considered was that of narrativity, the writing of one's life. It is not a static story, nor a set plot; rather, narrativity stresses the ongoing activity of writing one's life. Christianity has always included the practice of narrativity. In settled times this activity may entail appropriating fairly fixed narratives, while in times of great change this activity may involve crafting quite new narratives. Narrativity, in most Christian forms, is surrounded by the ecclesia; in communion and community in reflection and working together, the Christian life is constantly written. There are, of course, many forms of narratives, and each narrative has its own distinctiveness, if not its own uniqueness. As with the narratives we read in books or see in films, different meanings can be attached and different interpretations offered. Yet the meanings and interpretations are always set in context of the narrative itself. Women are writing new narratives because they must.

Within these narratives certain ideas appear and reappear in various ways. Ideas of the subject as active agent, ideas of creativity and religious symbols, ideas of understanding and naming experiences in new ways are woven through these narratives. Values emerge: the privileging of difference; the revelation of the connectedness we have and the task of nurturing these connections; the respect of embodiment and the

314

recognition that theology too is always embodied; and the valuing of friendship as a naming and vision of ultimacy.

It is these values that become the internal goods of the practice of narrativity. Women and men engaged in the practice of narrativity value connections, embodiment, creativity, and difference. It is important to understand that these values become ways of interpreting the world. Take the value of difference: engaged in feminist practices of theological education, women learn in various ways how to hear and appreciate difference. This may come through the sharing of a variety of stories, through open conflict, through enlarging knowledge about what goes on for different women around the world. If patriarchy creates and constructs some notion of essential identity, feminism deconstructs this universal category and replaces it with difference and specificity. This is not a matter simply of learning to see difference, but also of valuing and appreciating difference.

Another example might be that of connectedness. A woman engaged in practices of theological education will form her narrativity around connections to others, to God, to the world, as well as to the self. This connectedness will occur in rituals of community, in the emphasis on friendship, in classroom explorations of connectedness, and in social work for justice. The connectedness will be formed in women through images of God not as wholly disconnected other, but as a friend who is already connected. The idea of connectedness in feminist theology may shape the habits of one's daily life to use public transportation, to recycle, to spend time with friends in rest and recreation. The dual ideas of God as friend and of the earth as our home reinforce our solidarity with all and move our action toward greater flourishing. As a lens through which we understand reality, connectedness will be valued for its own intrinsic satisfaction. Women and men will learn the arts of nurturing connection, and the many ways that connections become distorted and broken.

Feminist theology works to provide tools for constructing new narratives for women and for clearing discursive spaces for women to enact their ongoing narrativity. That women must rewrite their lives in new ways must be understood as arising directly within the context of cultural patterns of change. Women, as I have already mentioned, lack narratives of themselves in theological education as well as in culture. Feminist theology provides important symbolic frames and values as resources to do this saving work. Yet, as we have seen, there are some preferred dimensions of narrativity represented in feminist theology: the valuing of contextuality, the privileging of difference, the naming of

315

women's experiences, and the concern for moral agency. In feminist theology, symbols function in a quite practical way to enable the feminist practice of narrativity in theological education.

The practice of ekklesiality incorporates and expands many of the ideas in the practice of narrativity. Women and men engage in a variety of ekklesial practices, from struggles with ordination in established denominations, to development of alternative forms of community, to creation of feminist liturgies, to participation in spirituality groups. Feminist ecclesiology finds its spaces in a wide variety of places. Feminist ecclesiology, as we have seen, can be named symbolically in the denunciation of sin and the annunciation of grace.

The use of symbols such as sin and grace have allowed us to examine how it is that feminist theology constructs the ekklesia. The church as space for the denunciation of sin and annunciation of grace functions sacramentally as a visible sign of God's invisible grace. In invoking these symbols from the tradition, feminist theology also reworks the symbols in order to help women and men resist patriarchy and to shape new forms of flourishing. The ekklesia, for women and men, exists as the counter-public of justice, the community of friends, and the spirituality of connectedness.

Ideas of justice, connectedness, embodiment, and openness, represented in these symbols, are the internal goods of the practice of the ekklesia. Within the church, as within the world, justice is a necessary though not sufficient condition of friendship. Connectedness runs through both friendship and justice, for the connectedness of justice is the possibility that each may determine her or his own life and have a say in determining life together. The internal goods in the practice of ecclesiology are themselves connected and parallel to those of narrativity: values of mutuality and friendship, connectedness and embodiment, concreteness and transformation.

Once again, then, we can understand the saving work of feminist theology as expressing, criticizing, and guiding the practice of ekklesia. It is important to note that feminist theology provides an understanding of ekklesia within the broader context of the culture. The ekklesia, as sacrament, represents redemptive community to the world. And the very understanding of sin and grace symbolizes not only an understanding of church but also an understanding of culture. Indeed, ideas function within ecclesiology not so much to demarcate separate spaces of church and world, but to exemplify and express ongoing relations of ekklesia and world.

The critical and creative work of theology is itself a practice within feminist liberationist Christianity. Envisioned by one student as a "crazy quilt," feminist theology works to critically resist oppression and dehumanization and to construct ideas, symbols, and other resources for survival and human flourishing. As a type of understanding, feminist theology arises out of emancipatory praxis. Joining the ethical and the epistemological, feminist theory is a pragmatic critical theory.

Central to the saving work of feminist theology as a pragmatic critical theory is symbolic construction. The symbolic construction of feminist theology works to emancipate from oppression and sin, to envision new spaces of flourishing, and to produce new ways of being in the world. Feminist theology deconstructs oppressive symbols and oppressive functions of symbols of God. Exploring different experiences of God and world, feminist theology opens up new meanings and functions through the symbol of God. Feminist theology works to envision transformation through new symbols of God and to develop discourses of God that are themselves transformative.

As with the practices of narrativity and ekklesiality, certain ideas and values are expressed. Theology envisions a God, as well as a church and a subject, that is fundamentally known through connections, mutuality, and friendship. Openness and the desire to appreciate difference name a fundamental perspective of theology's work. Justice is itself the binding quality of theology's own internal relations between ethics and epistemology.

Theology is saving work, and as such it is aimed at saving the present and finding new possibilities for the future. The idea of feminist theology as a practice can be best understood through rhetoric as a type of understanding aimed at action. To fashion theology as rhetoric is to attend self-consciously to the practical effectiveness of ideas. Feminists fashion different rhetorical strategies to accomplish saving work.

Feminist theology offers a rather holistic vision of what actually goes on in theological education. Out of the practices of narrativity, ekklesia, and theology such a particular vision arises. It is based on new images, values, and relations. Just as other historic forms of Christianity have continued practices such as these and changed them in relation to form, function, and meaning, so also has feminism transformed practices of Christianity. These practices create a way of being in the world for Christianity and shape, as we have seen, the nature and import of theological education.

Educational Process in Feminist Practices

The concentration on practices enables us to think about education in new ways. To identify practices as the sites of learning in theological education is to avoid some common "divisions" in thinking about education and to require the development of new language to name the process of education. In a way, it avoids some of the problems in our usual way of talking about education, and it also provides us with new ways of thinking about education as a process and not simply as a product. . . .

Feminist theorists of education have often pointed out that "knowing" for women has to be understood in terms of physical presence, relationships with students and faculty, and connections between feelings and ideas. The book *Women's Ways of Knowing* identifies the following kinds of knowledge: received, subjective (in terms of the inner voice and the quest for self), procedural (reason as well as separate and connected knowing), and constructed. The authors suggest that dominant models of education hinder women's process of education because the educational models continue to be based on modern assumptions of epistemology. The text then offers some suggestions for reconceiving knowledge and education based on the actual practices of women. Likewise, Patricia Hill Collins in *Black Feminist Thought* develops what she calls an "Afrocentric feminist epistemology" based on the practices of concrete experience as a criterion of meaning, the use of dialogue in assessing knowledge claims, the ethic of caring, and an ethic of accountability.

But developing new models of "knowing" is not unique to feminism. Historically, as David Kelsey has suggested, there are quite different forms of epistemology in relation to theology. Some of the contemporary theological models discussed in chapter 4 are concerned with developing new models of knowing, given the pluralism of culture and anti-foundationalism of contemporary epistemology. David Tracy and George Lindbeck use hermeneutical and linguistic theories to provide new understandings of "knowing" within what they call religious traditions. Susan Hekman, in *Gender and Knowledge,* relates complementary postmodern and feminist forms of epistemology.

It has been the argument of this text that one of the distinctive characteristics of feminist practices is that they provide the resource for new forms of knowing and for new understandings of theological education. To focus on specific practices, as we have done in this text, allows us both to enlarge the nature of "knowing" beyond that utilized in modern theological education and to name some specific components of the education process in which this "knowing" is engaged. In the context of our investigation of feminist practices at least three themes emerge within each practice: imagination, dialogue, and justice.

Utilizing these themes, I want to move toward conceiving education as a process and not merely a product. I want to contend that feminist theology both requires and contributes a process of education that is a training in imagination, dialogue, and justice, even as it is an insemination of ideas from the past.

Justice

At the conclusion of *God's Fierce Whimsy*, the women of the Mud Flower Collective contend that "the fundamental goal of theological education must be the doing of justice." Likewise, Elisabeth Schüssler Fiorenza places the doing of justice at the center of theological education:

> I have argued that theology and theological education must be conceived as a transformative discursive praxis that critically reflects on the concrete historical-political configurations and theological practices of Christian communities which have engendered and still engender the exclusion and dehumanization of "the others" of free born, educated and propertied men in Western society. At the same time it must seek to articulate alternative communal visions and values for the human community on the brink of atomic annihilation. Such a conception of theology cannot just limit itself to a critical reflection on religious and ecclesial practices. It is foremost a critical reflection on the social-cultural-political practices in which religious communities have been and still are embedded and to which they contribute.

Justice, as a basic theme of theological education, is central to each practice of feminist theological education. In narrativity a communicative possibility of justice prevails: each person gets a voice in self-determination. The activity of writing one's life in relation to self, others, and earth is an act of being drawn out, learning to shape and be shaped in right relationship. In the practice of ekklesia the church as a counterpublic of justice names a space in which ways of justice are modeled and formed. Justice, as we have seen, defines the nature and mission of the ekklesia. And in the feminist practice of theology, justice is central to the braiding together of ethics and epistemology in the formation of new

319

meanings and functions of symbols and the development of new discursive practices.

Likewise, in terms of the questions of subject, culture, and symbol that I introduced in chapter 1, justice is an important theme. In contemporary theology, visions of justice are central to the new symbols and new meanings of symbols in theology. Justice as a key to symbolic life of Christianity is represented not only in feminist theology but also in African American, Latin American, and other forms of liberation theology. Within the various theologies of liberation movements, the symbolic construction of justice seeks to express the dialectical movement within the function of Christian symbols: justice enables us to name faith, and faith symbols reconceived as justice allow us to envision new spaces of life together.

One of the quests of this book has been to understand the broader cultural context of contemporary theological education. I have suggested that the very presence of women, in great diversity, represents many of the cultural struggles of the day. The struggle for justice in American culture and in the world is centrally involved in hearing voices that have been marginalized, but also envisioning new spaces in church and culture for the living out of justice. Thus justice demands, in a sense, the focus on particular human subjects, the participation of different voices, and the articulation of different concerns and needs.

But theological education is not just *about* justice, it is, in a sense, justice itself. We need to conceive of theological education as the doing of justice, with justice as a central theme, along with "ordered" learning, imaginative envisioning, and dialogue. In American history the parallel referent, and that which feminist theology continues, is the understanding of education as the training of citizens. Justice names not simply the goal but the process itself. . . .

Dialogue

Thus justice, as a theme of education, is intertwined with solidarity, communication, and dialogue. Dialogue, within Welch's conception of communicative ethics, is not abstract dialogue. Welch is critical of Habermas and others who focus on the ideal of conversation, assuming that the "other" has simply been "excluded" from the conversation. Welch asks, "If the inclusion of women and minorities is simply a matter of extension, why has it been so long in coming?" Dialogue requires real interaction among embodied persons, with openness and respect for mutual critique.

In theological education this material interaction might be envisioned by the creation of dialogical spaces. Theological education is a series of quite physical spaces: classrooms, hallways, and worship places, and sites of spirituality group and committee meetings. These physical spaces are filled with the bodies of students, faculty, and staff, representing many differences that have come to mark and define the present constitution of American Christianity and American culture.

The spaces of theological education, filled with persons who are different and seeking justice, are already "dialogical" places where lives meet, and where bodies interact on physical, emotional, and linguistic levels. In feminist theological education, these spaces are places where solidarity begins and where freedom occurs. As Maxine Greene has suggested, "We might think of freedom as an opening of spaces as well as perspectives." Within feminist theological education, education is a dialogical process of concrete encounter with others enacted through classes, worship, committees. Education is about social interaction, and even reason within education is dialogical and communicative. . . .

Imagination

With the stress on material as well as discursive practices leading to transformation and the struggle and desire for new hope of justice, imagination is central to education. Imagination, the ability to think the new, is an act of survival. Yet the imagination is rarely explicit in the educational process and is usually relegated to a few small elective courses emphasizing how to use music in worship.

Feminist theology, as we have seen, makes imagination central, since the saving work of theology requires new imaginative visions. Indeed the very notion of a pragmatic critical theory requires imaginative reconstruction as well as analytical explanation. Central to feminist theological practice is recognizing the unrealized possibilities in a situation. Imagination, Iris Young tells us, "is the faculty of transforming the experience of what is into a projection of what could be, the faculty that frees thought to form ideas and norms." And feminist ecclesiology is based on imagination in terms of envisioning the church in new spaces. Narrativity is also imaginative: the ability to imagine new possibilities for our lives and for the world.

Feminist theologies are replete with calls to the imagination, such as this from Marjorie Procter-Smith: "Anamnesis for women requires the creation of feminist imagination, which permits women to appropriate the past and to envision our future." Elisabeth Schüssler Fiorenza has suggested that an important step in biblical hermeneutics and in theological education is the creative visualization of the text. Sallie McFague, Rita Nakashima Brock, and Rosemary Radford Ruether have all modeled what it is to imagine new symbols and new meanings for symbols of God.

Within feminist theology and feminist practices of theological education, this need and quest for reimagining means not only specific acts of reconstruction but also the inclusion of literature and poetry as sources of theological reflection. In many cases these *are* the written documents by women, and their use is central to the inclusion of "tradition" in feminist theology. But such prose and poetry not only represent what women wrote but also teach us an imaginative process of reconstructing women's lives, the church, and the very nature of reflection as aimed toward the future. Feminist theology includes poetic revisioning, aesthetic production, and imaginative construction.

It is ironic, in some ways, that modern theology and theological education have paid so little explicit attention to imagination and methods of imaginative revisioning. Modern theology, in thinkers such as Barth and Schleiermacher, Tillich and Rahner, and the Niebuhr brothers used imaginative revisioning to allow theology as the discourse of faith to survive the onslaught of modern rationality. Yet with the rare exception of thinkers such as Samuel Coleridge and Jonathan Edwards, the dimensions of imagination, beauty, and aesthetics were not emphasized as central to modern theological method. . . .

Conclusion: The Warning and Hope of Utopian Realism

Throughout this book I have tried to identify what is special or unique in what women do in feminist practices of theological education and the vision of education (as well as Christianity) that arises out of these practices. I have consciously attempted to provide ways of naming what is among us, and far too often not seen, or is belittled, since it does not fit the dominant discourse about theological education.

But I would not be faithful to the women engaged in feminist practices of theological education if I did not end the book with a warning that this vision is still utopian, that it is the speaking of largely still *unrealized* possibilities in our midst even as it is expressed and constituted among us. Many feminist works have focused on the difficulties of women in theological education who engage in feminist practices (and those who don't consciously engage as well!).

In traveling around the United States and Canada researching this book, I was often struck by both the utopian hope and the factual realism that women expressed about the role of feminist practices within theological education. Women, and men, struggle to hold both the joyous hope of resistance and community together with the frustrating realism of continued oppression and belittlement in theological education. This struggle of hope and realism names, as well, my own experience as a woman in theological education. Very early on in my research, as I began to realize how my own struggles were repeated in countless times and ways, I read Gail Griffin's *Calling: Essays on Teaching in the Mother Tongue,* which identifies the struggles to deal with the feminist movement on a college campus. One of the ways she symbolizes the complexities and paradoxes within the struggle is by the following story from *Alice in Wonderland.*

> The table was a large one, but the three were all crowded together at one corner of it. "No room, no room!" they cried out when they saw Alice coming. "There's plenty of room!" said Alice, indignantly, and she sat down in a large arm-chair at one end of the table.
> "Have some wine," the March Hare said, in an encouraging tone.
> Alice looked all round the table, but there was nothing on it but tea. "I don't see any wine," she remarked.
> "There isn't any," said the March Hare.
> "Then it wasn't very civil of you to offer it," said Alice, angrily.
> "It wasn't very civil of you to sit down without being invited," said the March Hare.
> "I didn't know it was your table," said Alice; "it's laid for great many more than three."

Women engaged in feminist practices come to the laden table of theological education ready to contribute, to feast, to talk, and to participate. Though the table, laden with the rich food of concepts, categories, symbols, practices, relationships, seems to invite women, they are often told that they haven't really been invited. There is still a dominant group and discourse that claims ownership of theological education, that adjudicates the discourse, that decides what is civil and what is rude, and that parcels out the riches of the table. Part of our struggle is that the table is abundant and inviting, but the March Hares tell us that despite appearances, we aren't invited.

But like Alice, we know that we *are already* at the table. The question is, how do we respond to the resources present in theological education, in the midst of all the mixed messages of beckoning and dismissal? In a chapter on theological education in her book *But She Said*, Elisabeth Schüssler Fiorenza contends that women not only have to move from lay to professional persona but from a "feminine supportive, marginal, silent, private *persona* to a masculine, assertive, central, speaking, public, one." Women are supposed to master the discourses and disciplines of theological education and assume the subject position of an elite white Eurocentric male. Schüssler Fiorenza observes that women actually have three possibilities. The first possibility is that women can assume the masculine position and learn to do it like a man. The second possibility is that women can totally reject this subject position and try to find preferred "feminine" ways. This position usually refuses the resources within the academy, including the resources of changing the system. A third possibility is for women to become "bilingual" and learn the male system in order to transform it. Schüssler Fiorenza calls women who follow the third option *resident aliens*. A resident alien, Schüssler Fiorenza suggests, is both an insider and outsider, "insider by virtue of residence or patriarchal affiliation to a male citizen or institution; outsider in terms of language, experience, culture, and history."

Certainly I advocate the third position. It is not easy, but neither are the other positions that Schüssler Fiorenza identifies. To deny what one has experienced and learned as a particular woman and try to act in ways that deny or contradict one's memories and desires is to become alienated from one's own history. To reject the structures in which we find ourselves, and all the resources on that abundant table, is to forgo the solidarity with the earth and with all those for whom the structures must change in order to secure survival, let alone flourish. But the position of a resident alien is difficult, for one never really is home, except where one can create even partial visions of a home with a table to which all are readily and eagerly invited.

CPSIA information can be obtained at www.ICGtesting.com
Printed in the USA
LVOW091956090911

245637LV00001B/206/A

9 780687 012473